KEEP YOUR HANDS OFF EIZOUKEN!

03

STORY AND ART BY

大童澄瞳

SUMITO OOWARA

CONTENTS

KEEP YOUR HANDS OFF EIZOUKEN! VOL. 3
TRANSLATED BY KUMAR SIVASUBRAMANIAN
SPECIAL THANKS FOR TRANSLATION ASSISTANCE: CHITOKU TESHIMA
LETTERING AND RETOUCH BY SUSIE LEE AND STUDIO CUTIE
EDITED BY CARL GUSTAV HORN

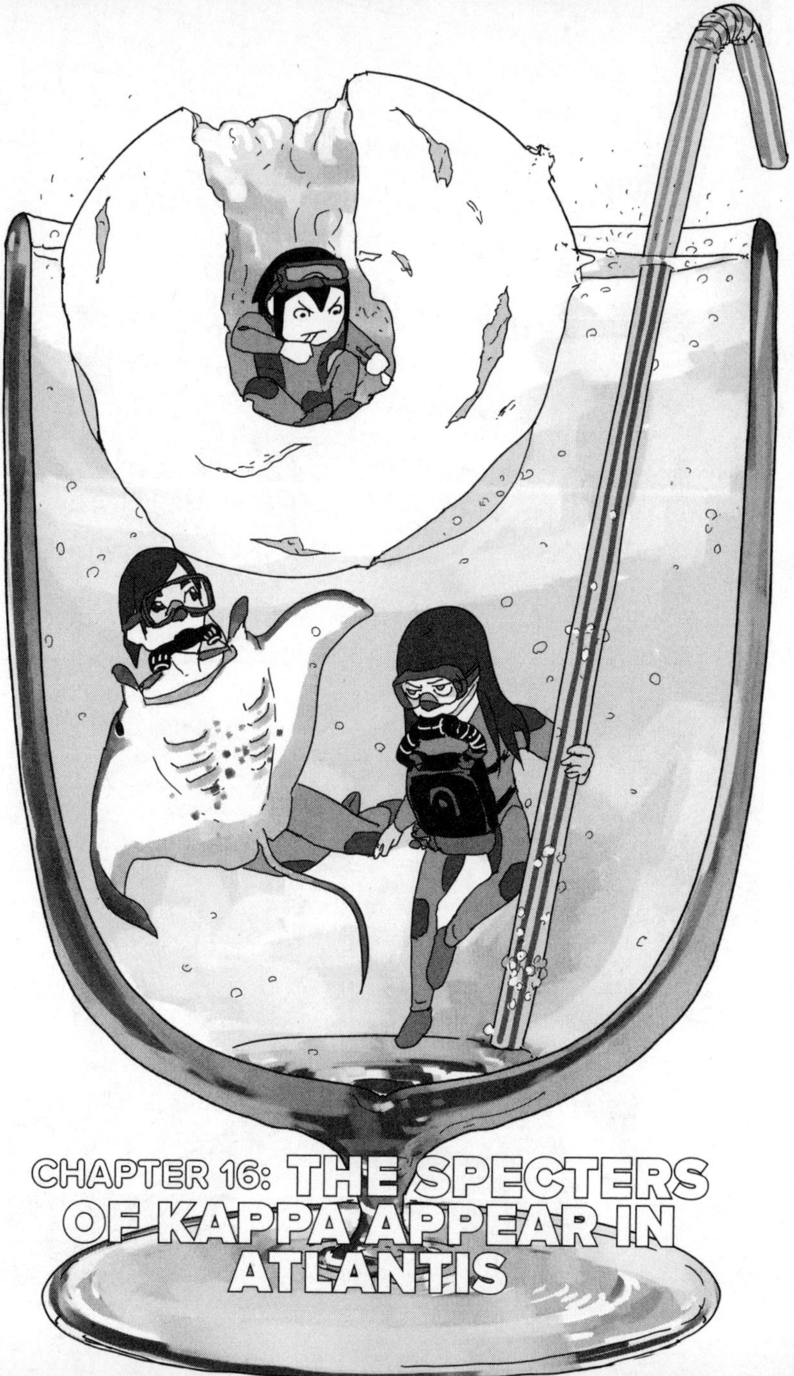

CHAPTER 16: THE SPECTERS OF KAPPA APPEAR IN ATLANTIS

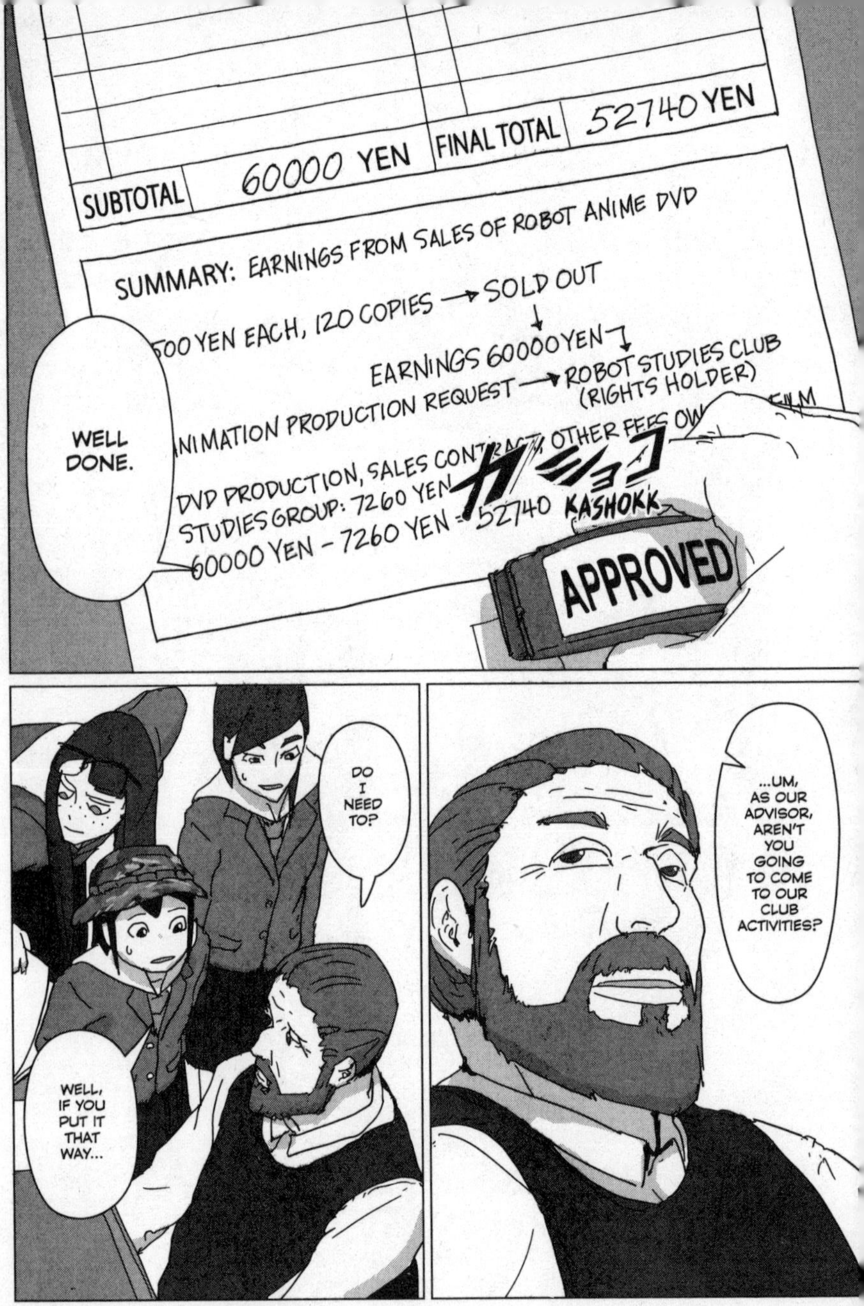

SUBTOTAL
60000 YEN
FINAL TOTAL
52740 YEN
SUMMARY: EARNINGS FROM SALES OF ROBOT ANIME DVD
500 YEN EACH, 120 COPIES → SOLD OUT
EARNINGS 60000 YEN
ANIMATION PRODUCTION REQUEST → ROBOT STUDIES CLUB (RIGHTS HOLDER)
DVD PRODUCTION, SALES CONTRACT, OTHER FEES OW
STUDIES GROUP: 7260 YEN
60000 YEN - 7260 YEN = 52740
WELL DONE.
ガショコ
KASHOKK
APPROVED
...UM, AS OUR ADVISOR, AREN'T YOU GOING TO COME TO OUR CLUB ACTIVITIES?
DO I NEED TO?
WELL, IF YOU PUT IT THAT WAY...

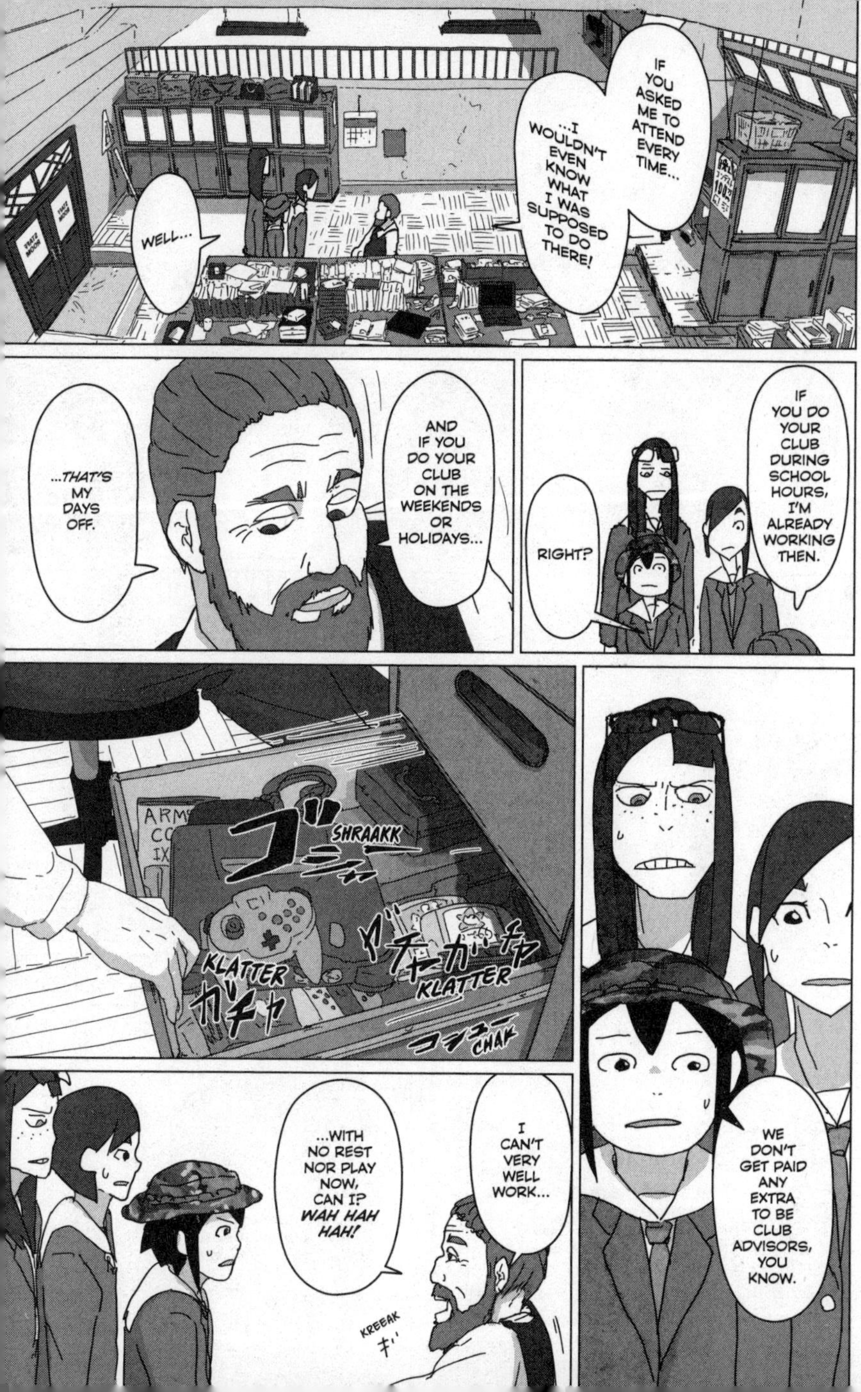
IF YOU ASKED ME TO ATTEND EVERY TIME...
...I WOULDN'T EVEN KNOW WHAT I WAS SUPPOSED TO DO THERE!
WELL...
IF YOU DO YOUR CLUB DURING SCHOOL HOURS, I'M ALREADY WORKING THEN.
RIGHT?
AND IF YOU DO YOUR CLUB ON THE WEEKENDS OR HOLIDAYS...
...THAT'S MY DAYS OFF.
WE DON'T GET PAID ANY EXTRA TO BE CLUB ADVISORS, YOU KNOW.
ゴシャ SHRAAKK
ガチャガチャ KLATTER
ガチャ KLATTER
コシュー CHAK
I CAN'T VERY WELL WORK...
...WITH NO REST NOR PLAY NOW, CAN I? *WAH HAH HAH!*
KREEAK ギ

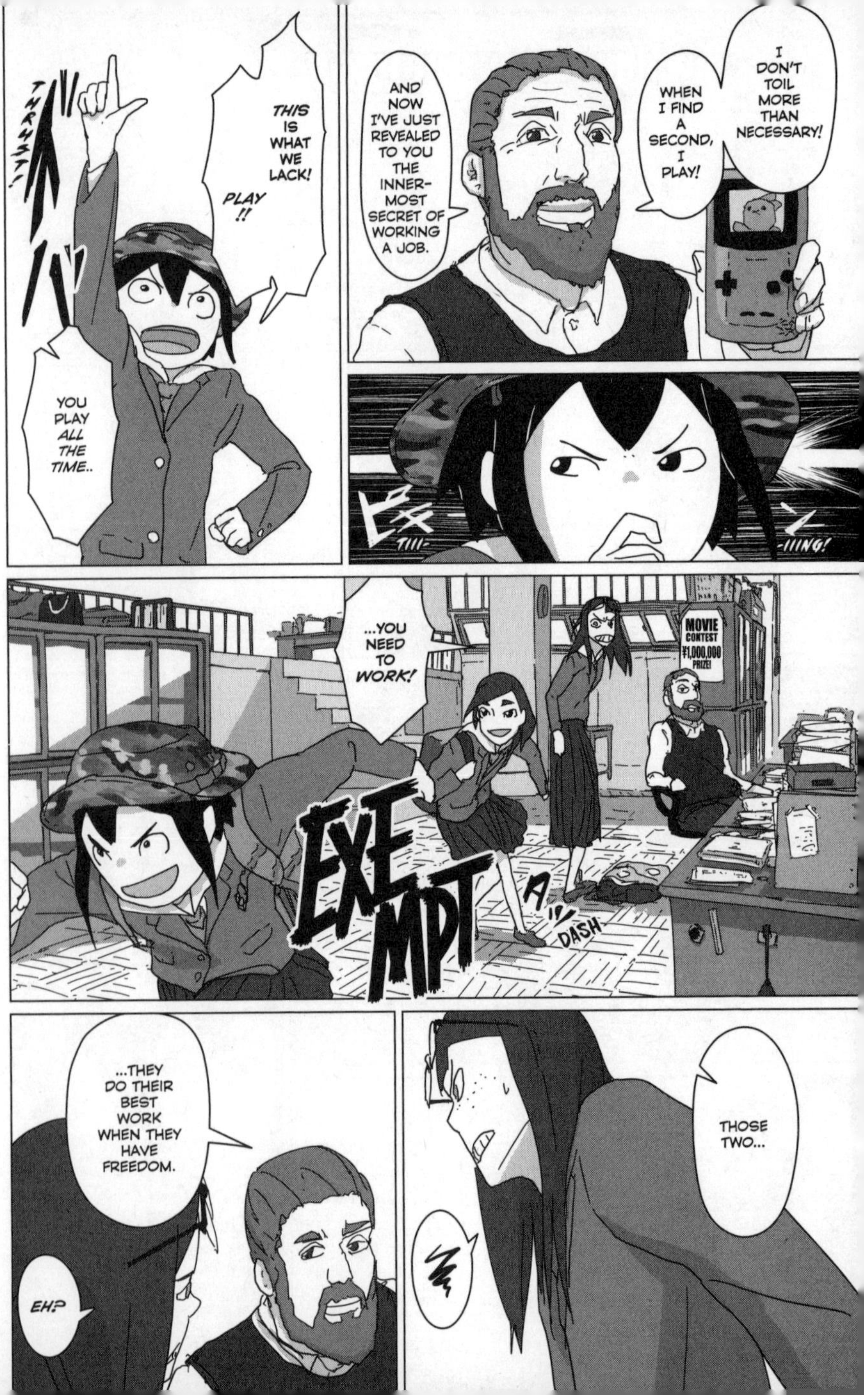
I DON'T TOIL MORE THAN NECESSARY!
WHEN I FIND A SECOND, I PLAY!
AND NOW I'VE JUST REVEALED TO YOU THE INNER-MOST SECRET OF WORKING A JOB.
TIII-
-IIING!
THRUST!
THIS IS WHAT WE LACK!
PLAY !!
YOU PLAY *ALL THE TIME*..
MOVIE CONTEST ¥1,000,000 PRIZE!
...YOU NEED TO *WORK!*
EXEMPT
A
DASH
THOSE TWO...
...THEY DO THEIR BEST WORK WHEN THEY HAVE FREEDOM.
EH?

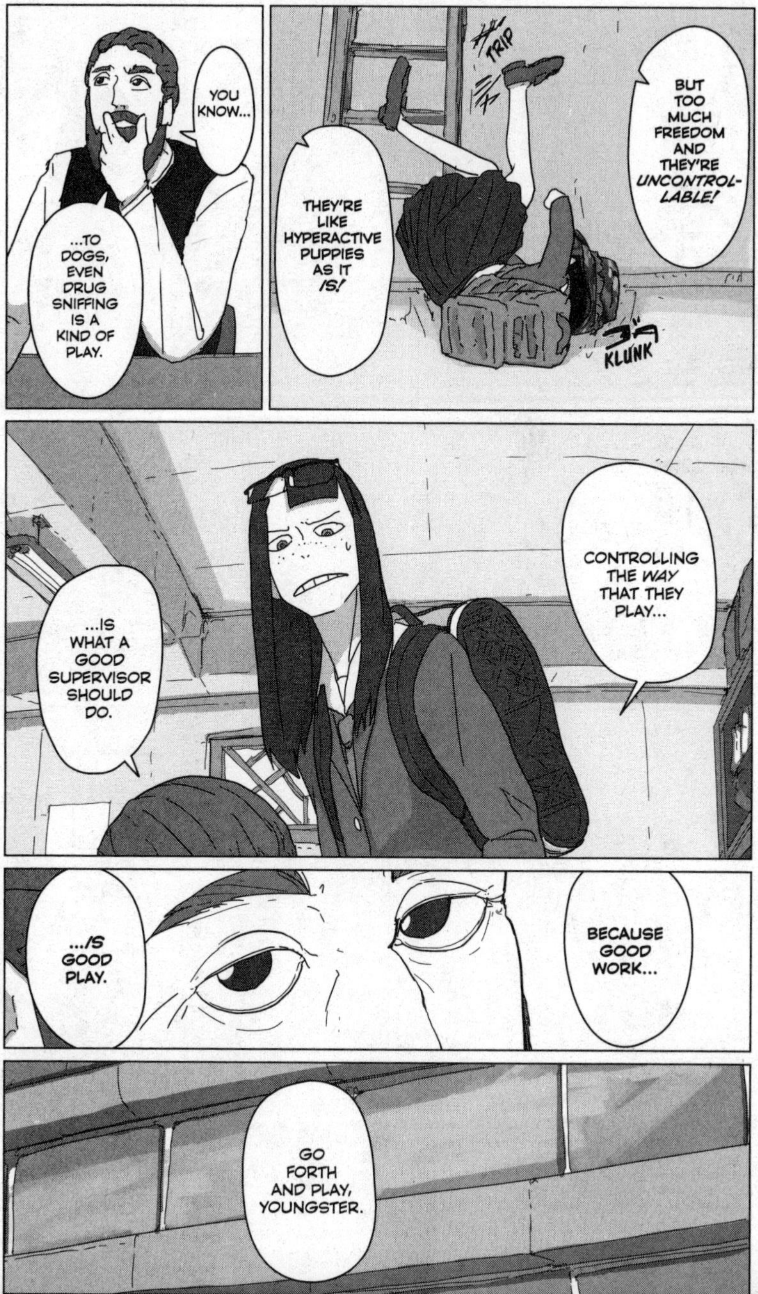
BUT TOO MUCH FREEDOM AND THEY'RE *UNCONTROLLABLE!*
TRIP
THEY'RE LIKE HYPERACTIVE PUPPIES AS IT *IS!*
KLUNK
YOU KNOW...
...TO DOGS, EVEN DRUG SNIFFING IS A KIND OF PLAY.
CONTROLLING THE *WAY* THAT THEY PLAY...
...IS WHAT A GOOD SUPERVISOR SHOULD DO.
BECAUSE GOOD WORK...
...*IS* GOOD PLAY.
GO FORTH AND PLAY, YOUNGSTER.

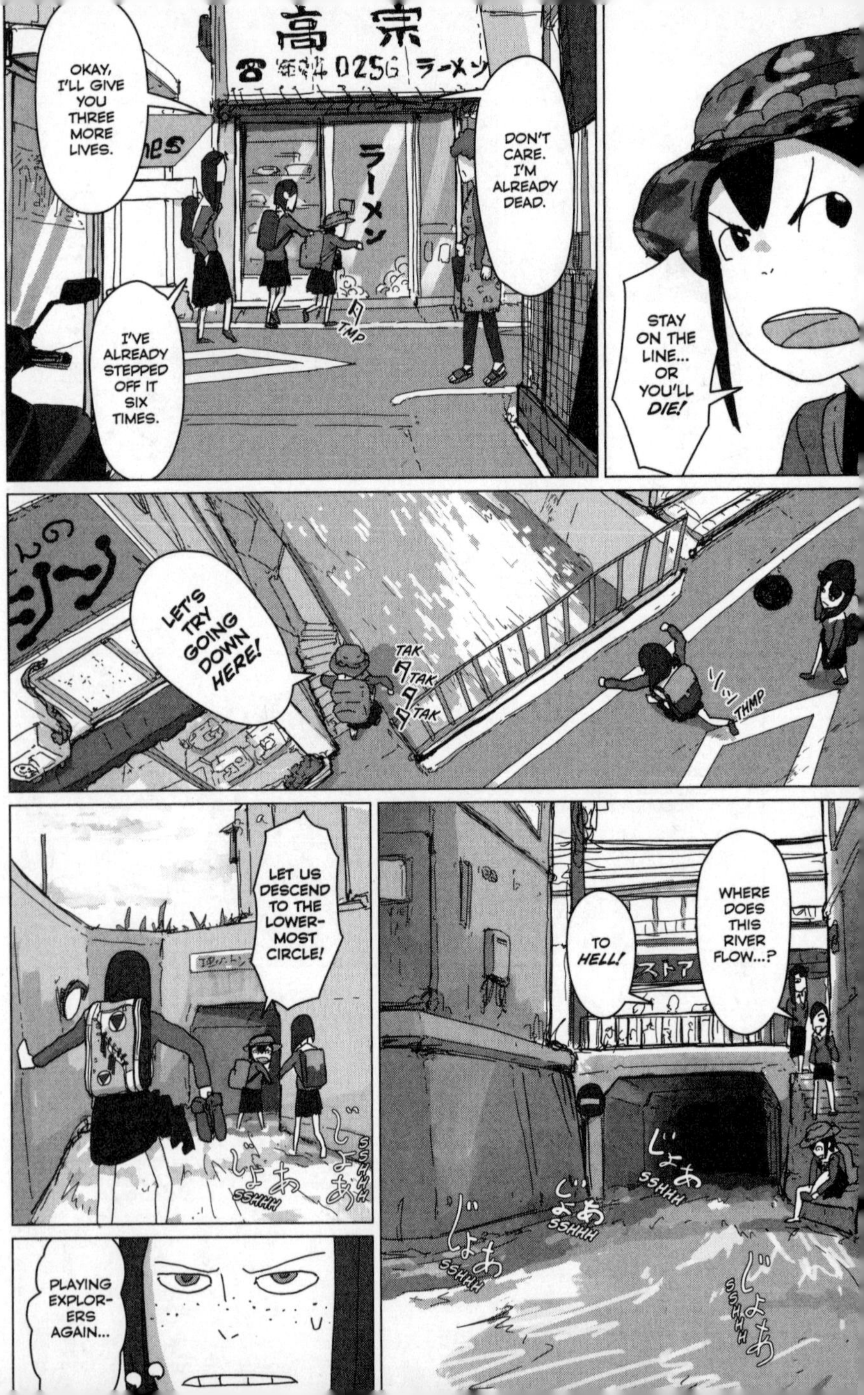
STAY ON THE LINE... OR YOU'LL DIE!
DON'T CARE. I'M ALREADY DEAD.
OKAY, I'LL GIVE YOU THREE MORE LIVES.
I'VE ALREADY STEPPED OFF IT SIX TIMES.
TMP
THMP
LET'S TRY GOING DOWN HERE!
TAK TAK TAK
WHERE DOES THIS RIVER FLOW...?
TO HELL!
SSHHH
LET US DESCEND TO THE LOWER-MOST CIRCLE!
SSHHH
PLAYING EXPLORERS AGAIN...

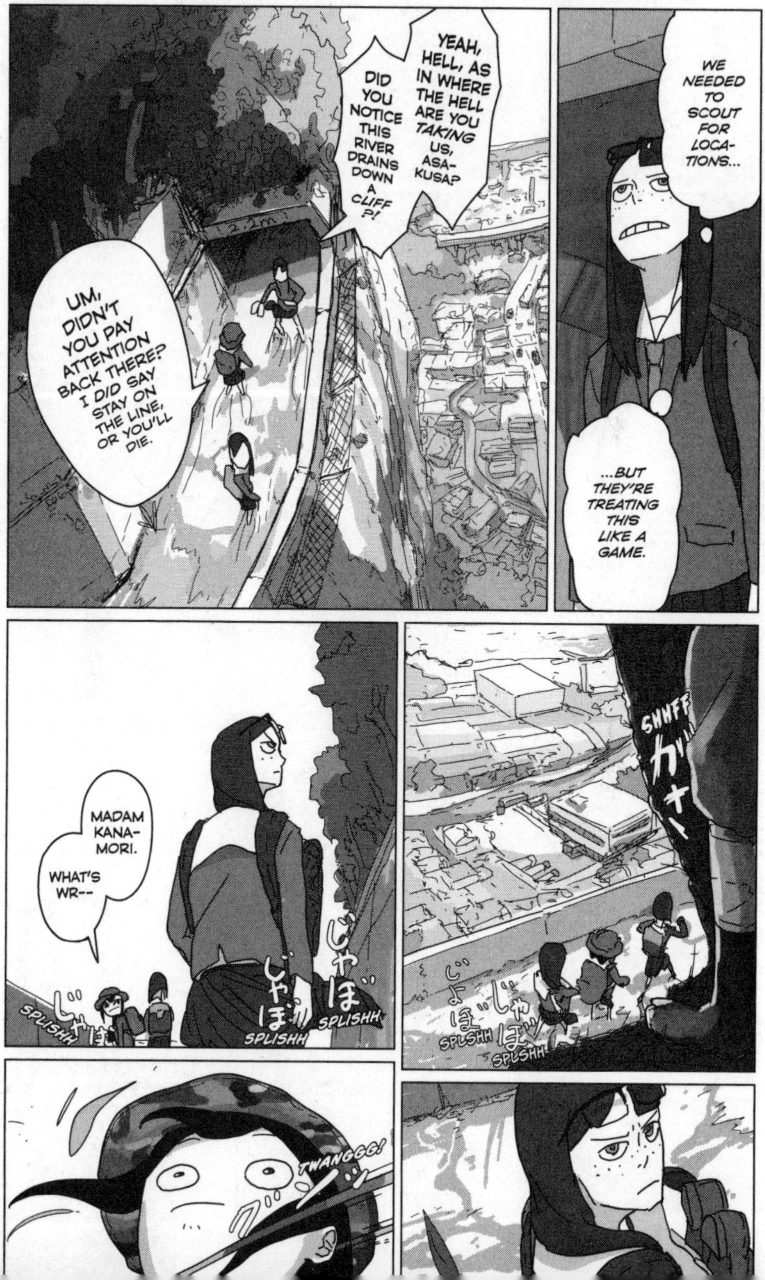
WE NEEDED TO SCOUT FOR LOCA-TIONS...
...BUT THEY'RE TREATING THIS LIKE A GAME.
YEAH, HELL, AS IN WHERE THE HELL ARE YOU *TAKING* US, ASA-KUSA?
DID YOU NOTICE THIS RIVER DRAINS DOWN A *CLIFF* ?!
UM, DIDN'T YOU PAY ATTENTION BACK THERE? I *DID* SAY STAY ON THE LINE, OR YOU'LL DIE.
SHHFF
SPLSHH
SPLSHH
MADAM KANA-MORI.
WHAT'S WR--
SPLISHH
SPLISHH
SPLISHH
TWANGGG!

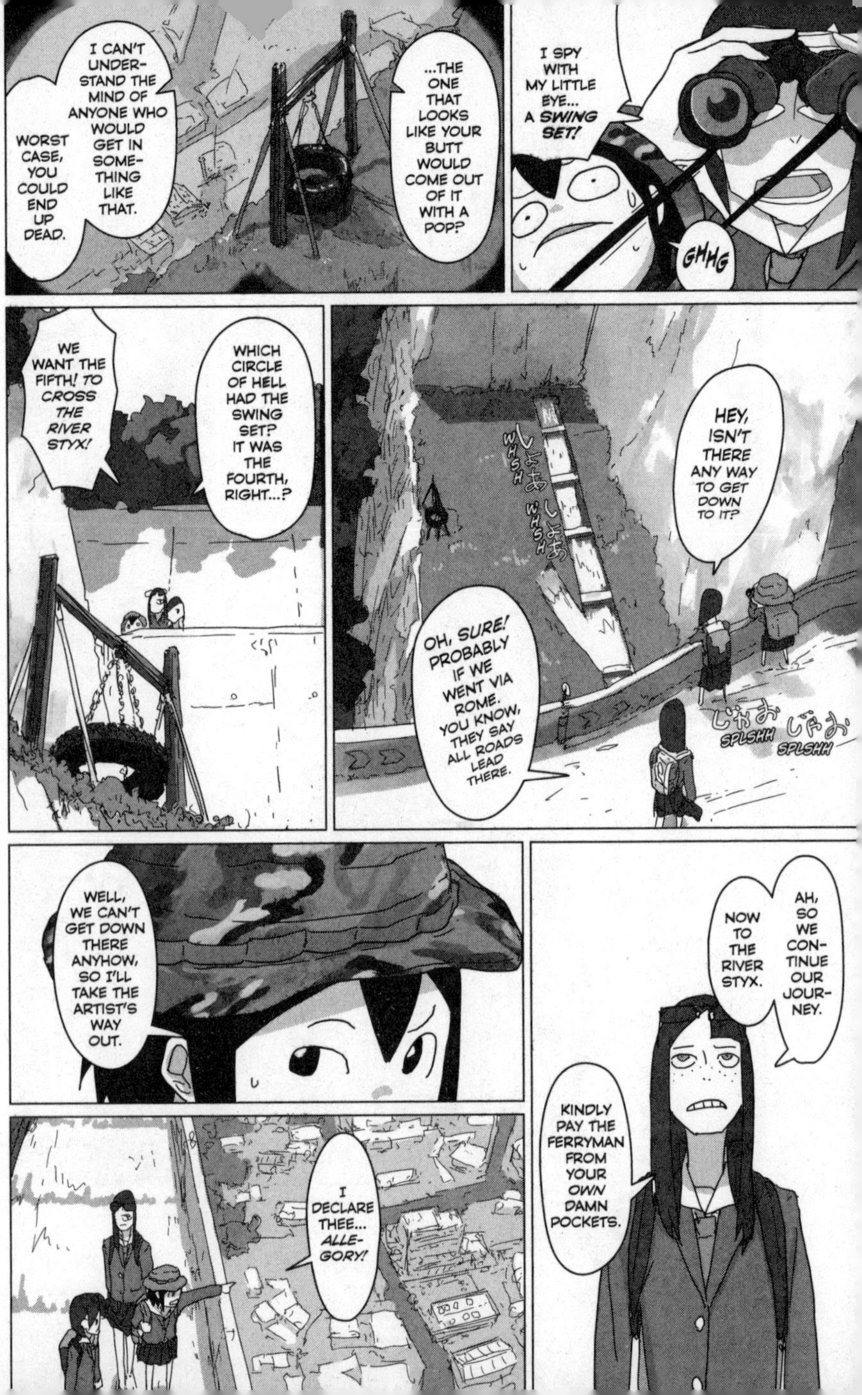
I SPY WITH MY LITTLE EYE... A *SWING SET!*
GHHG
...THE ONE THAT LOOKS LIKE YOUR BUTT WOULD COME OUT OF IT WITH A POP?
I CAN'T UNDERSTAND THE MIND OF ANYONE WHO WOULD GET IN SOMETHING LIKE THAT.
WORST CASE, YOU COULD END UP DEAD.
HEY, ISN'T THERE ANY WAY TO GET DOWN TO IT?
WHSH WHSH
OH, *SURE!* PROBABLY IF WE WENT VIA ROME. YOU KNOW, THEY SAY ALL ROADS LEAD THERE.
SPLSHH SPLSHH
WHICH CIRCLE OF HELL HAD THE SWING SET? IT WAS THE FOURTH, RIGHT...?
WE WANT THE FIFTH! *TO CROSS THE RIVER STYX!*
AH, SO WE CONTINUE OUR JOURNEY.
NOW TO THE RIVER STYX.
KINDLY PAY THE FERRYMAN FROM YOUR *OWN* DAMN POCKETS.
WELL, WE CAN'T GET DOWN THERE ANYHOW, SO I'LL TAKE THE ARTIST'S WAY OUT.
I DECLARE THEE... *ALLEGORY!*

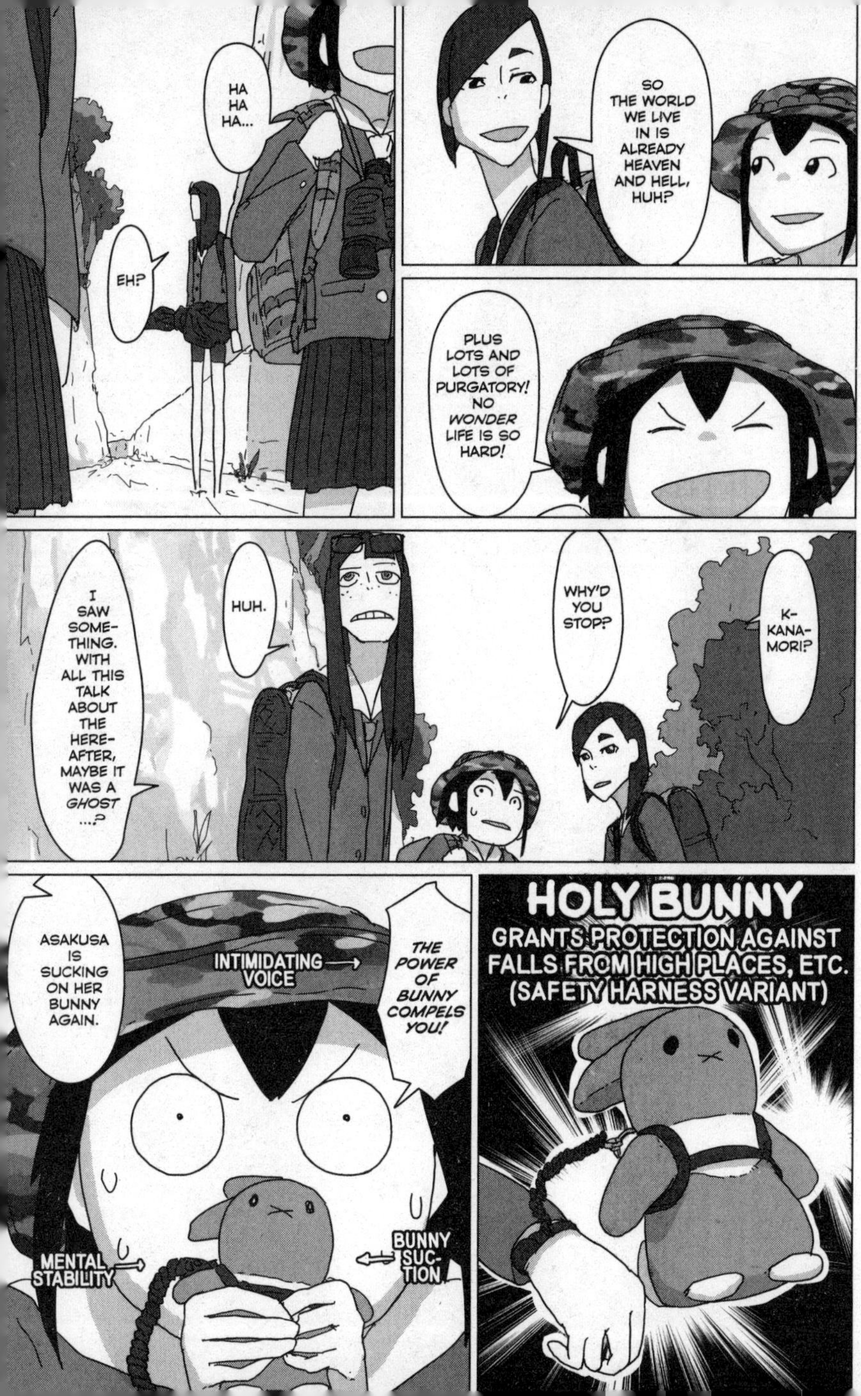
SO THE WORLD WE LIVE IN IS ALREADY HEAVEN AND HELL, HUH?
PLUS LOTS AND LOTS OF PURGATORY! NO WONDER LIFE IS SO HARD!
HA HA HA...
EH?
K-KANAMORI?
WHY'D YOU STOP?
HUH.
I SAW SOMETHING. WITH ALL THIS TALK ABOUT THE HEREAFTER, MAYBE IT WAS A GHOST ...?
HOLY BUNNY
GRANTS PROTECTION AGAINST FALLS FROM HIGH PLACES, ETC. (SAFETY HARNESS VARIANT)
THE POWER OF BUNNY COMPELS YOU!
INTIMIDATING VOICE
ASAKUSA IS SUCKING ON HER BUNNY AGAIN.
BUNNY SUCTION
MENTAL STABILITY

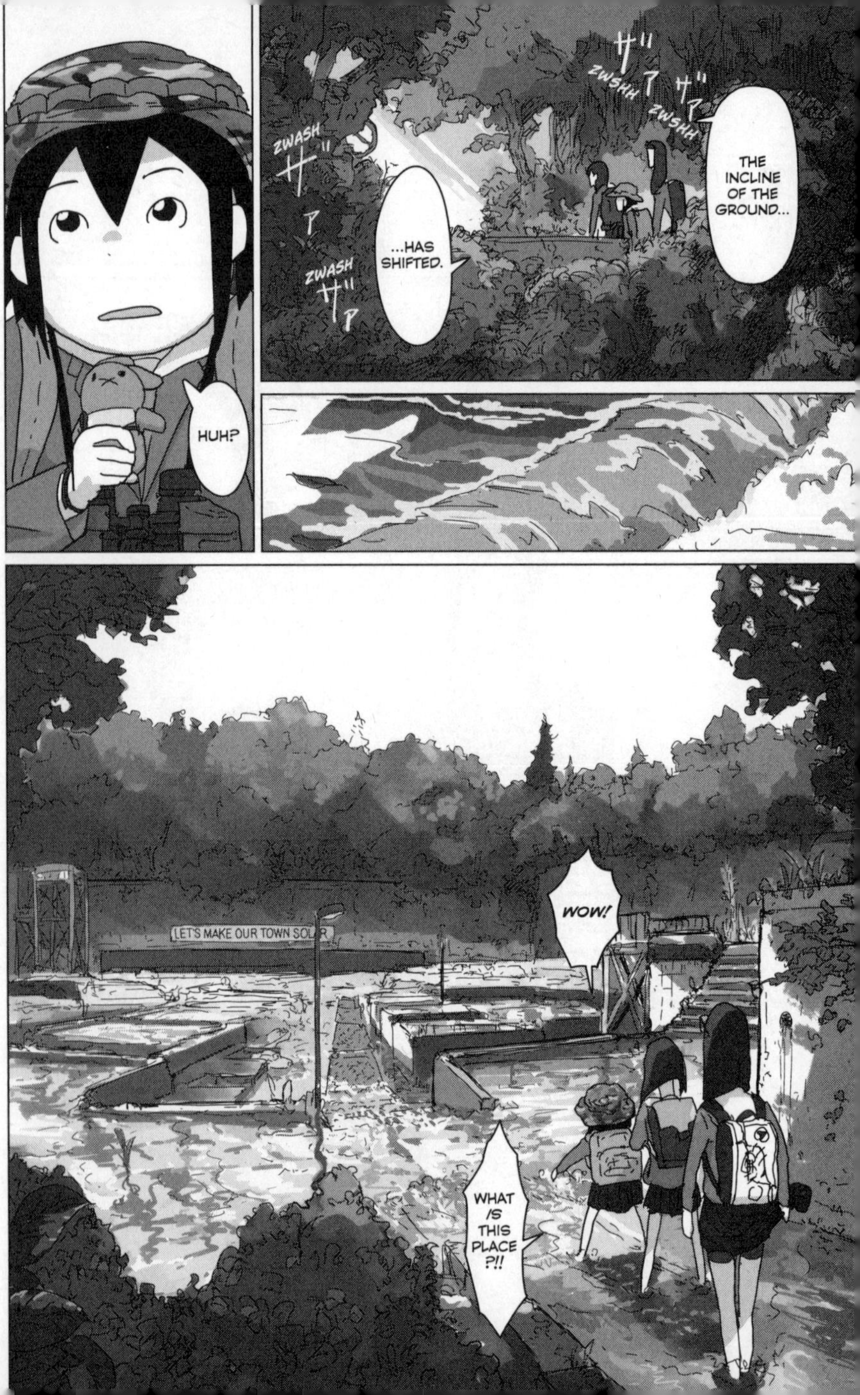
ZWSHH
ZWSHH
THE INCLINE OF THE GROUND...
...HAS SHIFTED.
ZWASH
ZWASH
HUH?
WOW!
LET'S MAKE OUR TOWN SOLAR
WHAT IS THIS PLACE?!!

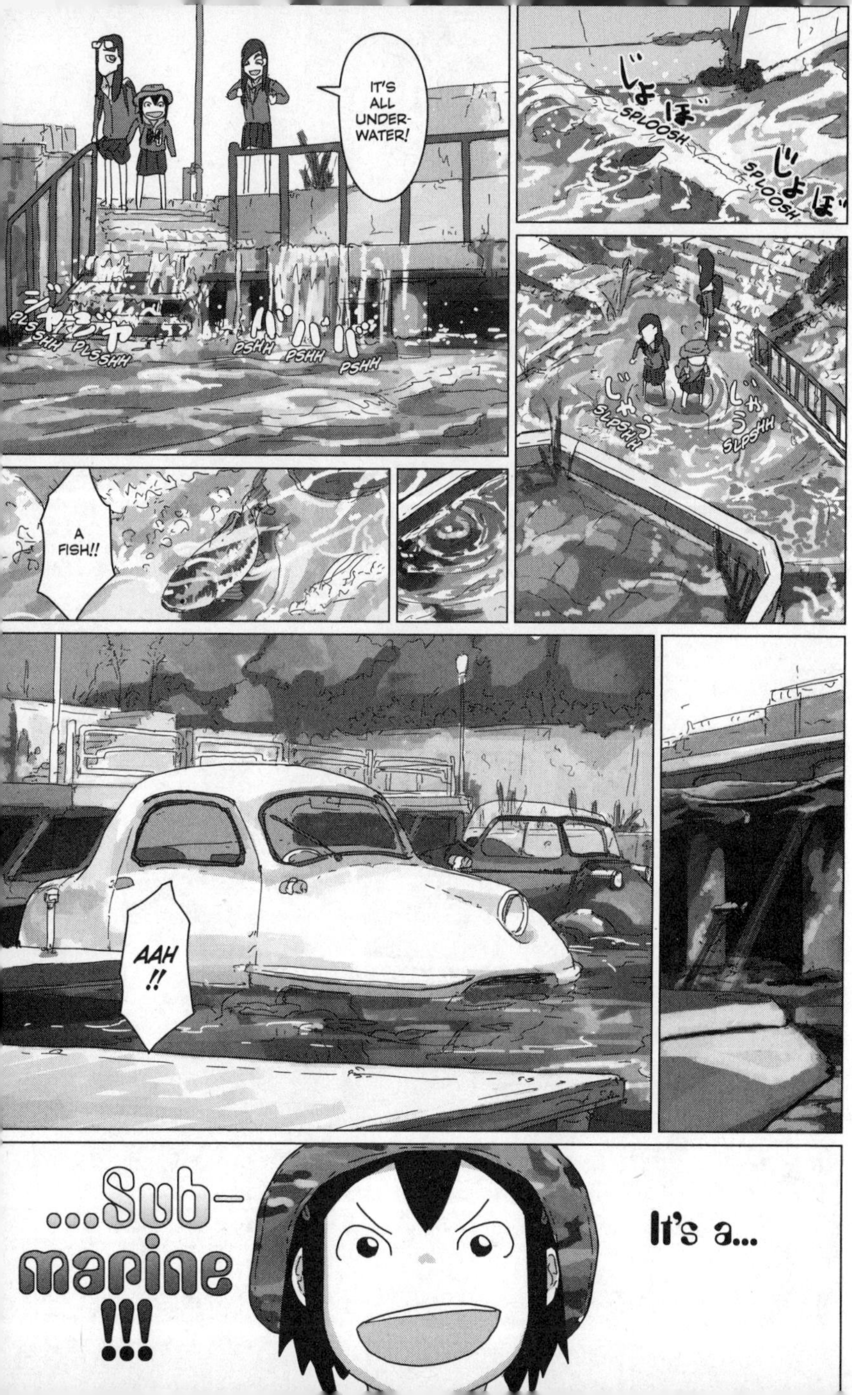
じょぼ
SPLOOSH
じょぼ
SPLOOSH
じゅう
SLPSHH
じゅう
SLPSHH
IT'S ALL UNDER-WATER!
ジャジャ
PLSSHH
PLSSHH
ドバババ
PSHH
PSHH
PSHH
A FISH!!
AAH!!
It's a...
...Sub-marine!!!

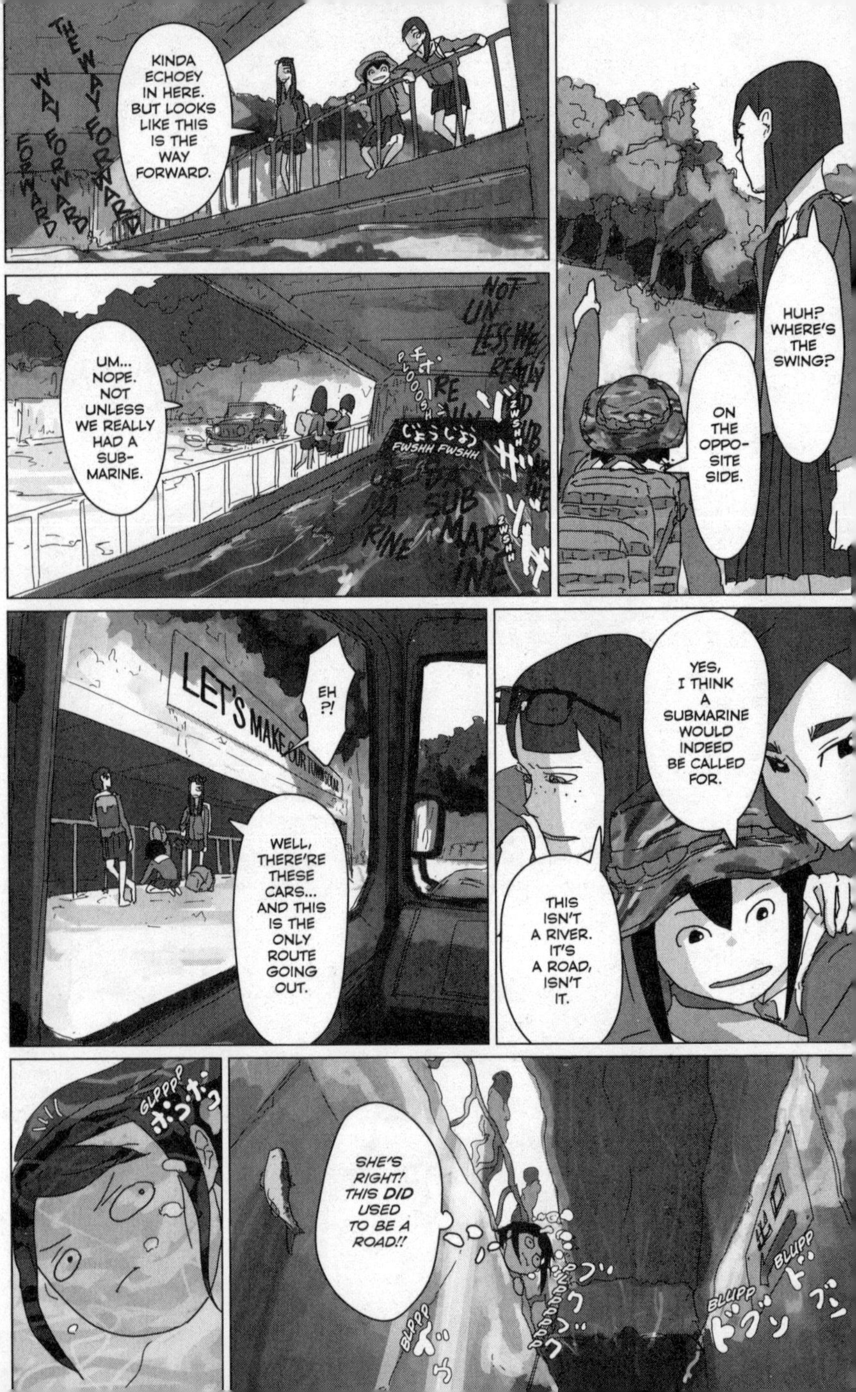

HUH? WHERE'S THE SWING?
ON THE OPPOSITE SIDE.
THE WAY FORWARD
WAY FORWARD
FORWARD
KINDA ECHOEY IN HERE. BUT LOOKS LIKE THIS IS THE WAY FORWARD.
NOT UNLESS WE REALLY
PLOOOOSH
FWSHH FWSHH
ZWSHH
ZWSHH
SUBMARINE
UM... NOPE. NOT UNLESS WE REALLY HAD A SUBMARINE.
YES, I THINK A SUBMARINE WOULD INDEED BE CALLED FOR.
THIS ISN'T A RIVER. IT'S A ROAD, ISN'T IT.
LET'S MAKE
EH ?!
WELL, THERE'RE THESE CARS... AND THIS IS THE ONLY ROUTE GOING OUT.
SHE'S RIGHT! THIS DID USED TO BE A ROAD!!
BLUPP
BLUPP
BLPPP
GLPPPP

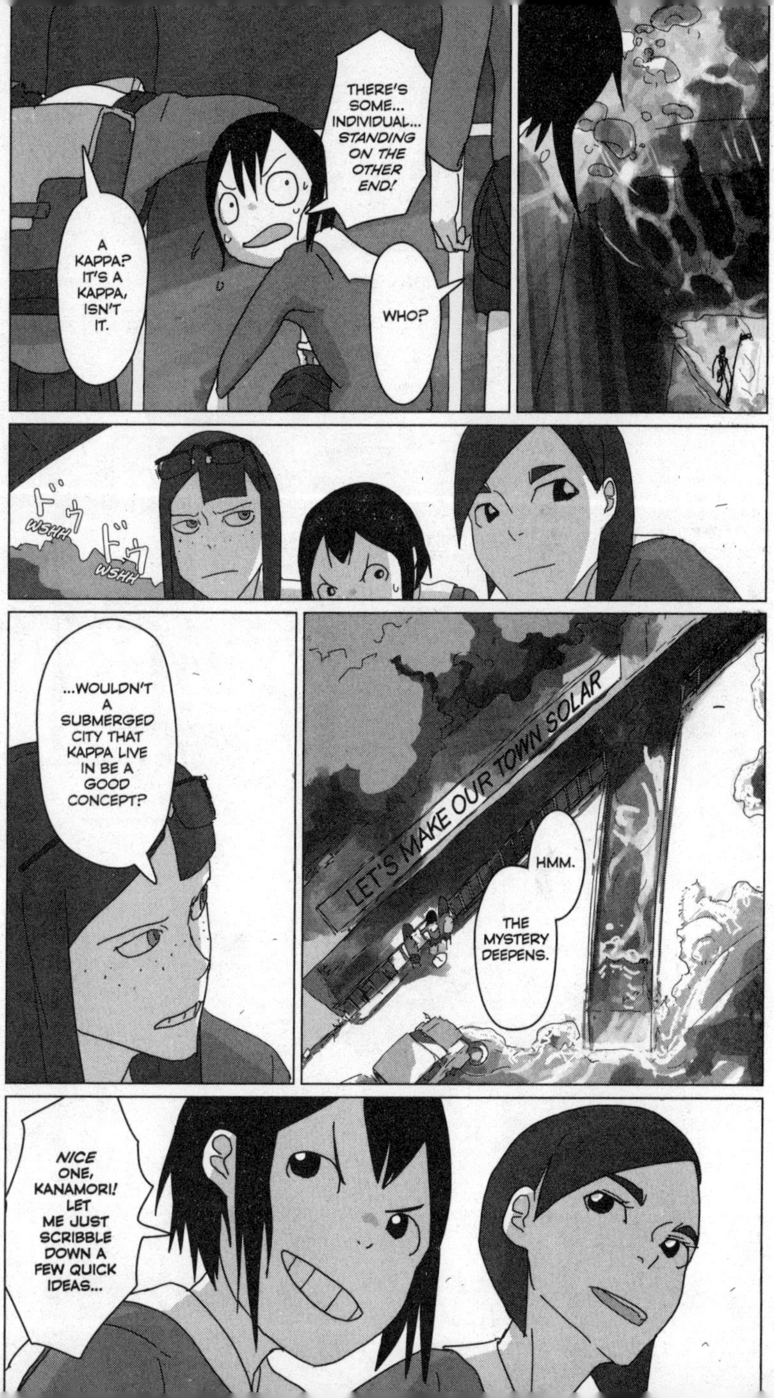
THERE'S SOME... INDIVIDUAL... STANDING ON THE OTHER END!
WHO?
A KAPPA? IT'S A KAPPA, ISN'T IT.
ドゥ
WSHH
ドゥ
WSHH
LET'S MAKE OUR TOWN SOLAR
HMM.
THE MYSTERY DEEPENS.
...WOULDN'T A SUBMERGED CITY THAT KAPPA LIVE IN BE A GOOD CONCEPT?
NICE ONE, KANAMORI! LET ME JUST SCRIBBLE DOWN A FEW QUICK IDEAS...

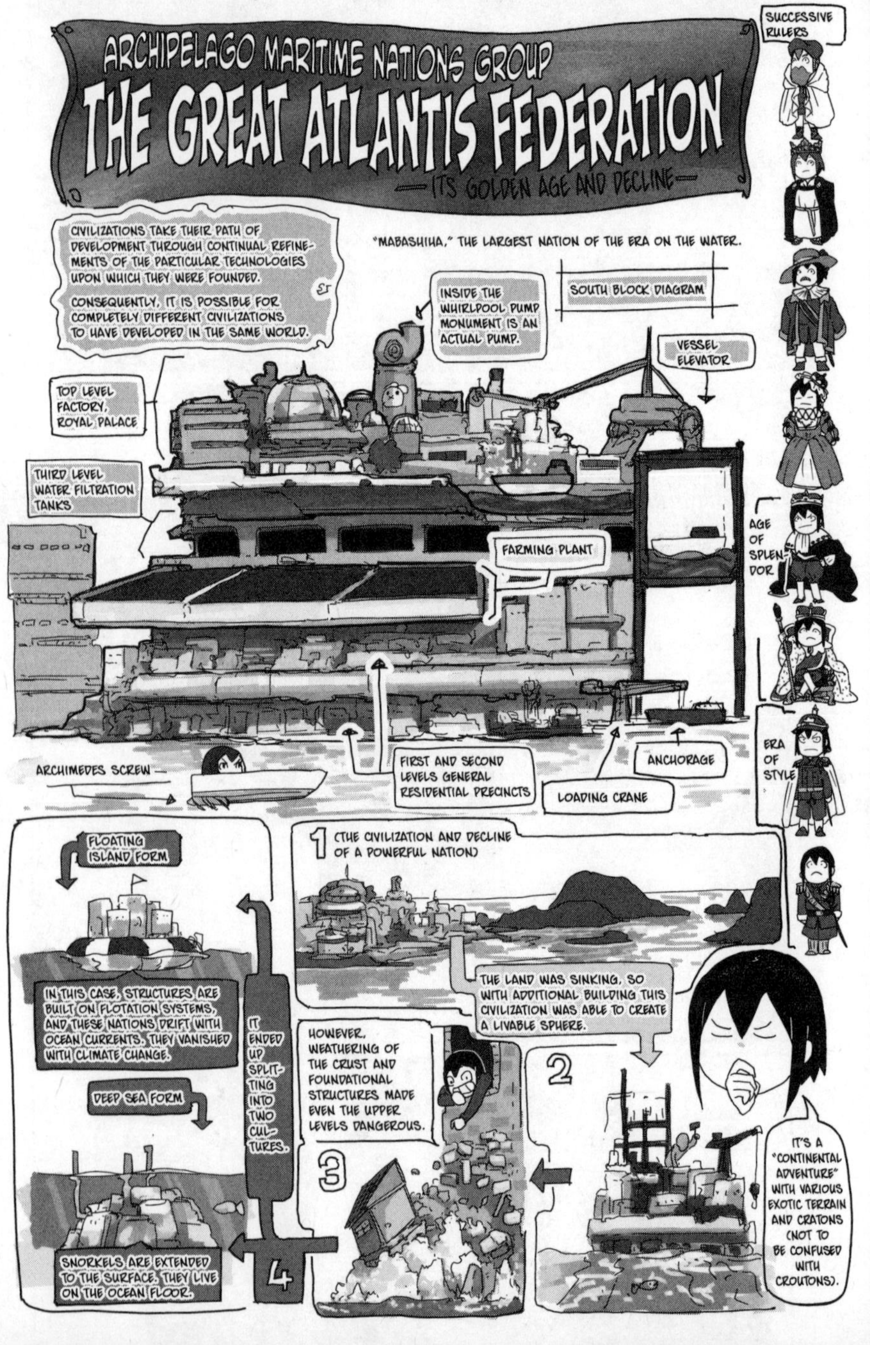
ARCHIPELAGO MARITIME NATIONS GROUP
THE GREAT ATLANTIS FEDERATION
—ITS GOLDEN AGE AND DECLINE—
SUCCESSIVE RULERS
AGE OF SPLENDOR
ERA OF STYLE
"MABASHIHA," THE LARGEST NATION OF THE ERA ON THE WATER.
SOUTH BLOCK DIAGRAM
CIVILIZATIONS TAKE THEIR PATH OF DEVELOPMENT THROUGH CONTINUAL REFINEMENTS OF THE PARTICULAR TECHNOLOGIES UPON WHICH THEY WERE FOUNDED.
CONSEQUENTLY, IT IS POSSIBLE FOR COMPLETELY DIFFERENT CIVILIZATIONS TO HAVE DEVELOPED IN THE SAME WORLD.
INSIDE THE WHIRLPOOL PUMP MONUMENT IS AN ACTUAL PUMP.
VESSEL ELEVATOR
TOP LEVEL FACTORY, ROYAL PALACE
THIRD LEVEL WATER FILTRATION TANKS
FARMING PLANT
ARCHIMEDES SCREW
FIRST AND SECOND LEVELS GENERAL RESIDENTIAL PRECINCTS
ANCHORAGE
LOADING CRANE
1 (THE CIVILIZATION AND DECLINE OF A POWERFUL NATION)
THE LAND WAS SINKING, SO WITH ADDITIONAL BUILDING THIS CIVILIZATION WAS ABLE TO CREATE A LIVABLE SPHERE.
2
IT'S A "CONTINENTAL ADVENTURE" WITH VARIOUS EXOTIC TERRAIN AND CRATONS (NOT TO BE CONFUSED WITH CROUTONS).
3
HOWEVER, WEATHERING OF THE CRUST AND FOUNDATIONAL STRUCTURES MADE EVEN THE UPPER LEVELS DANGEROUS.
4
IT ENDED UP SPLITTING INTO TWO CULTURES.
FLOATING ISLAND FORM
IN THIS CASE, STRUCTURES ARE BUILT ON FLOTATION SYSTEMS, AND THESE NATIONS DRIFT WITH OCEAN CURRENTS. THEY VANISHED WITH CLIMATE CHANGE.
DEEP SEA FORM
SNORKELS ARE EXTENDED TO THE SURFACE. THEY LIVE ON THE OCEAN FLOOR.

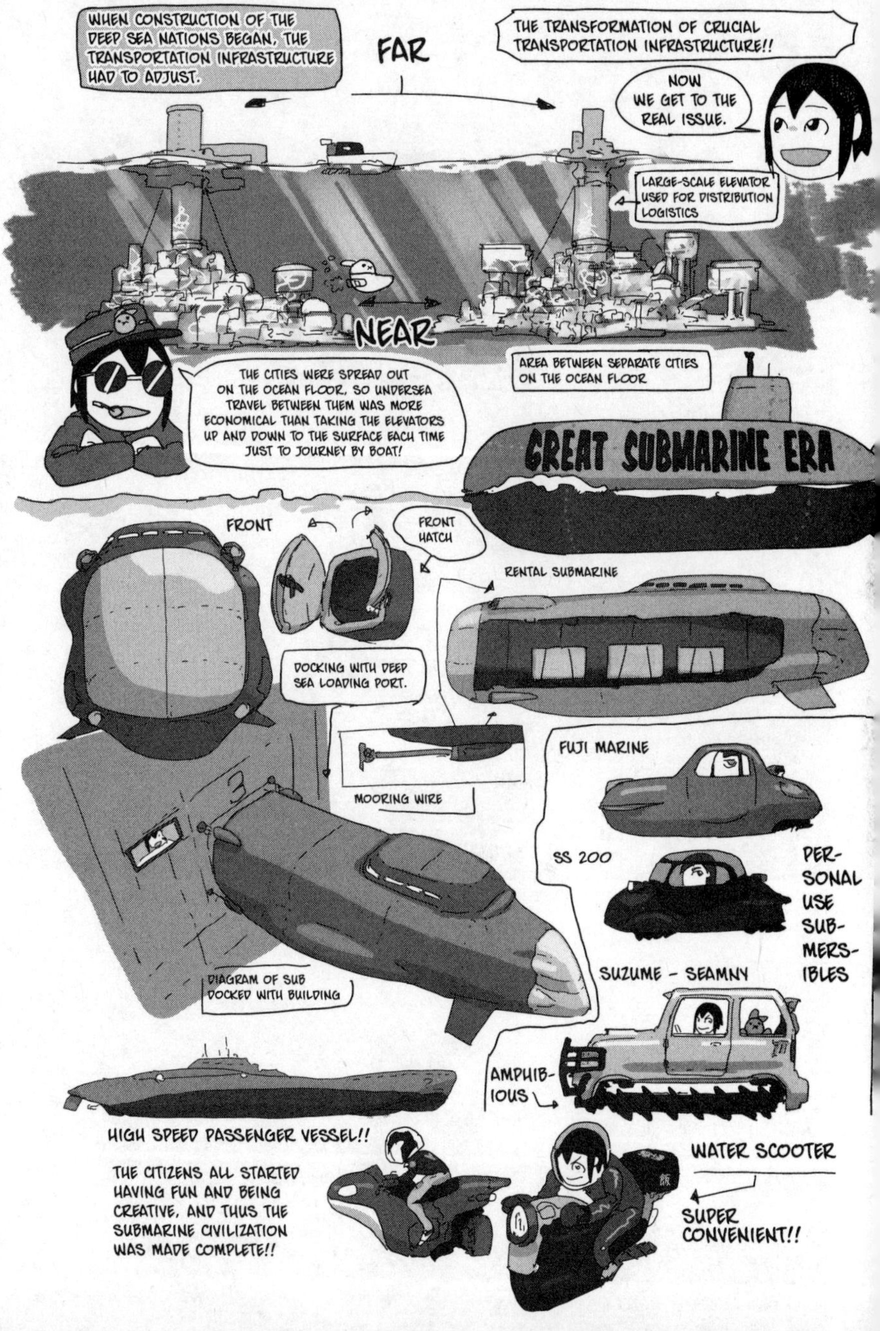

THE TRANSFORMATION OF CRUCIAL TRANSPORTATION INFRASTRUCTURE!!
NOW WE GET TO THE REAL ISSUE.
WHEN CONSTRUCTION OF THE DEEP SEA NATIONS BEGAN, THE TRANSPORTATION INFRASTRUCTURE HAD TO ADJUST.
FAR
LARGE-SCALE ELEVATOR USED FOR DISTRIBUTION LOGISTICS
NEAR
AREA BETWEEN SEPARATE CITIES ON THE OCEAN FLOOR
THE CITIES WERE SPREAD OUT ON THE OCEAN FLOOR, SO UNDERSEA TRAVEL BETWEEN THEM WAS MORE ECONOMICAL THAN TAKING THE ELEVATORS UP AND DOWN TO THE SURFACE EACH TIME JUST TO JOURNEY BY BOAT!
GREAT SUBMARINE ERA
RENTAL SUBMARINE
FRONT HATCH
FRONT
DOCKING WITH DEEP SEA LOADING PORT.
MOORING WIRE
FUJI MARINE
PERSONAL USE SUBMERSIBLES
SS 200
SUZUME - SEAMNY
AMPHIBIOUS
DIAGRAM OF SUB DOCKED WITH BUILDING
HIGH SPEED PASSENGER VESSEL!!
WATER SCOOTER
SUPER CONVENIENT!!
THE CITIZENS ALL STARTED HAVING FUN AND BEING CREATIVE, AND THUS THE SUBMARINE CIVILIZATION WAS MADE COMPLETE!!

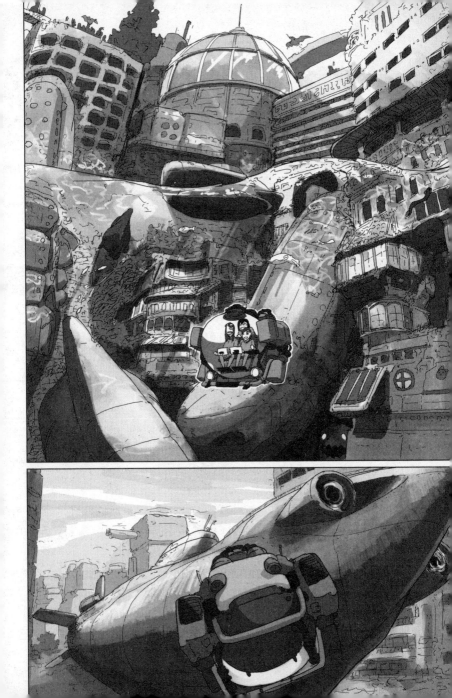

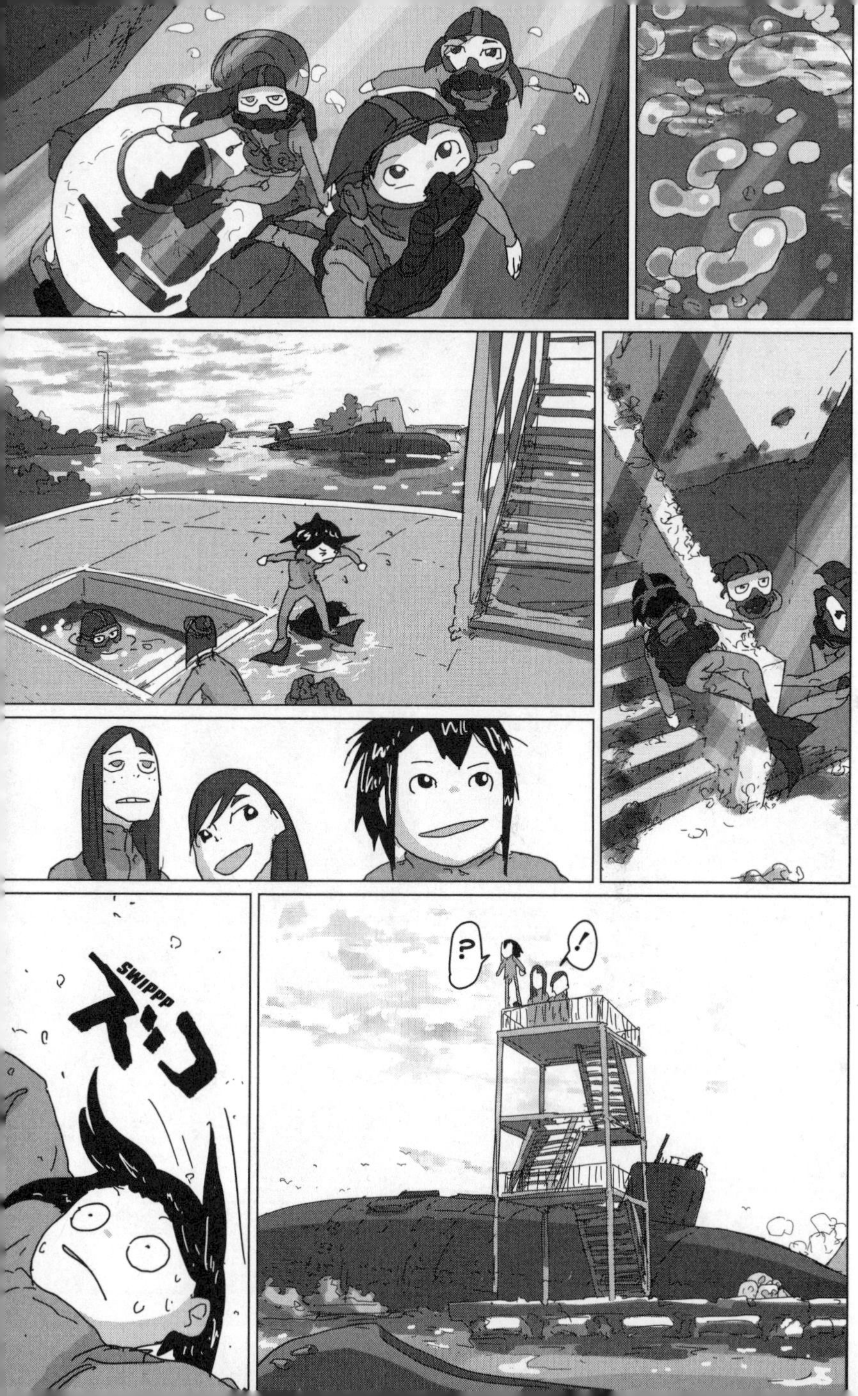
!
?
SWIPPP
ズン

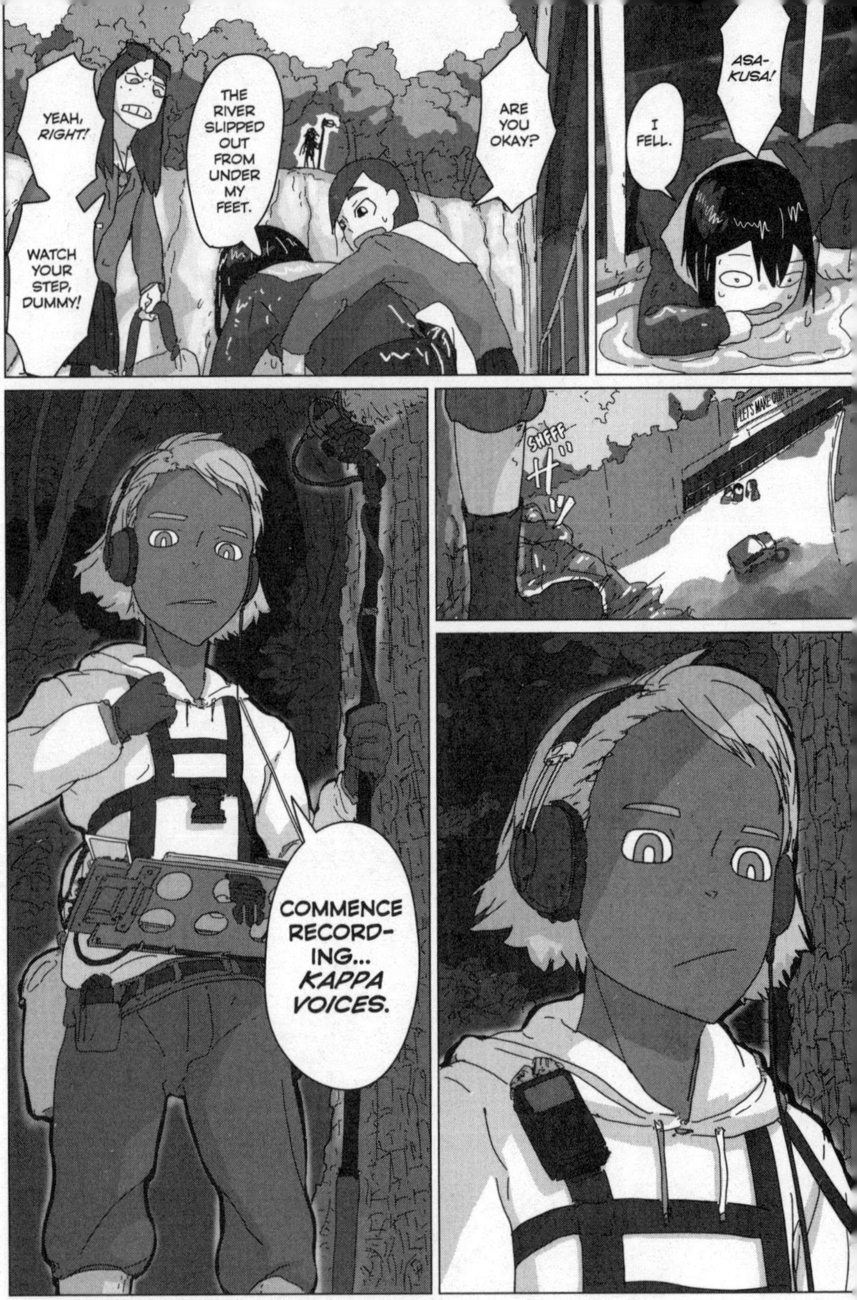
ASA-KUSA!
I FELL.
ARE YOU OKAY?
THE RIVER SLIPPED OUT FROM UNDER MY FEET.
YEAH, *RIGHT!*
WATCH YOUR STEP, DUMMY!
LET'S MAKE OUR
SHFFF
COMMENCE RECORDING... *KAPPA VOICES.*

CHAPTER 17: TREASURE HEIST!

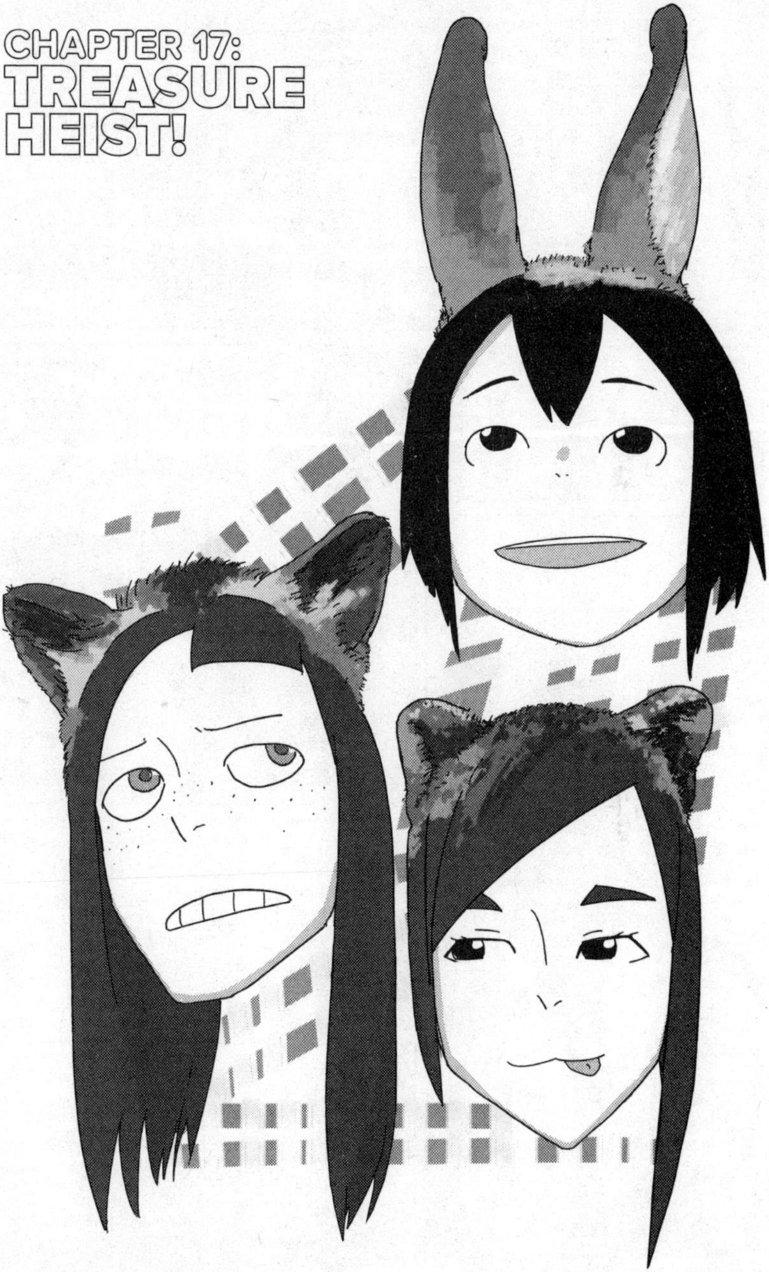

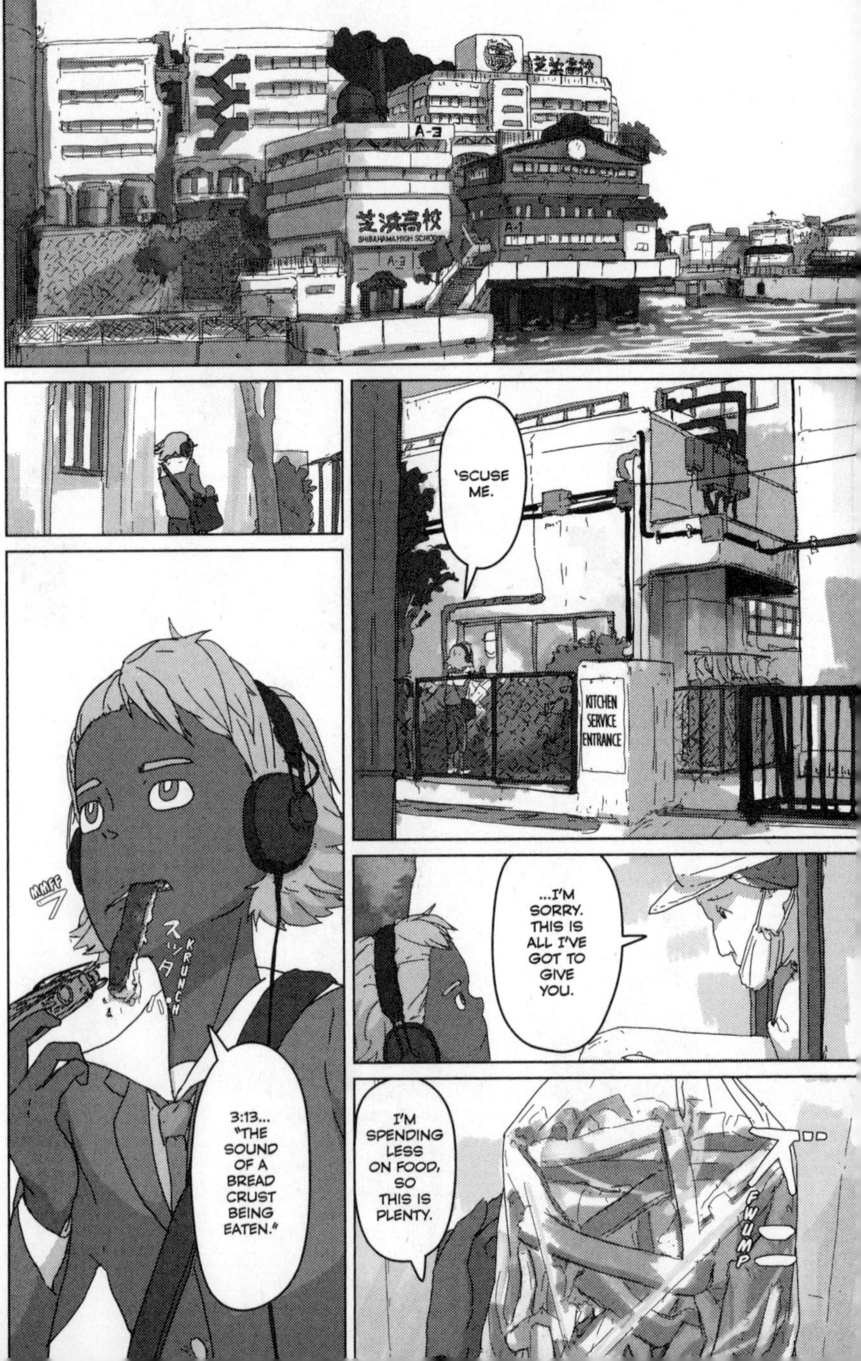

芝浜高校
A-3
芝浜高校
SHIBAHAMA HIGH SCHOOL
A3
A-1
'SCUSE ME.
KITCHEN SERVICE ENTRANCE
...I'M SORRY. THIS IS ALL I'VE GOT TO GIVE YOU.
I'M SPENDING LESS ON FOOD, SO THIS IS PLENTY.
FWUMP
MMFF
KRUNCH
3:13... "THE SOUND OF A BREAD CRUST BEING EATEN."

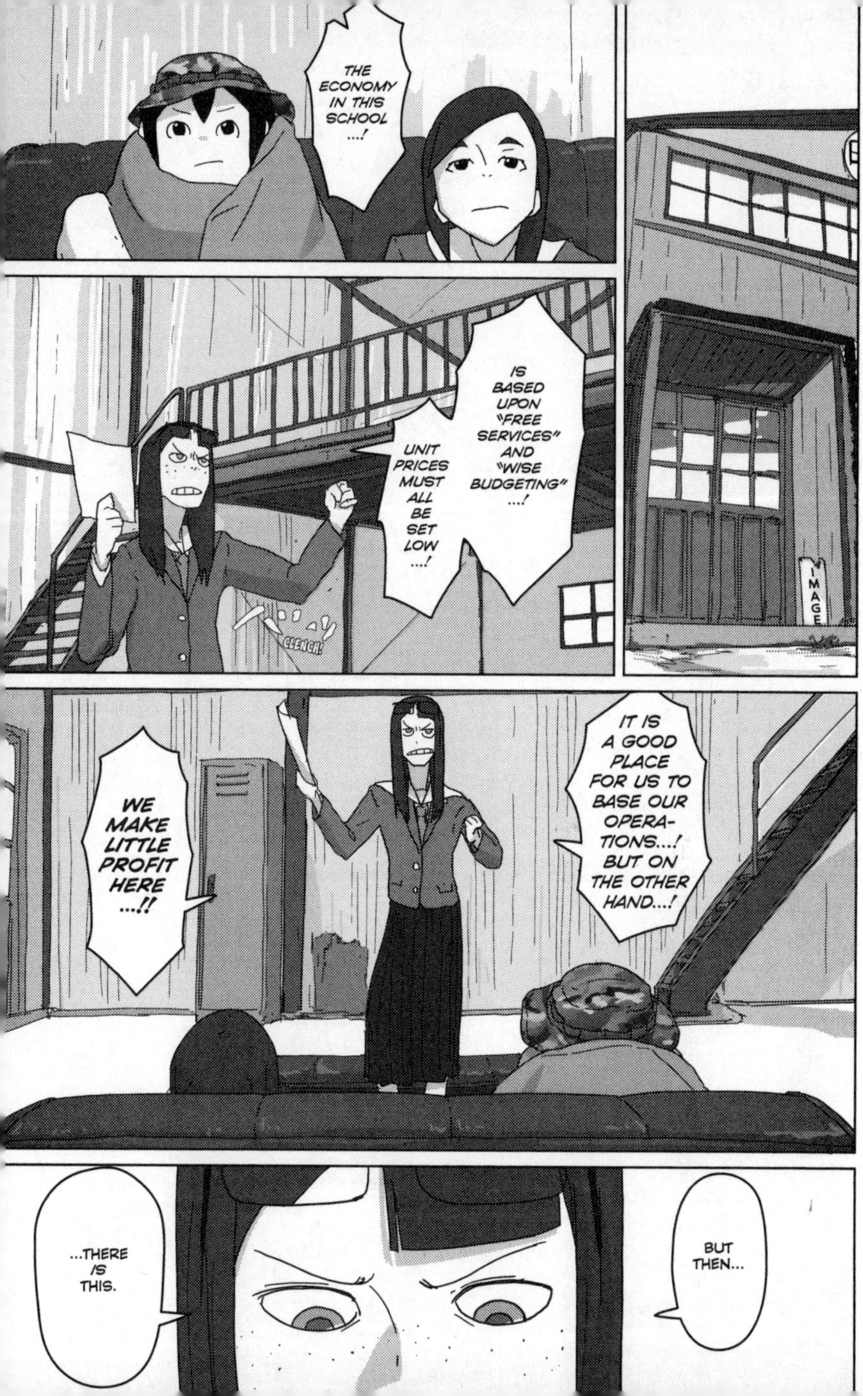
IMAGE
THE ECONOMY IN THIS SCHOOL ...!
IS BASED UPON "FREE SERVICES" AND "WISE BUDGETING" ...!
UNIT PRICES MUST ALL BE SET LOW ...!
CLENCH!
IT IS A GOOD PLACE FOR US TO BASE OUR OPERATIONS...! BUT ON THE OTHER HAND...!
WE MAKE LITTLE PROFIT HERE ...!!
BUT THEN...
...THERE IS THIS.

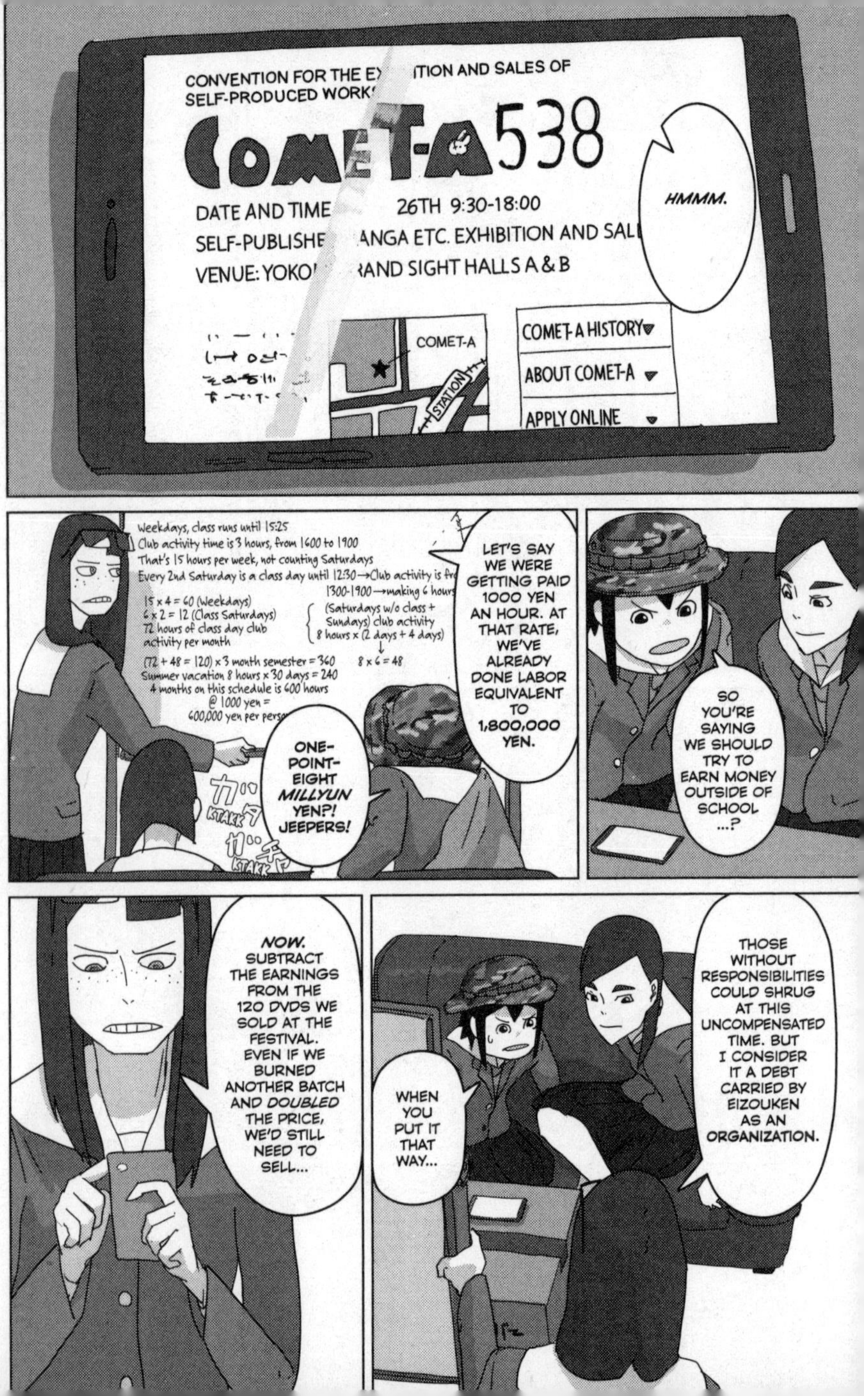
CONVENTION FOR THE EX ITION AND SALES OF
SELF-PRODUCED WORKS
COMET-A 538
DATE AND TIME 26TH 9:30-18:00
SELF-PUBLISHE ANGA ETC. EXHIBITION AND SAL
VENUE: YOKO RAND SIGHT HALLS A & B
COMET-A
STATION
COMET-A HISTORY
ABOUT COMET-A
APPLY ONLINE
HMMM.
SO YOU'RE SAYING WE SHOULD TRY TO EARN MONEY OUTSIDE OF SCHOOL ...?
LET'S SAY WE WERE GETTING PAID 1000 YEN AN HOUR. AT THAT RATE, WE'VE ALREADY DONE LABOR EQUIVALENT TO 1,800,000 YEN.
Weekdays, class runs until 15:25
Club activity time is 3 hours, from 1600 to 1900
That's 15 hours per week, not counting Saturdays
Every 2nd Saturday is a class day until 12:30→Club activity is fr
1300-1900→making 6 hours
15 x 4 = 60 (Weekdays)
6 x 2 = 12 (Class Saturdays)
72 hours of class day club activity per month
(Saturdays w/o class + Sundays) club activity
8 hours x (2 days + 4 days)
8 x 6 = 48
(72 + 48 = 120) x 3 month semester = 360
Summer vacation 8 hours x 30 days = 240
4 months on this schedule is 600 hours
@ 1000 yen =
600,000 yen per perso
ONE-POINT-EIGHT MILLYUN YEN?! JEEPERS!
KTAKK
KTAKK
THOSE WITHOUT RESPONSIBILITIES COULD SHRUG AT THIS UNCOMPENSATED TIME. BUT I CONSIDER IT A DEBT CARRIED BY EIZOUKEN AS AN ORGANIZATION.
WHEN YOU PUT IT THAT WAY...
NOW. SUBTRACT THE EARNINGS FROM THE 120 DVDS WE SOLD AT THE FESTIVAL. EVEN IF WE BURNED ANOTHER BATCH AND DOUBLED THE PRICE, WE'D STILL NEED TO SELL...

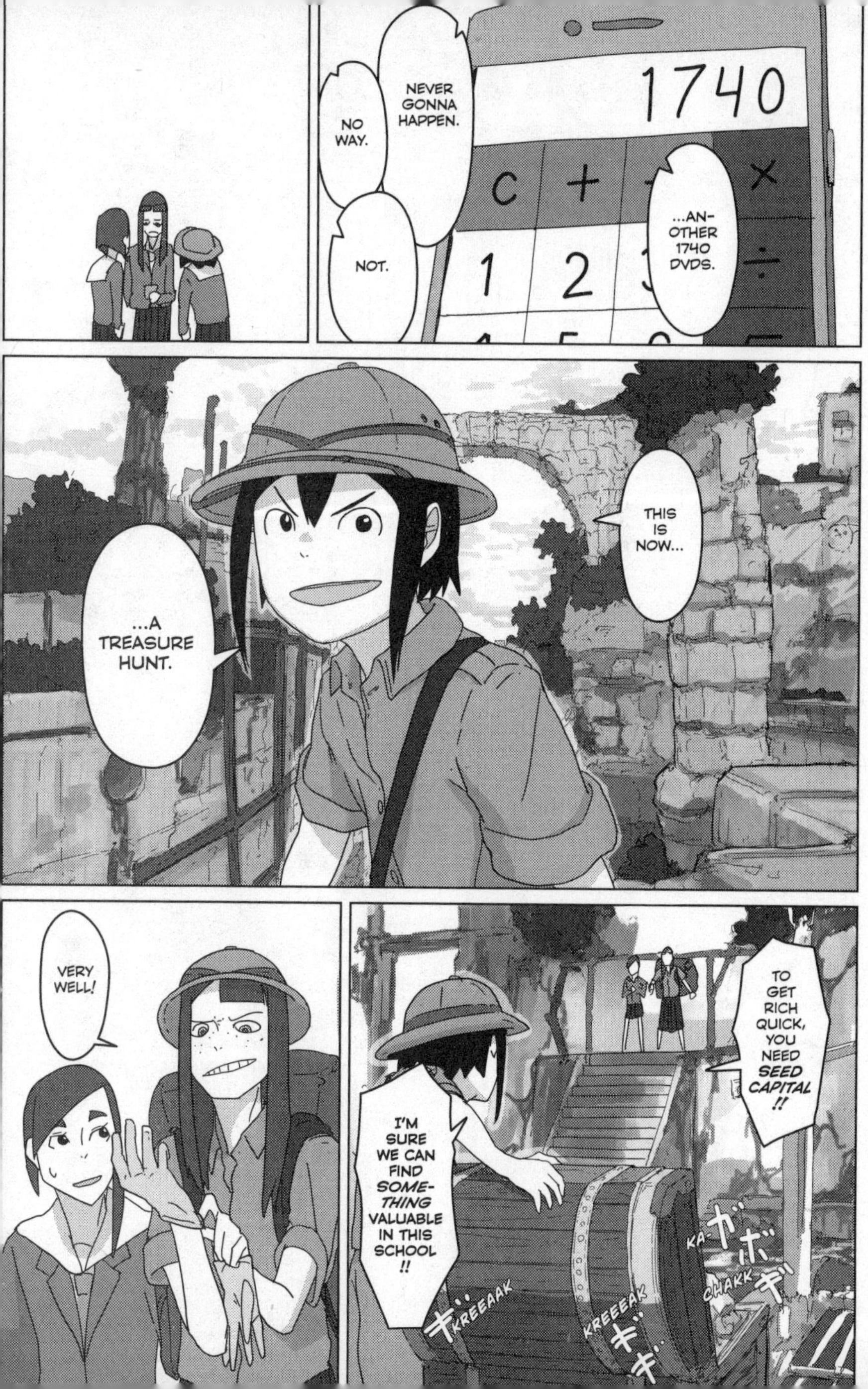
1740
...AN-OTHER 1740 DVDS.
NEVER GONNA HAPPEN.
NO WAY.
NOT.
THIS IS NOW...
...A TREASURE HUNT.
TO GET RICH QUICK, YOU NEED *SEED CAPITAL* !!
I'M SURE WE CAN FIND *SOME-THING* VALUABLE IN THIS SCHOOL !!
KA-CHAKK ガボギ
KREEEAK ギギ
KREEAAK ギ
VERY WELL!

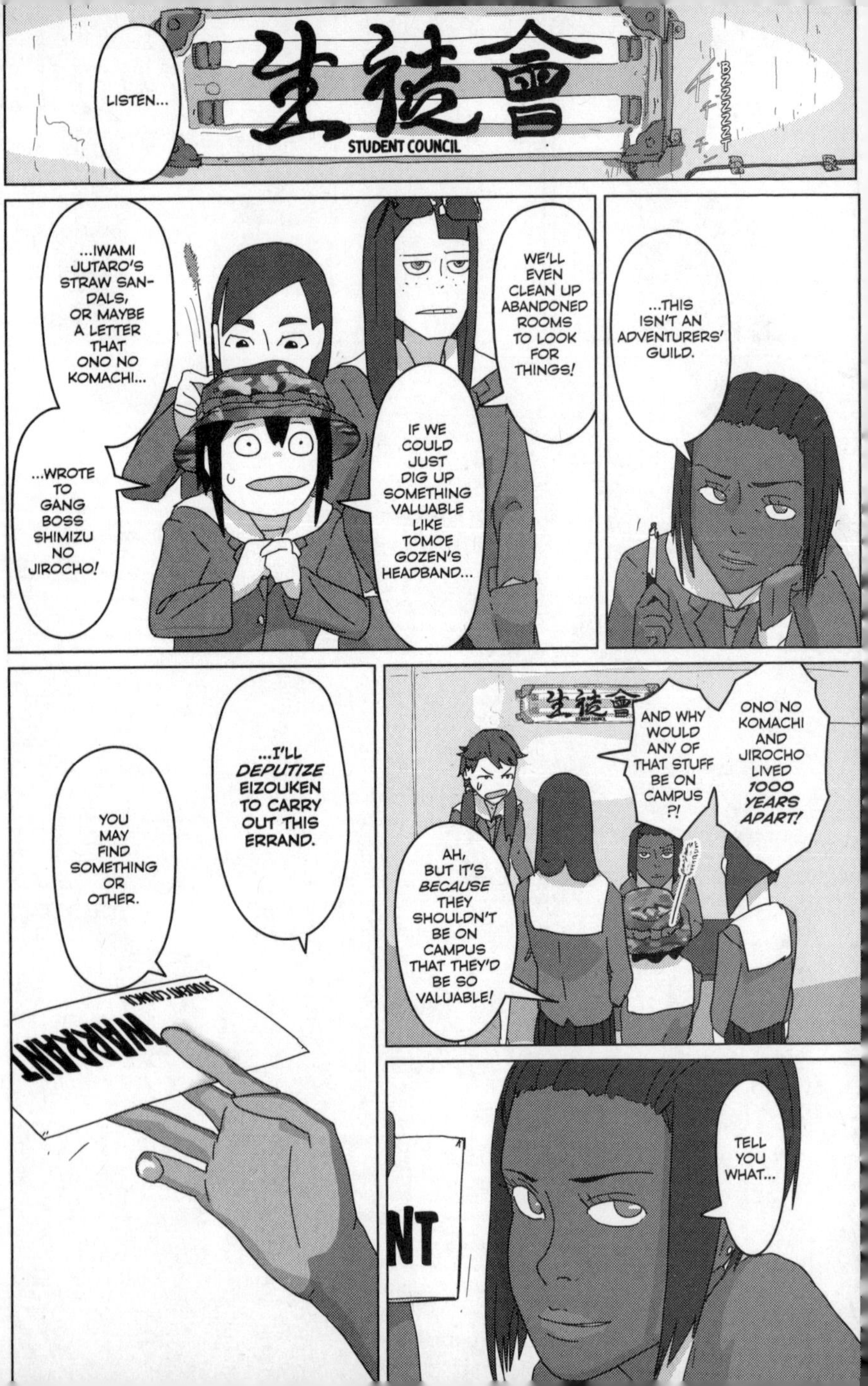

生徒會
STUDENT COUNCIL
BZZZZZT
チチチン
LISTEN...
...THIS ISN'T AN ADVENTURERS' GUILD.
WE'LL EVEN CLEAN UP ABANDONED ROOMS TO LOOK FOR THINGS!
IF WE COULD JUST DIG UP SOMETHING VALUABLE LIKE TOMOE GOZEN'S HEADBAND...
...IWAMI JUTARO'S STRAW SAN-DALS, OR MAYBE A LETTER THAT ONO NO KOMACHI...
...WROTE TO GANG BOSS SHIMIZU NO JIROCHO!
生徒會
ONO NO KOMACHI AND JIROCHO LIVED *1000 YEARS APART!*
AND WHY WOULD ANY OF THAT STUFF BE ON CAMPUS ?!
AH, BUT IT'S *BECAUSE* THEY SHOULDN'T BE ON CAMPUS THAT THEY'D BE SO VALUABLE!
TELL YOU WHAT...
...I'LL *DEPUTIZE* EIZOUKEN TO CARRY OUT THIS ERRAND.
YOU MAY FIND SOMETHING OR OTHER.
STUDENT COUNCIL
WARRANT

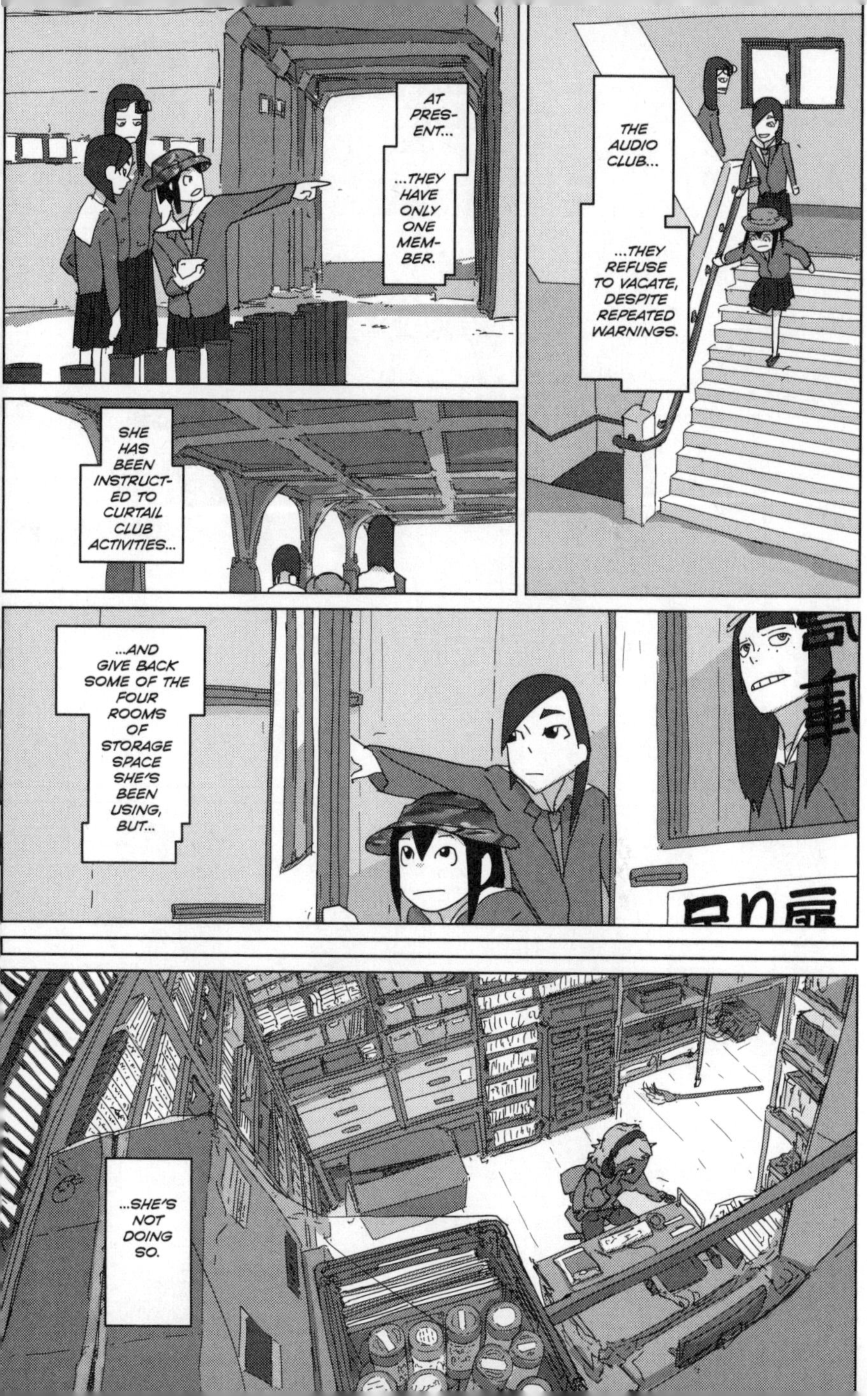
THE AUDIO CLUB...
...THEY REFUSE TO VACATE, DESPITE REPEATED WARNINGS.
AT PRESENT...
...THEY HAVE ONLY ONE MEMBER.
SHE HAS BEEN INSTRUCTED TO CURTAIL CLUB ACTIVITIES...
...AND GIVE BACK SOME OF THE FOUR ROOMS OF STORAGE SPACE SHE'S BEEN USING, BUT...
...SHE'S NOT DOING SO.

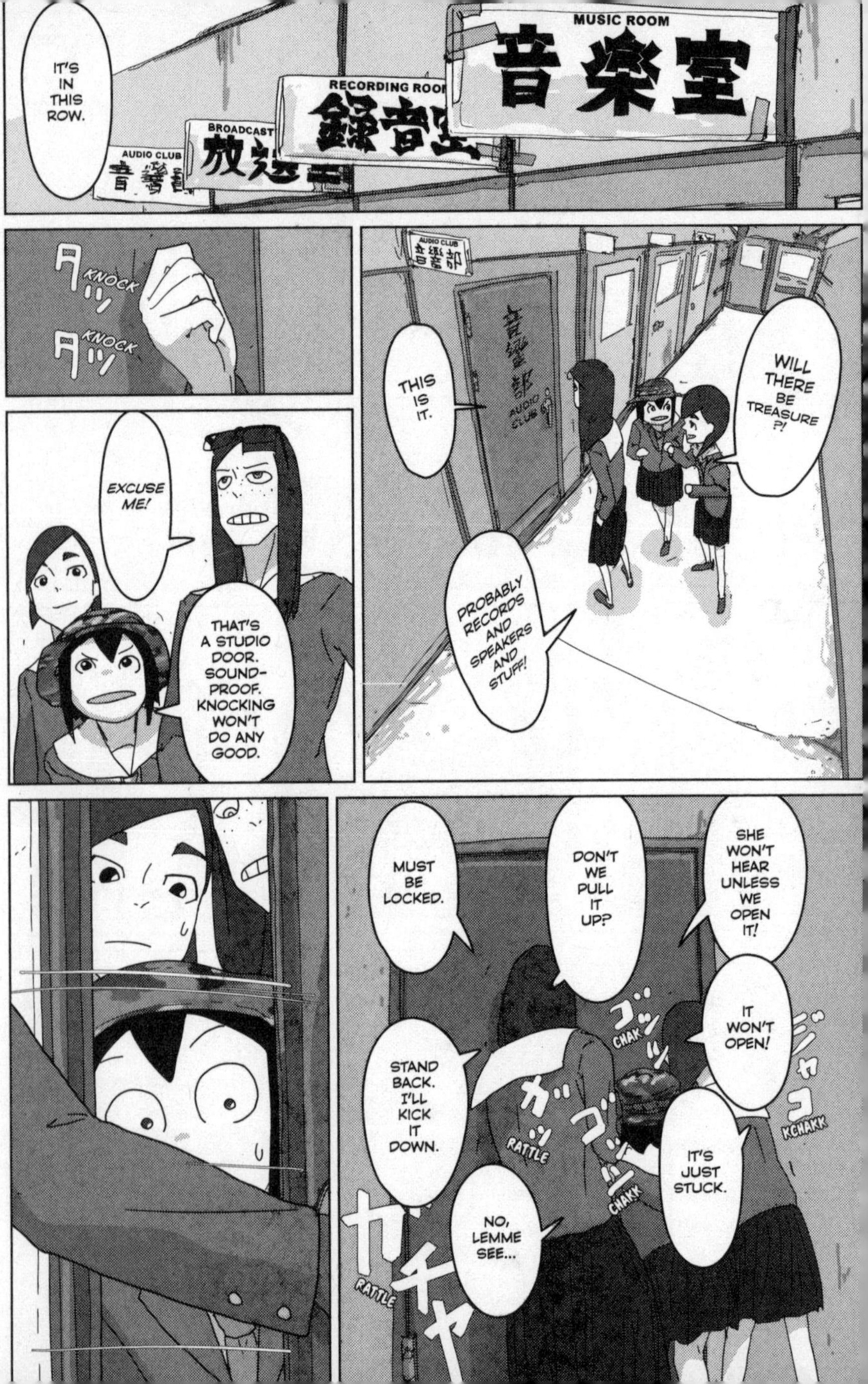
MUSIC ROOM
音楽室
RECORDING ROOM
録音室
BROADCAST
AUDIO CLUB
IT'S IN THIS ROW.
WILL THERE BE TREASURE?!
AUDIO CLUB
音響部
音響部
AUDIO CLUB
THIS IS IT.
PROBABLY RECORDS AND SPEAKERS AND STUFF!
タッ
KNOCK
タッ
KNOCK
EXCUSE ME!
THAT'S A STUDIO DOOR. SOUNDPROOF. KNOCKING WON'T DO ANY GOOD.
SHE WON'T HEAR UNLESS WE OPEN IT!
DON'T WE PULL IT UP?
MUST BE LOCKED.
IT WON'T OPEN!
ジャコ
KCHAKK
ゴッ
CHAK
STAND BACK. I'LL KICK IT DOWN.
IT'S JUST STUCK.
ガッ
RATTLE
ゴッ
CHAKK
NO, LEMME SEE...
ガチャ
RATTLE

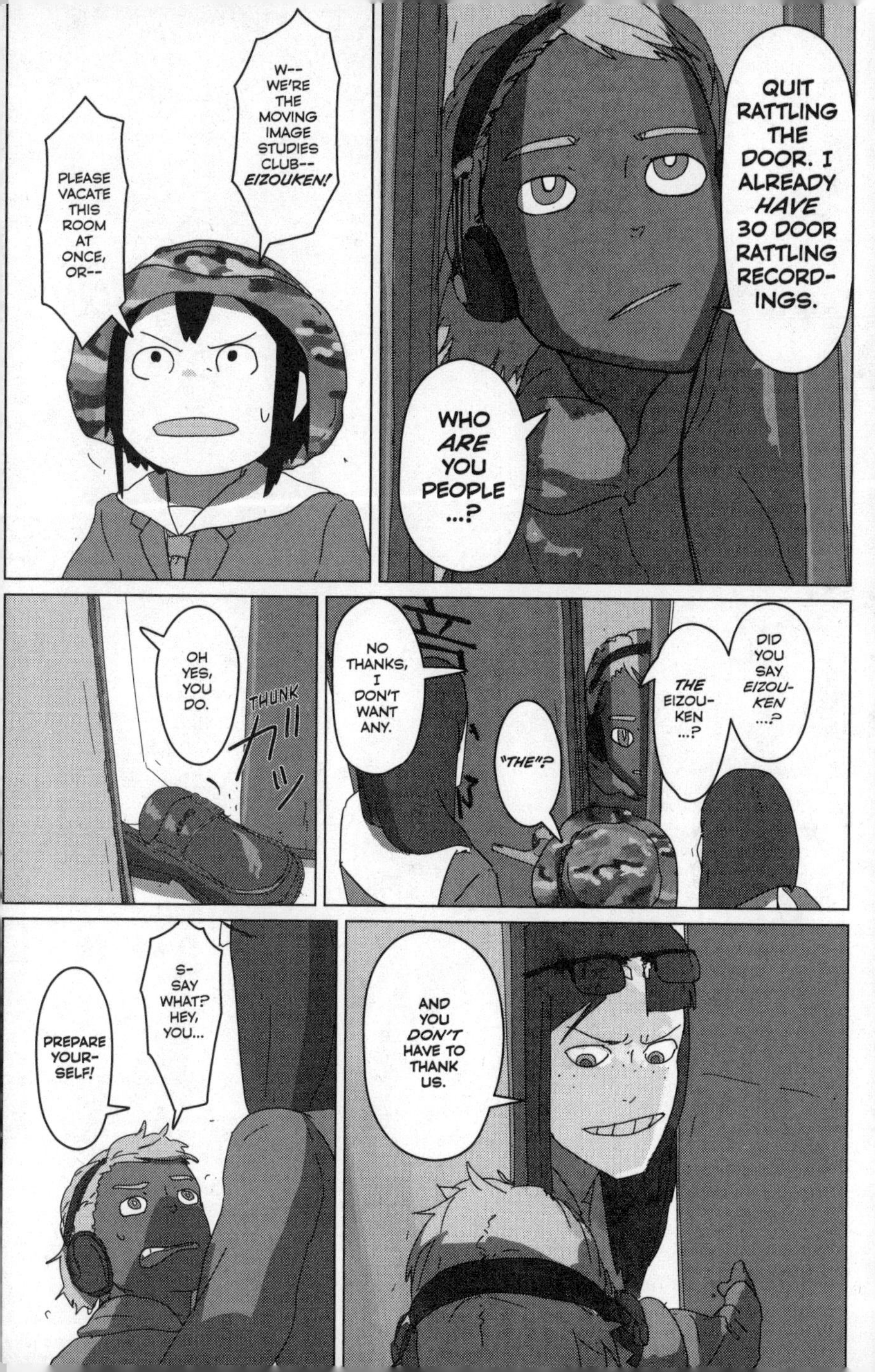
QUIT RATTLING THE DOOR. I ALREADY *HAVE* 30 DOOR RATTLING RECORDINGS.
WHO *ARE* YOU PEOPLE ...?
W-- WE'RE THE MOVING IMAGE STUDIES CLUB-- *EIZOUKEN!*
PLEASE VACATE THIS ROOM AT ONCE, OR--
DID YOU SAY *EIZOUKEN* ...?
THE EIZOUKEN ...?
NO THANKS, I DON'T WANT ANY.
"THE"?
OH YES, YOU DO.
THUNK
AND YOU *DON'T* HAVE TO THANK US.
S- SAY WHAT? HEY, YOU...
PREPARE YOURSELF!

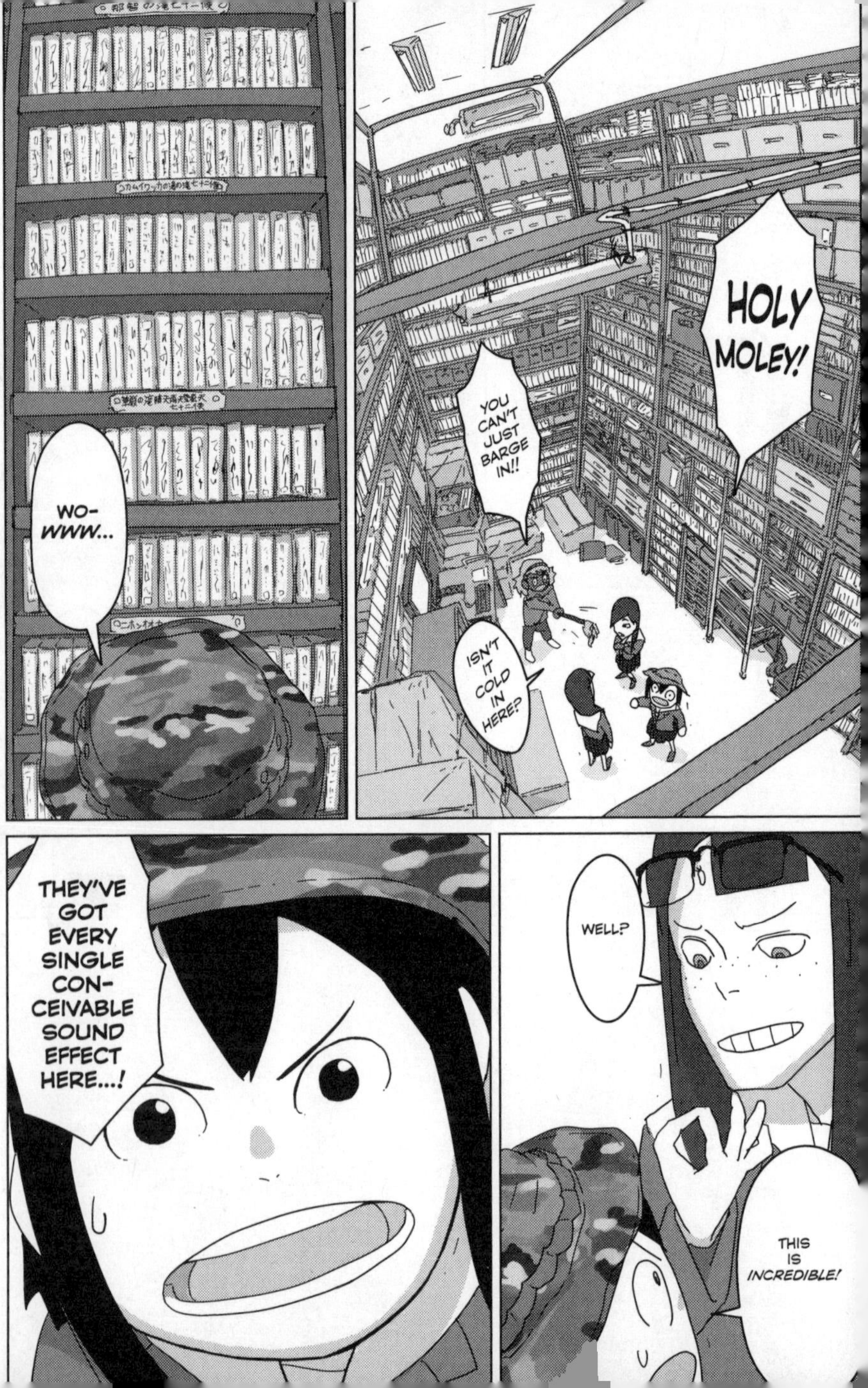
HOLY MOLEY!
YOU CAN'T JUST BARGE IN!!
ISN'T IT COLD IN HERE?
WO-WWW...
WELL?
THIS IS INCREDIBLE!
THEY'VE GOT EVERY SINGLE CON-CEIVABLE SOUND EFFECT HERE...!

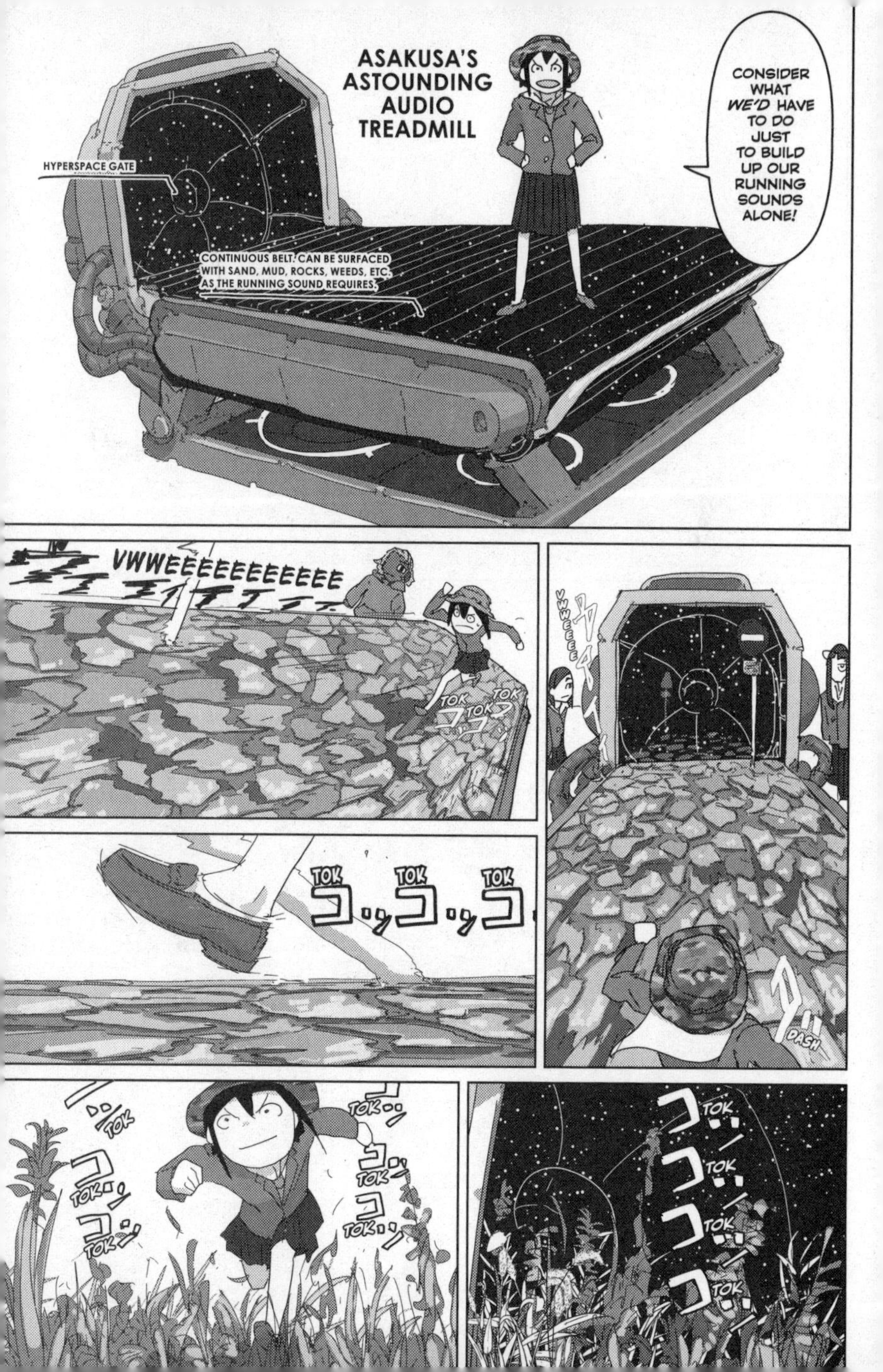
CONSIDER WHAT *WE'D* HAVE TO DO JUST TO BUILD UP OUR RUNNING SOUNDS ALONE!
ASAKUSA'S ASTOUNDING AUDIO TREADMILL
HYPERSPACE GATE
CONTINUOUS BELT. CAN BE SURFACED WITH SAND, MUD, ROCKS, WEEDS, ETC. AS THE RUNNING SOUND REQUIRES.
VWWEEEEE
DASH
VWWEEEEEEEEEEEE
TOK TOK TOK
TOK TOK TOK
TOK TOK TOK TOK
TOK TOK TOK TOK TOK TOK

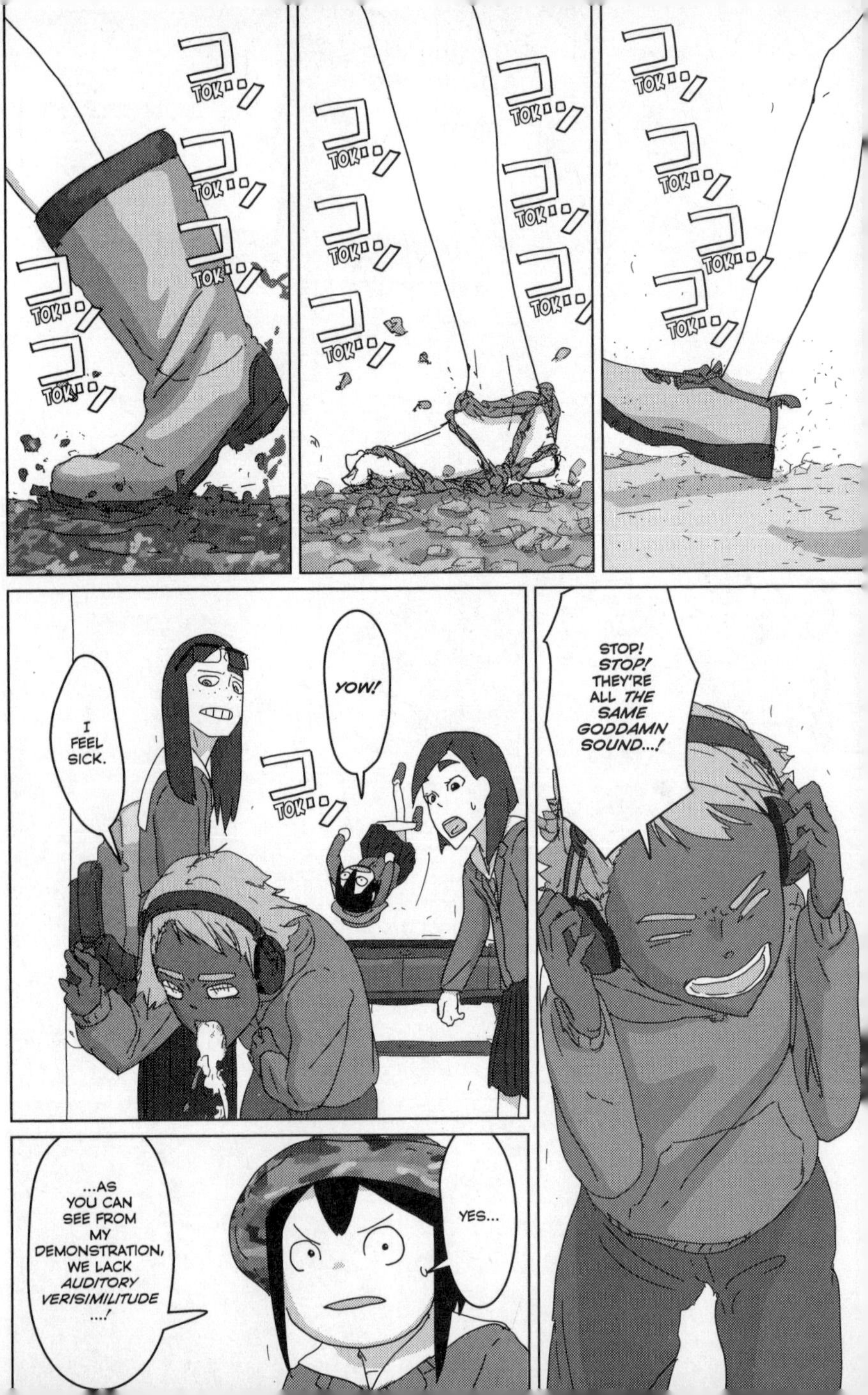
TOK..
TOK..
TOK..
TOK..
TOK..
TOK..
TOK..
TOK..
TOK..
TOK..
TOK..
TOK..
TOK..
TOK..
TOK..
STOP! *STOP!* THEY'RE ALL *THE SAME* GODDAMN SOUND...!
YOW!
TOK..
I FEEL SICK.
YES...
...AS YOU CAN SEE FROM MY DEMONSTRATION, WE LACK *AUDITORY VERISIMILITUDE* ...!

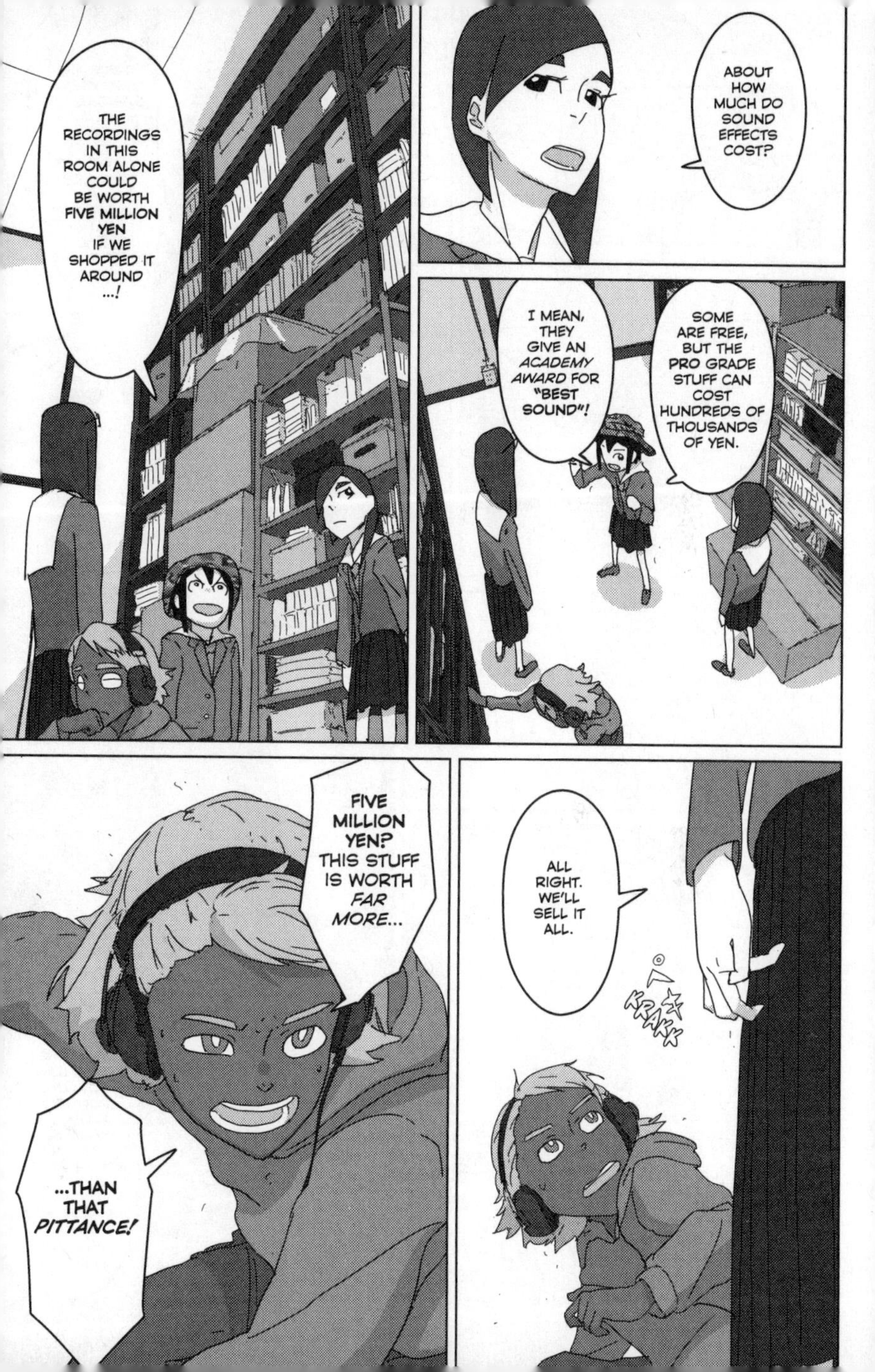
ABOUT HOW MUCH DO SOUND EFFECTS COST?
SOME ARE FREE, BUT THE PRO GRADE STUFF CAN COST HUNDREDS OF THOUSANDS OF YEN.
I MEAN, THEY GIVE AN *ACADEMY AWARD* FOR "BEST SOUND"!
THE RECORDINGS IN THIS ROOM ALONE COULD BE WORTH FIVE MILLION YEN IF WE SHOPPED IT AROUND ...!
ALL RIGHT. WE'LL SELL IT ALL.
KRAKK
FIVE MILLION YEN? THIS STUFF IS WORTH *FAR MORE...*
...THAN THAT *PITTANCE!*

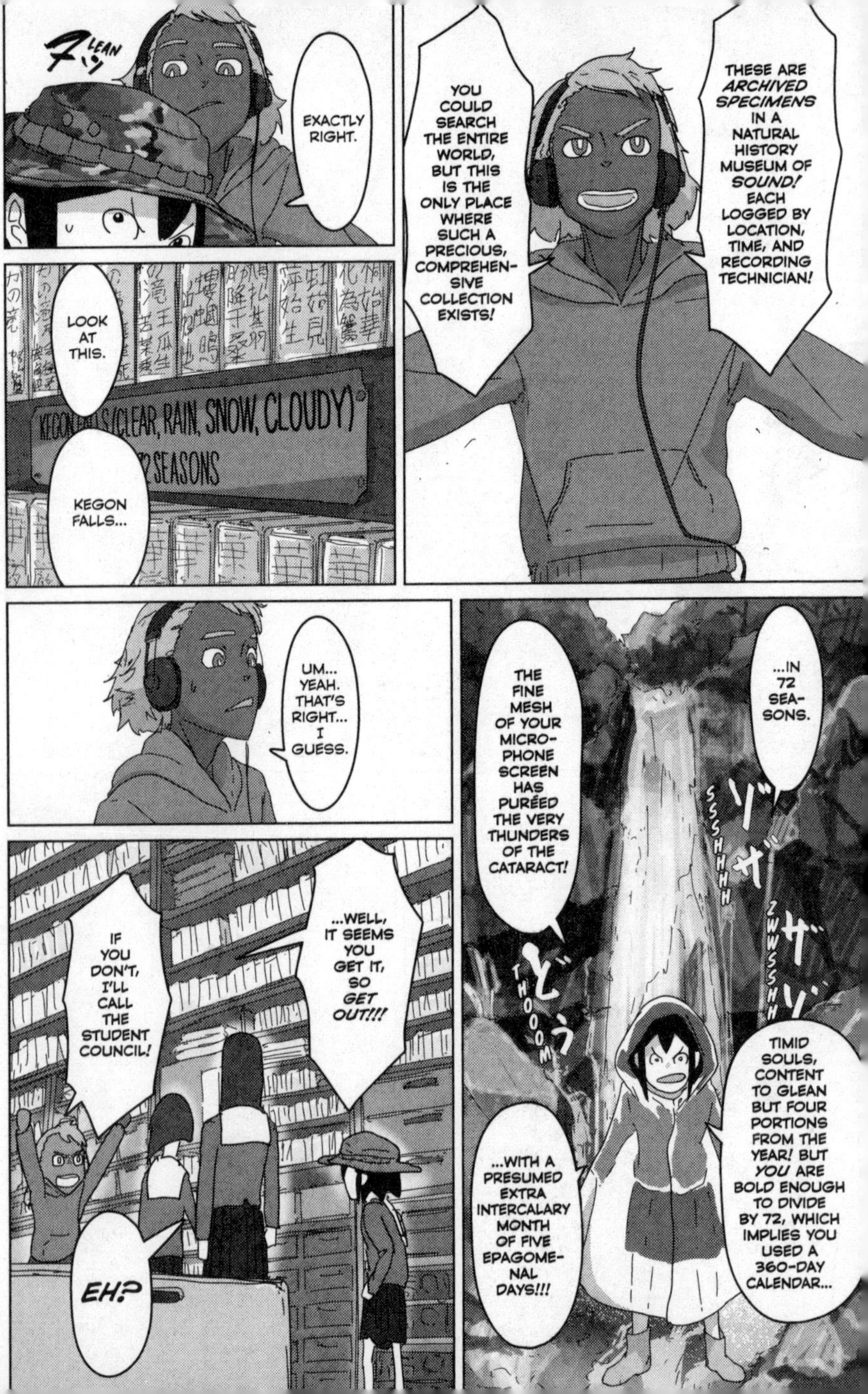

THESE ARE *ARCHIVED SPECIMENS* IN A NATURAL HISTORY MUSEUM OF *SOUND!* EACH LOGGED BY LOCATION, TIME, AND RECORDING TECHNICIAN!
YOU COULD SEARCH THE ENTIRE WORLD, BUT THIS IS THE ONLY PLACE WHERE SUCH A PRECIOUS, COMPREHENSIVE COLLECTION EXISTS!
LEAN
EXACTLY RIGHT.
LOOK AT THIS.
KEGON (CLEAR, RAIN, SNOW, CLOUDY)
SEASONS
KEGON FALLS...
...IN 72 SEASONS.
THE FINE MESH OF YOUR MICROPHONE SCREEN HAS PURÉED THE VERY THUNDERS OF THE CATARACT!
SSSHHHH
ZWSSHH
THOOOOM
TIMID SOULS, CONTENT TO GLEAN BUT FOUR PORTIONS FROM THE YEAR! BUT *YOU* ARE BOLD ENOUGH TO DIVIDE BY 72, WHICH IMPLIES YOU USED A 360-DAY CALENDAR...
...WITH A PRESUMED EXTRA INTERCALARY MONTH OF FIVE EPAGOMENAL DAYS!!!
UM... YEAH. THAT'S RIGHT... I GUESS.
...WELL, IT SEEMS YOU GET IT, SO *GET OUT!!!*
IF YOU DON'T, I'LL CALL THE STUDENT COUNCIL!
EH?

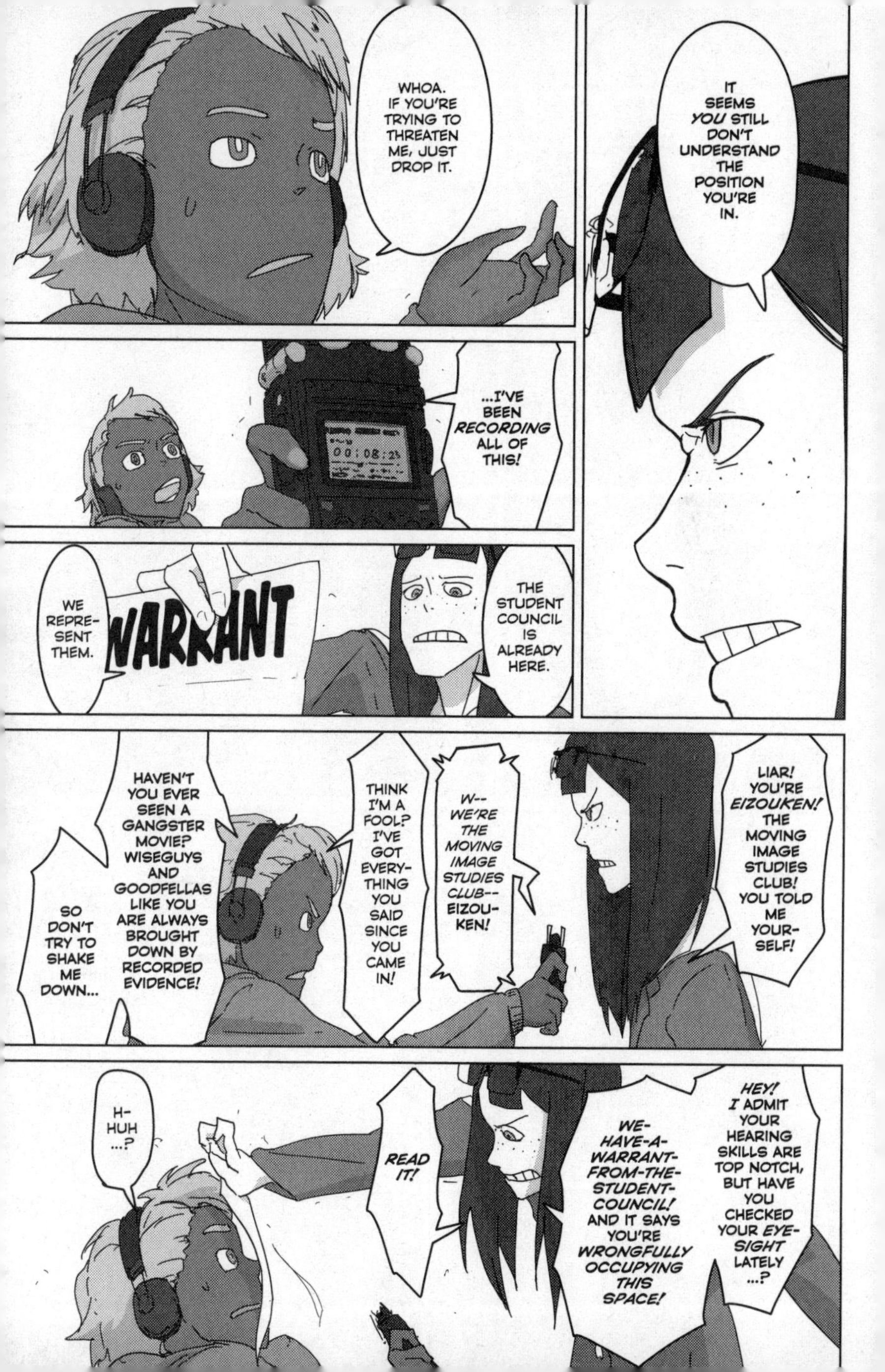
IT SEEMS YOU STILL DON'T UNDERSTAND THE POSITION YOU'RE IN.
WHOA. IF YOU'RE TRYING TO THREATEN ME, JUST DROP IT.
...I'VE BEEN RECORDING ALL OF THIS!
THE STUDENT COUNCIL IS ALREADY HERE.
WE REPRESENT THEM.
WARRANT
LIAR! YOU'RE EIZOUKEN! THE MOVING IMAGE STUDIES CLUB! YOU TOLD ME YOURSELF!
W-- WE'RE THE MOVING IMAGE STUDIES CLUB-- EIZOUKEN!
THINK I'M A FOOL? I'VE GOT EVERYTHING YOU SAID SINCE YOU CAME IN!
HAVEN'T YOU EVER SEEN A GANGSTER MOVIE? WISEGUYS AND GOODFELLAS LIKE YOU ARE ALWAYS BROUGHT DOWN BY RECORDED EVIDENCE!
SO DON'T TRY TO SHAKE ME DOWN...
HEY! I ADMIT YOUR HEARING SKILLS ARE TOP NOTCH, BUT HAVE YOU CHECKED YOUR EYESIGHT LATELY ...?
WE-HAVE-A-WARRANT-FROM-THE-STUDENT-COUNCIL! AND IT SAYS YOU'RE WRONGFULLY OCCUPYING THIS SPACE!
READ IT!
H-HUH ...?

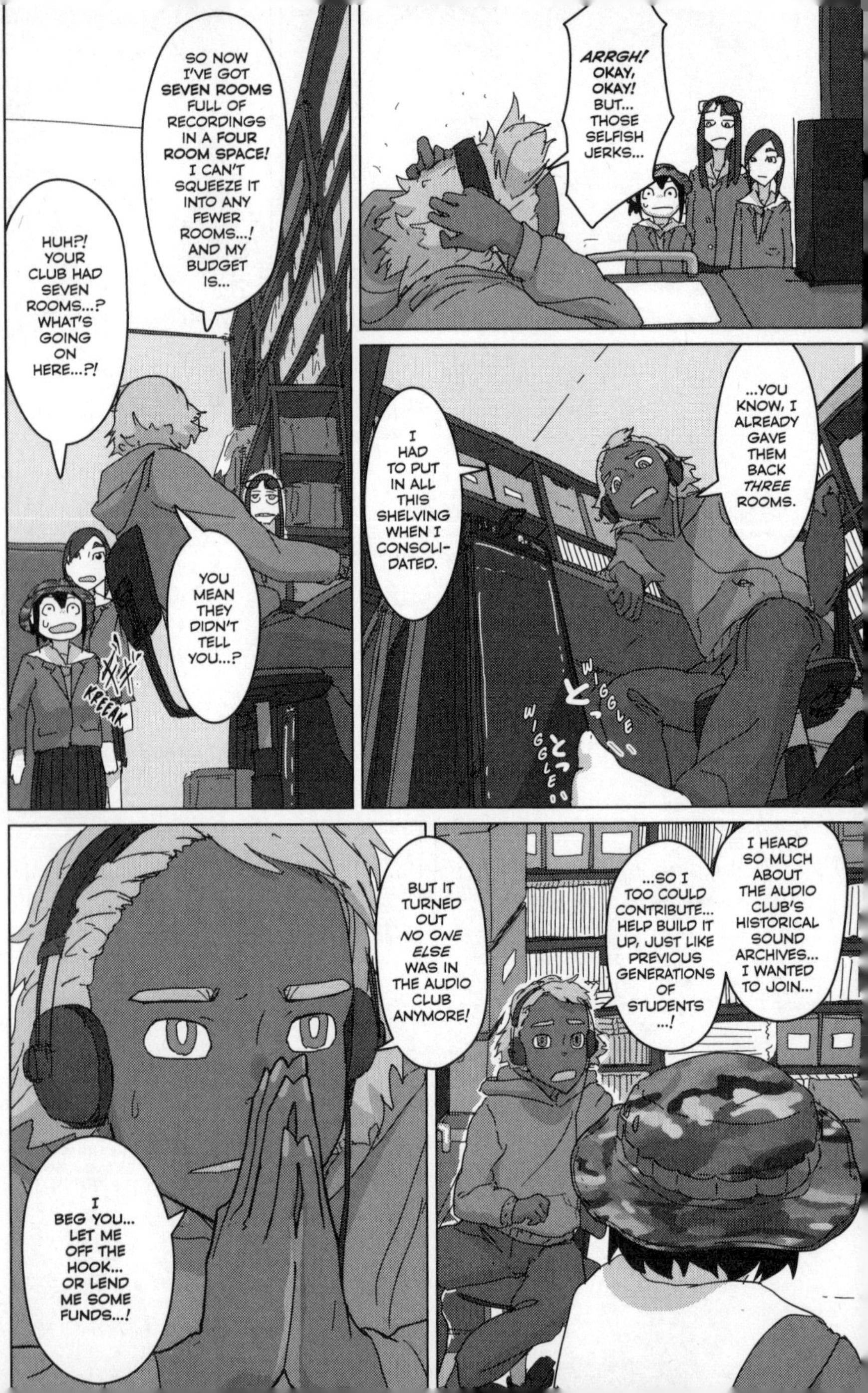
ARRGH! OKAY, OKAY! BUT... THOSE SELFISH JERKS...
...YOU KNOW, I ALREADY GAVE THEM BACK THREE ROOMS.
I HAD TO PUT IN ALL THIS SHELVING WHEN I CONSOLIDATED.
WIGGLE
WIGGLE
SO NOW I'VE GOT SEVEN ROOMS FULL OF RECORDINGS IN A FOUR ROOM SPACE! I CAN'T SQUEEZE IT INTO ANY FEWER ROOMS...! AND MY BUDGET IS...
HUH?! YOUR CLUB HAD SEVEN ROOMS...? WHAT'S GOING ON HERE...?!
YOU MEAN THEY DIDN'T TELL YOU...?
KREEAK
I HEARD SO MUCH ABOUT THE AUDIO CLUB'S HISTORICAL SOUND ARCHIVES... I WANTED TO JOIN...
...SO I TOO COULD CONTRIBUTE... HELP BUILD IT UP, JUST LIKE PREVIOUS GENERATIONS OF STUDENTS ...!
BUT IT TURNED OUT NO ONE ELSE WAS IN THE AUDIO CLUB ANYMORE!
I BEG YOU... LET ME OFF THE HOOK... OR LEND ME SOME FUNDS...!

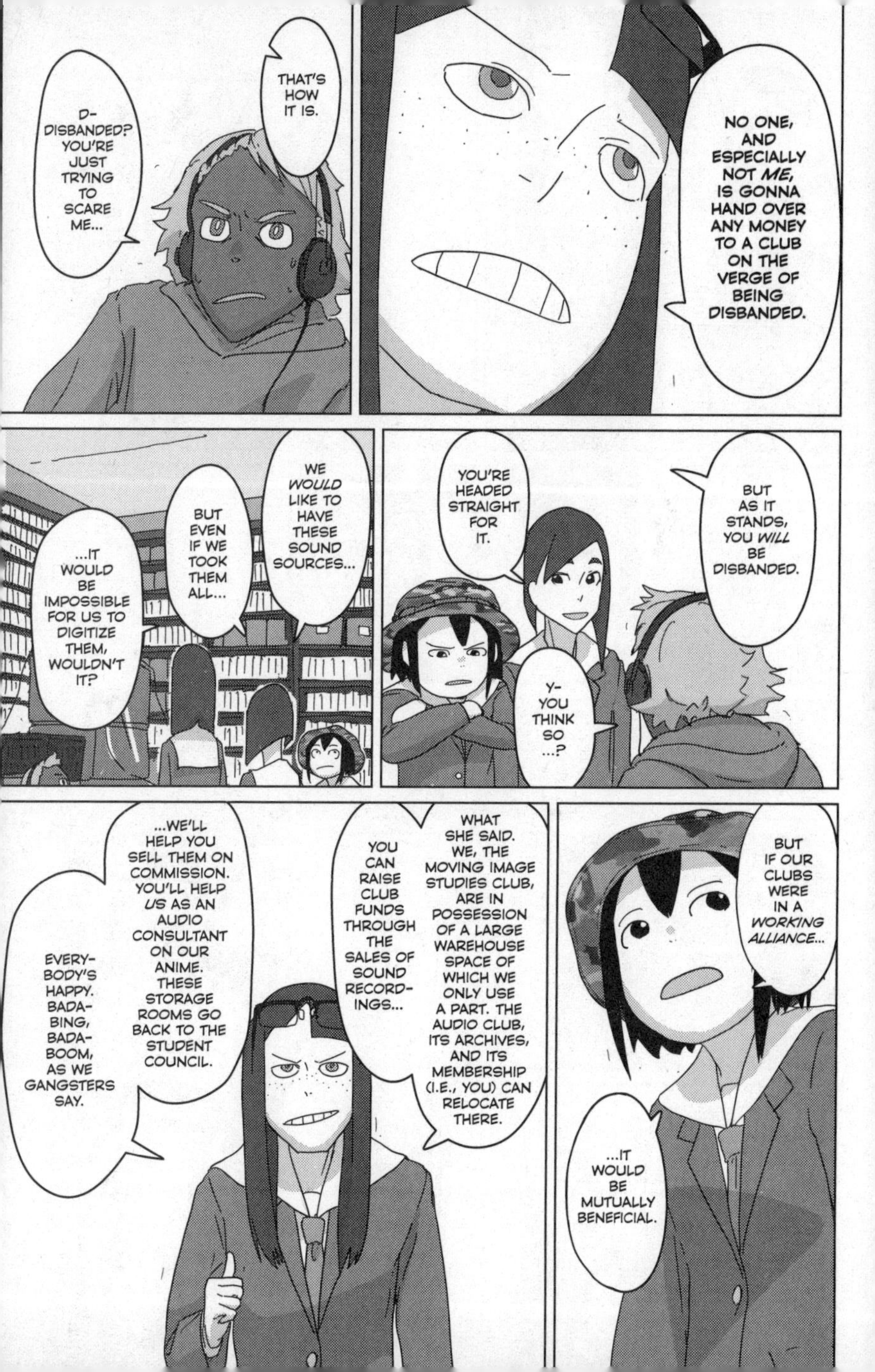
NO ONE, AND ESPECIALLY NOT *ME*, IS GONNA HAND OVER ANY MONEY TO A CLUB ON THE VERGE OF BEING DISBANDED.
THAT'S HOW IT IS.
D-DISBANDED? YOU'RE JUST TRYING TO SCARE ME...
BUT AS IT STANDS, YOU *WILL* BE DISBANDED.
YOU'RE HEADED STRAIGHT FOR IT.
Y-YOU THINK SO ...?
WE *WOULD* LIKE TO HAVE THESE SOUND SOURCES...
BUT EVEN IF WE TOOK THEM ALL...
...IT WOULD BE IMPOSSIBLE FOR US TO DIGITIZE THEM, WOULDN'T IT?
BUT IF OUR CLUBS WERE IN A *WORKING ALLIANCE*...
...IT WOULD BE MUTUALLY BENEFICIAL.
WHAT SHE SAID. WE, THE MOVING IMAGE STUDIES CLUB, ARE IN POSSESSION OF A LARGE WAREHOUSE SPACE OF WHICH WE ONLY USE A PART. THE AUDIO CLUB, ITS ARCHIVES, AND ITS MEMBERSHIP (I.E., YOU) CAN RELOCATE THERE.
YOU CAN RAISE CLUB FUNDS THROUGH THE SALES OF SOUND RECORD-INGS...
...WE'LL HELP YOU SELL THEM ON COMMISSION. YOU'LL HELP *US* AS AN AUDIO CONSULTANT ON OUR ANIME. THESE STORAGE ROOMS GO BACK TO THE STUDENT COUNCIL.
EVERY-BODY'S HAPPY. BADA-BING, BADA-BOOM, AS WE GANGSTERS SAY.

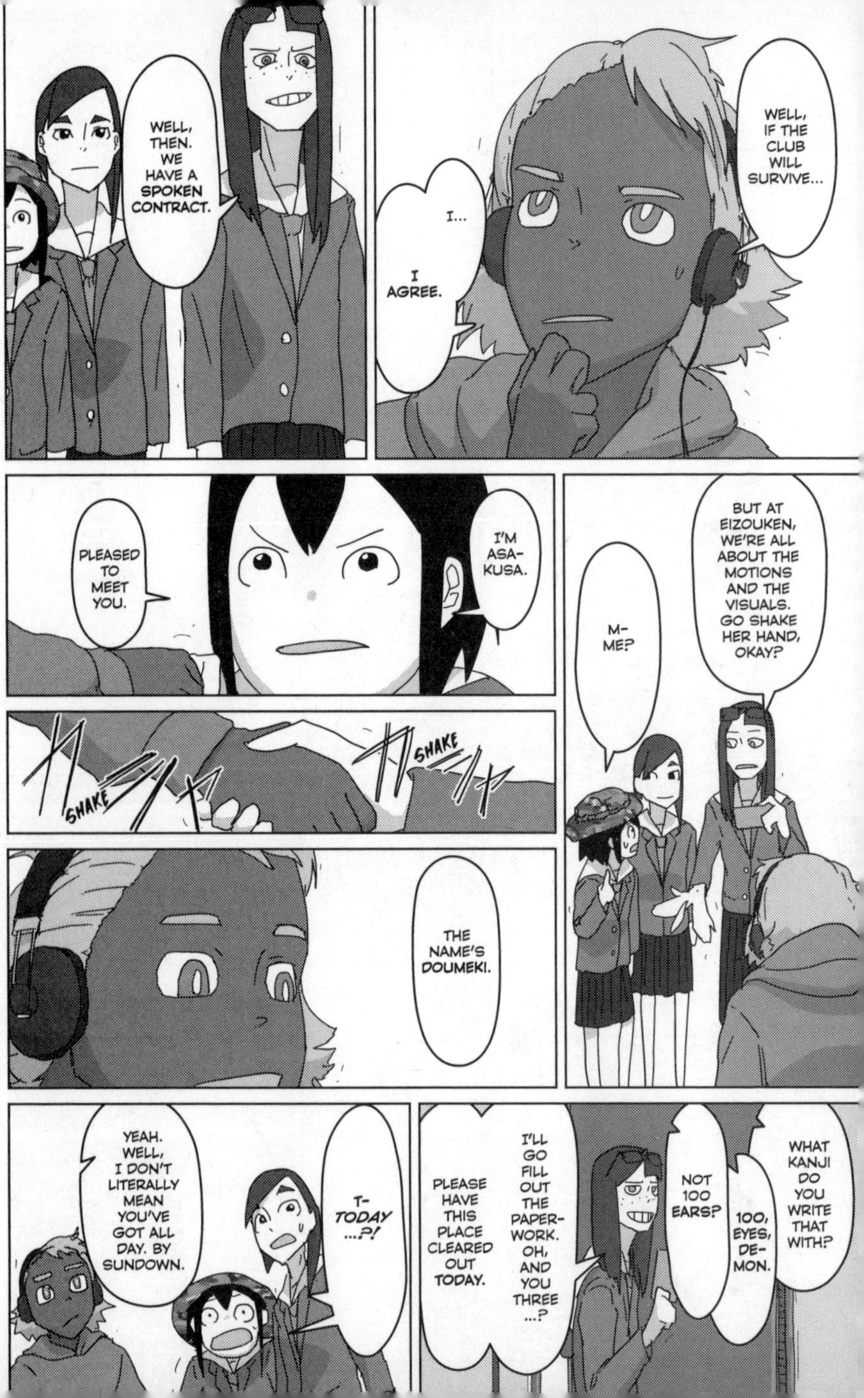
WELL, IF THE CLUB WILL SURVIVE...
I... I AGREE.
WELL, THEN. WE HAVE A SPOKEN CONTRACT.
BUT AT EIZOUKEN, WE'RE ALL ABOUT THE MOTIONS AND THE VISUALS. GO SHAKE HER HAND, OKAY?
M-ME?
I'M ASA-KUSA.
PLEASED TO MEET YOU.
SHAKE
SHAKE
THE NAME'S DOUMEKI.
WHAT KANJI DO YOU WRITE THAT WITH?
100, EYES, DE-MON.
NOT 100 EARS?
I'LL GO FILL OUT THE PAPER-WORK. OH, AND YOU THREE ...?
PLEASE HAVE THIS PLACE CLEARED OUT TODAY.
T-TODAY ...?!
YEAH. WELL, I DON'T LITERALLY MEAN YOU'VE GOT ALL DAY. BY SUNDOWN.

CHAPTER 18:
HUNT FOR SOUND!

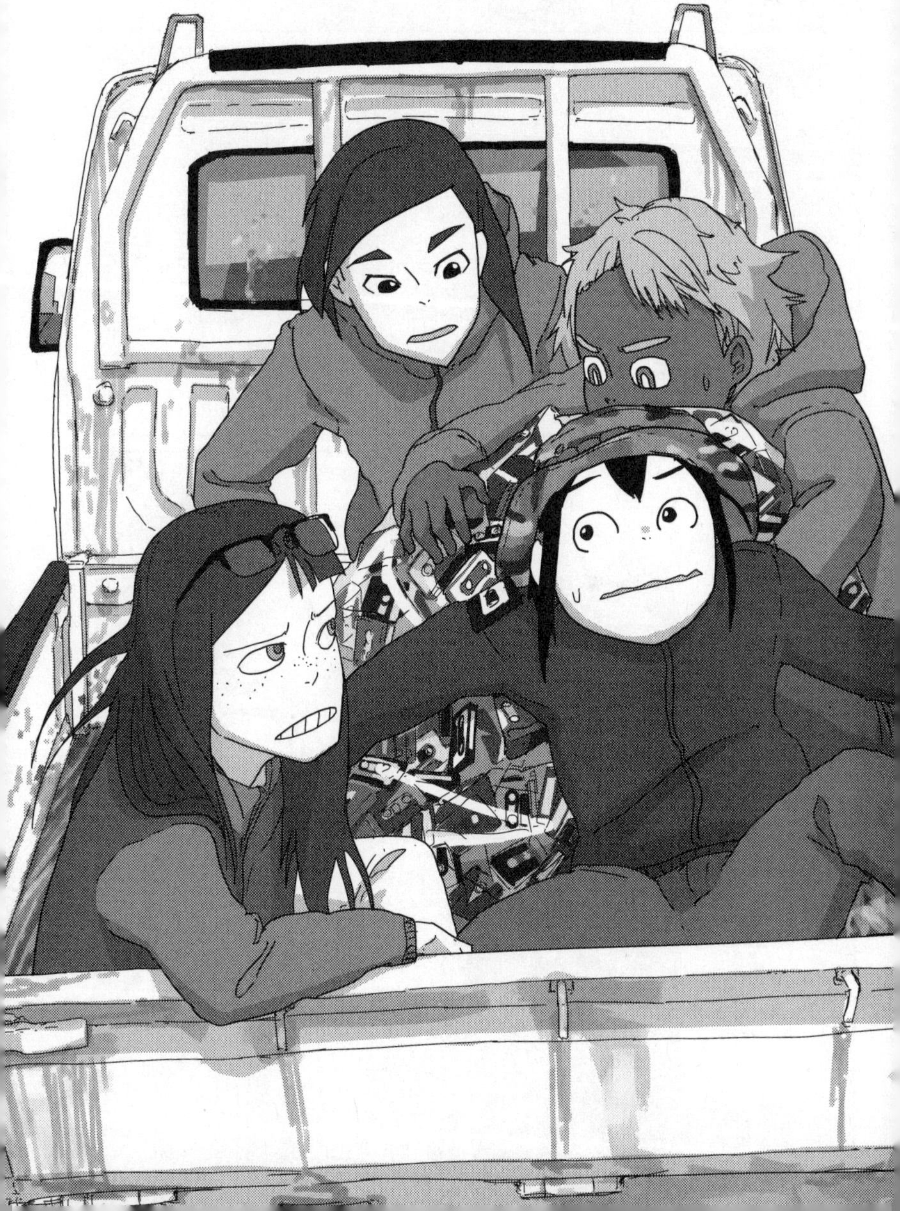

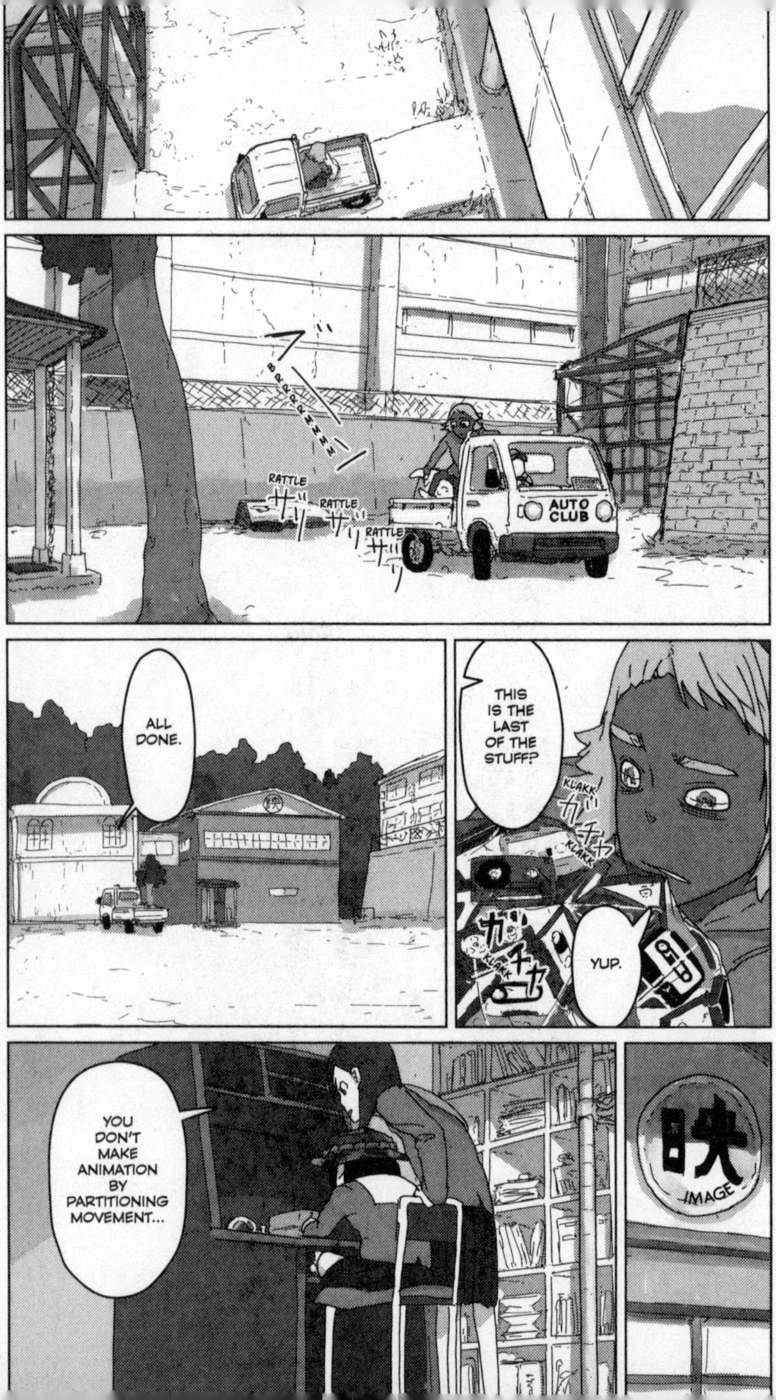
BRRRRMMMM
RATTLE
RATTLE
RATTLE
THIS IS THE LAST OF THE STUFF?
KLAKK
KLAKK
KLAKK
YUP.
ALL DONE.
映
IMAGE
YOU DON'T MAKE ANIMATION BY PARTITIONING MOVEMENT...

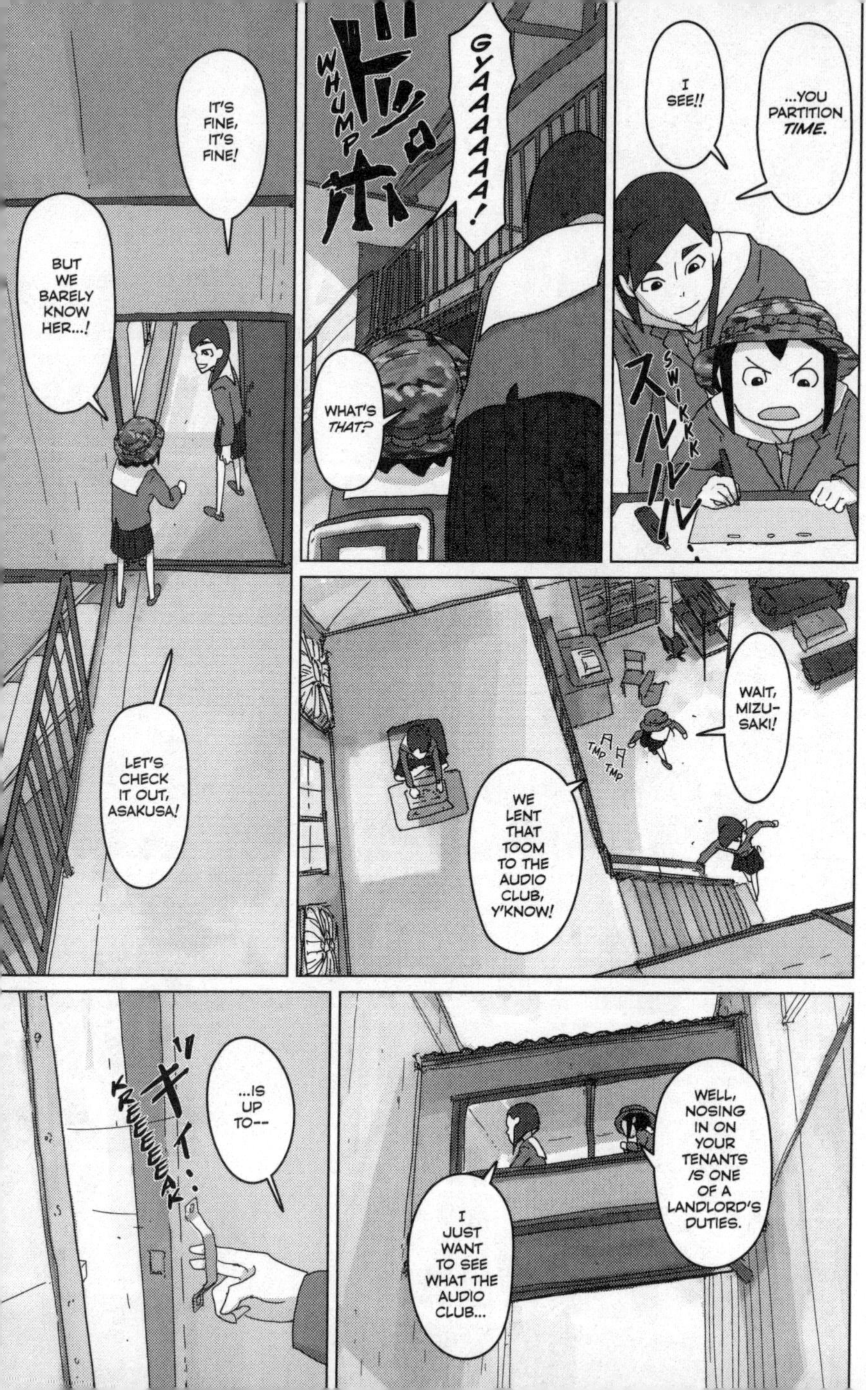
...YOU PARTITION TIME.
I SEE!!
SWIKKK
GYAAAAAAA!
WHUMP
WHAT'S THAT?
WAIT, MIZUSAKI!
TMP TMP
WE LENT THAT TOOM TO THE AUDIO CLUB, Y'KNOW!
LET'S CHECK IT OUT, ASAKUSA!
BUT WE BARELY KNOW HER...!
IT'S FINE, IT'S FINE!
WELL, NOSING IN ON YOUR TENANTS /S ONE OF A LANDLORD'S DUTIES.
I JUST WANT TO SEE WHAT THE AUDIO CLUB...
...IS UP TO--
KREEEEAK

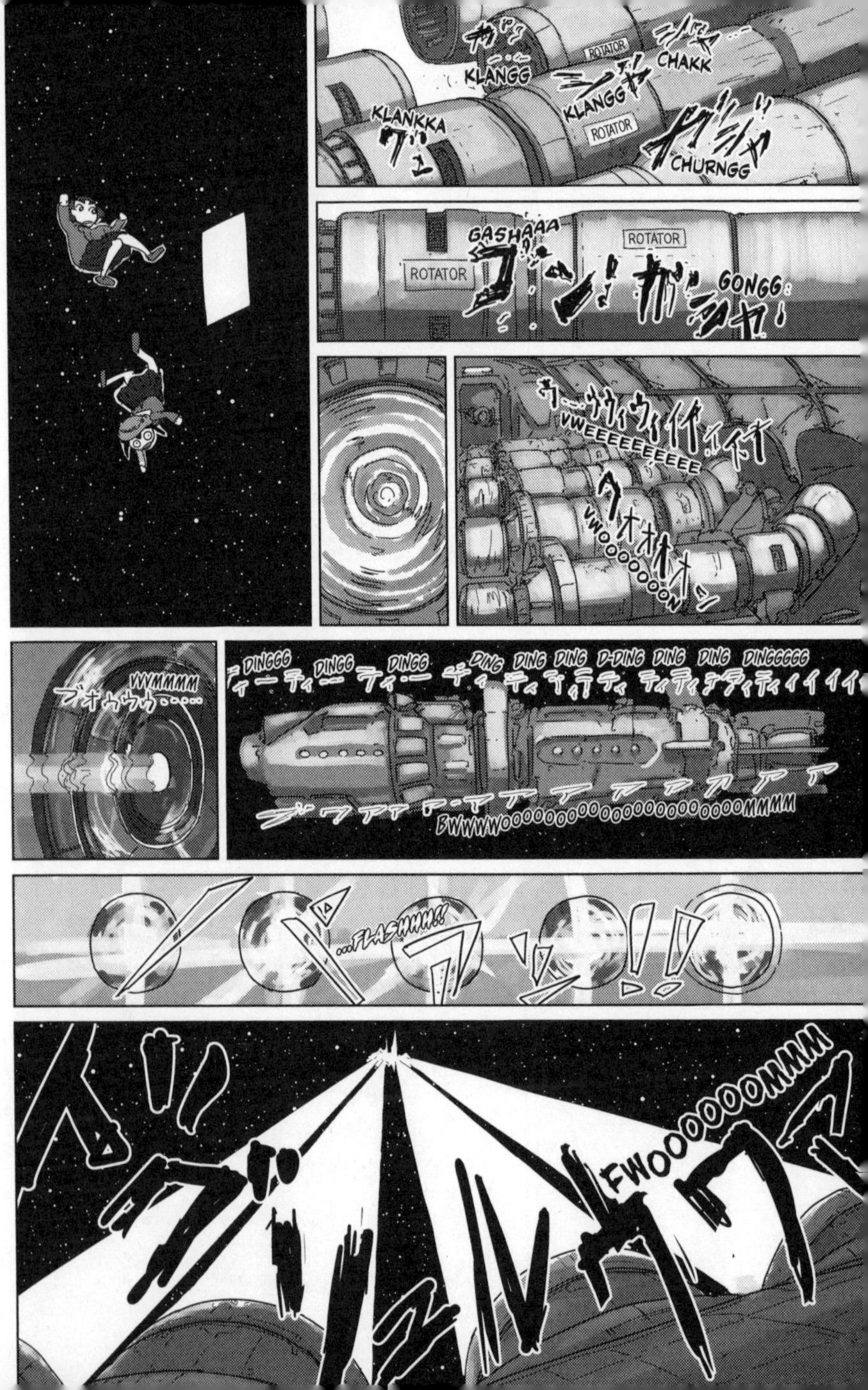
CHAKK
ROTATOR
KLANGG
KLANGG
ROTATOR
CHURNGG
KLANKKA
GONGG
ROTATOR
GASHAAA
ROTATOR
VWEEEEEEEEEEE
VWOOOOOOOON
DINGGG DINGG DINGG DING DING DING D-DING DING DING DINGGGGG
BWWWWOOOOOOOOOOOOOOOOOOOOMMMM
VWMMMM
...FLASHHH!!
FWOOOOOOMMM

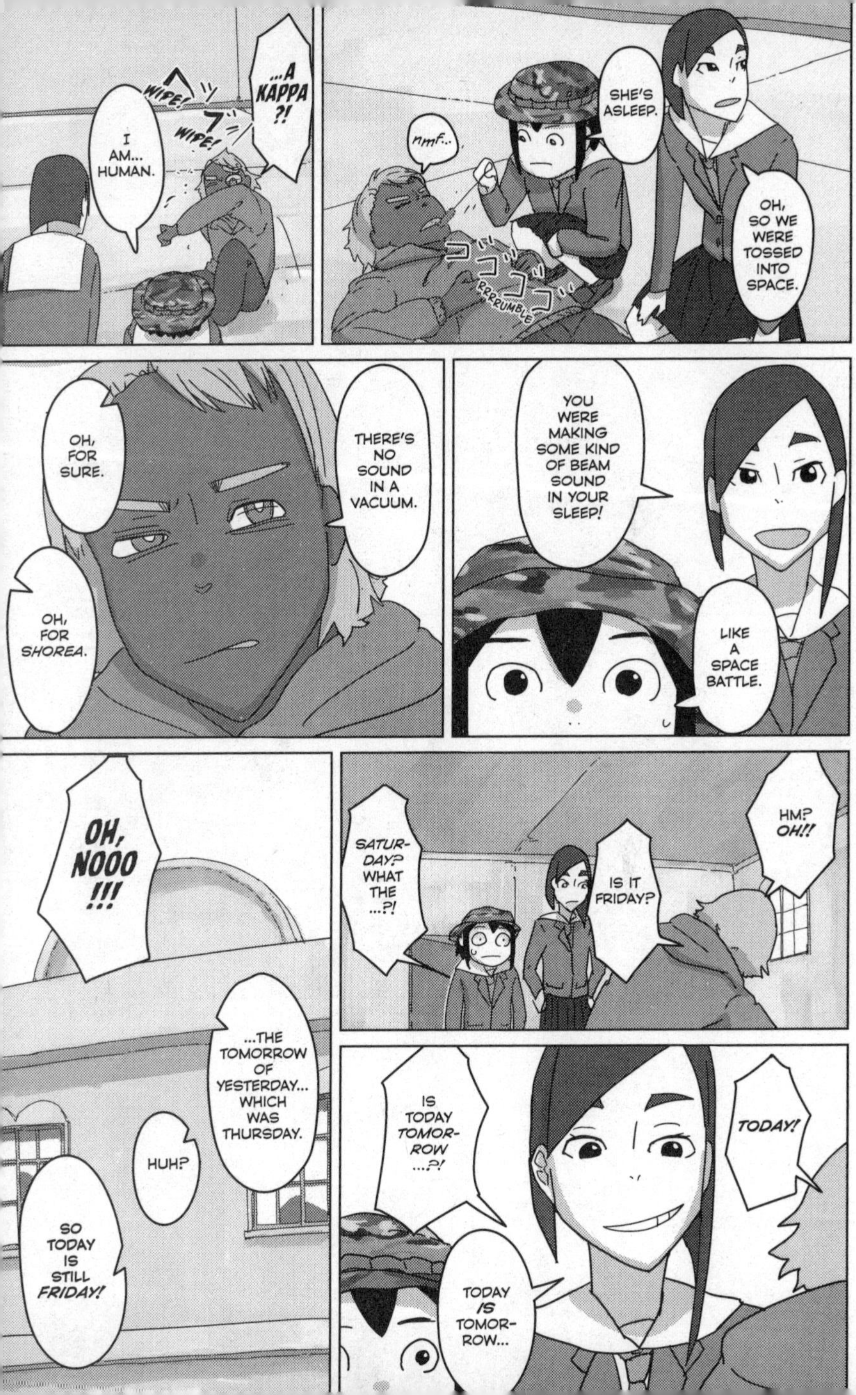
SHE'S ASLEEP.
OH, SO WE WERE TOSSED INTO SPACE.
nmf..
RRRUMBLE
...A KAPPA?!
WIPE!
WIPE!
I AM... HUMAN.
YOU WERE MAKING SOME KIND OF BEAM SOUND IN YOUR SLEEP!
LIKE A SPACE BATTLE.
THERE'S NO SOUND IN A VACUUM.
OH, FOR SURE.
OH, FOR SHOREA.
HM? OH!!
IS IT FRIDAY?
SATURDAY? WHAT THE ...?!
TODAY!
IS TODAY TOMORROW ...?!
TODAY IS TOMORROW...
OH, NOOO!!!
...THE TOMORROW OF YESTERDAY... WHICH WAS THURSDAY.
HUH?
SO TODAY IS STILL FRIDAY!

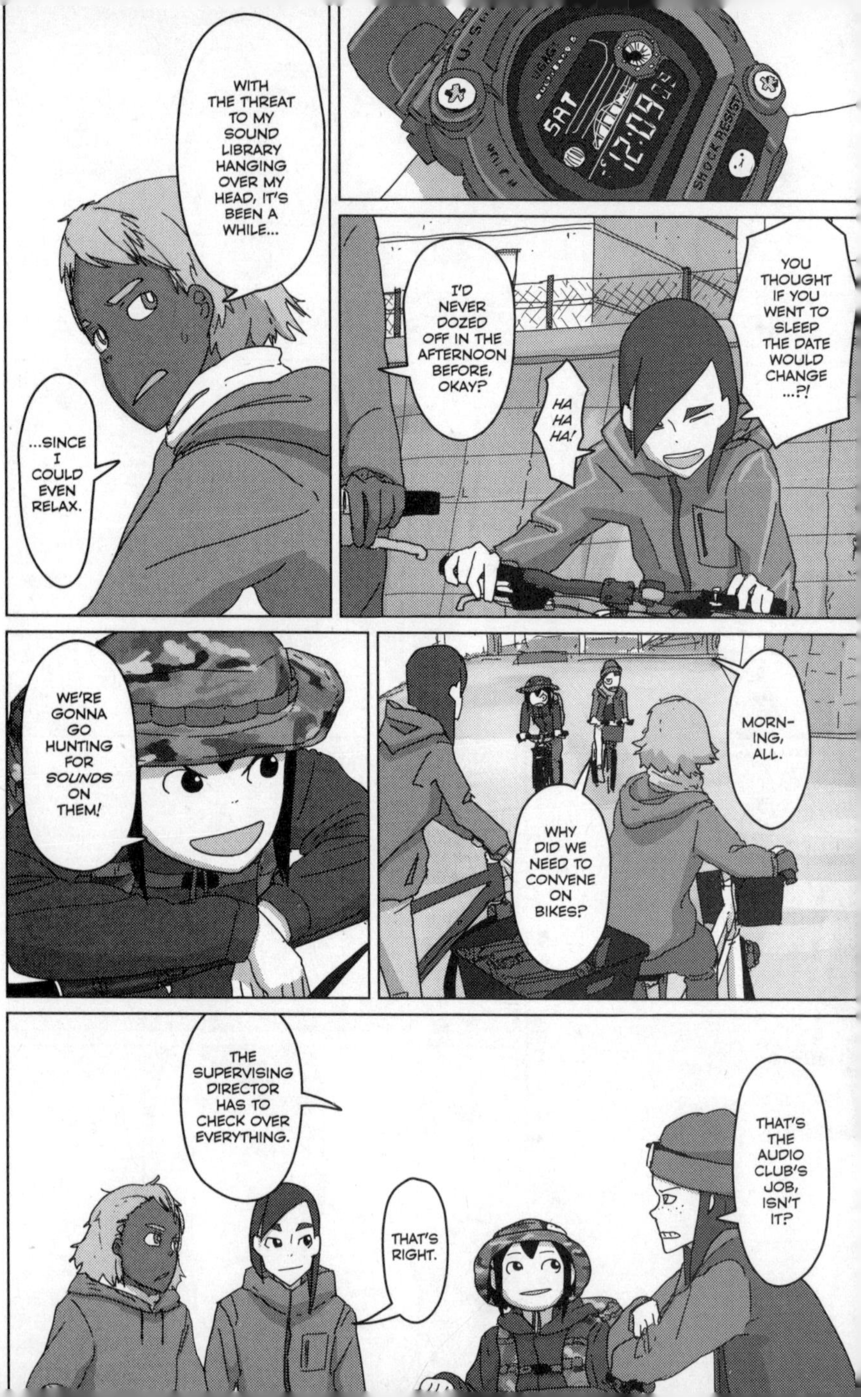
YOU THOUGHT IF YOU WENT TO SLEEP THE DATE WOULD CHANGE ...?!
HA HA HA!
I'D NEVER DOZED OFF IN THE AFTERNOON BEFORE, OKAY?
WITH THE THREAT TO MY SOUND LIBRARY HANGING OVER MY HEAD, IT'S BEEN A WHILE...
...SINCE I COULD EVEN RELAX.
MORNING, ALL.
WHY DID WE NEED TO CONVENE ON BIKES?
WE'RE GONNA GO HUNTING FOR *SOUNDS* ON THEM!
THAT'S THE AUDIO CLUB'S JOB, ISN'T IT?
THAT'S RIGHT.
THE SUPERVISING DIRECTOR HAS TO CHECK OVER EVERYTHING.

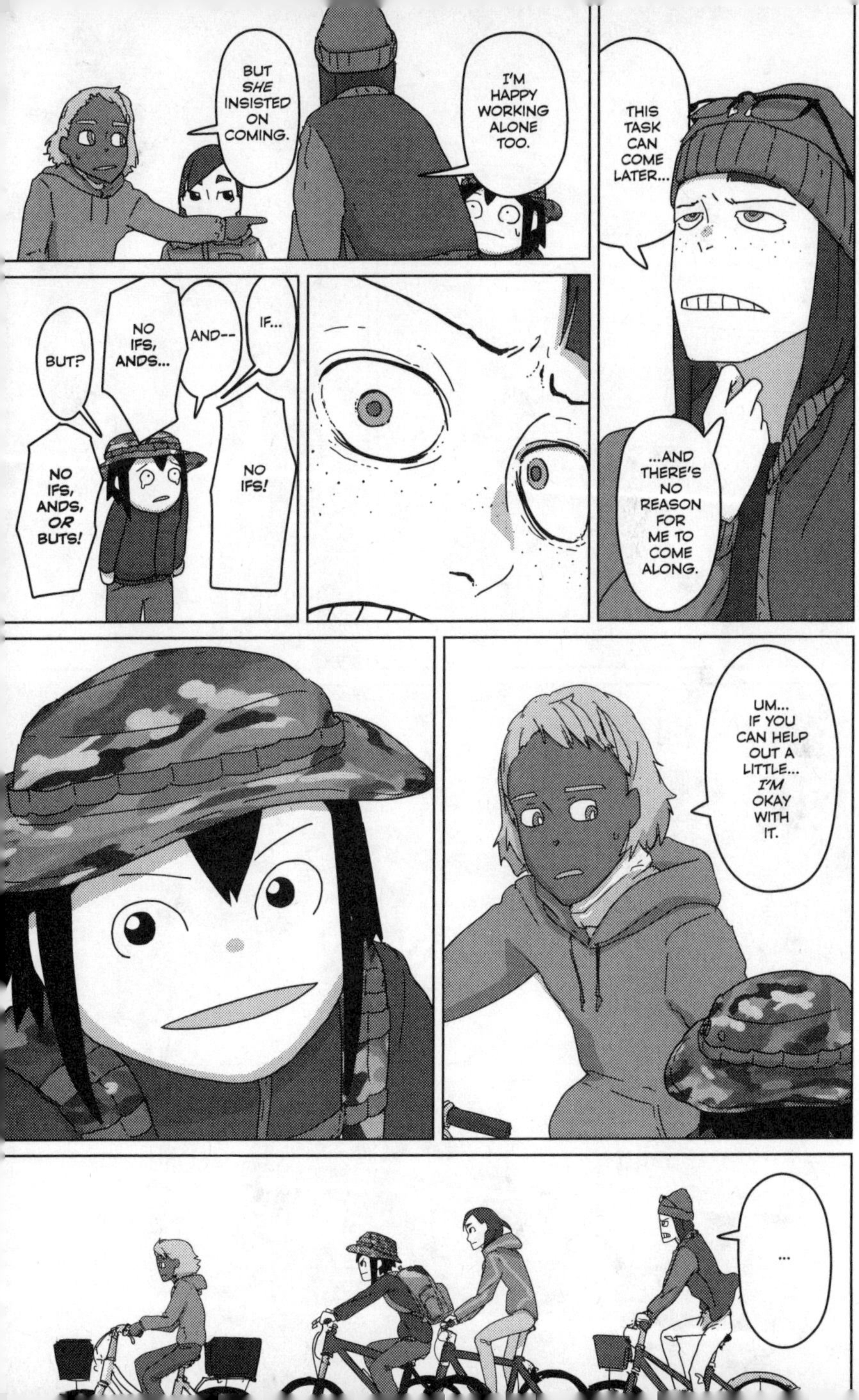
THIS TASK CAN COME LATER...
...AND THERE'S NO REASON FOR ME TO COME ALONG.
I'M HAPPY WORKING ALONE TOO.
BUT *SHE* INSISTED ON COMING.
IF...
NO IFS!
AND--
NO IFS, ANDS...
BUT?
NO IFS, ANDS, *OR* BUTS!
UM... IF YOU CAN HELP OUT A LITTLE... *I'M* OKAY WITH IT.
...

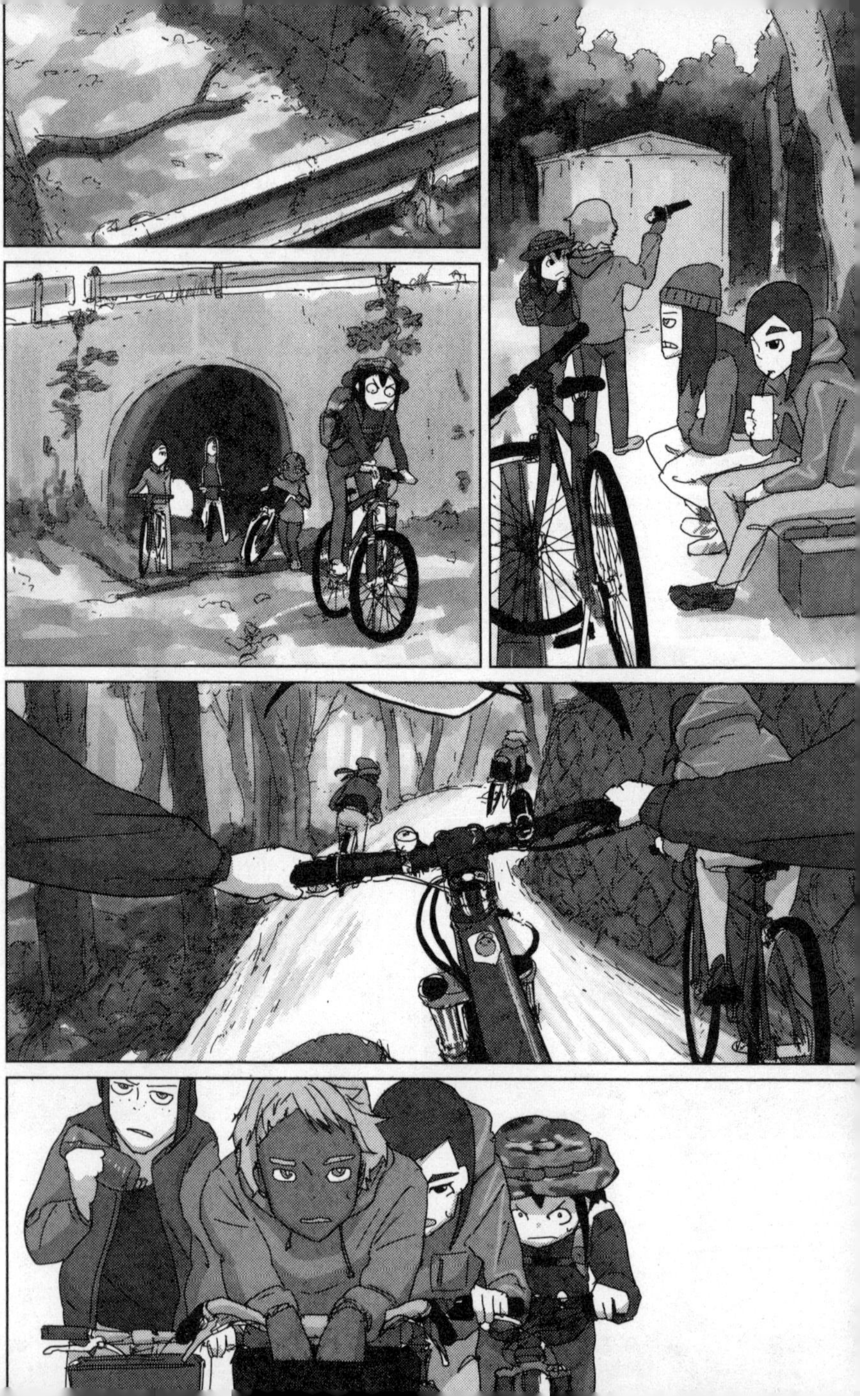

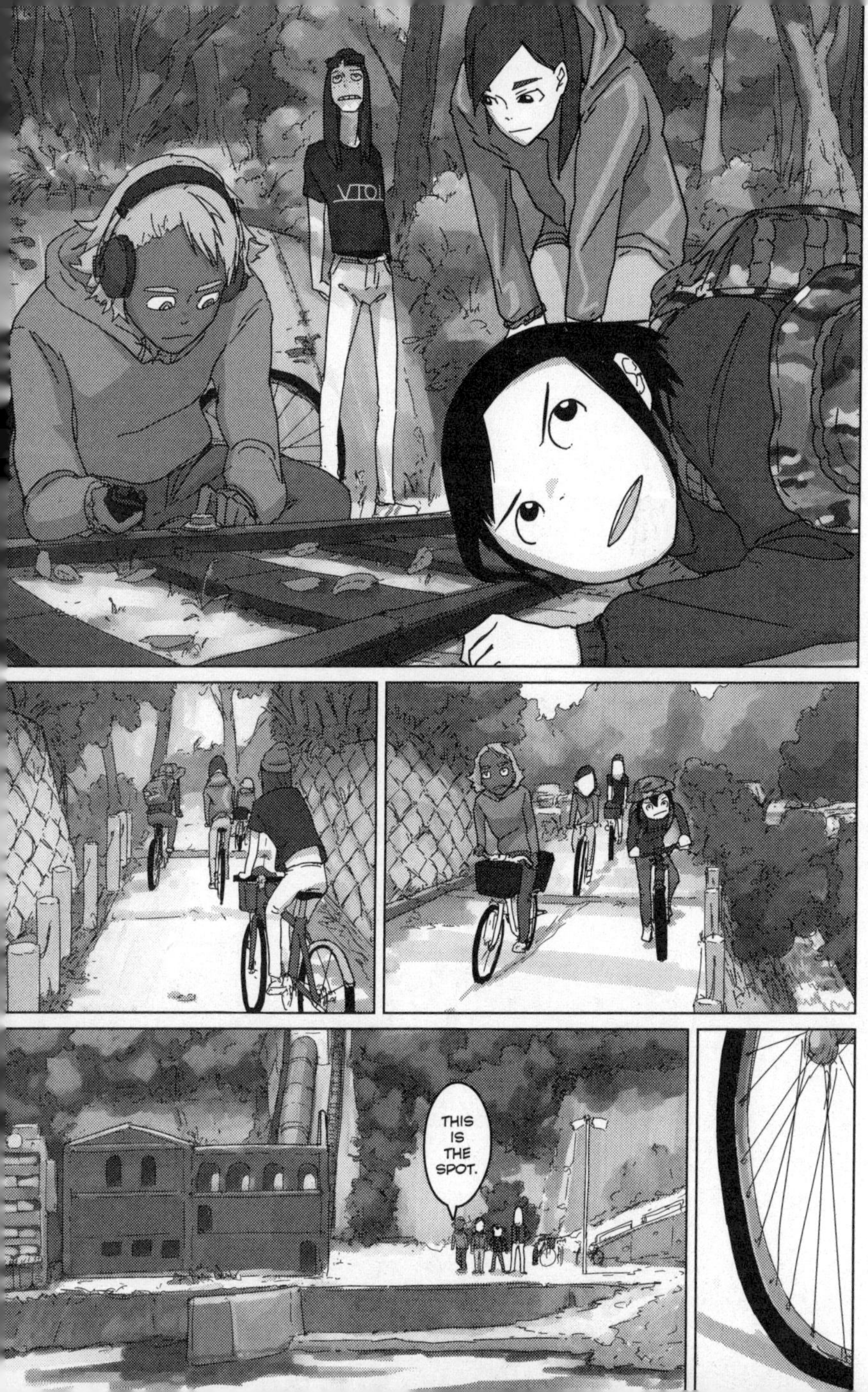
THIS IS THE SPOT.

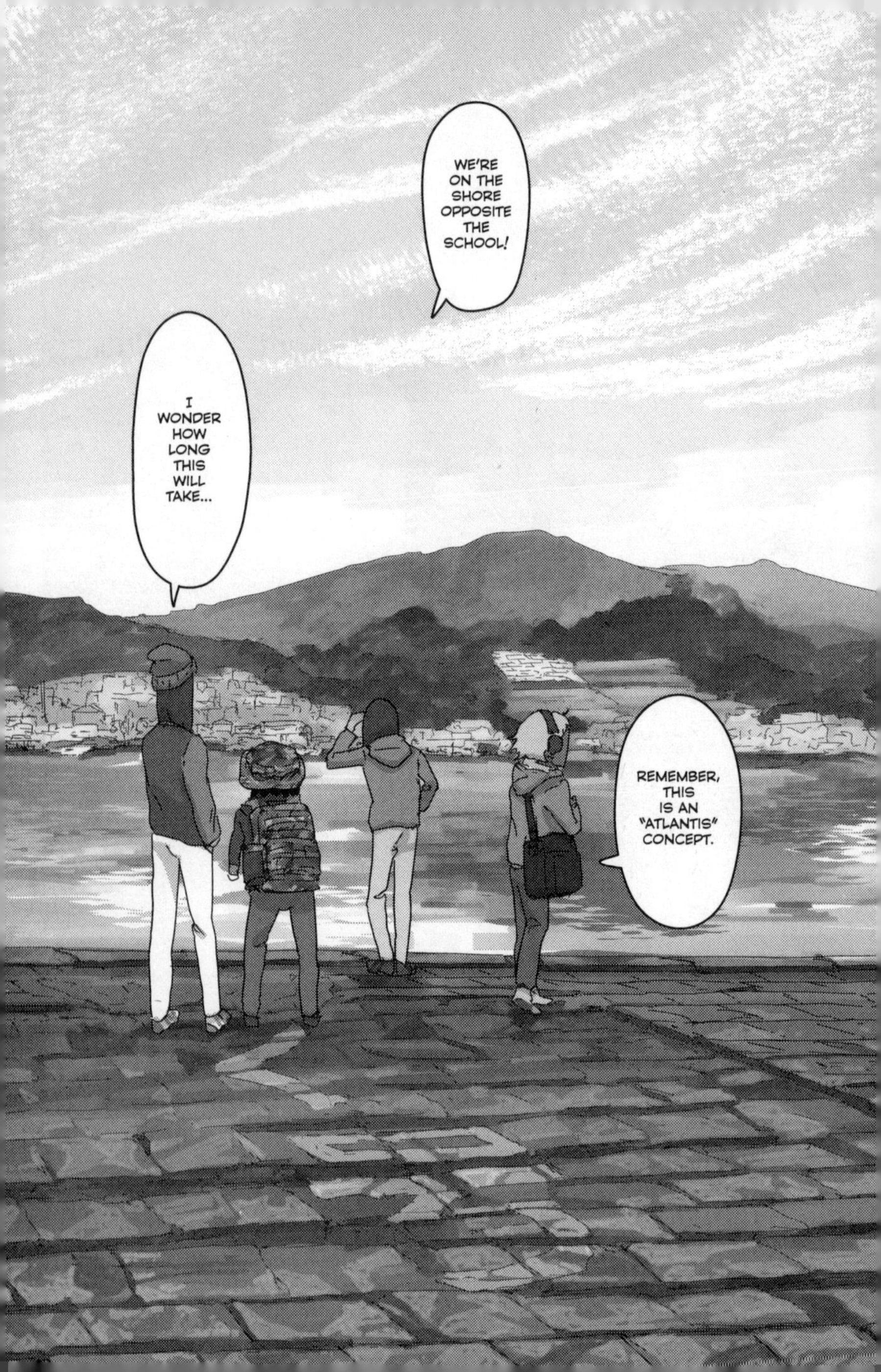
WE'RE ON THE SHORE OPPOSITE THE SCHOOL!
I WONDER HOW LONG THIS WILL TAKE...
REMEMBER, THIS IS AN "ATLANTIS" CONCEPT.

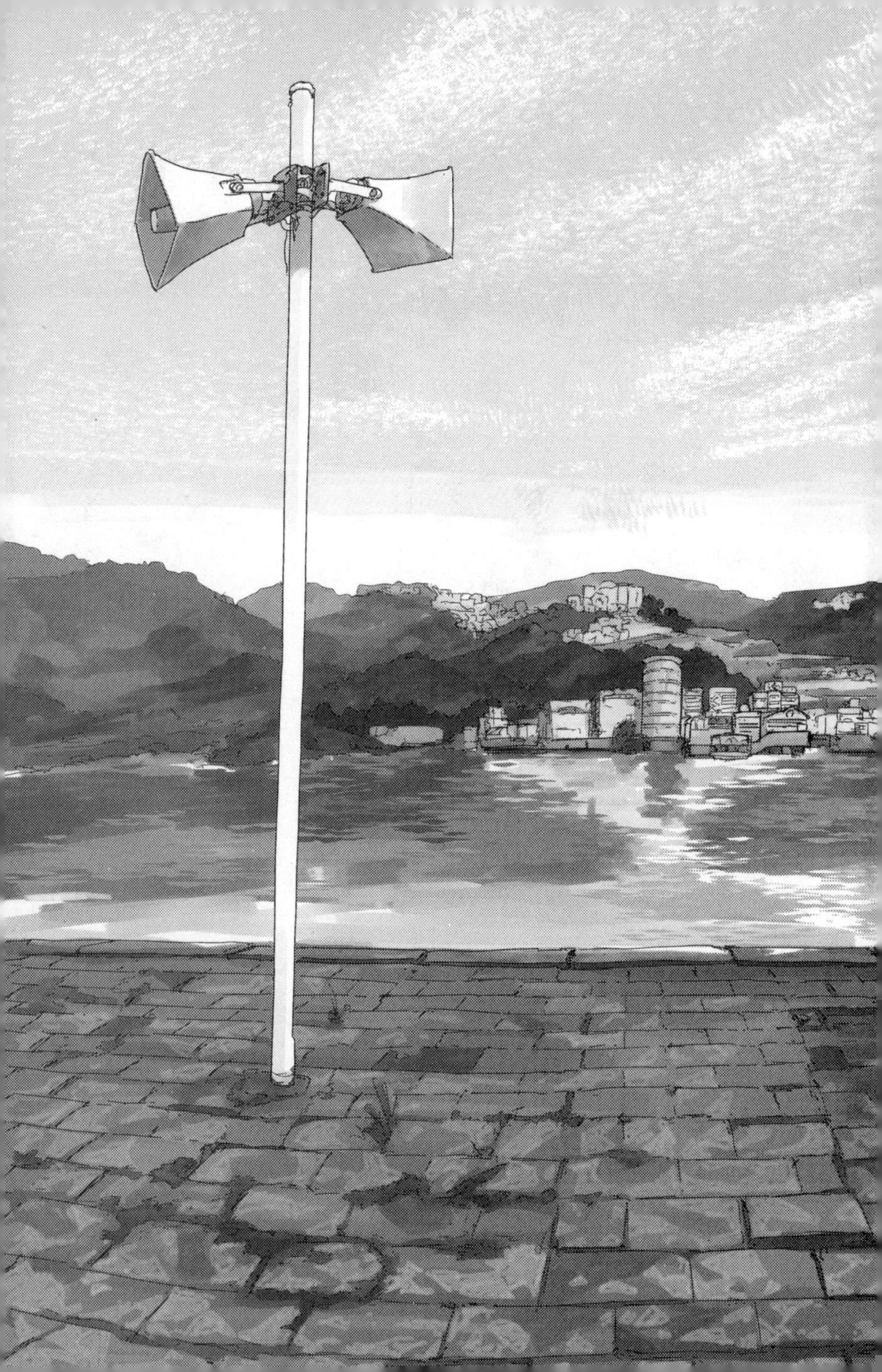

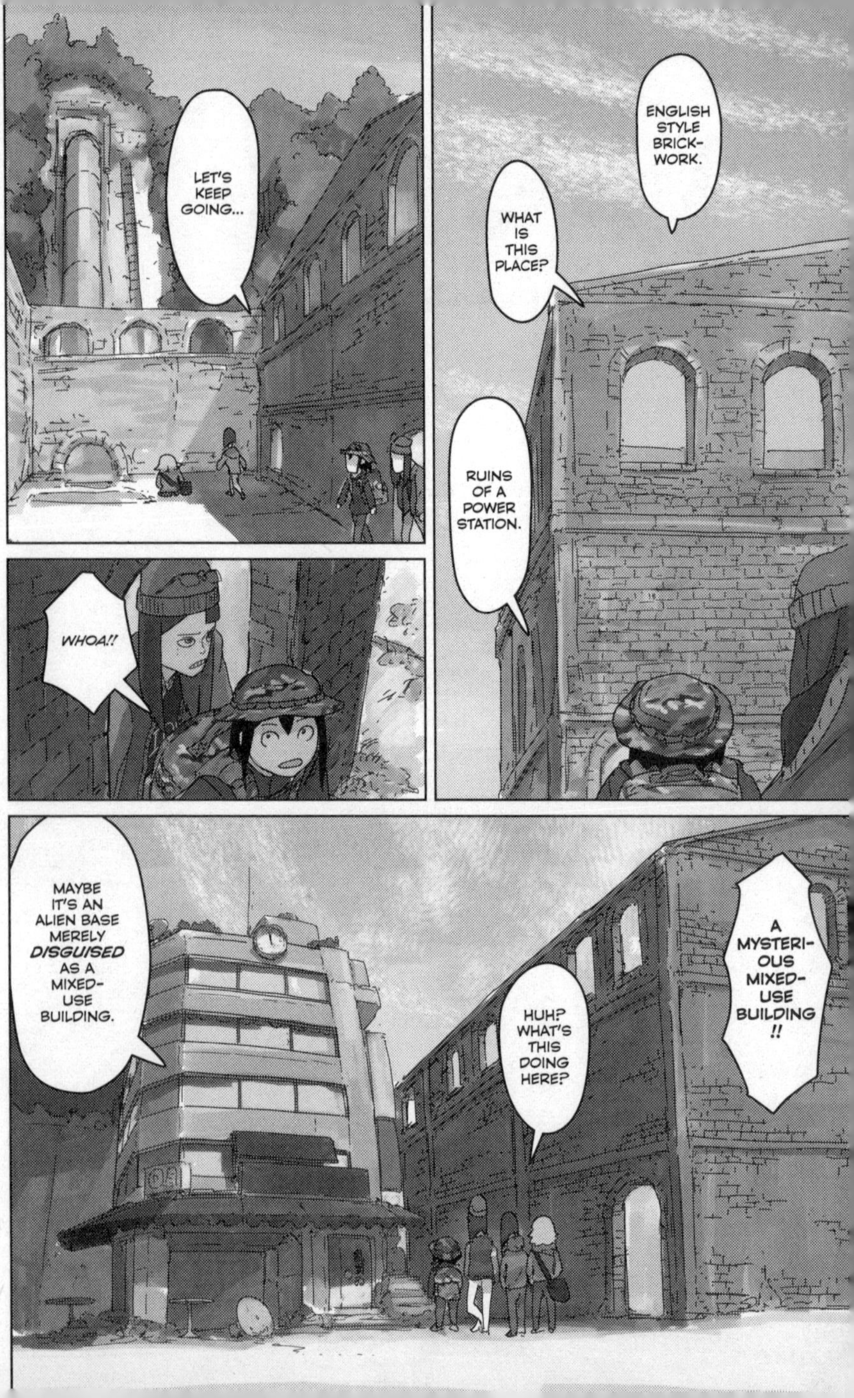
ENGLISH STYLE BRICK-WORK.
WHAT IS THIS PLACE?
RUINS OF A POWER STATION.
LET'S KEEP GOING...
WHOA!!
A MYSTERIOUS MIXED-USE BUILDING!!
HUH? WHAT'S THIS DOING HERE?
MAYBE IT'S AN ALIEN BASE MERELY DISGUISED AS A MIXED-USE BUILDING.

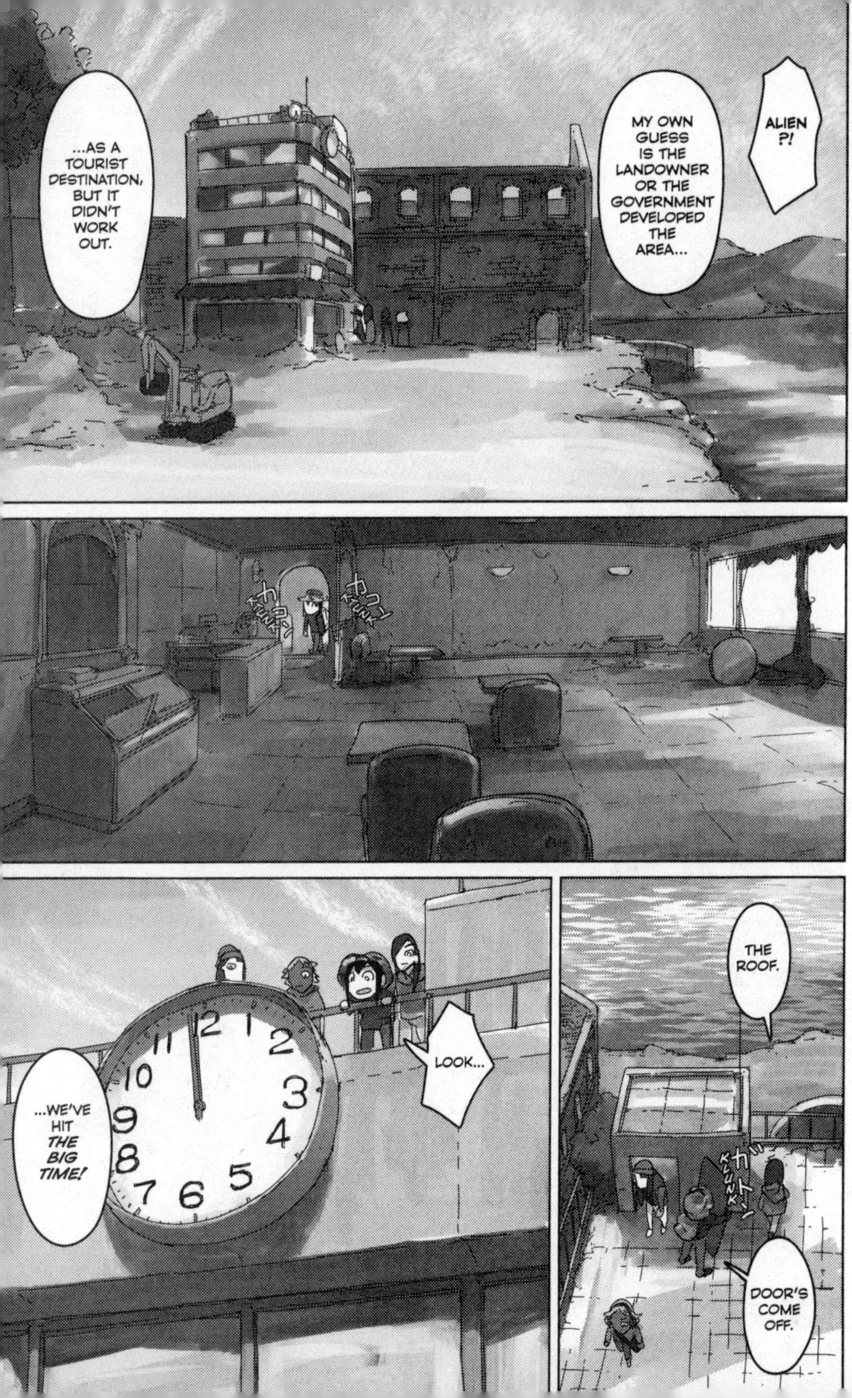
ALIEN ?!
MY OWN GUESS IS THE LANDOWNER OR THE GOVERNMENT DEVELOPED THE AREA...
...AS A TOURIST DESTINATION, BUT IT DIDN'T WORK OUT.
KRUNK
KRUNK
THE ROOF.
KRUNK
DOOR'S COME OFF.
LOOK...
...WE'VE HIT *THE BIG TIME!*

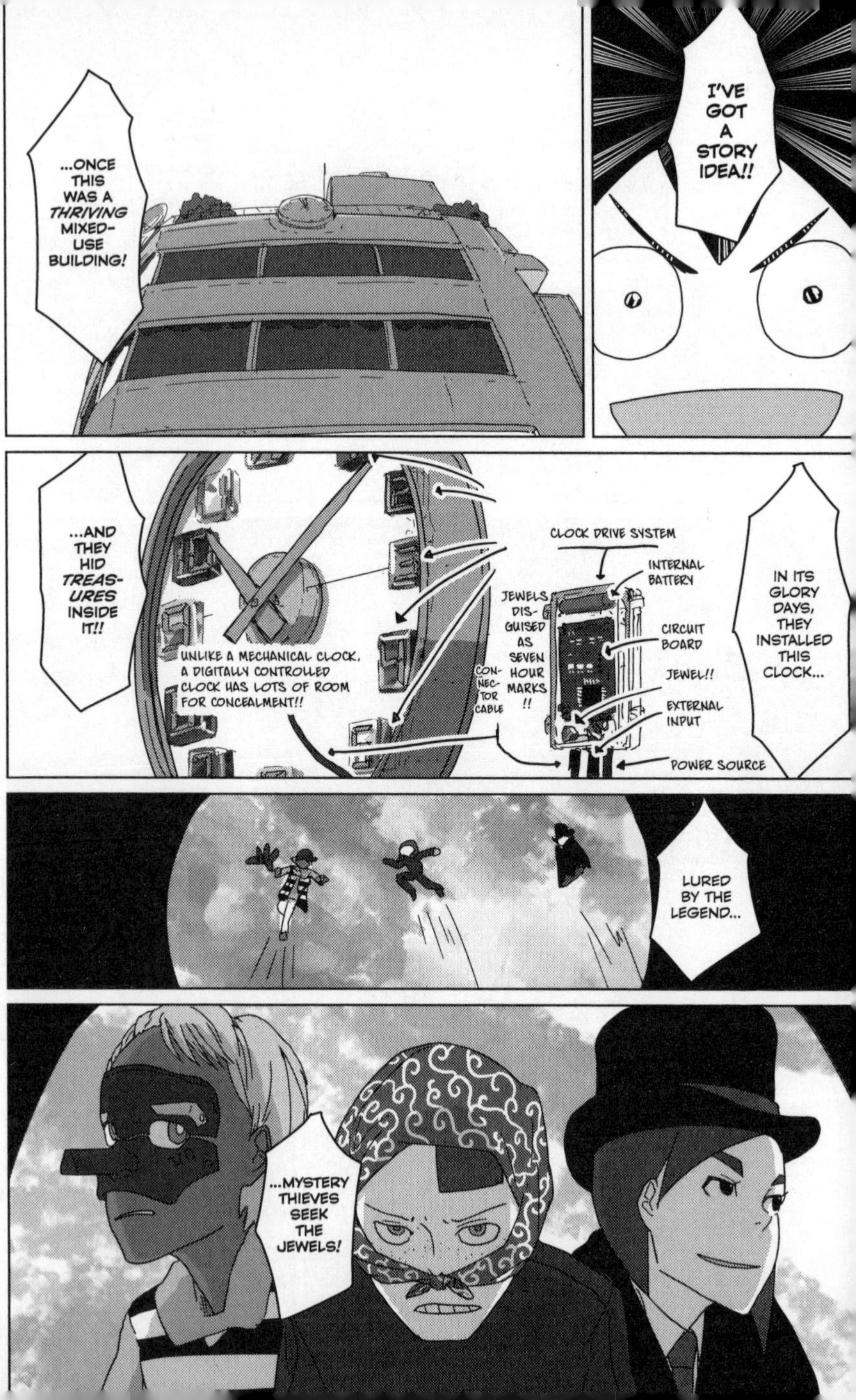
I'VE GOT A STORY IDEA!!
...ONCE THIS WAS A *THRIVING* MIXED-USE BUILDING!
IN ITS GLORY DAYS, THEY INSTALLED THIS CLOCK...
CLOCK DRIVE SYSTEM
INTERNAL BATTERY
CIRCUIT BOARD
JEWEL!!
EXTERNAL INPUT
POWER SOURCE
JEWELS DIS-GUISED AS SEVEN HOUR MARKS !!
CON-NEC-TOR CABLE
UNLIKE A MECHANICAL CLOCK, A DIGITALLY CONTROLLED CLOCK HAS LOTS OF ROOM FOR CONCEALMENT!!
...AND THEY HID *TREAS-URES* INSIDE IT!!
LURED BY THE LEGEND...
...MYSTERY THIEVES SEEK THE JEWELS!

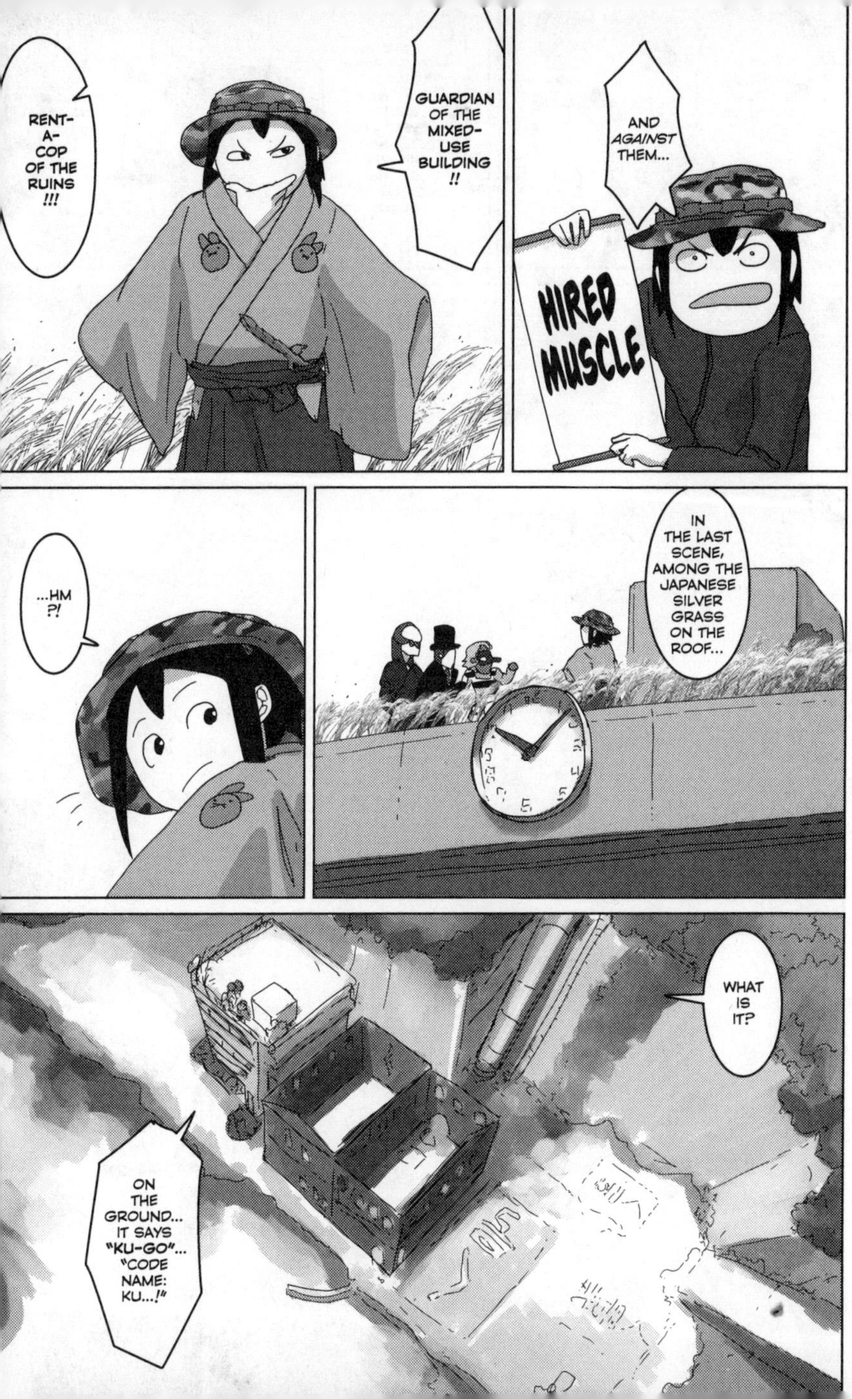
AND *AGAINST* THEM...
HIRED MUSCLE
GUARDIAN OF THE MIXED-USE BUILDING !!
RENT-A-COP OF THE RUINS !!!
IN THE LAST SCENE, AMONG THE JAPANESE SILVER GRASS ON THE ROOF...
...HM ?!
WHAT IS IT?
ON THE GROUND... IT SAYS "KU-GO"... "CODE NAME: KU...!"

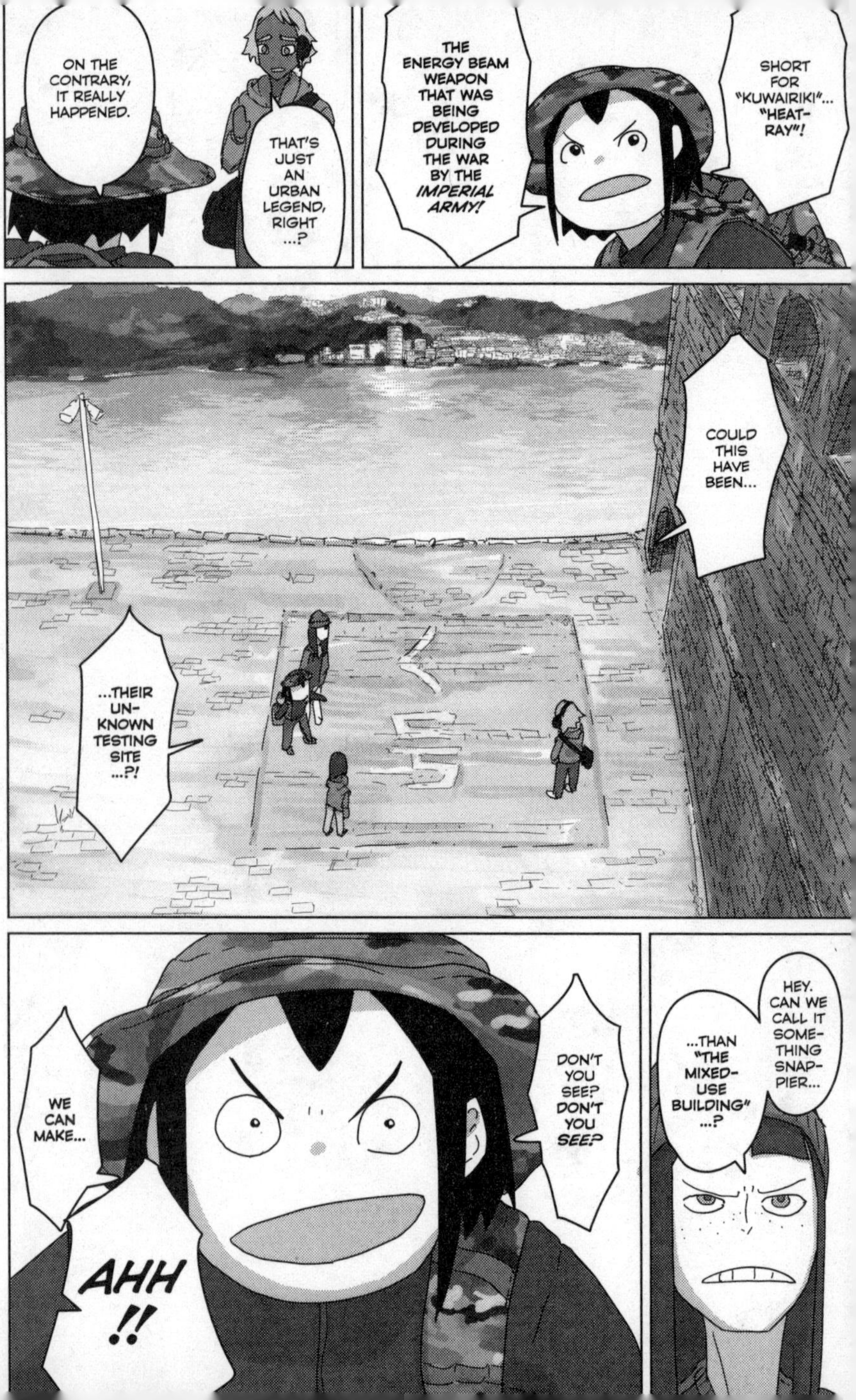
SHORT FOR "KUWAIRIKI"... "HEAT-RAY"!
THE ENERGY BEAM WEAPON THAT WAS BEING DEVELOPED DURING THE WAR BY THE *IMPERIAL ARMY!*
THAT'S JUST AN URBAN LEGEND, RIGHT ...?
ON THE CONTRARY, IT REALLY HAPPENED.
COULD THIS HAVE BEEN...
...THEIR UN-KNOWN TESTING SITE ...?!
HEY. CAN WE CALL IT SOME-THING SNAP-PIER...
...THAN "THE MIXED-USE BUILDING" ...?
DON'T YOU SEE? DON'T YOU *SEE?*
WE CAN MAKE...
AHH !!

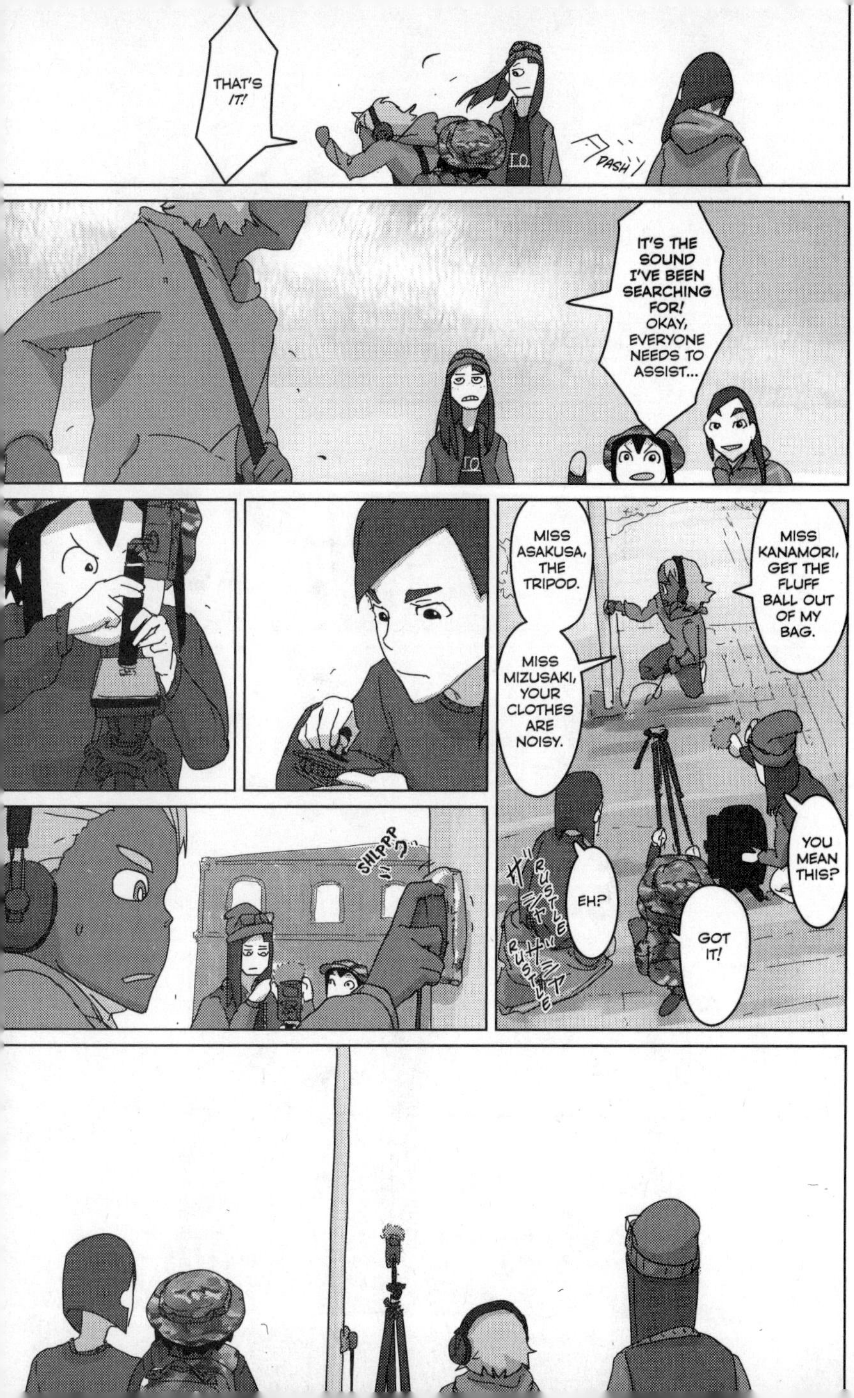
THAT'S IT!
DASH
IT'S THE SOUND I'VE BEEN SEARCHING FOR! OKAY, EVERYONE NEEDS TO ASSIST...
MISS KANAMORI, GET THE FLUFF BALL OUT OF MY BAG.
MISS ASAKUSA, THE TRIPOD.
MISS MIZUSAKI, YOUR CLOTHES ARE NOISY.
YOU MEAN THIS?
EH?
GOT IT!
RUSTLE
RUSTLE
SHLPPP

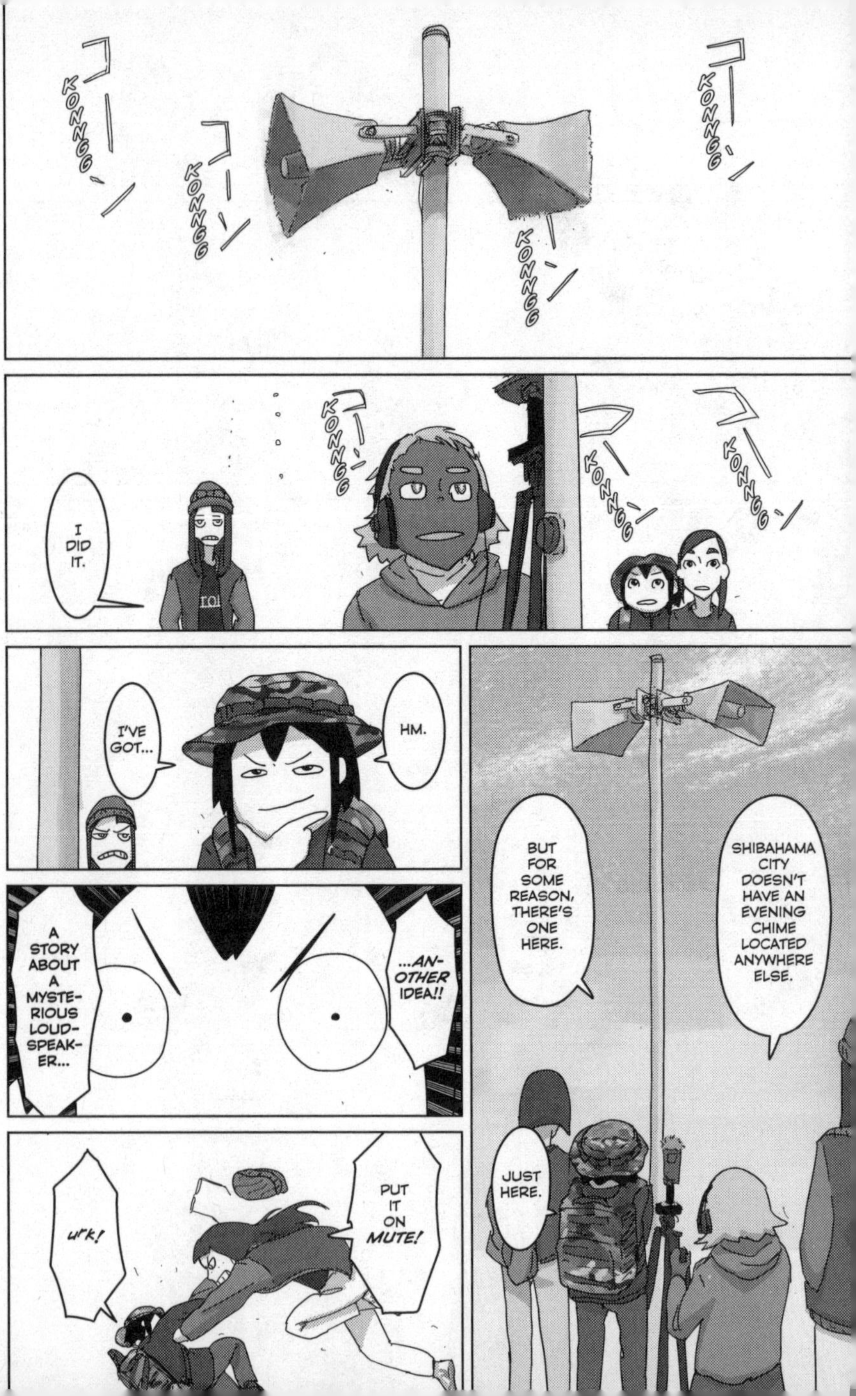
KONNGG
KONNGG
KONNGG
KONNGG
KONNGG
KONNGG
KONNGG
I DID IT.
SHIBAHAMA CITY DOESN'T HAVE AN EVENING CHIME LOCATED ANYWHERE ELSE.
BUT FOR SOME REASON, THERE'S ONE HERE.
JUST HERE.
HM.
I'VE GOT...
...ANOTHER IDEA!!
A STORY ABOUT A MYSTERIOUS LOUDSPEAKER...
PUT IT ON MUTE!
urk!

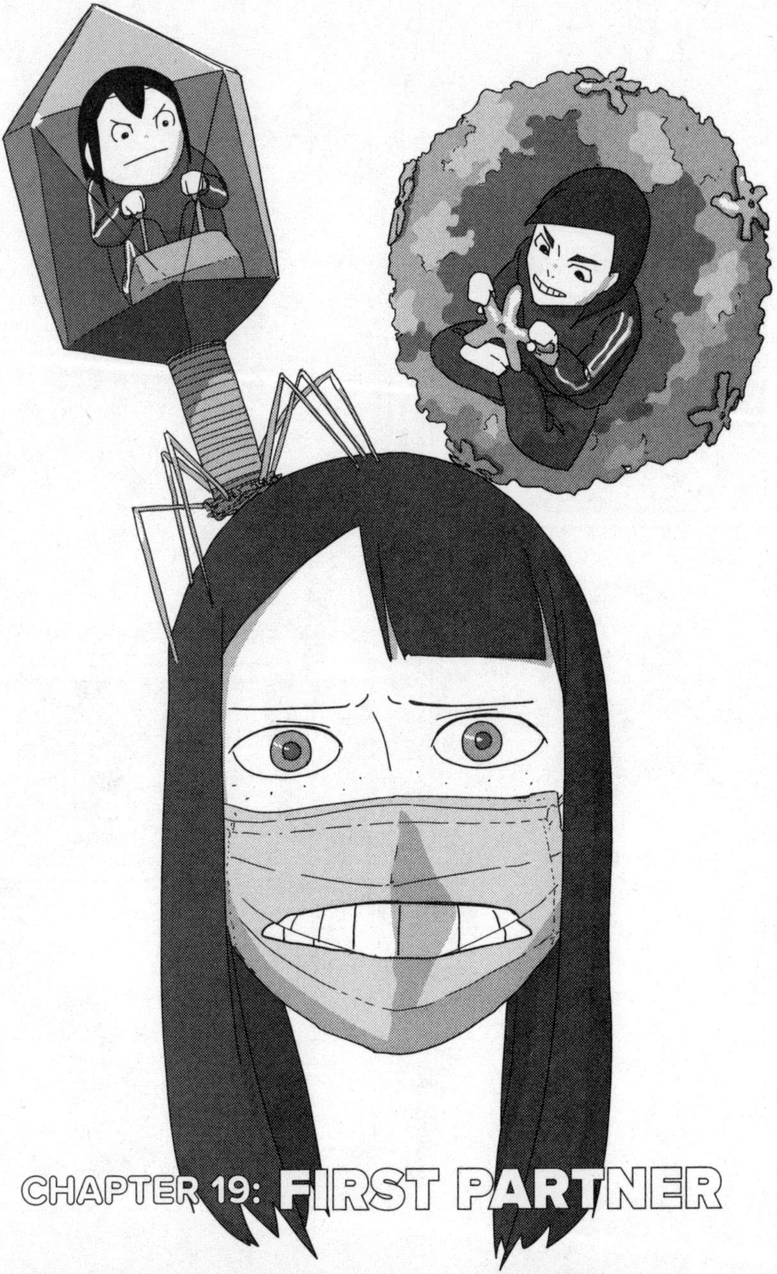

CHAPTER 19: FIRST PARTNER

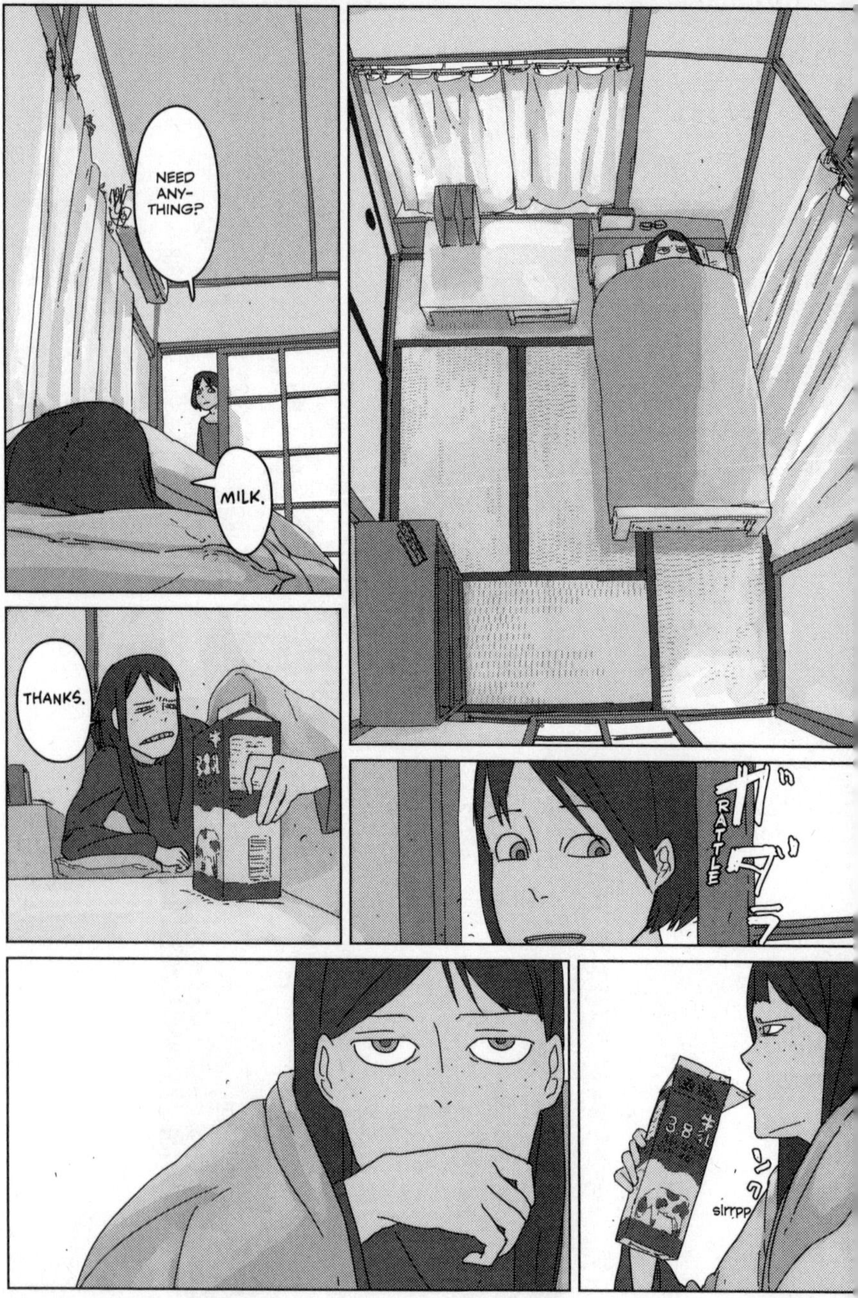
NEED ANY-THING?
MILK.
RATTLE
THANKS.
slrrpp

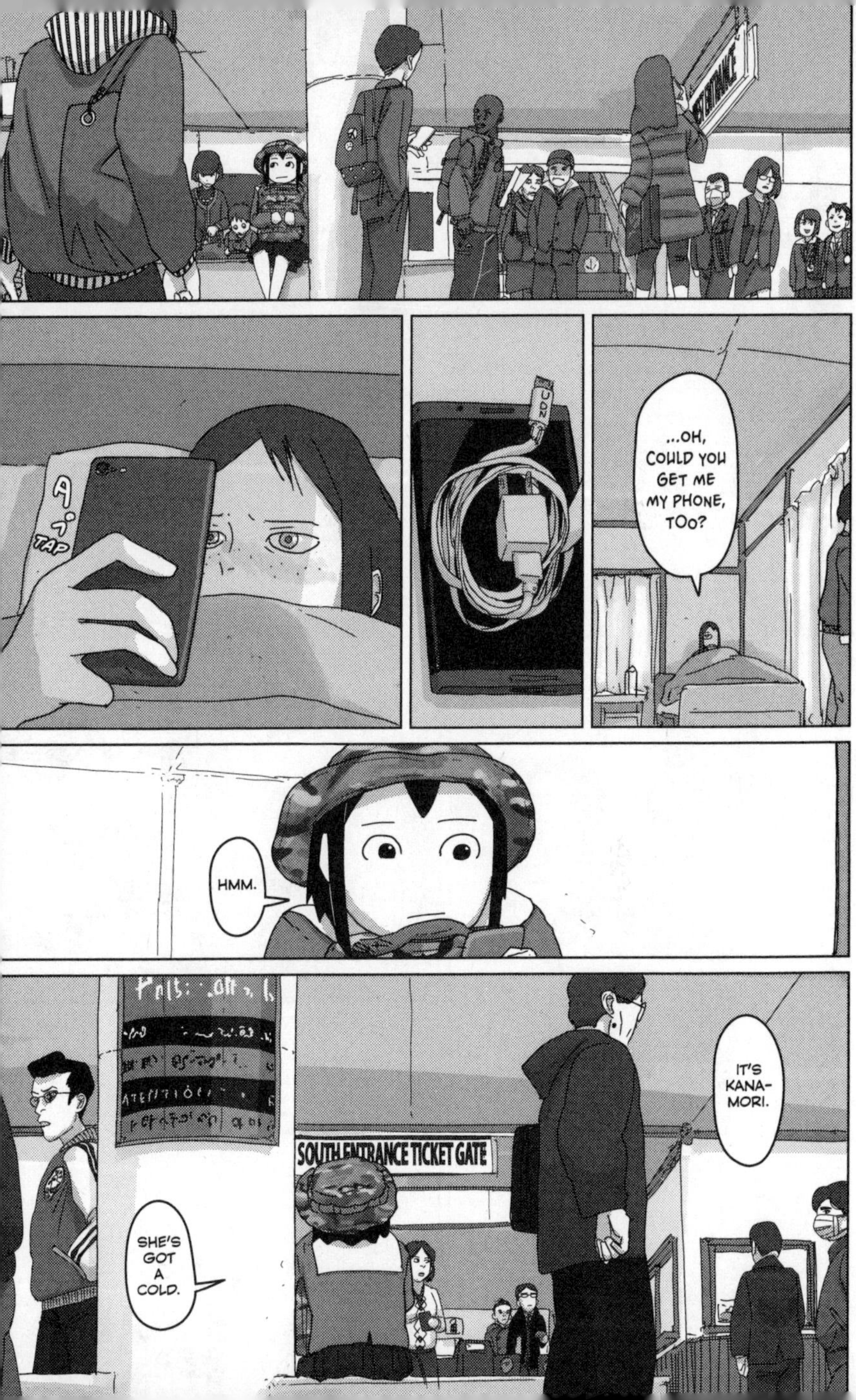
...OH, COULD YOU GET ME MY PHONE, TOO?
UDN
TAP
HMM.
IT'S KANA-MORI.
SOUTH ENTRANCE TICKET GATE
SHE'S GOT A COLD.

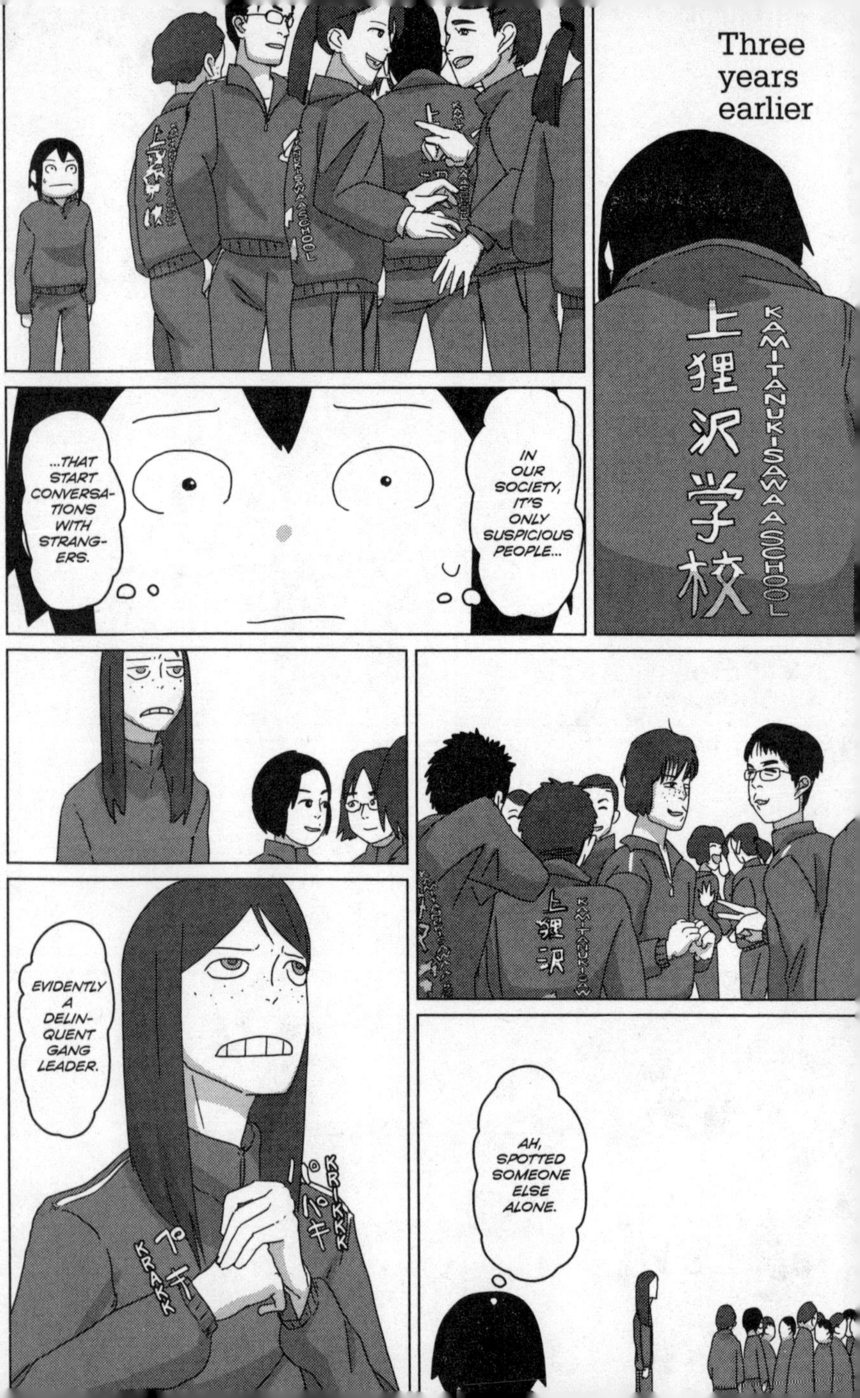
Three years earlier
上狸沢学校
KAMITANUKISAWASCHOOL
IN OUR SOCIETY, IT'S ONLY SUSPICIOUS PEOPLE...
...THAT START CONVERSATIONS WITH STRANGERS.
上狸沢
KAMITANUKISAW
AH, SPOTTED SOMEONE ELSE ALONE.
EVIDENTLY A DELINQUENT GANG LEADER.
パキ KRIKKK
ペキ KRAKK

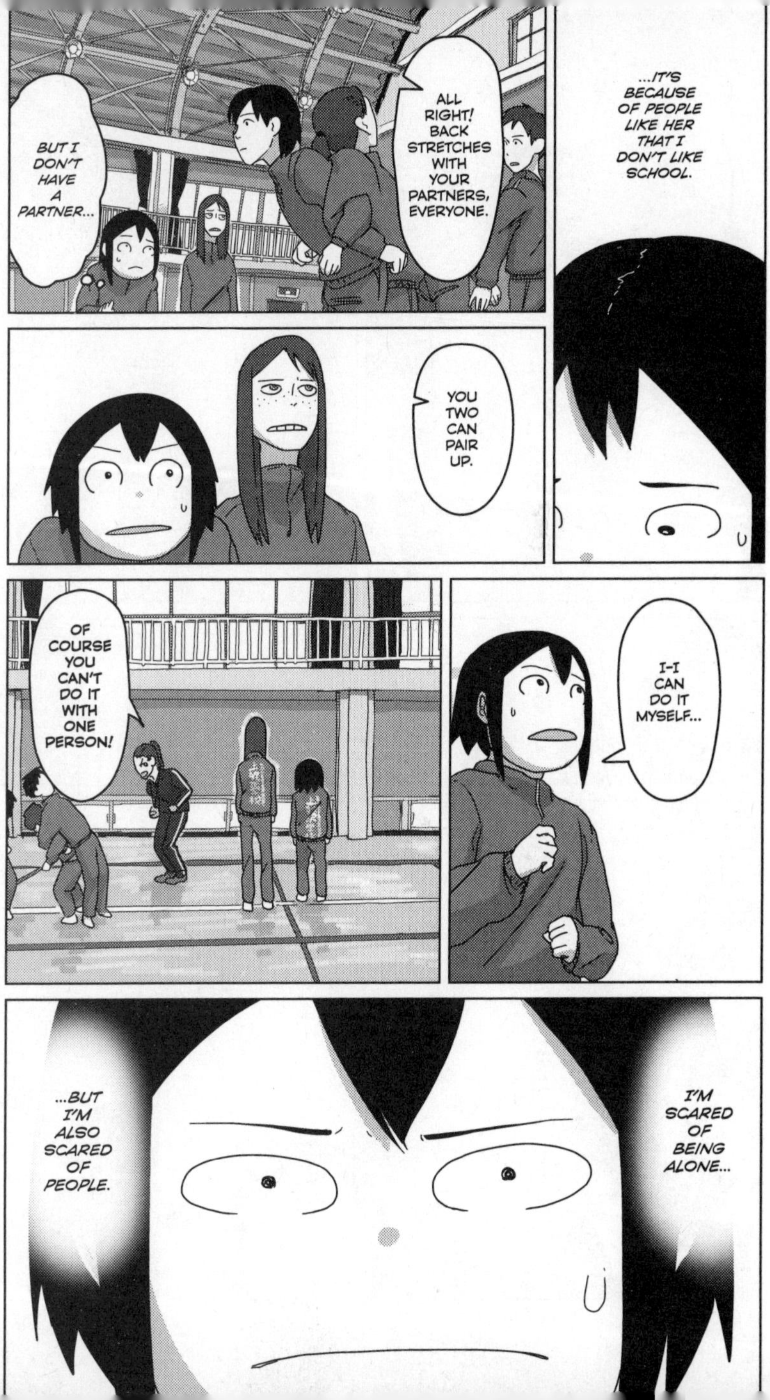
...IT'S BECAUSE OF PEOPLE LIKE HER THAT I DON'T LIKE SCHOOL.
ALL RIGHT! BACK STRETCHES WITH YOUR PARTNERS, EVERYONE.
BUT I DON'T HAVE A PARTNER...
YOU TWO CAN PAIR UP.
I-I CAN DO IT MYSELF...
OF COURSE YOU CAN'T DO IT WITH ONE PERSON!
I'M SCARED OF BEING ALONE...
...BUT I'M ALSO SCARED OF PEOPLE.

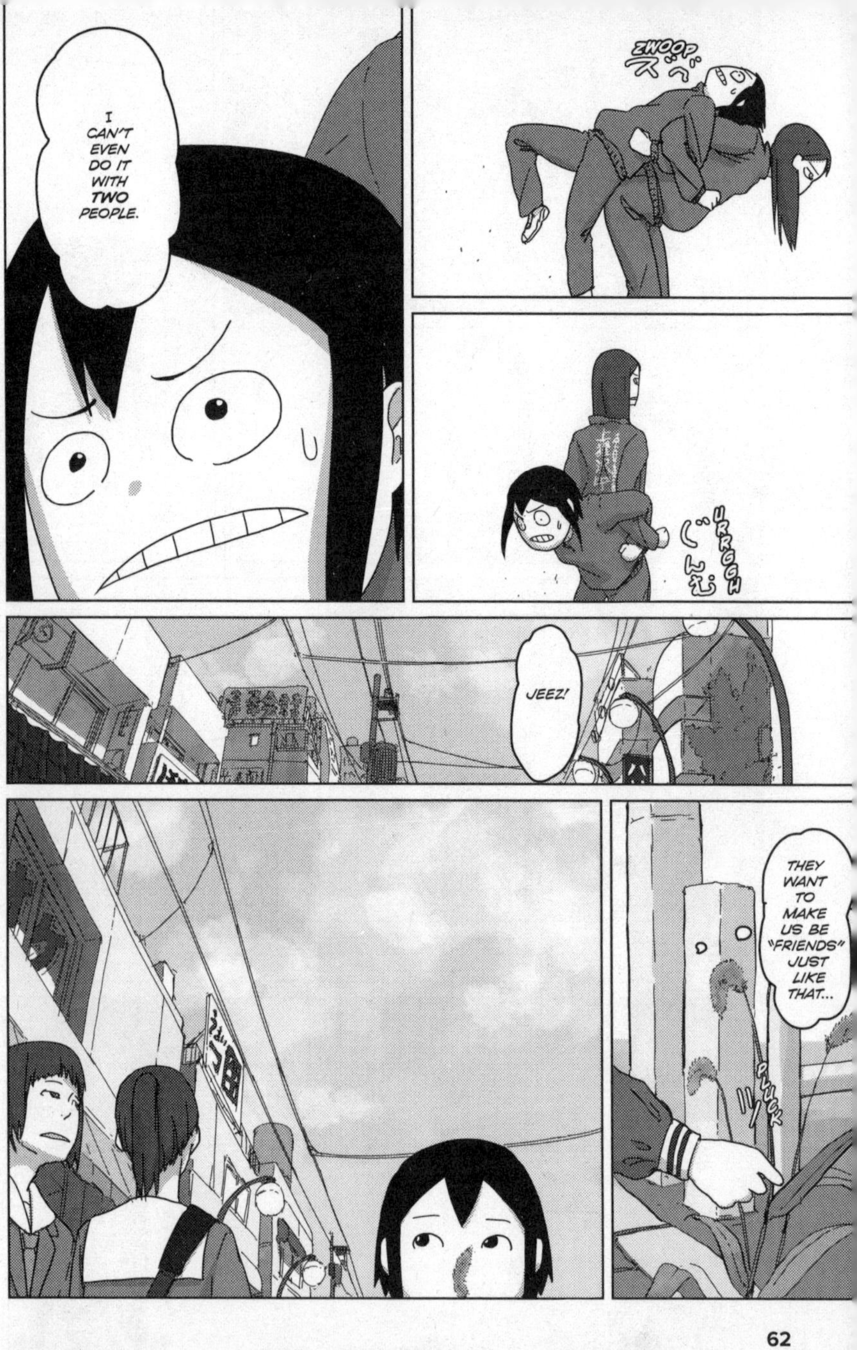
ZWOOP
URRGH
I CAN'T EVEN DO IT WITH **TWO** PEOPLE.
JEEZ!
THEY WANT TO MAKE US BE "FRIENDS" JUST LIKE THAT...
PLUCK

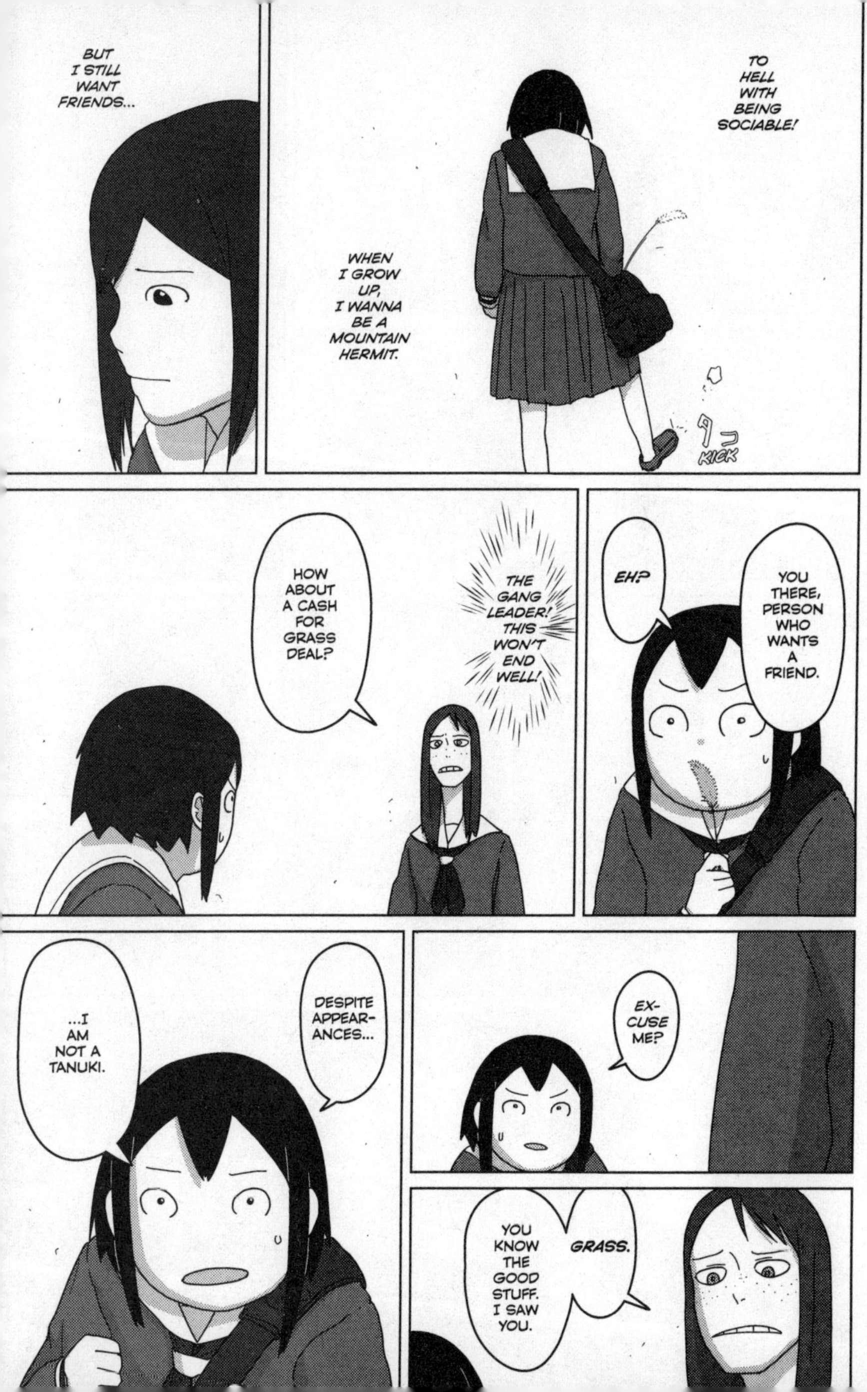
TO HELL WITH BEING SOCIABLE!
WHEN I GROW UP, I WANNA BE A MOUNTAIN HERMIT.
KICK
BUT I STILL WANT FRIENDS...
YOU THERE, PERSON WHO WANTS A FRIEND.
EH?
THE GANG LEADER! THIS WON'T END WELL!
HOW ABOUT A CASH FOR GRASS DEAL?
EXCUSE ME?
YOU KNOW THE GOOD STUFF. I SAW YOU.
GRASS.
DESPITE APPEARANCES...
...I AM NOT A TANUKI.

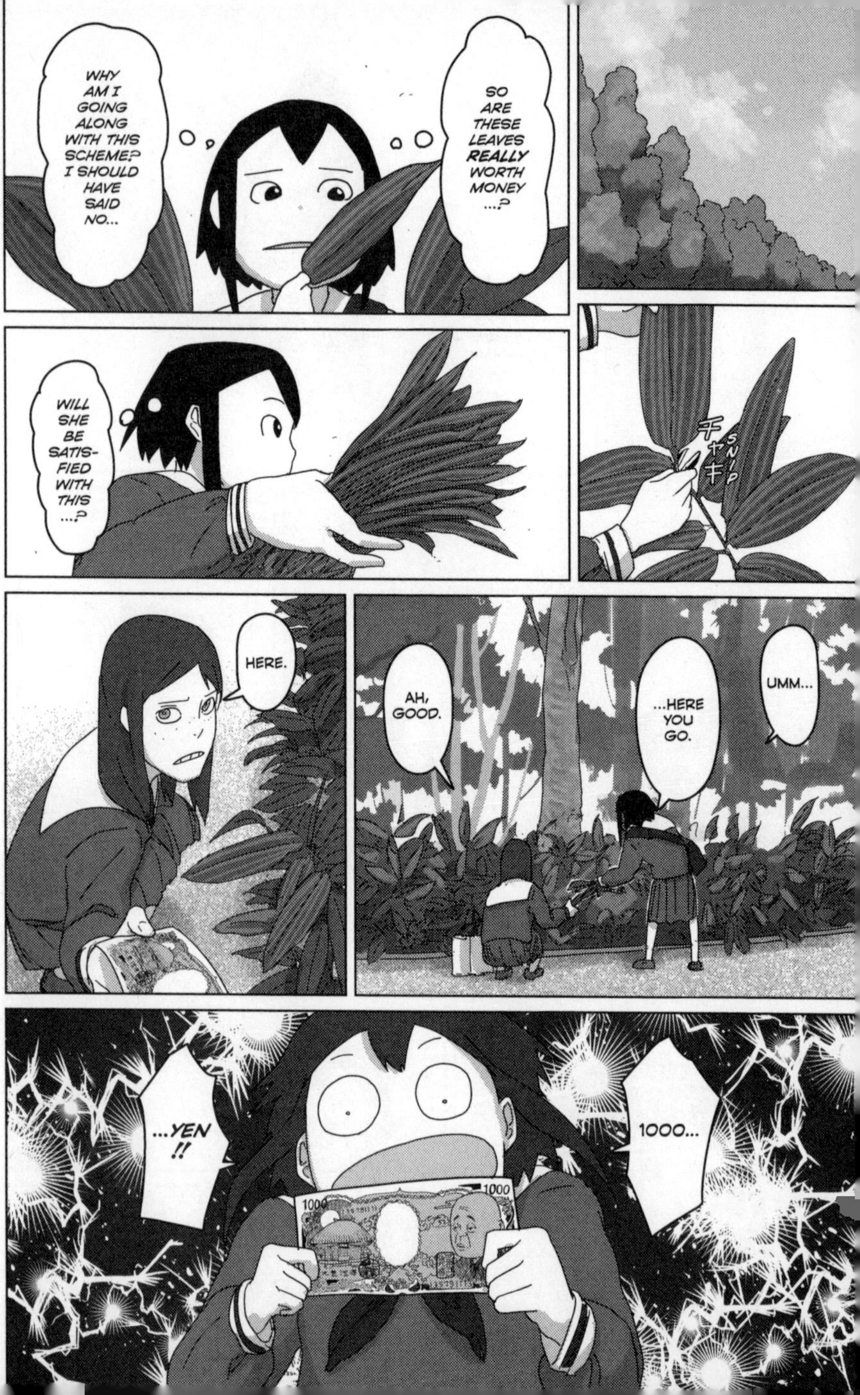
SO ARE THESE LEAVES REALLY WORTH MONEY ...?
WHY AM I GOING ALONG WITH THIS SCHEME? I SHOULD HAVE SAID NO...
チャキ
SNIP
WILL SHE BE SATIS-FIED WITH THIS ...?
UMM...
...HERE YOU GO.
AH, GOOD.
HERE.
1000...
...YEN !!

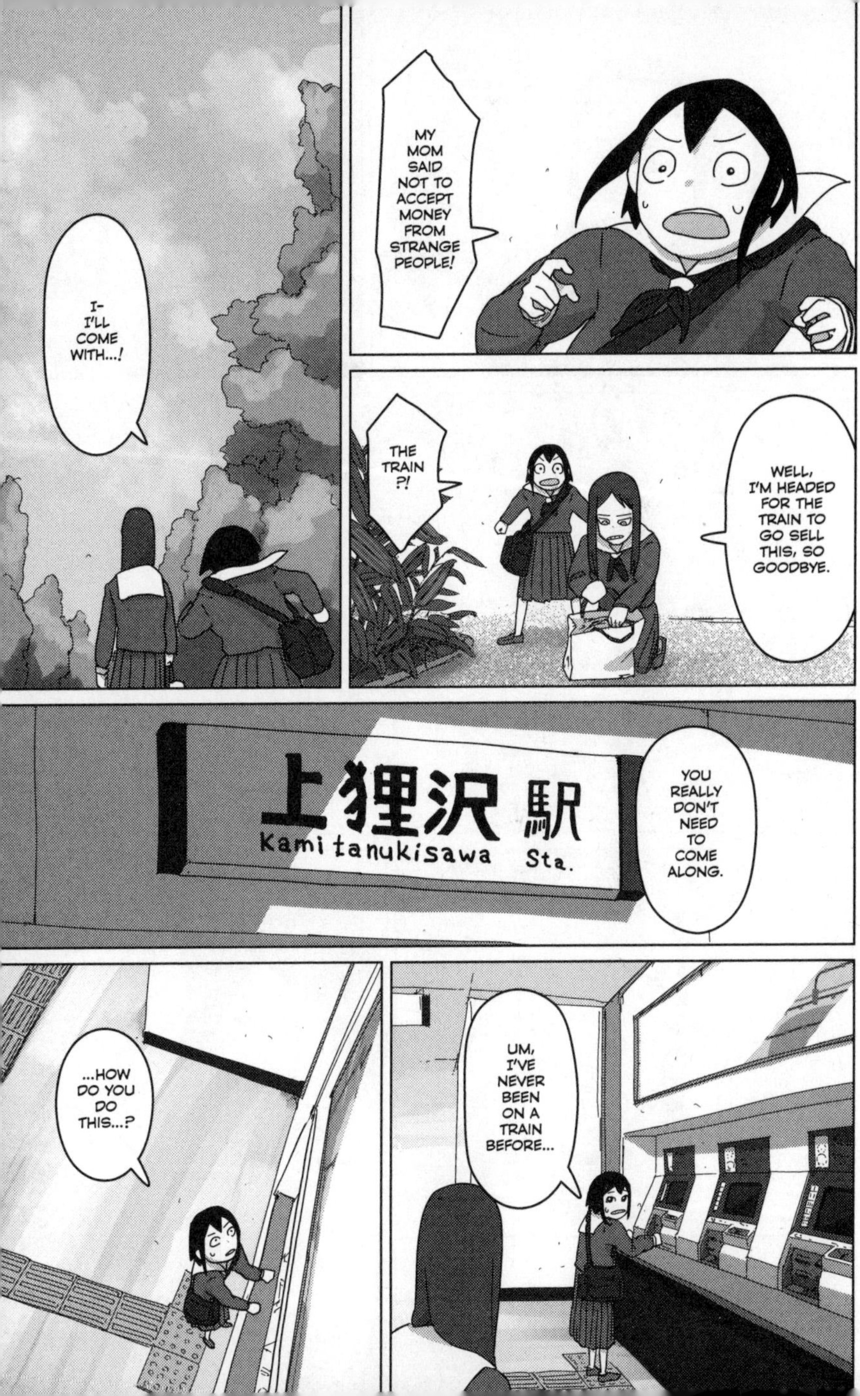
MY MOM SAID NOT TO ACCEPT MONEY FROM STRANGE PEOPLE!
WELL, I'M HEADED FOR THE TRAIN TO GO SELL THIS, SO GOODBYE.
THE TRAIN ?!
I- I'LL COME WITH...!
YOU REALLY DON'T NEED TO COME ALONG.
上狸沢駅
Kami tanukisawa Sta.
UM, I'VE NEVER BEEN ON A TRAIN BEFORE...
...HOW DO YOU DO THIS...?

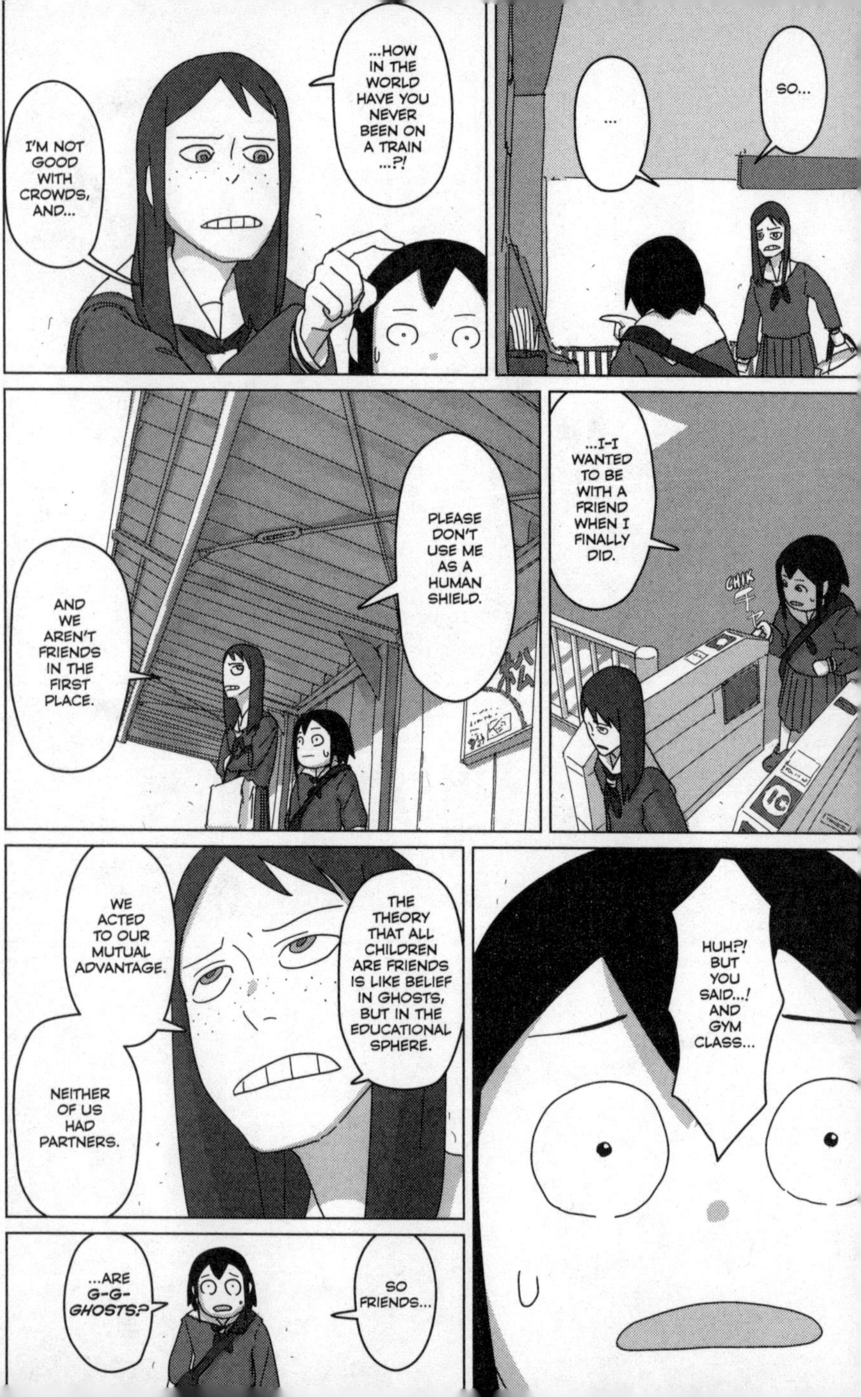
SO...
...
...HOW IN THE WORLD HAVE YOU NEVER BEEN ON A TRAIN ...?!
I'M NOT GOOD WITH CROWDS, AND...
...I-I WANTED TO BE WITH A FRIEND WHEN I FINALLY DID.
CHIK
PLEASE DON'T USE ME AS A HUMAN SHIELD.
AND WE AREN'T FRIENDS IN THE FIRST PLACE.
HUH?! BUT YOU SAID...! AND GYM CLASS...
WE ACTED TO OUR MUTUAL ADVANTAGE.
NEITHER OF US HAD PARTNERS.
THE THEORY THAT ALL CHILDREN ARE FRIENDS IS LIKE BELIEF IN GHOSTS, BUT IN THE EDUCATIONAL SPHERE.
SO FRIENDS...
...ARE G-G-GHOSTS?

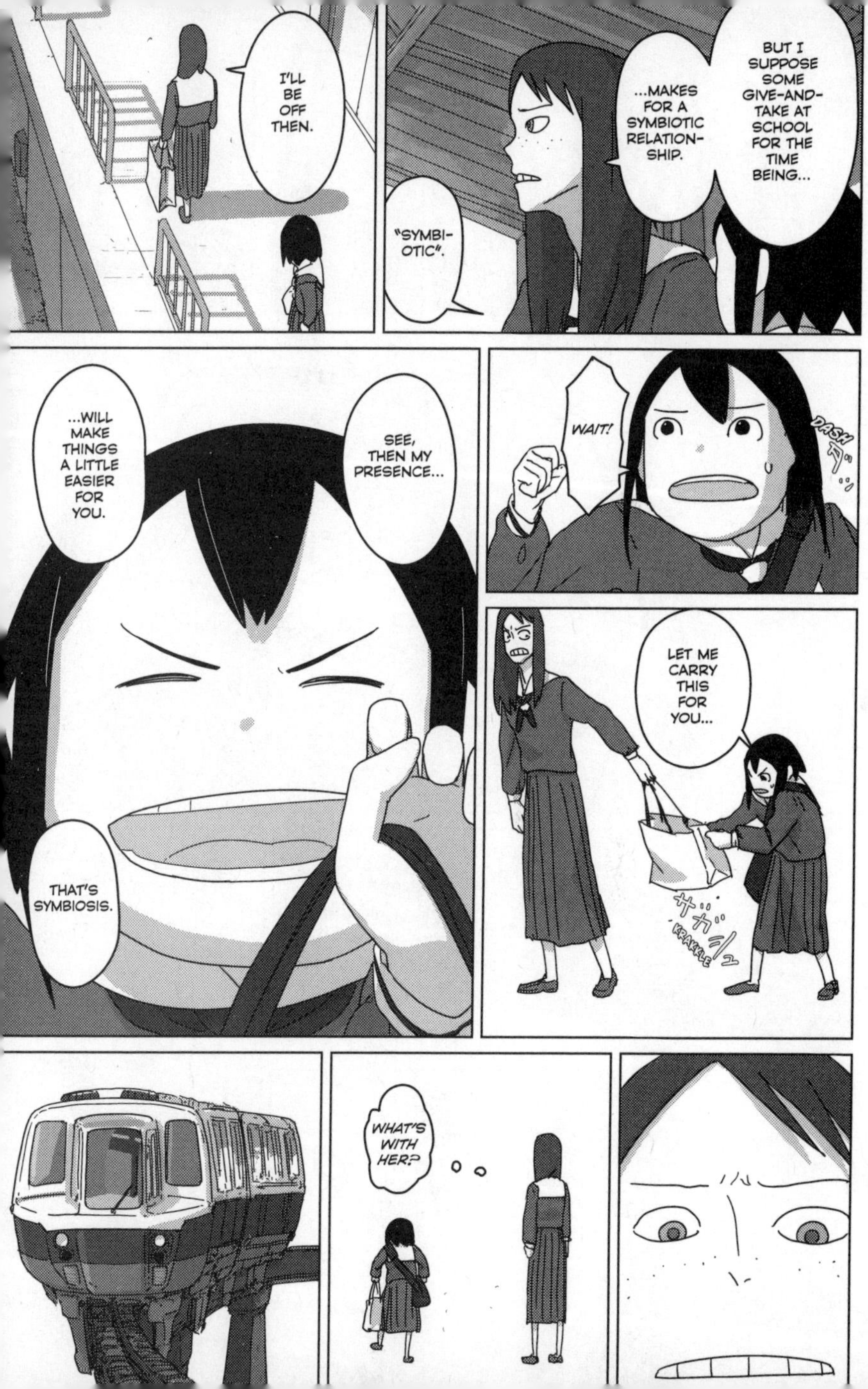
BUT I SUPPOSE SOME GIVE-AND-TAKE AT SCHOOL FOR THE TIME BEING...
...MAKES FOR A SYMBIOTIC RELATION-SHIP.
"SYMBI-OTIC".
I'LL BE OFF THEN.
WAIT!
DASH
LET ME CARRY THIS FOR YOU...
KRAKKLE
SEE, THEN MY PRESENCE...
...WILL MAKE THINGS A LITTLE EASIER FOR YOU.
THAT'S SYMBIOSIS.
WHAT'S WITH HER?

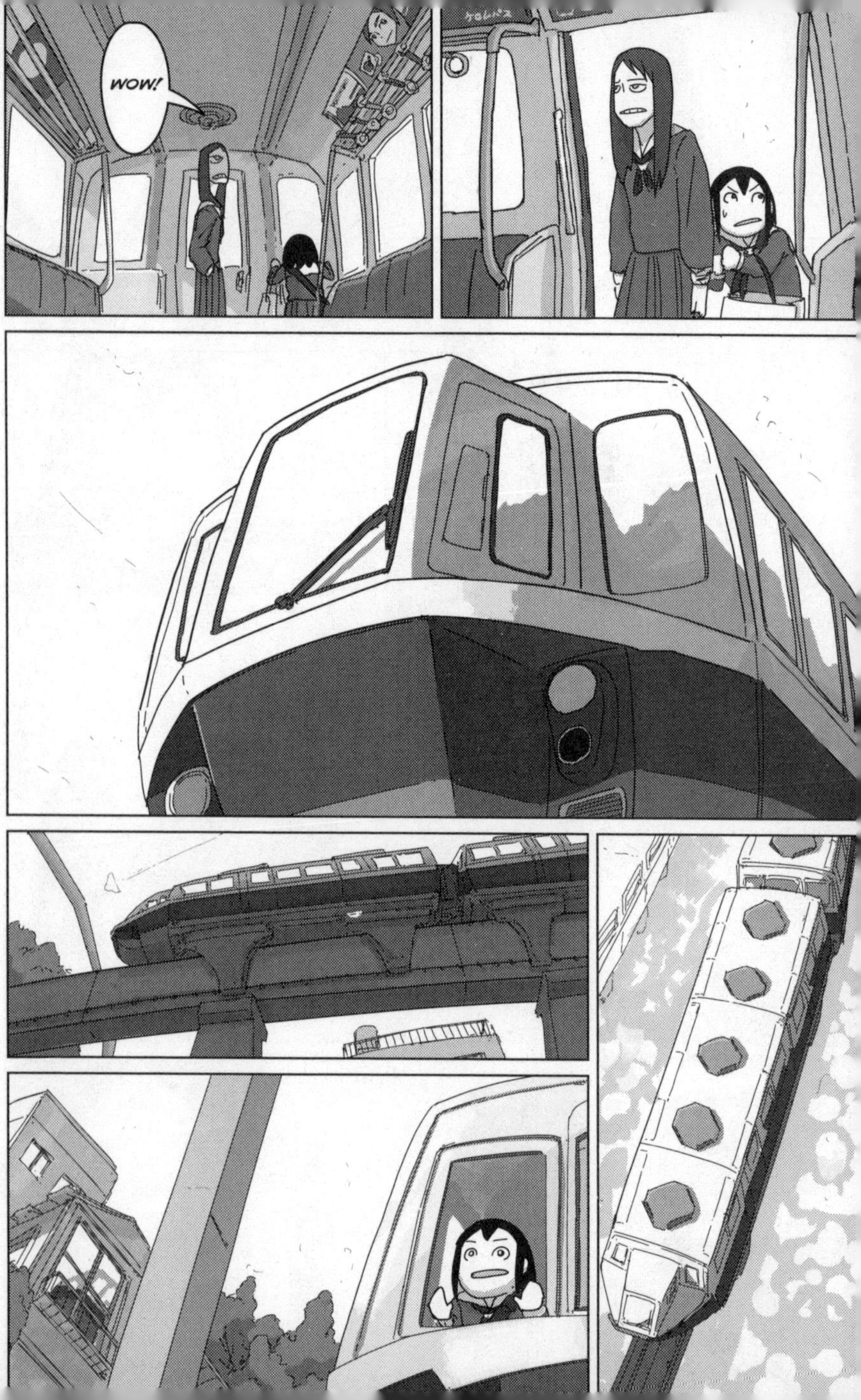
WOW!

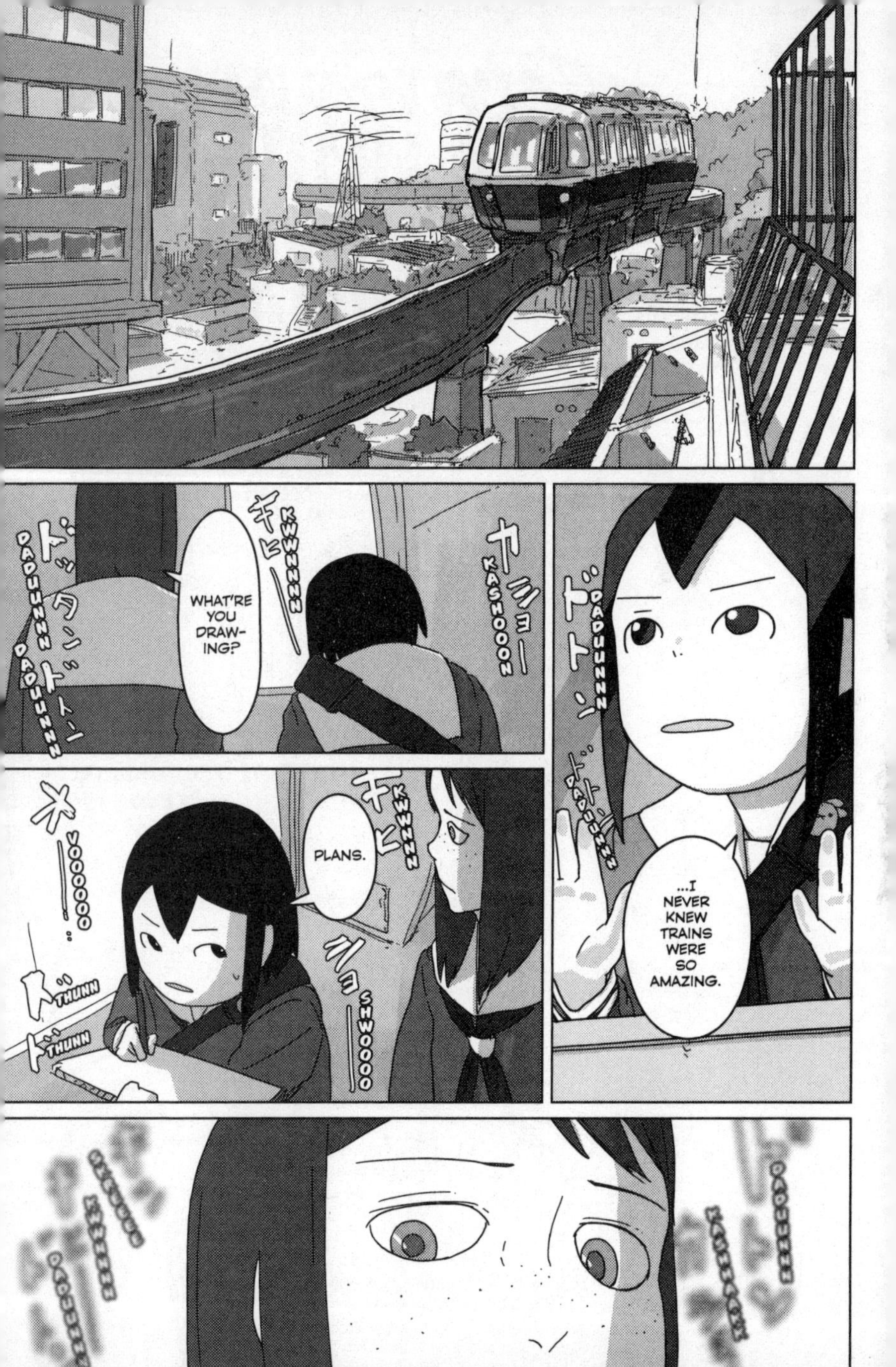
DADUNNN
...I NEVER KNEW TRAINS WERE SO AMAZING.
DADUNNN
KASHOOOON
KWWNNNN
WHAT'RE YOU DRAWING?
DADUNNN DADUNNN
KWWNNN
PLANS.
SHWOOOOO
VOOOOOO
THUNN
THUNN

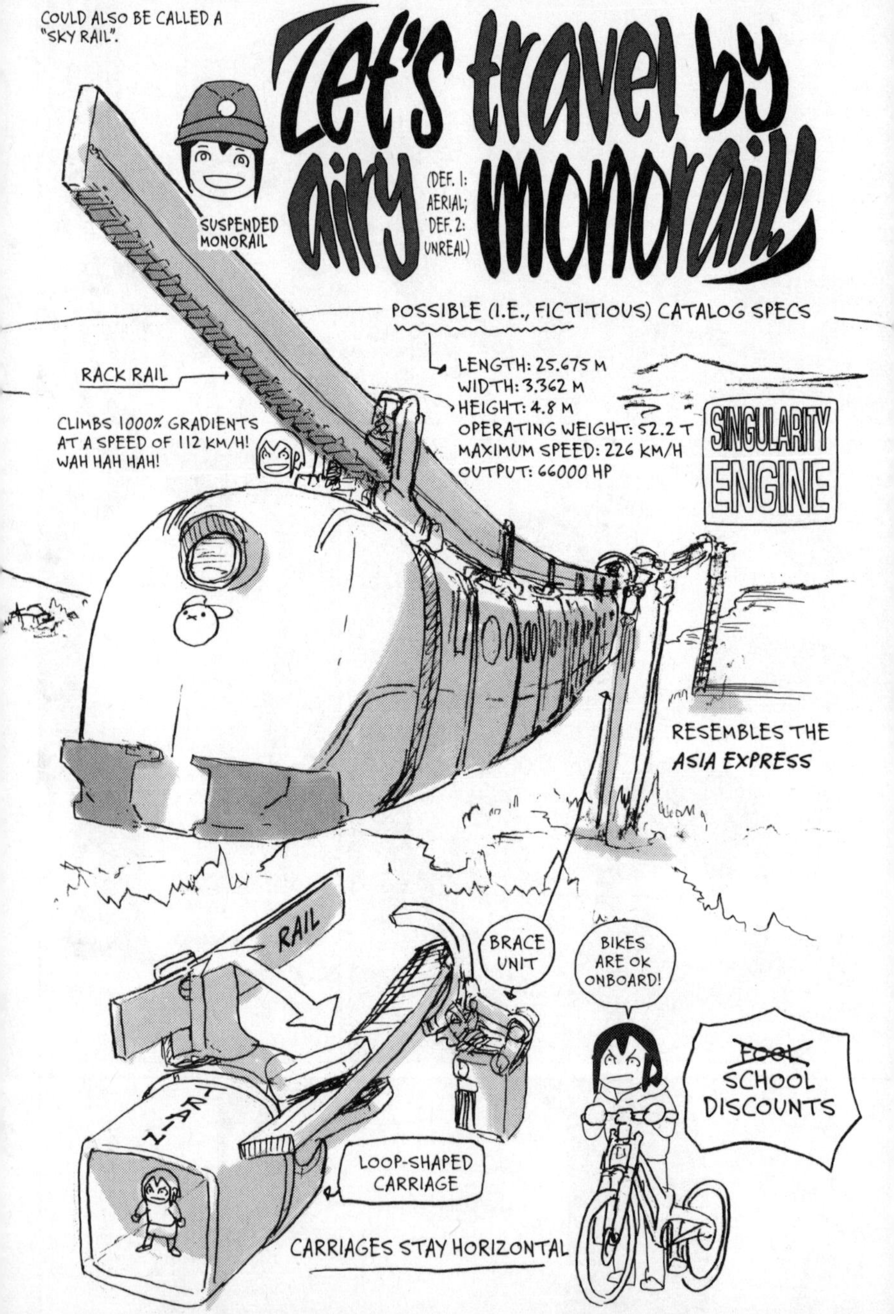

COULD ALSO BE CALLED A "SKY RAIL".
Let's travel by airy monorail!
(DEF. 1: AERIAL; DEF. 2: UNREAL)
SUSPENDED MONORAIL
POSSIBLE (I.E., FICTITIOUS) CATALOG SPECS
LENGTH: 25.675 M
WIDTH: 3.362 M
HEIGHT: 4.8 M
OPERATING WEIGHT: 52.2 T
MAXIMUM SPEED: 226 KM/H
OUTPUT: 66000 HP
SINGULARITY ENGINE
RACK RAIL
CLIMBS 1000% GRADIENTS AT A SPEED OF 112 KM/H! WAH HAH HAH!
RESEMBLES THE ASIA EXPRESS
RAIL
TRAIN
BRACE UNIT
BIKES ARE OK ONBOARD!
~~FOOL~~ SCHOOL DISCOUNTS
LOOP-SHAPED CARRIAGE
CARRIAGES STAY HORIZONTAL

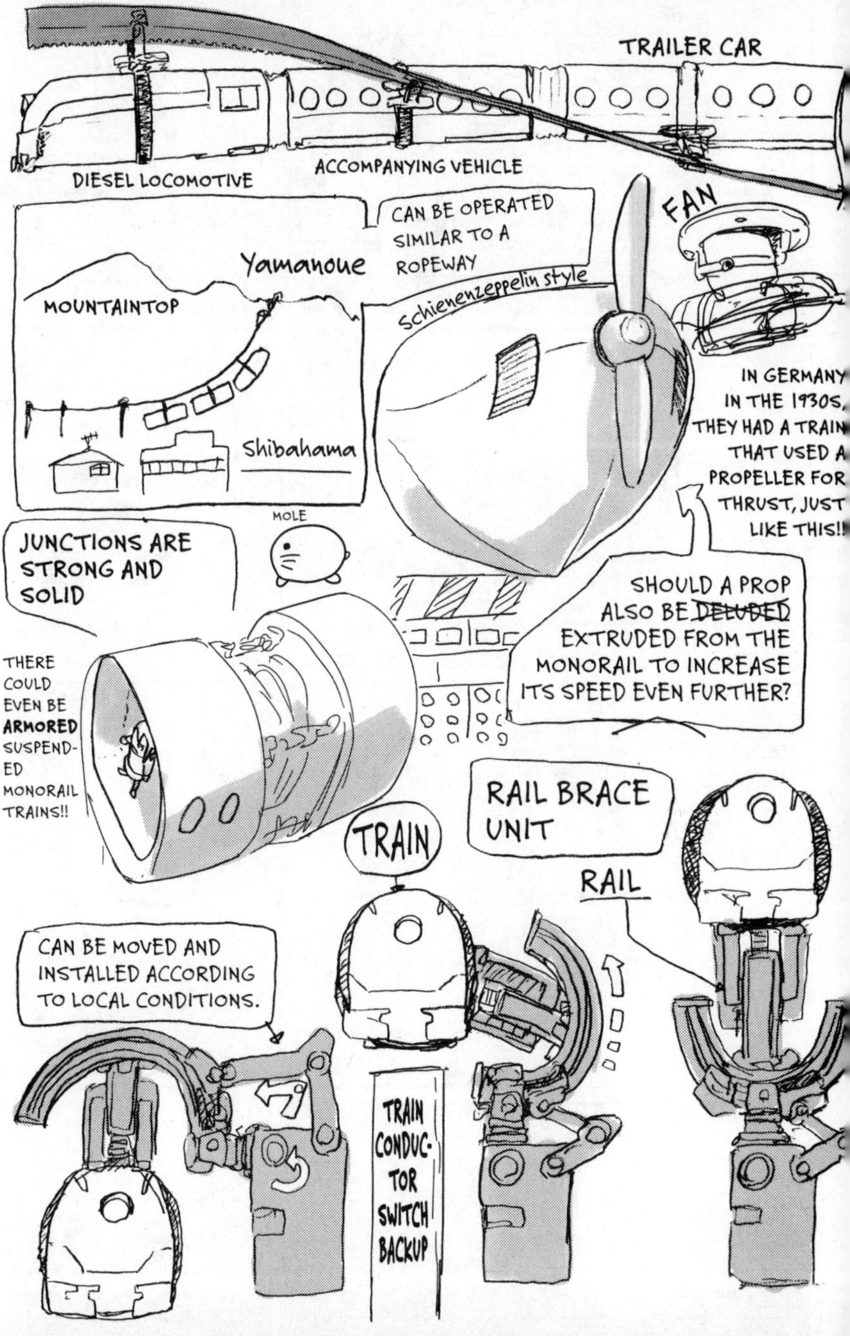
TRAILER CAR
ACCOMPANYING VEHICLE
DIESEL LOCOMOTIVE
FAN
CAN BE OPERATED SIMILAR TO A ROPEWAY
Yamanoue
MOUNTAINTOP
Shibahama
Schienenzeppelin style
IN GERMANY IN THE 1930S, THEY HAD A TRAIN THAT USED A PROPELLER FOR THRUST, JUST LIKE THIS!!
MOLE
JUNCTIONS ARE STRONG AND SOLID
SHOULD A PROP ALSO BE ~~DELUDED~~ EXTRUDED FROM THE MONORAIL TO INCREASE ITS SPEED EVEN FURTHER?
THERE COULD EVEN BE **ARMORED** SUSPEND-ED MONORAIL TRAINS!!
RAIL BRACE UNIT
TRAIN
RAIL
CAN BE MOVED AND INSTALLED ACCORDING TO LOCAL CONDITIONS.
TRAIN CONDUC-TOR SWITCH BACKUP

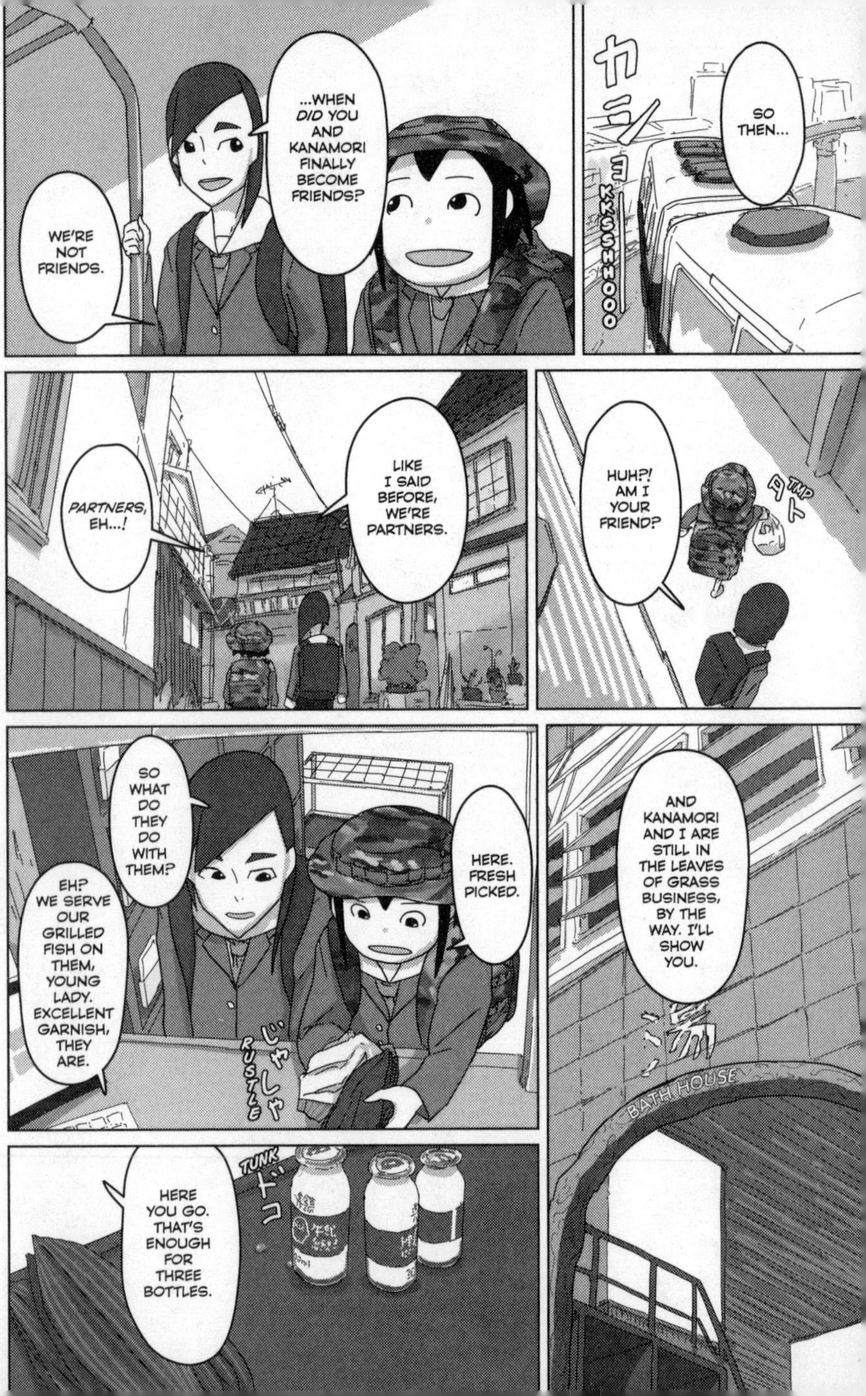
KKSSHOOO
SO THEN...
...WHEN DID YOU AND KANAMORI FINALLY BECOME FRIENDS?
WE'RE NOT FRIENDS.
HUH?! AM I YOUR FRIEND?
TMP
LIKE I SAID BEFORE, WE'RE PARTNERS.
PARTNERS, EH...!
AND KANAMORI AND I ARE STILL IN THE LEAVES OF GRASS BUSINESS, BY THE WAY. I'LL SHOW YOU.
BATH HOUSE
HERE. FRESH PICKED.
SO WHAT DO THEY DO WITH THEM?
EH? WE SERVE OUR GRILLED FISH ON THEM, YOUNG LADY. EXCELLENT GARNISH, THEY ARE.
RUSTLE
TUNK
HERE YOU GO. THAT'S ENOUGH FOR THREE BOTTLES.

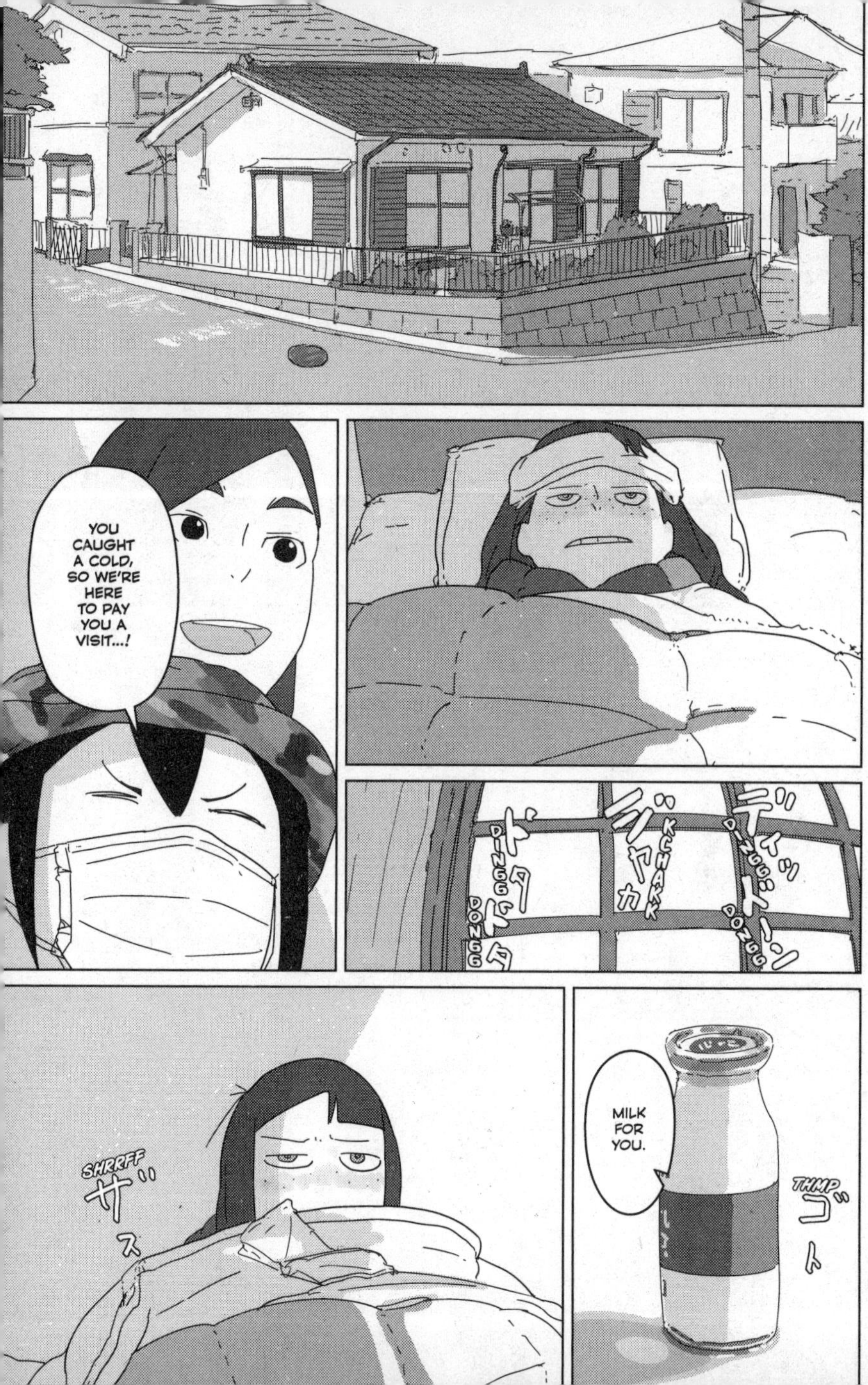
DINGG DONGG
KCHAKK
DINGG DONGG
YOU CAUGHT A COLD, SO WE'RE HERE TO PAY YOU A VISIT...!
MILK FOR YOU.
THMP
SHRRFF

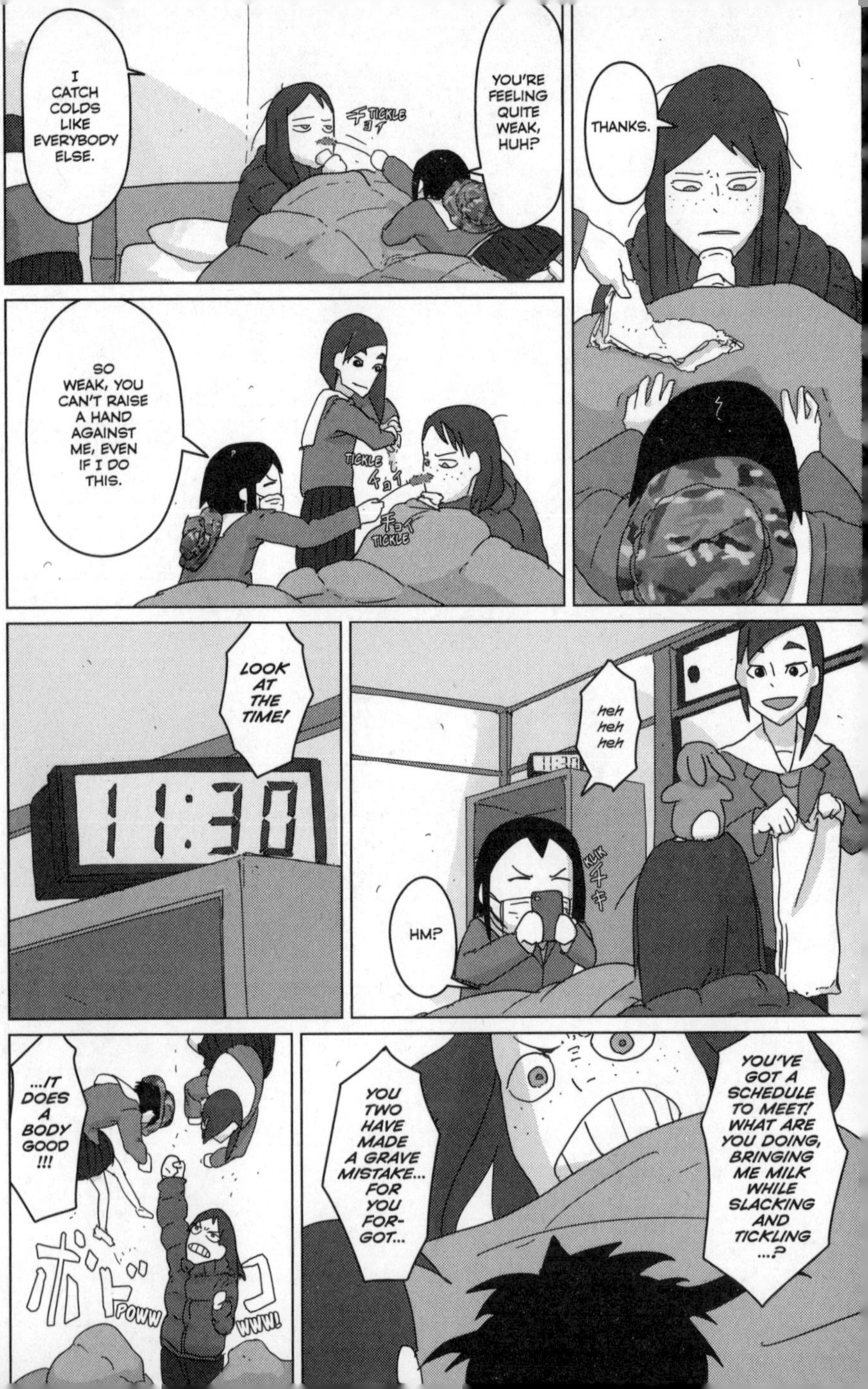
THANKS.
YOU'RE FEELING QUITE WEAK, HUH?
TICKLE
I CATCH COLDS LIKE EVERYBODY ELSE.
SO WEAK, YOU CAN'T RAISE A HAND AGAINST ME, EVEN IF I DO THIS.
TICKLE
TICKLE
heh heh heh
KUK
HM?
LOOK AT THE TIME!
11:30
YOU'VE GOT A SCHEDULE TO MEET! WHAT ARE YOU DOING, BRINGING ME MILK WHILE SLACKING AND TICKLING ...?
YOU TWO HAVE MADE A GRAVE MISTAKE... FOR YOU FOR-GOT...
...IT DOES A BODY GOOD !!!
POWW
WWW!

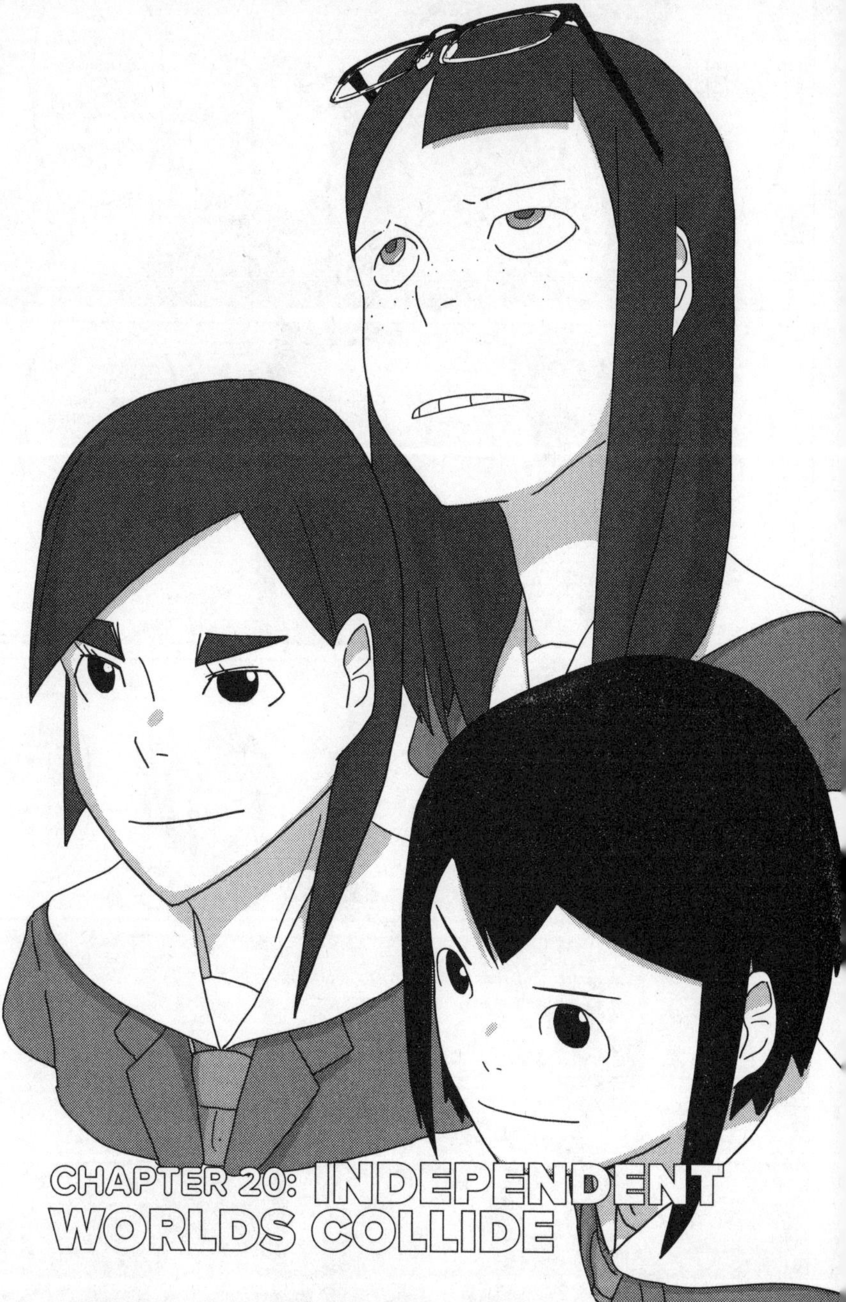

CHAPTER 20: INDEPENDENT WORLDS COLLIDE

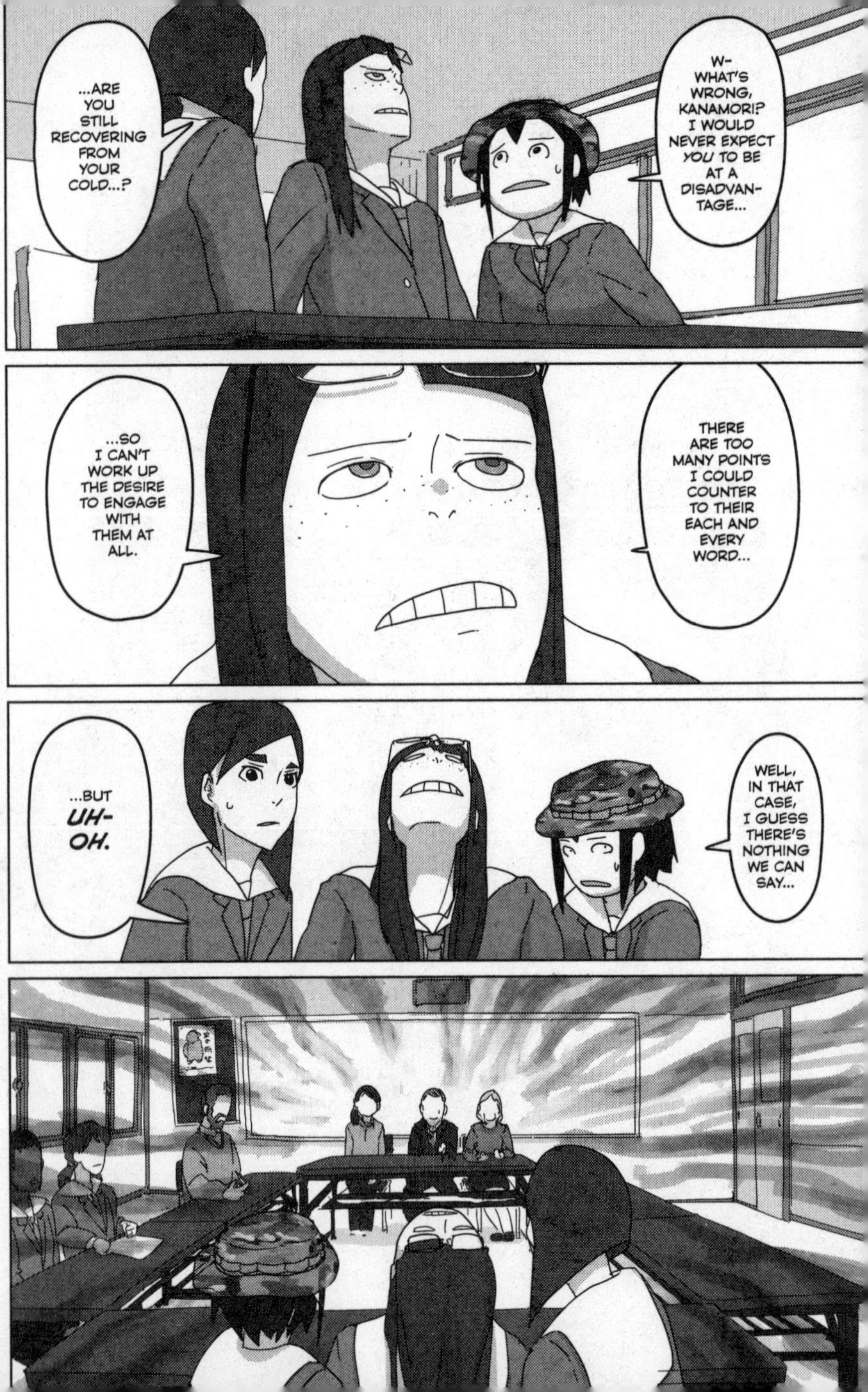
W- WHAT'S WRONG, KANAMORI!? I WOULD NEVER EXPECT *YOU* TO BE AT A DISADVANTAGE...
...ARE YOU STILL RECOVERING FROM YOUR COLD...?
THERE ARE TOO MANY POINTS I COULD COUNTER TO THEIR EACH AND EVERY WORD...
...SO I CAN'T WORK UP THE DESIRE TO ENGAGE WITH THEM AT ALL.
WELL, IN THAT CASE, I GUESS THERE'S NOTHING WE CAN SAY...
...BUT *UH-OH.*

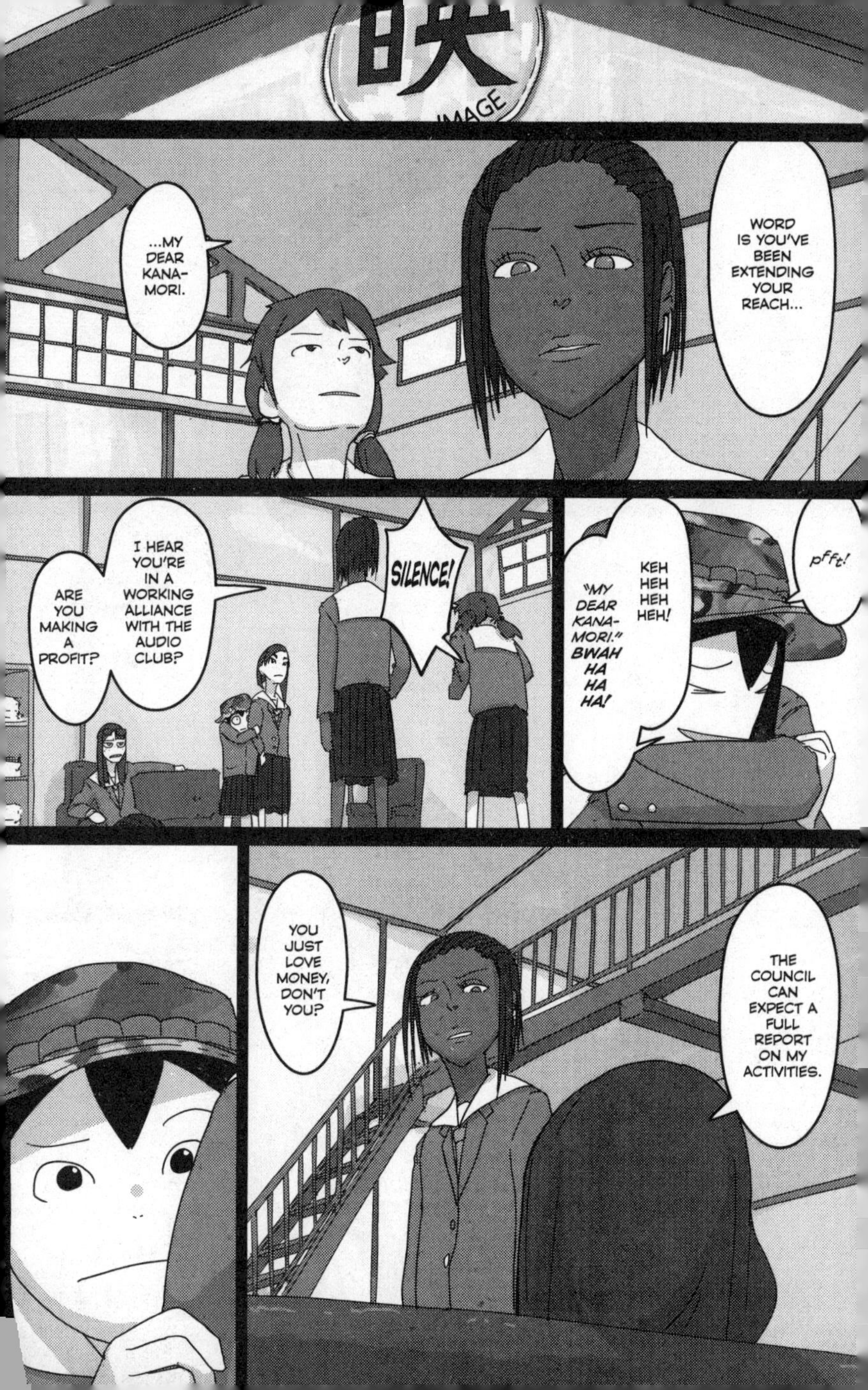
映
IMAGE
WORD IS YOU'VE BEEN EXTENDING YOUR REACH...
...MY DEAR KANA-MORI.
pfft!
KEH HEH HEH HEH!
"MY DEAR KANA-MORI." BWAH HA HA HA!
SILENCE!
I HEAR YOU'RE IN A WORKING ALLIANCE WITH THE AUDIO CLUB?
ARE YOU MAKING A PROFIT?
THE COUNCIL CAN EXPECT A FULL REPORT ON MY ACTIVITIES.
YOU JUST LOVE MONEY, DON'T YOU?

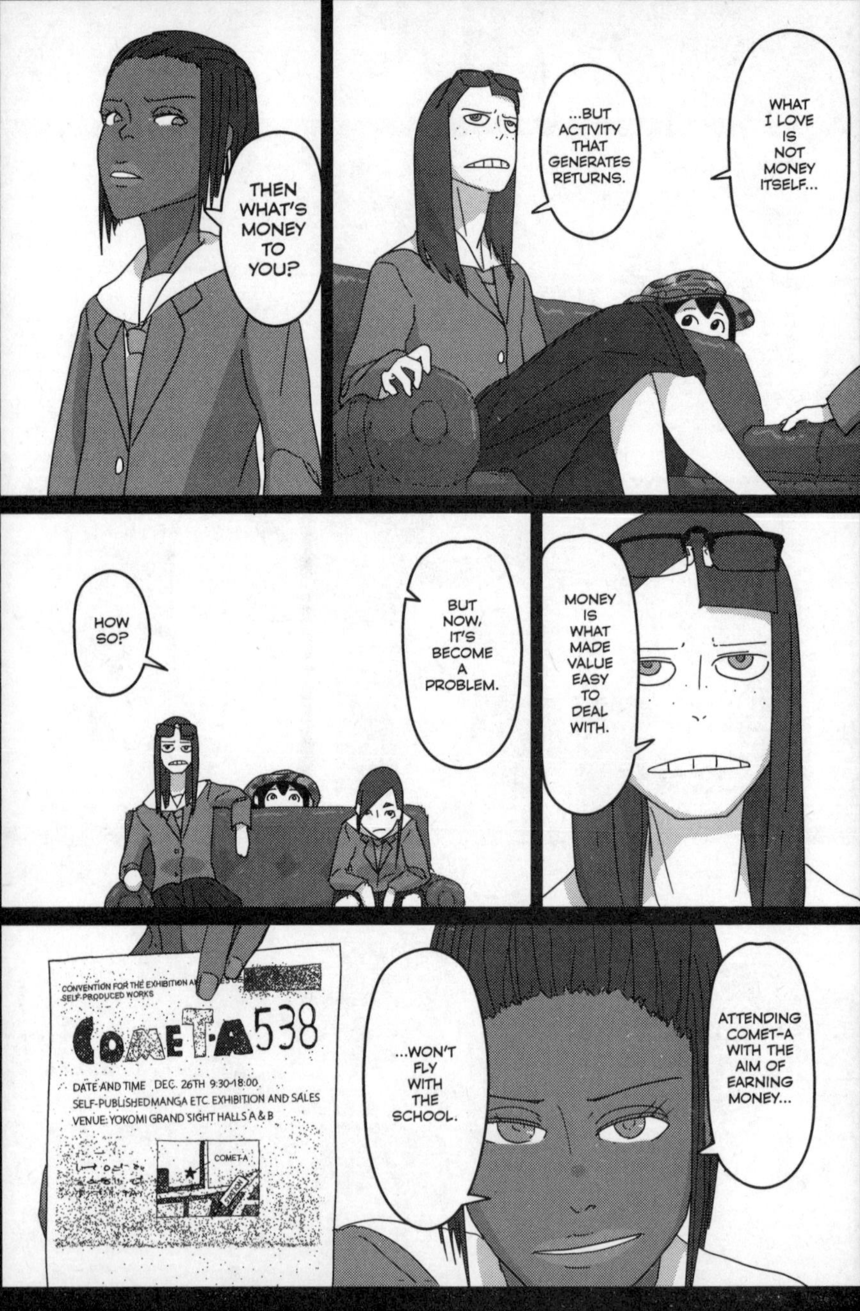
WHAT I LOVE IS NOT MONEY ITSELF...
...BUT ACTIVITY THAT GENERATES RETURNS.
THEN WHAT'S MONEY TO YOU?
MONEY IS WHAT MADE VALUE EASY TO DEAL WITH.
BUT NOW, IT'S BECOME A PROBLEM.
HOW SO?
ATTENDING COMET-A WITH THE AIM OF EARNING MONEY...
...WON'T FLY WITH THE SCHOOL.
CONVENTION FOR THE EXHIBITION A [redacted]
SELF-PRODUCED WORKS
COMET-A 538
DATE AND TIME DEC. 26TH 9:30-18:00
SELF-PUBLISHEDMANGA ETC. EXHIBITION AND SALES
VENUE: YOKOMI GRAND SIGHT HALLS A & B
COMET-A
STATION

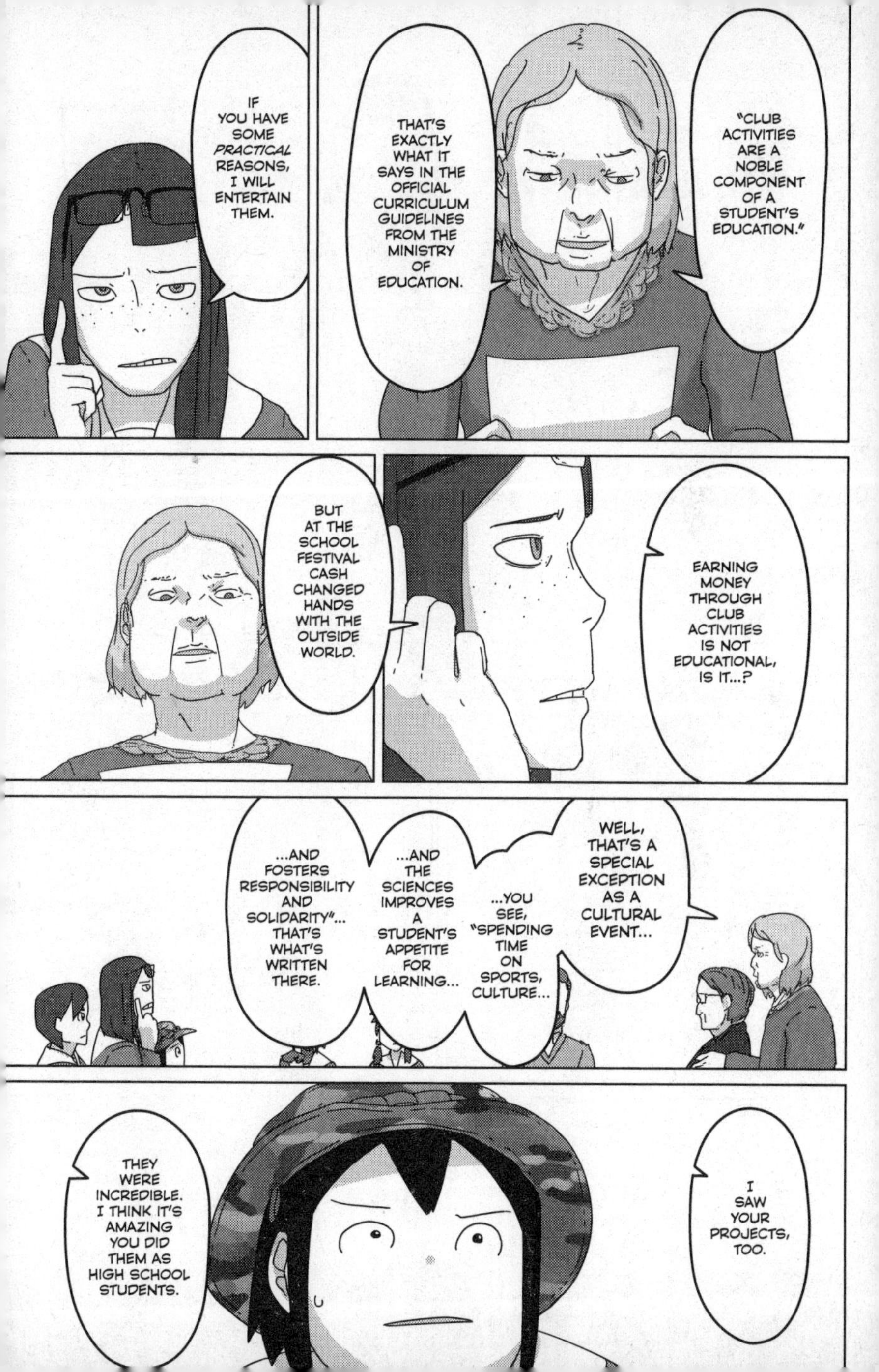
"CLUB ACTIVITIES ARE A NOBLE COMPONENT OF A STUDENT'S EDUCATION."
THAT'S EXACTLY WHAT IT SAYS IN THE OFFICIAL CURRICULUM GUIDELINES FROM THE MINISTRY OF EDUCATION.
IF YOU HAVE SOME *PRACTICAL* REASONS, I WILL ENTERTAIN THEM.
EARNING MONEY THROUGH CLUB ACTIVITIES IS NOT EDUCATIONAL, IS IT...?
BUT AT THE SCHOOL FESTIVAL CASH CHANGED HANDS WITH THE OUTSIDE WORLD.
WELL, THAT'S A SPECIAL EXCEPTION AS A CULTURAL EVENT...
...YOU SEE, "SPENDING TIME ON SPORTS, CULTURE...
...AND THE SCIENCES IMPROVES A STUDENT'S APPETITE FOR LEARNING...
...AND FOSTERS RESPONSIBILITY AND SOLIDARITY"... THAT'S WHAT'S WRITTEN THERE.
I SAW YOUR PROJECTS, TOO.
THEY WERE INCREDIBLE. I THINK IT'S AMAZING YOU DID THEM AS HIGH SCHOOL STUDENTS.

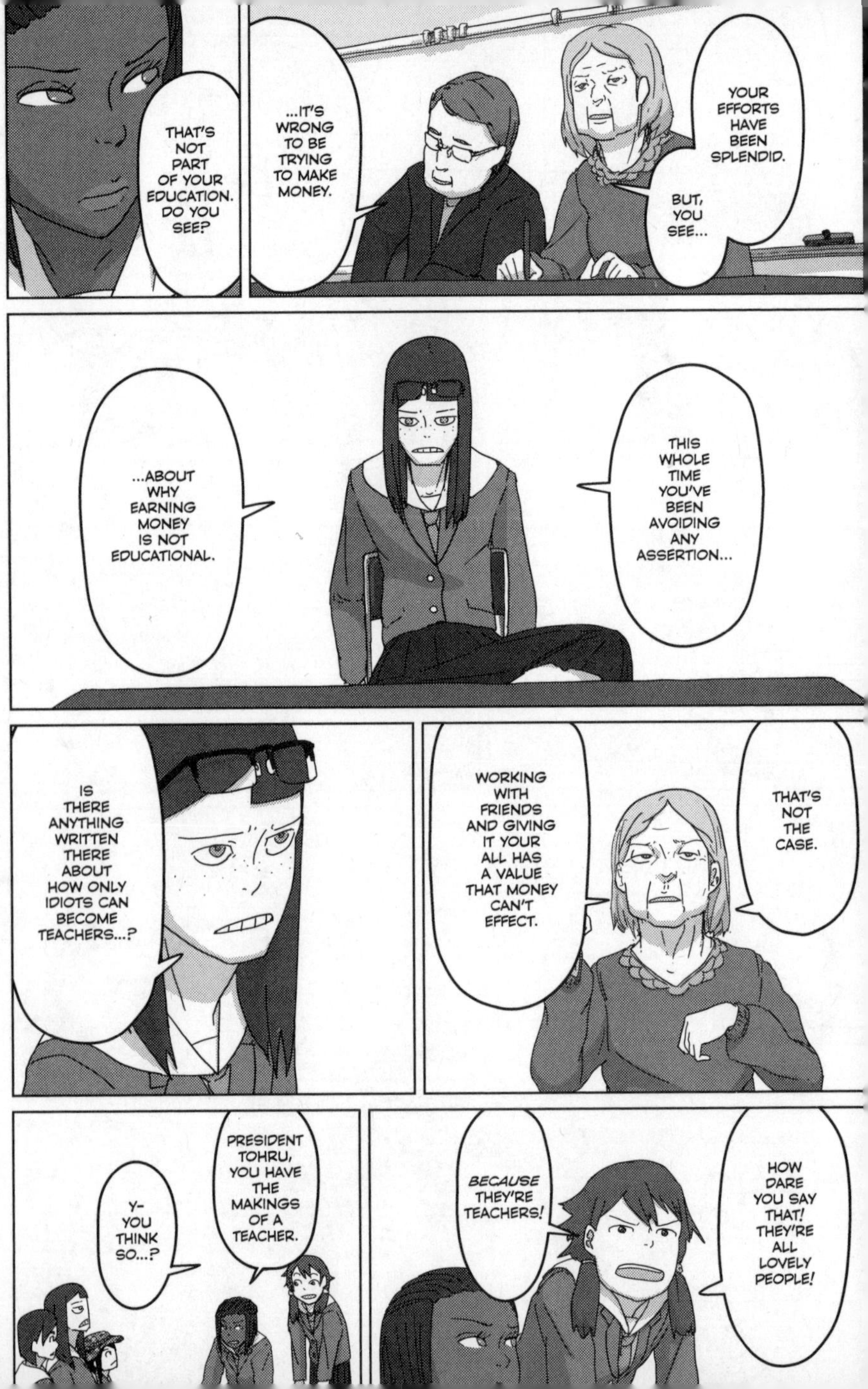
YOUR EFFORTS HAVE BEEN SPLENDID.
BUT, YOU SEE...
...IT'S WRONG TO BE TRYING TO MAKE MONEY.
THAT'S NOT PART OF YOUR EDUCATION. DO YOU SEE?
THIS WHOLE TIME YOU'VE BEEN AVOIDING ANY ASSERTION...
...ABOUT WHY EARNING MONEY IS NOT EDUCATIONAL.
THAT'S NOT THE CASE.
WORKING WITH FRIENDS AND GIVING IT YOUR ALL HAS A VALUE THAT MONEY CAN'T EFFECT.
IS THERE ANYTHING WRITTEN THERE ABOUT HOW ONLY IDIOTS CAN BECOME TEACHERS...?
HOW DARE YOU SAY THAT! THEY'RE ALL LOVELY PEOPLE!
BECAUSE THEY'RE TEACHERS!
PRESIDENT TOHRU, YOU HAVE THE MAKINGS OF A TEACHER.
Y-YOU THINK SO...?

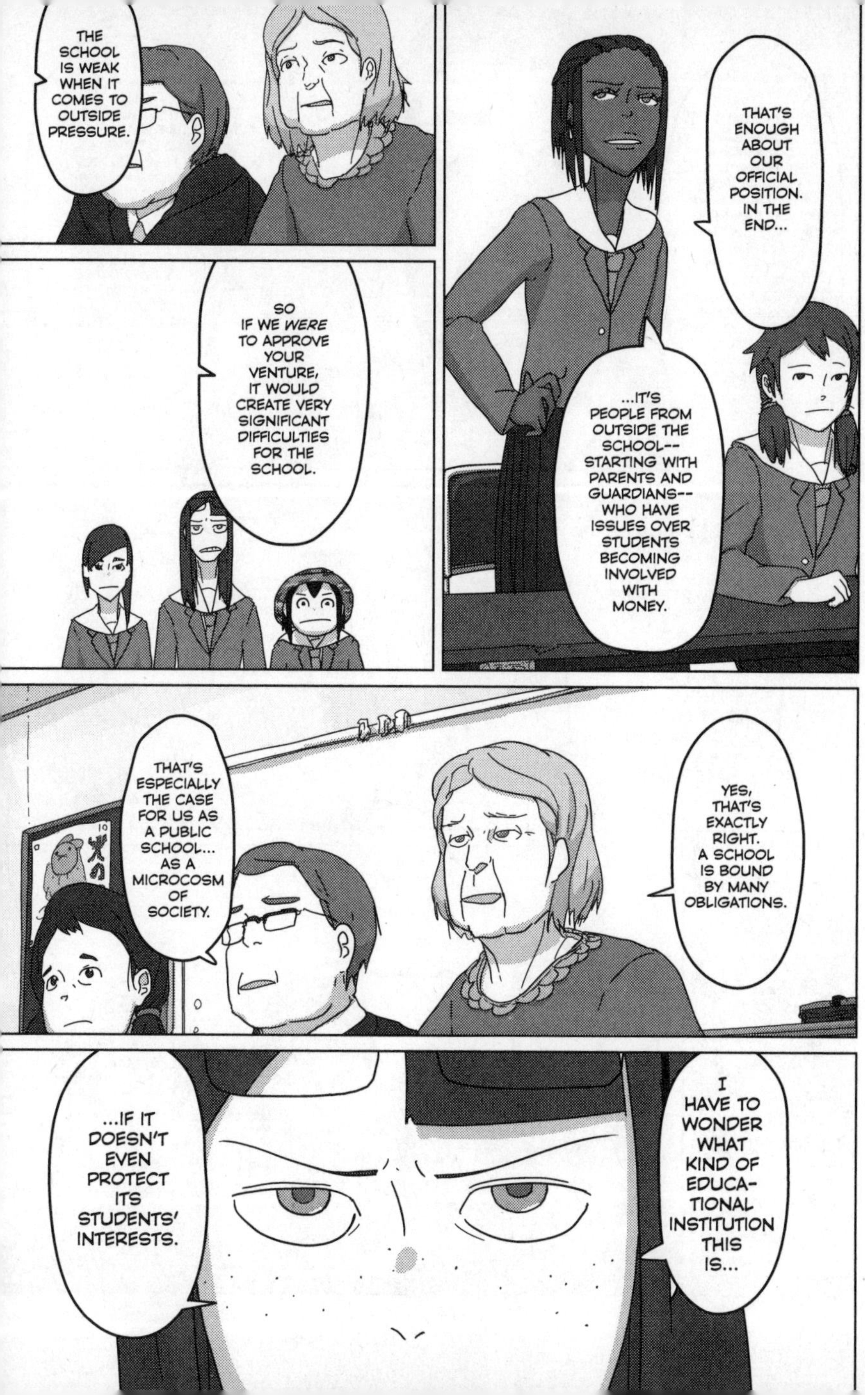
THAT'S ENOUGH ABOUT OUR OFFICIAL POSITION. IN THE END...
...IT'S PEOPLE FROM OUTSIDE THE SCHOOL-- STARTING WITH PARENTS AND GUARDIANS-- WHO HAVE ISSUES OVER STUDENTS BECOMING INVOLVED WITH MONEY.
THE SCHOOL IS WEAK WHEN IT COMES TO OUTSIDE PRESSURE.
SO IF WE *WERE* TO APPROVE YOUR VENTURE, IT WOULD CREATE VERY SIGNIFICANT DIFFICULTIES FOR THE SCHOOL.
THAT'S ESPECIALLY THE CASE FOR US AS A PUBLIC SCHOOL... AS A MICROCOSM OF SOCIETY.
YES, THAT'S EXACTLY RIGHT. A SCHOOL IS BOUND BY MANY OBLIGATIONS.
I HAVE TO WONDER WHAT KIND OF EDUCA- TIONAL INSTITUTION THIS IS...
...IF IT DOESN'T EVEN PROTECT ITS STUDENTS' INTERESTS.

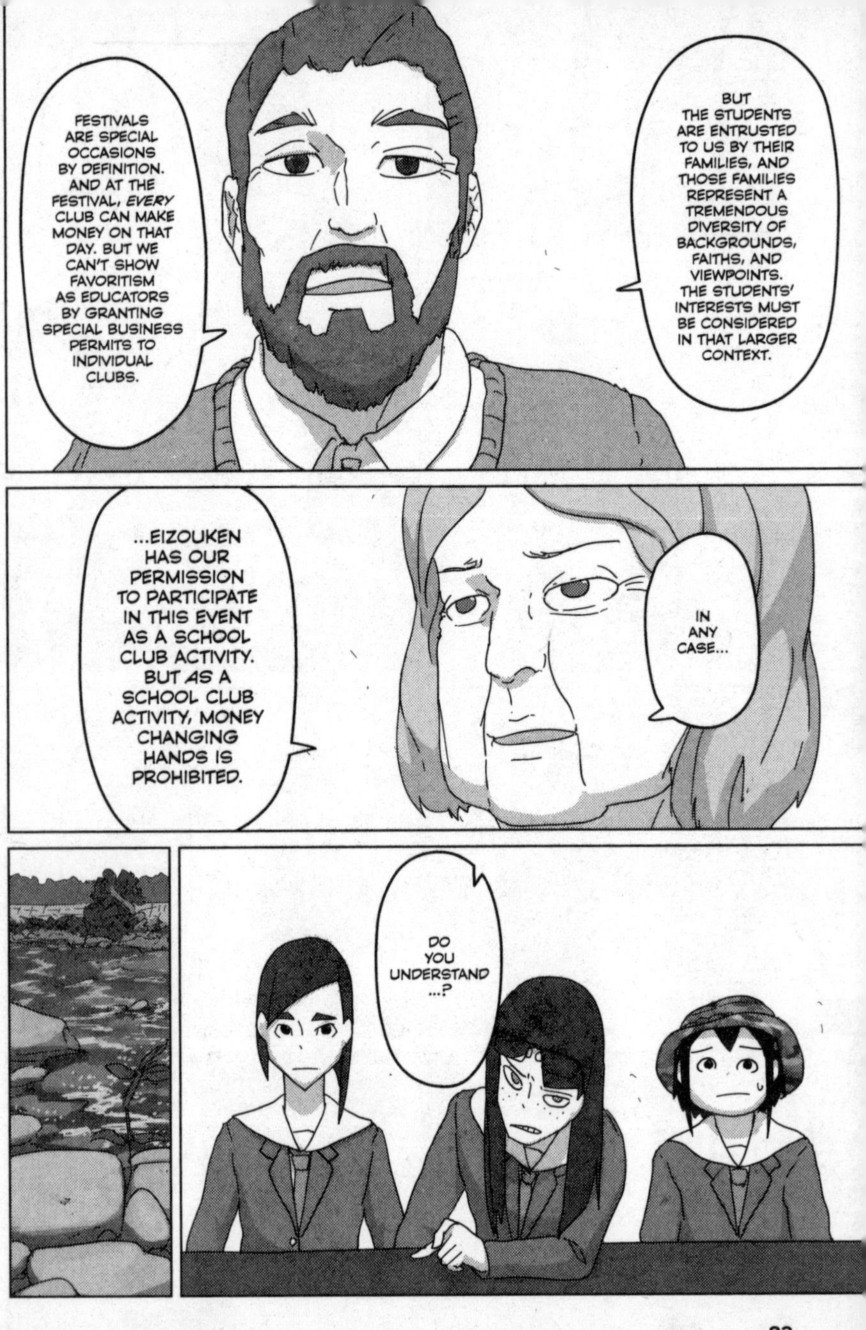
BUT THE STUDENTS ARE ENTRUSTED TO US BY THEIR FAMILIES, AND THOSE FAMILIES REPRESENT A TREMENDOUS DIVERSITY OF BACKGROUNDS, FAITHS, AND VIEWPOINTS. THE STUDENTS' INTERESTS MUST BE CONSIDERED IN THAT LARGER CONTEXT.
FESTIVALS ARE SPECIAL OCCASIONS BY DEFINITION. AND AT THE FESTIVAL, *EVERY* CLUB CAN MAKE MONEY ON THAT DAY. BUT WE CAN'T SHOW FAVORITISM AS EDUCATORS BY GRANTING SPECIAL BUSINESS PERMITS TO INDIVIDUAL CLUBS.
IN ANY CASE...
...EIZOUKEN HAS OUR PERMISSION TO PARTICIPATE IN THIS EVENT AS A SCHOOL CLUB ACTIVITY. BUT *AS* A SCHOOL CLUB ACTIVITY, MONEY CHANGING HANDS IS PROHIBITED.
DO YOU UNDERSTAND ...?

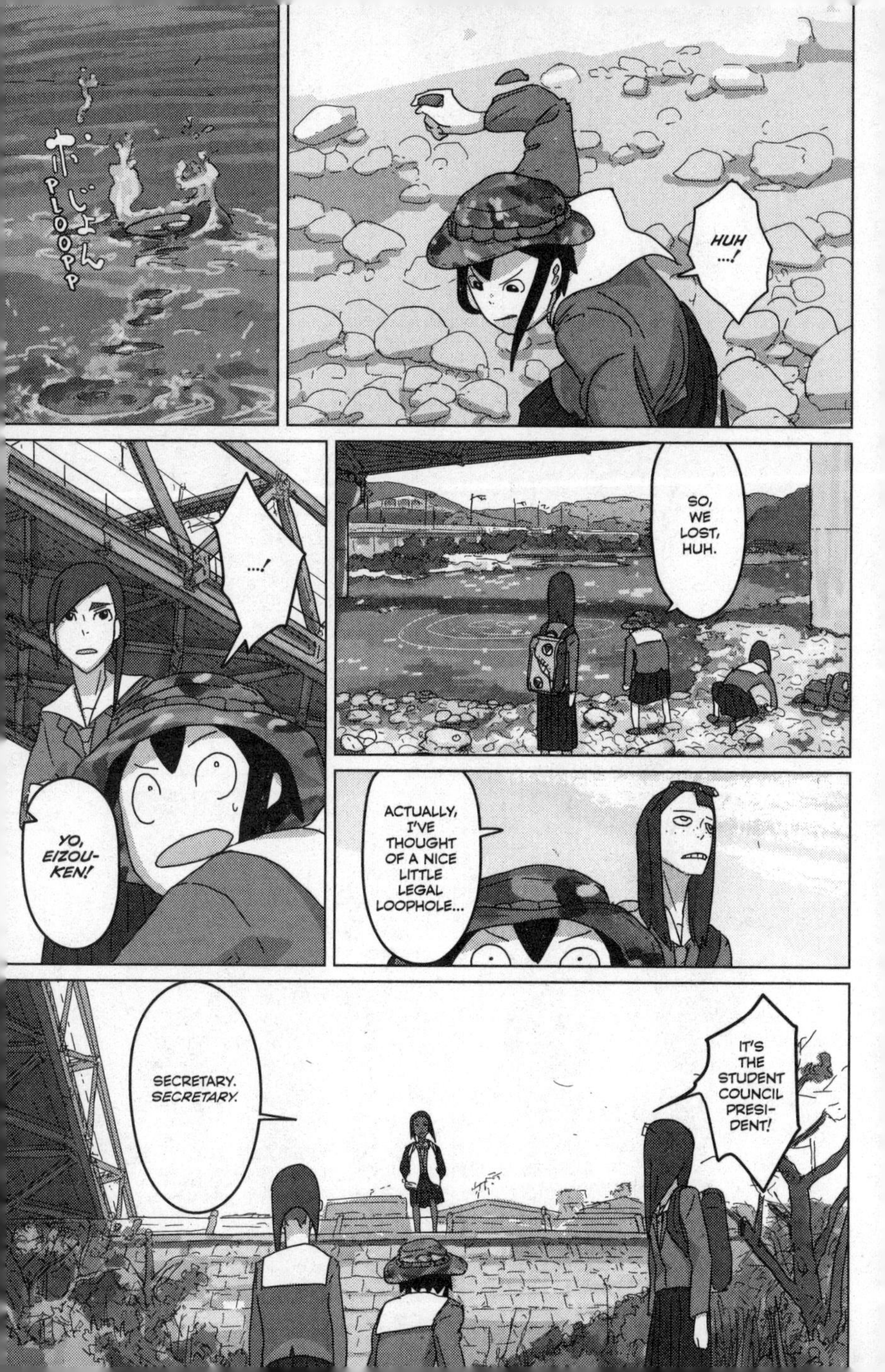
HUH ...!
PLOOPP
SO, WE LOST, HUH.
ACTUALLY, I'VE THOUGHT OF A NICE LITTLE LEGAL LOOPHOLE...
...!
YO, EIZOUKEN!
IT'S THE STUDENT COUNCIL PRESIDENT!
SECRETARY. SECRETARY.

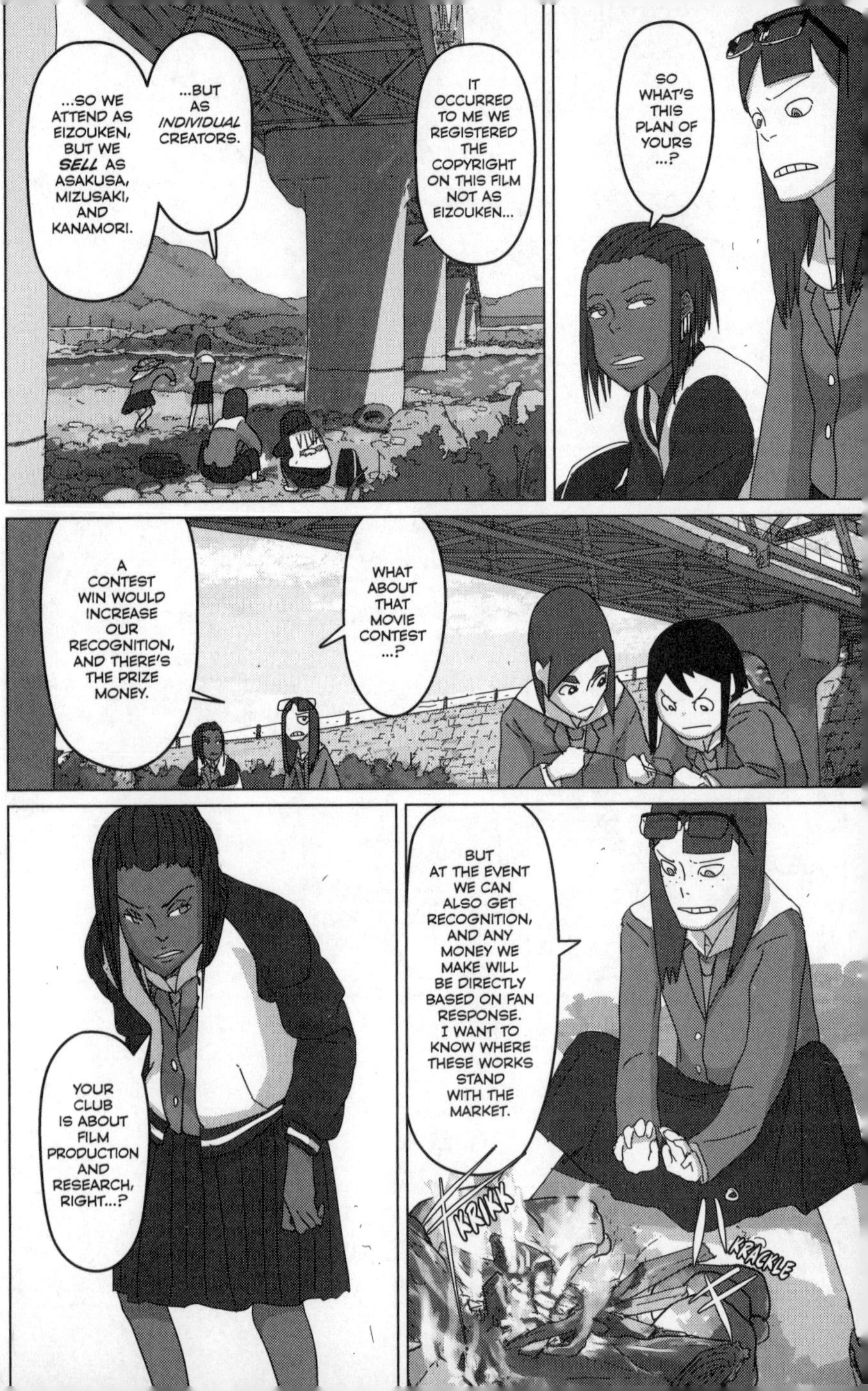

SO WHAT'S THIS PLAN OF YOURS ...?
IT OCCURRED TO ME WE REGISTERED THE COPYRIGHT ON THIS FILM NOT AS EIZOUKEN...
...BUT AS *INDIVIDUAL* CREATORS.
...SO WE ATTEND AS EIZOUKEN, BUT WE ***SELL*** AS ASAKUSA, MIZUSAKI, AND KANAMORI.
WHAT ABOUT THAT MOVIE CONTEST ...?
A CONTEST WIN WOULD INCREASE OUR RECOGNITION, AND THERE'S THE PRIZE MONEY.
BUT AT THE EVENT WE CAN ALSO GET RECOGNITION, AND ANY MONEY WE MAKE WILL BE DIRECTLY BASED ON FAN RESPONSE. I WANT TO KNOW WHERE THESE WORKS STAND WITH THE MARKET.
KRIKK
KRACKLE
YOUR CLUB IS ABOUT FILM PRODUCTION AND RESEARCH, RIGHT...?

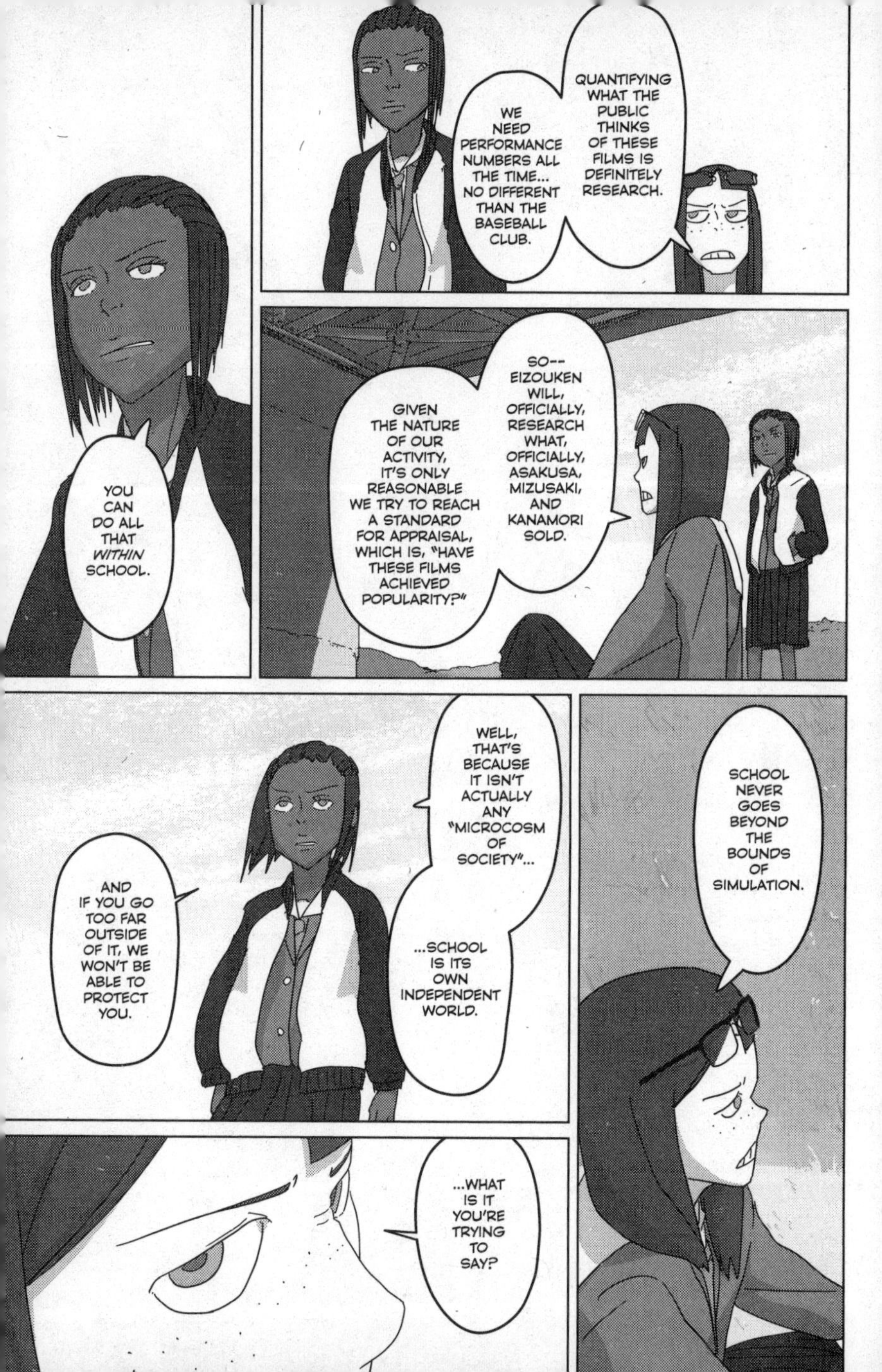
QUANTIFYING WHAT THE PUBLIC THINKS OF THESE FILMS IS DEFINITELY RESEARCH.
WE NEED PERFORMANCE NUMBERS ALL THE TIME... NO DIFFERENT THAN THE BASEBALL CLUB.
SO-- EIZOUKEN WILL, OFFICIALLY, RESEARCH WHAT, OFFICIALLY, ASAKUSA, MIZUSAKI, AND KANAMORI SOLD.
GIVEN THE NATURE OF OUR ACTIVITY, IT'S ONLY REASONABLE WE TRY TO REACH A STANDARD FOR APPRAISAL, WHICH IS, "HAVE THESE FILMS ACHIEVED POPULARITY?"
YOU CAN DO ALL THAT *WITHIN* SCHOOL.
SCHOOL NEVER GOES BEYOND THE BOUNDS OF SIMULATION.
WELL, THAT'S BECAUSE IT ISN'T ACTUALLY ANY "MICROCOSM OF SOCIETY"...
...SCHOOL IS ITS OWN INDEPENDENT WORLD.
AND IF YOU GO TOO FAR OUTSIDE OF IT, WE WON'T BE ABLE TO PROTECT YOU.
...WHAT IS IT YOU'RE TRYING TO SAY?

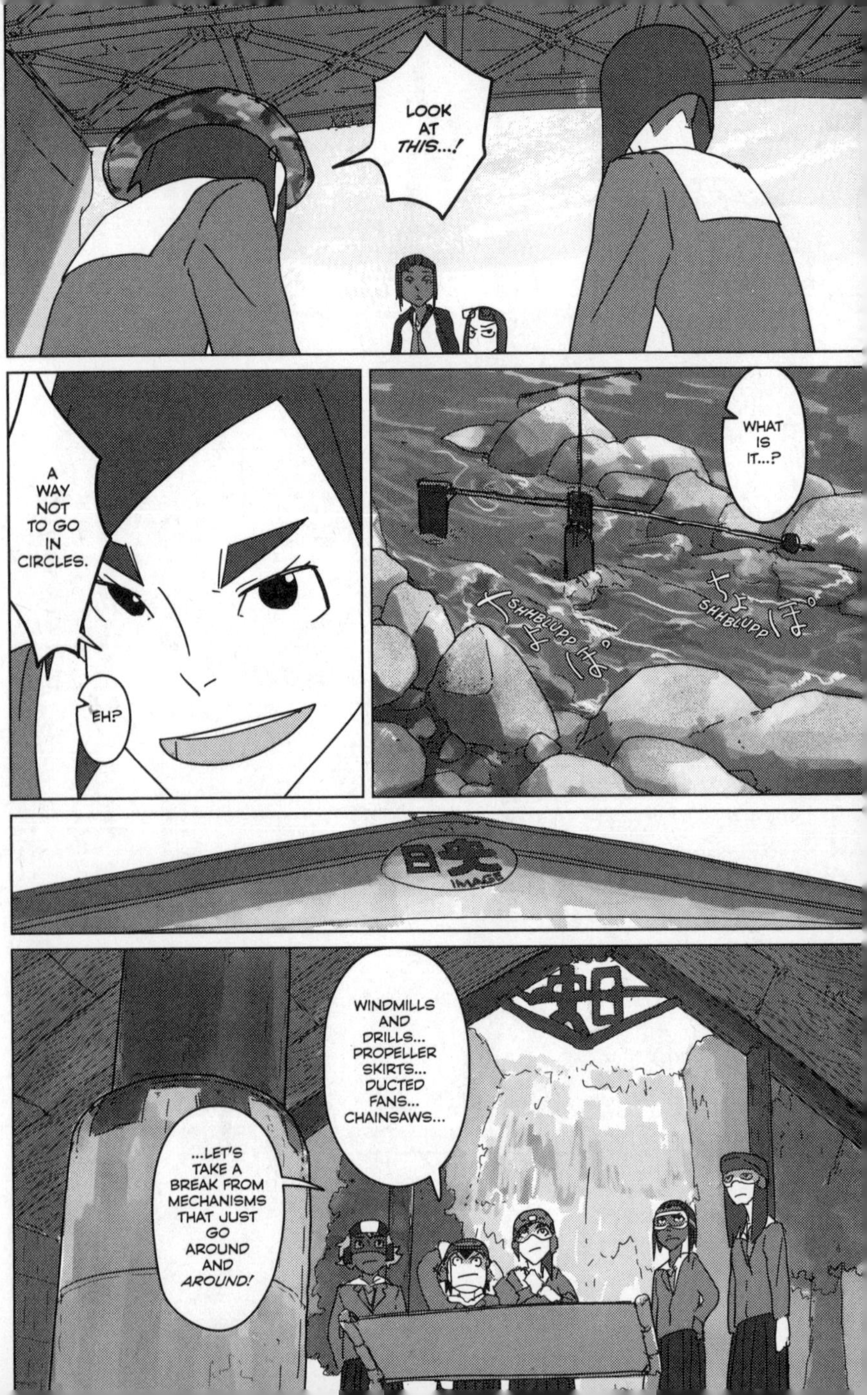
LOOK AT *THIS*...!
WHAT IS IT...?
ちょぽ
SHHBLUPP
ちょぽ
SHHBLUPP
A WAY NOT TO GO IN CIRCLES.
EH?
IMAGE
WINDMILLS AND DRILLS... PROPELLER SKIRTS... DUCTED FANS... CHAINSAWS...
...LET'S TAKE A BREAK FROM MECHANISMS THAT JUST GO AROUND AND *AROUND!*

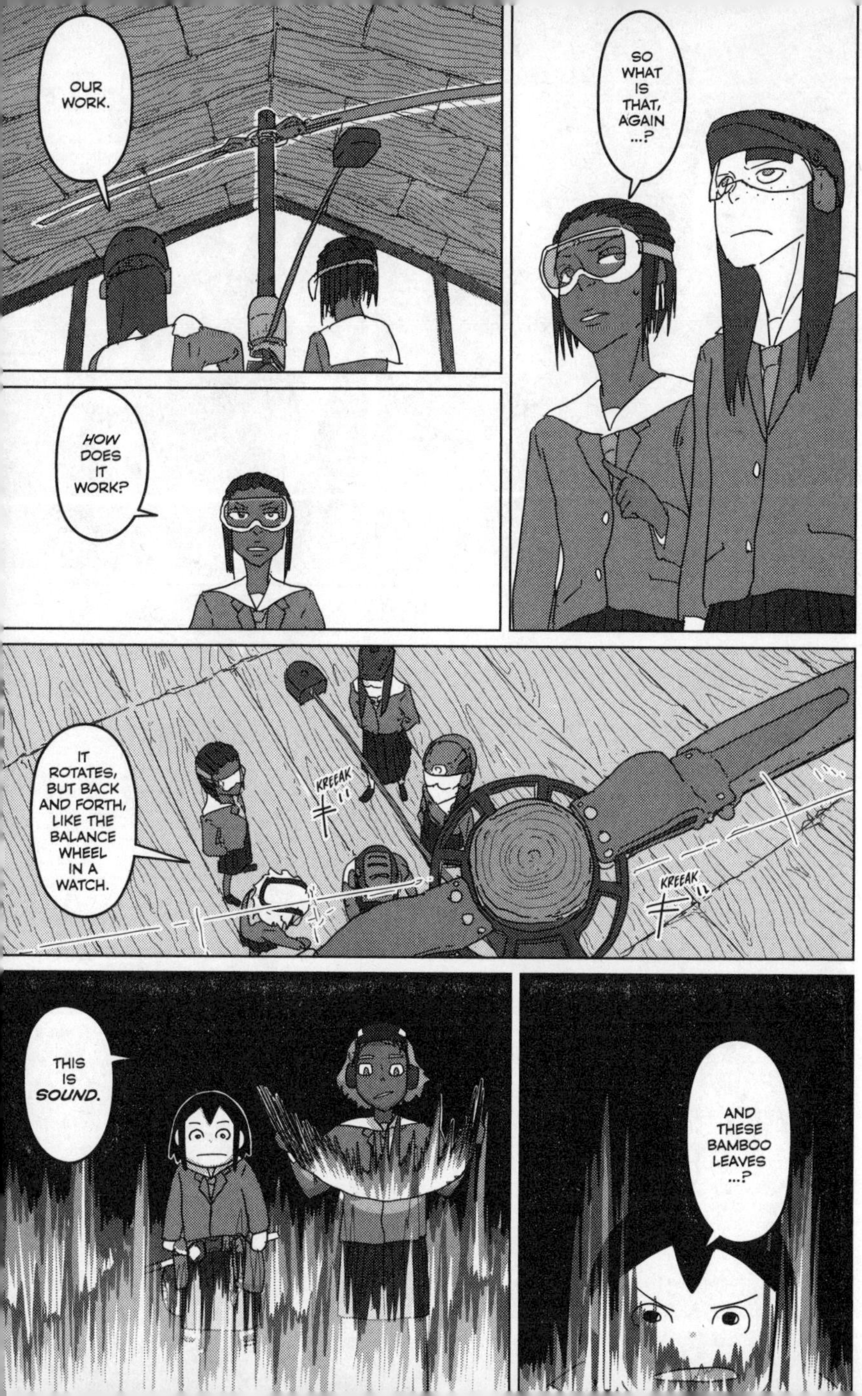
SO WHAT IS THAT, AGAIN ...?
OUR WORK.
HOW DOES IT WORK?
IT ROTATES, BUT BACK AND FORTH, LIKE THE BALANCE WHEEL IN A WATCH.
KREEAK
KREEAK
AND THESE BAMBOO LEAVES ...?
THIS IS SOUND.

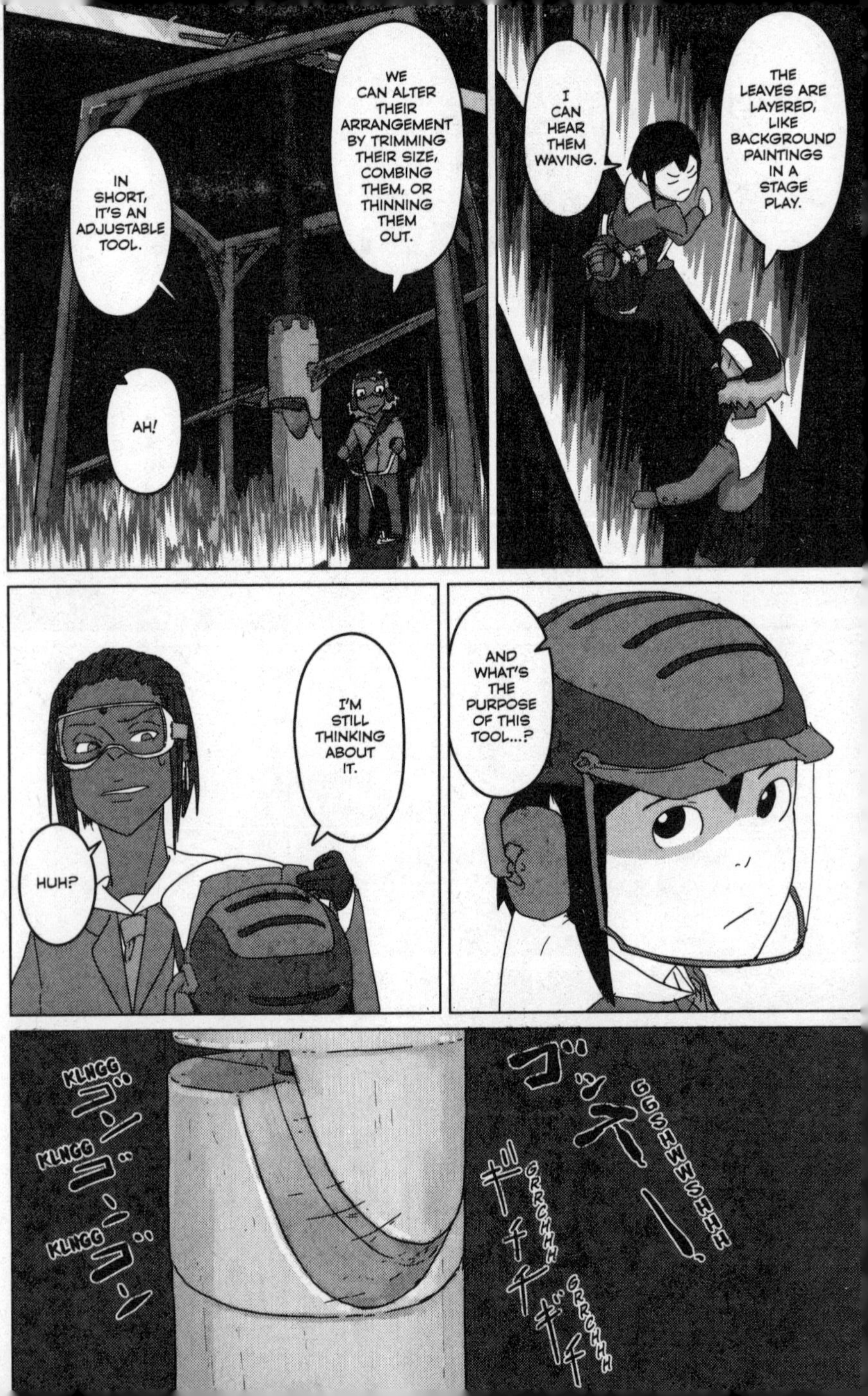
THE LEAVES ARE LAYERED, LIKE BACKGROUND PAINTINGS IN A STAGE PLAY.
I CAN HEAR THEM WAVING.
WE CAN ALTER THEIR ARRANGEMENT BY TRIMMING THEIR SIZE, COMBING THEM, OR THINNING THEM OUT.
IN SHORT, IT'S AN ADJUSTABLE TOOL.
AH!
AND WHAT'S THE PURPOSE OF THIS TOOL...?
I'M STILL THINKING ABOUT IT.
HUH?
GGSHWWSHHH
GRRCHHH
GRRCHHH
KLNGG
KLNGG
KLNGG

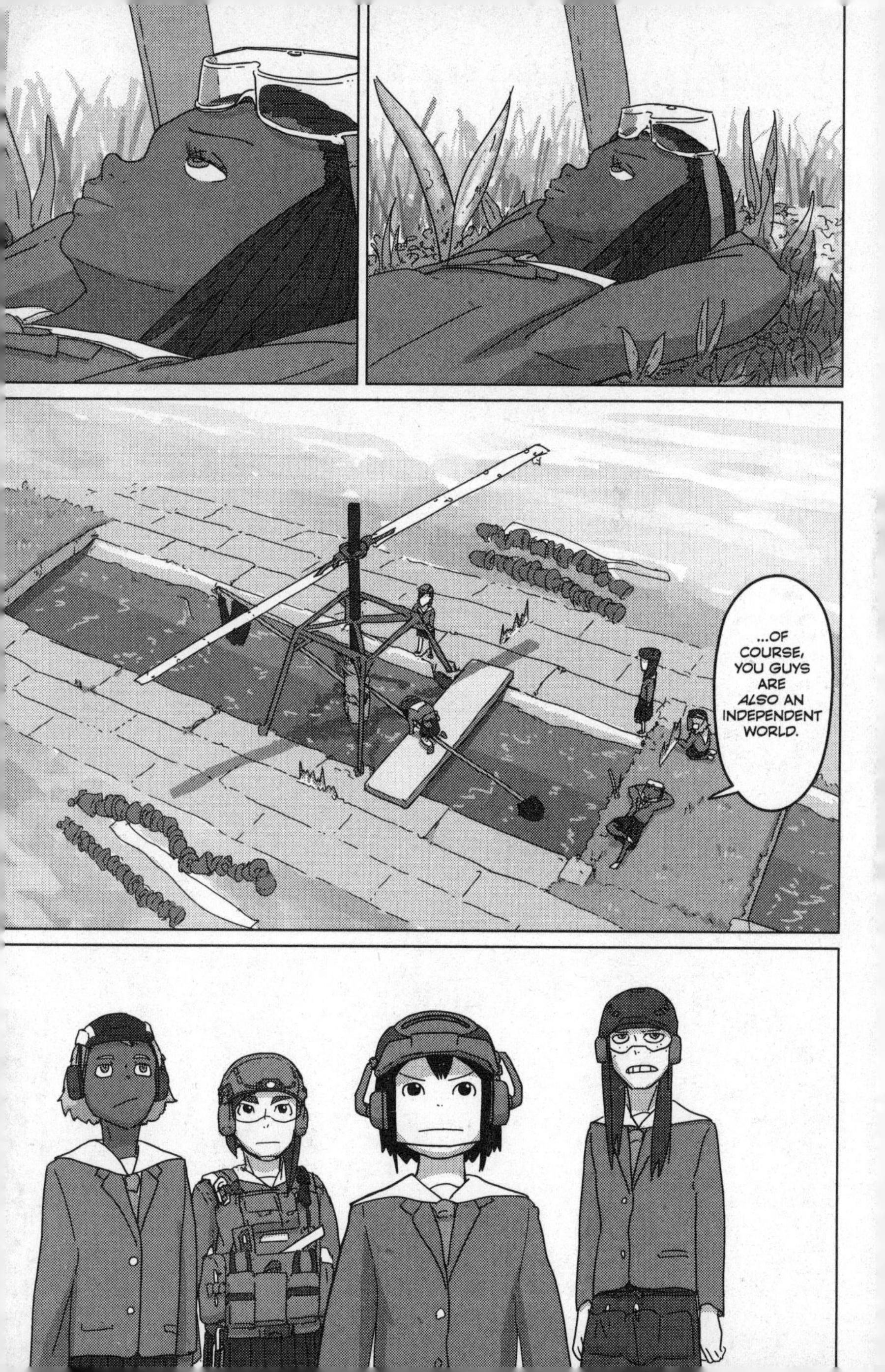
...OF COURSE, YOU GUYS ARE *ALSO* AN INDEPENDENT WORLD.

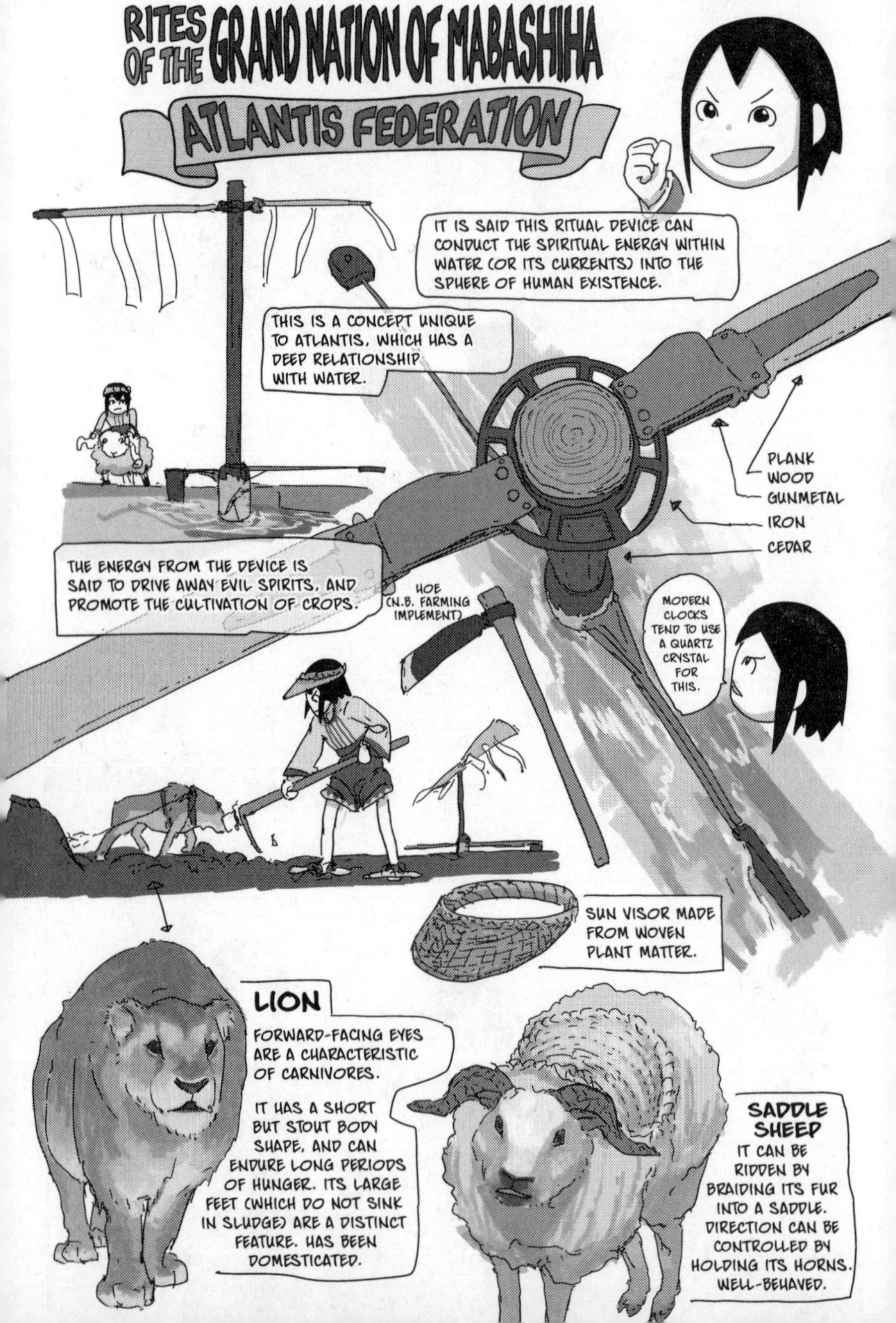
RITES OF THE GRAND NATION OF MABASHIHA
ATLANTIS FEDERATION
IT IS SAID THIS RITUAL DEVICE CAN CONDUCT THE SPIRITUAL ENERGY WITHIN WATER (OR ITS CURRENTS) INTO THE SPHERE OF HUMAN EXISTENCE.
THIS IS A CONCEPT UNIQUE TO ATLANTIS, WHICH HAS A DEEP RELATIONSHIP WITH WATER.
PLANK
WOOD
GUNMETAL
IRON
CEDAR
THE ENERGY FROM THE DEVICE IS SAID TO DRIVE AWAY EVIL SPIRITS, AND PROMOTE THE CULTIVATION OF CROPS.
HOE (N.B. FARMING IMPLEMENT)
MODERN CLOCKS TEND TO USE A QUARTZ CRYSTAL FOR THIS.
SUN VISOR MADE FROM WOVEN PLANT MATTER.
LION
FORWARD-FACING EYES ARE A CHARACTERISTIC OF CARNIVORES.
IT HAS A SHORT BUT STOUT BODY SHAPE, AND CAN ENDURE LONG PERIODS OF HUNGER. ITS LARGE FEET (WHICH DO NOT SINK IN SLUDGE) ARE A DISTINCT FEATURE. HAS BEEN DOMESTICATED.
SADDLE SHEEP
IT CAN BE RIDDEN BY BRAIDING ITS FUR INTO A SADDLE. DIRECTION CAN BE CONTROLLED BY HOLDING ITS HORNS. WELL-BEHAVED.

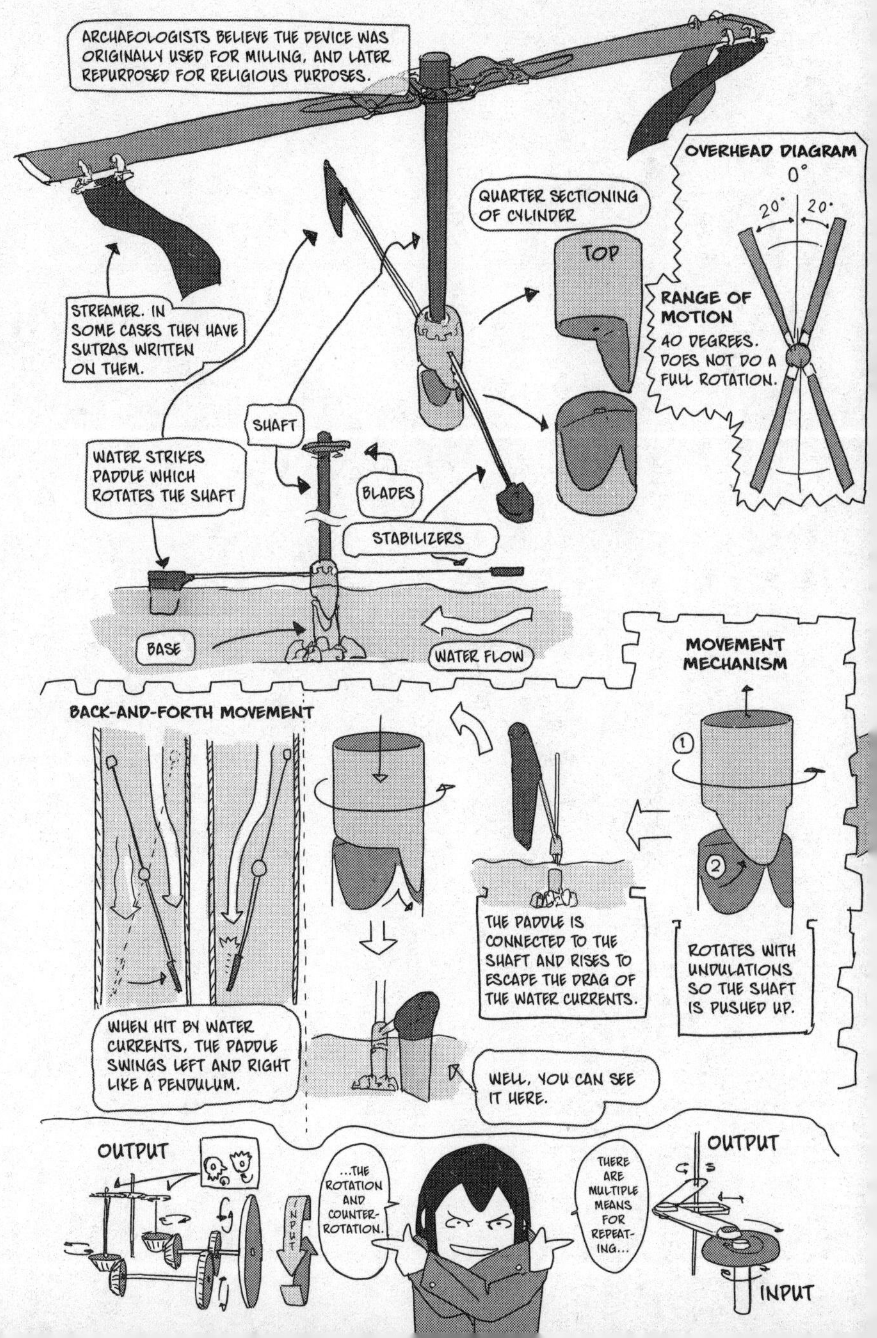

OVERHEAD DIAGRAM
0°
20°
20°
RANGE OF MOTION
40 DEGREES. DOES NOT DO A FULL ROTATION.
QUARTER SECTIONING OF CYLINDER
TOP
ARCHAEOLOGISTS BELIEVE THE DEVICE WAS ORIGINALLY USED FOR MILLING, AND LATER REPURPOSED FOR RELIGIOUS PURPOSES.
STREAMER. IN SOME CASES THEY HAVE SUTRAS WRITTEN ON THEM.
SHAFT
BLADES
WATER STRIKES PADDLE WHICH ROTATES THE SHAFT
STABILIZERS
WATER FLOW
BASE
MOVEMENT MECHANISM
1
2
ROTATES WITH UNDULATIONS SO THE SHAFT IS PUSHED UP.
THE PADDLE IS CONNECTED TO THE SHAFT AND RISES TO ESCAPE THE DRAG OF THE WATER CURRENTS.
WELL, YOU CAN SEE IT HERE.
BACK-AND-FORTH MOVEMENT
WHEN HIT BY WATER CURRENTS, THE PADDLE SWINGS LEFT AND RIGHT LIKE A PENDULUM.
OUTPUT
INPUT
THERE ARE MULTIPLE MEANS FOR REPEATING...
...THE ROTATION AND COUNTER-ROTATION.
INPUT
OUTPUT

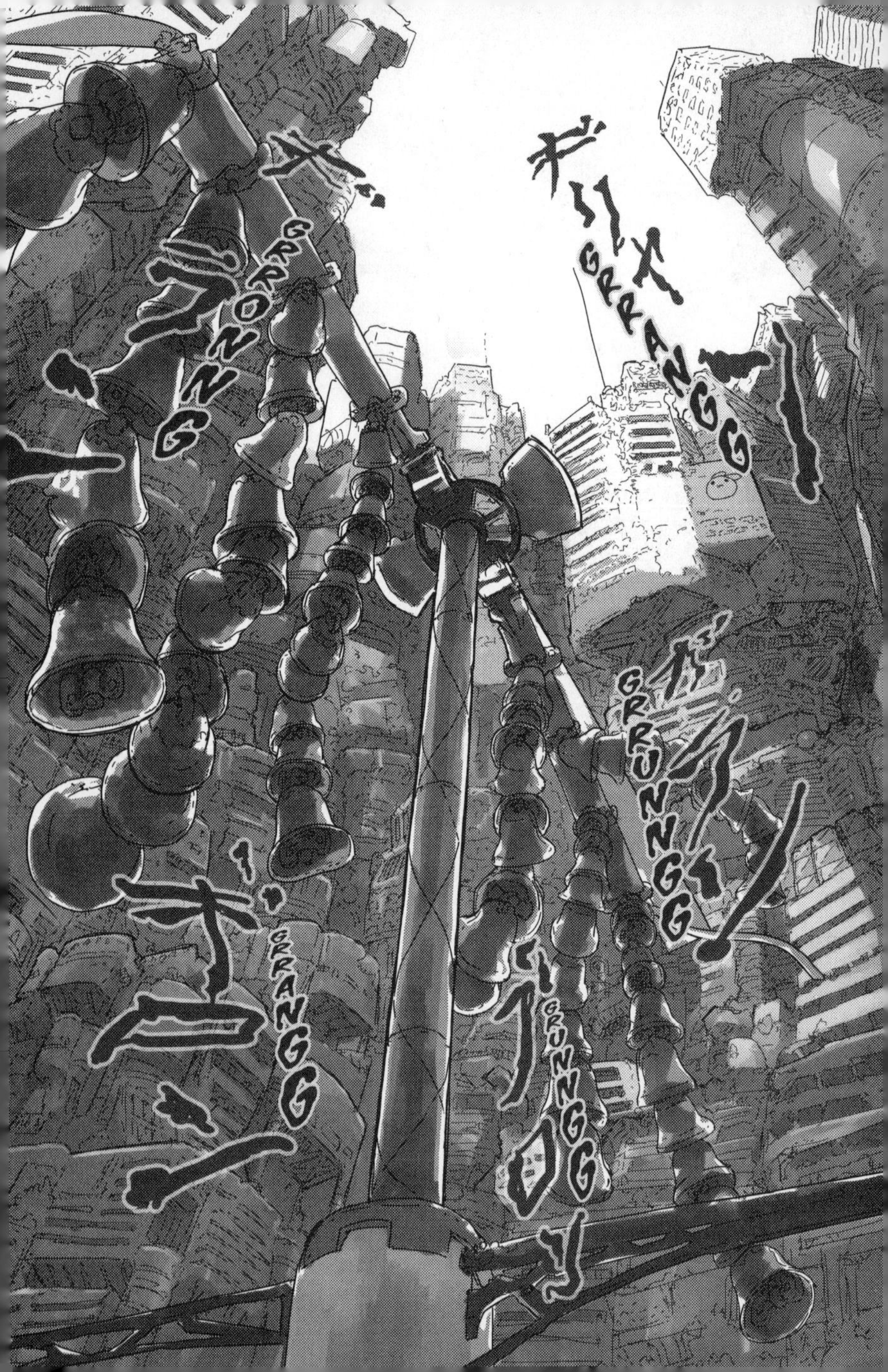
GRRANGG
GRRONNNG
GRRUNNGG
GRUNNGG
GRRANGG

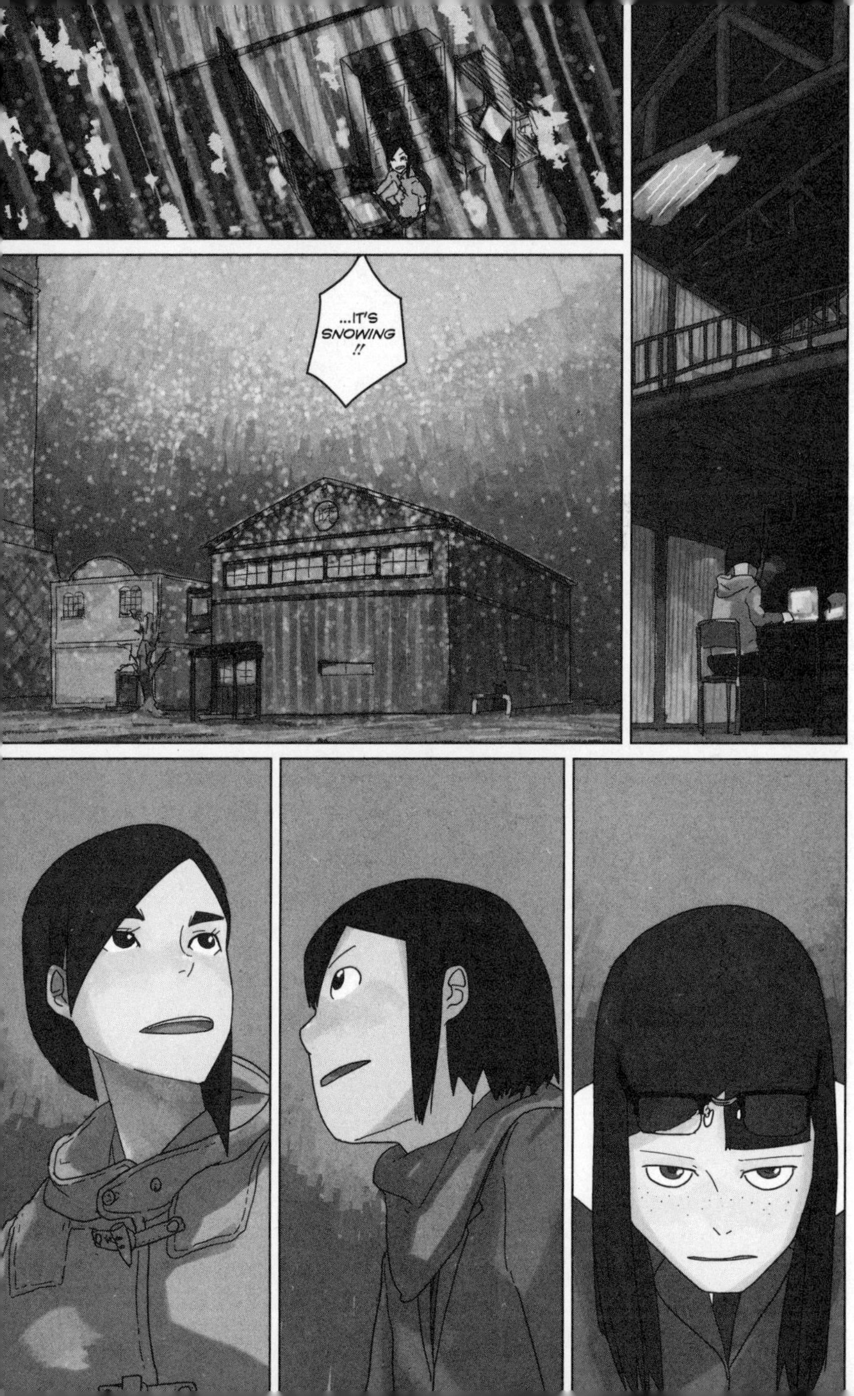
...IT'S SNOWING !!

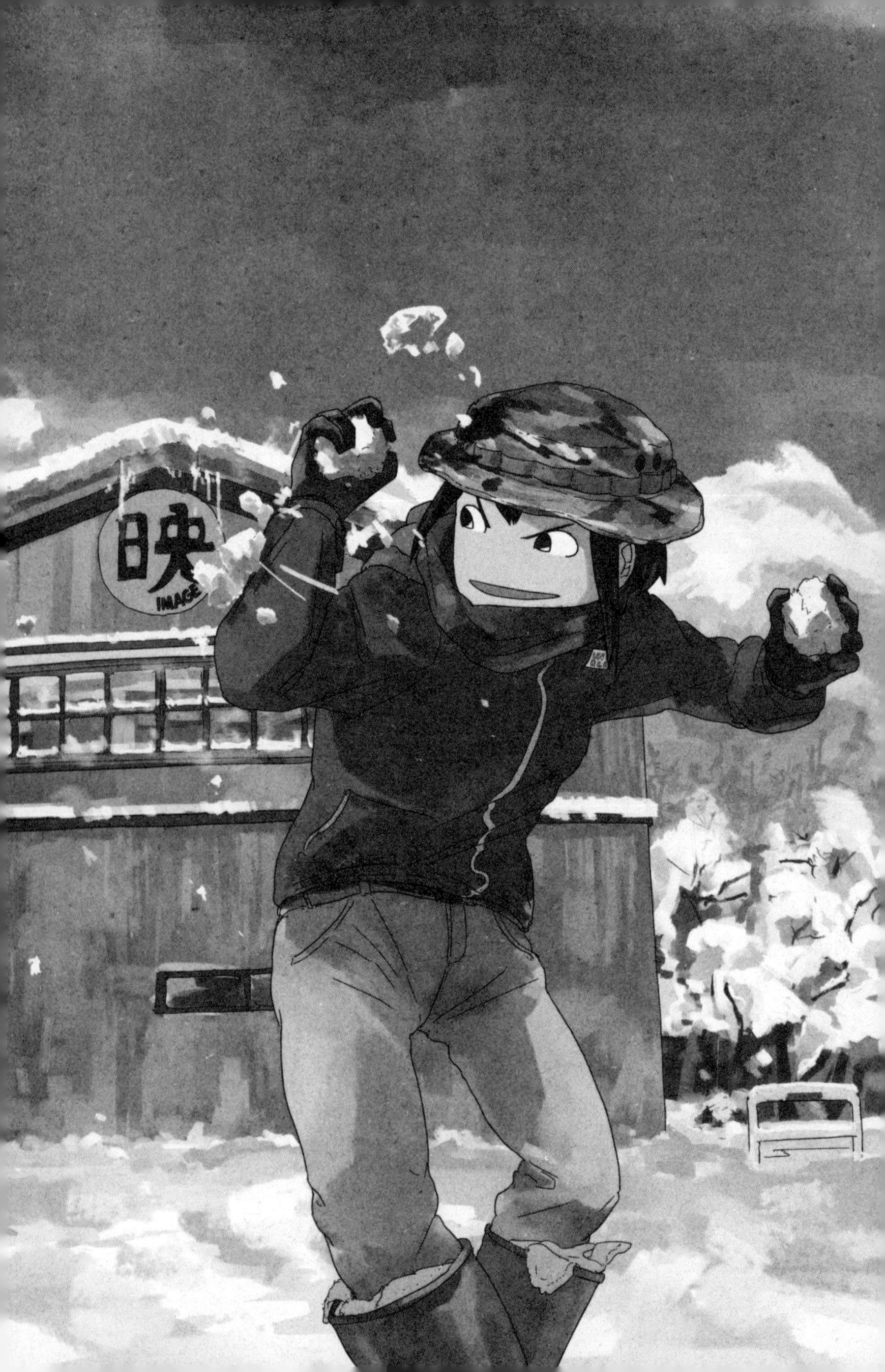
映
IMAGE

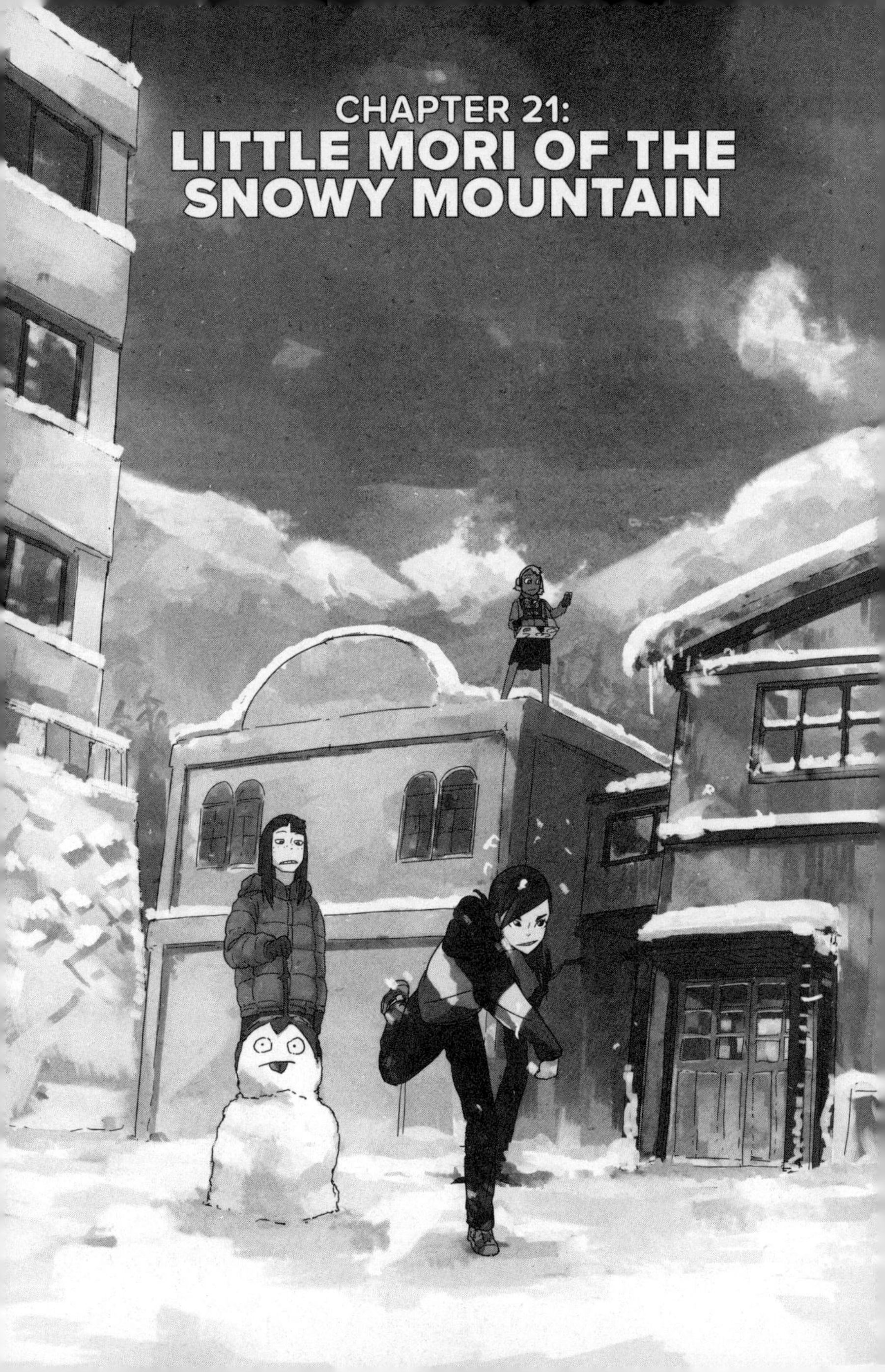
CHAPTER 21:
LITTLE MORI OF THE SNOWY MOUNTAIN

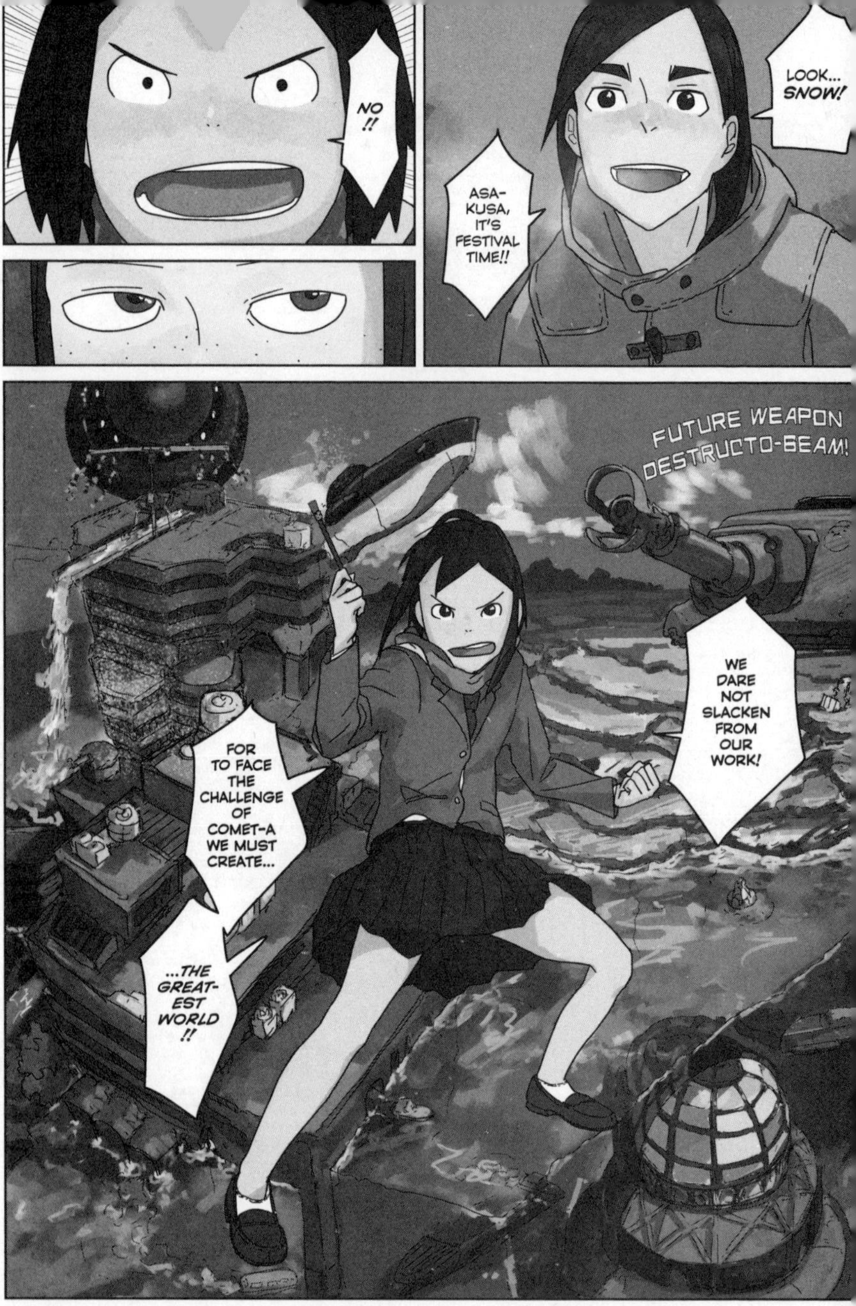
LOOK... SNOW!
ASA-KUSA, IT'S FESTIVAL TIME!!
NO!!
FUTURE WEAPON DESTRUCTO-BEAM!
WE DARE NOT SLACKEN FROM OUR WORK!
FOR TO FACE THE CHALLENGE OF COMET-A WE MUST CREATE...
...THE GREAT-EST WORLD!!

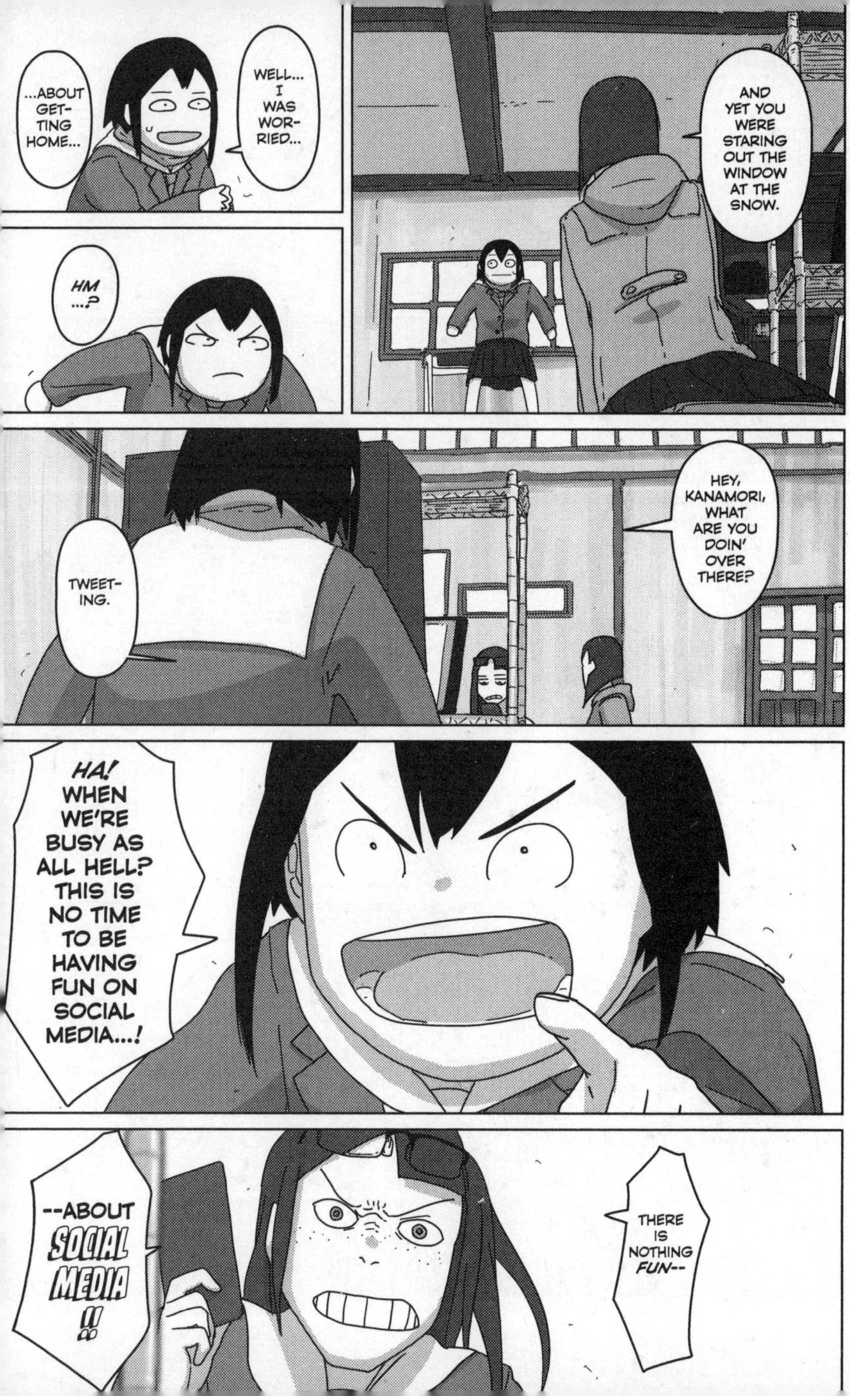
AND YET YOU WERE STARING OUT THE WINDOW AT THE SNOW.
WELL... I WAS WOR-RIED...
...ABOUT GET-TING HOME...
HM ...?
HEY, KANAMORI, WHAT ARE YOU DOIN' OVER THERE?
TWEET-ING.
HA! WHEN WE'RE BUSY AS ALL HELL? THIS IS NO TIME TO BE HAVING FUN ON SOCIAL MEDIA....!
THERE IS NOTHING FUN--
--ABOUT SOCIAL MEDIA !!

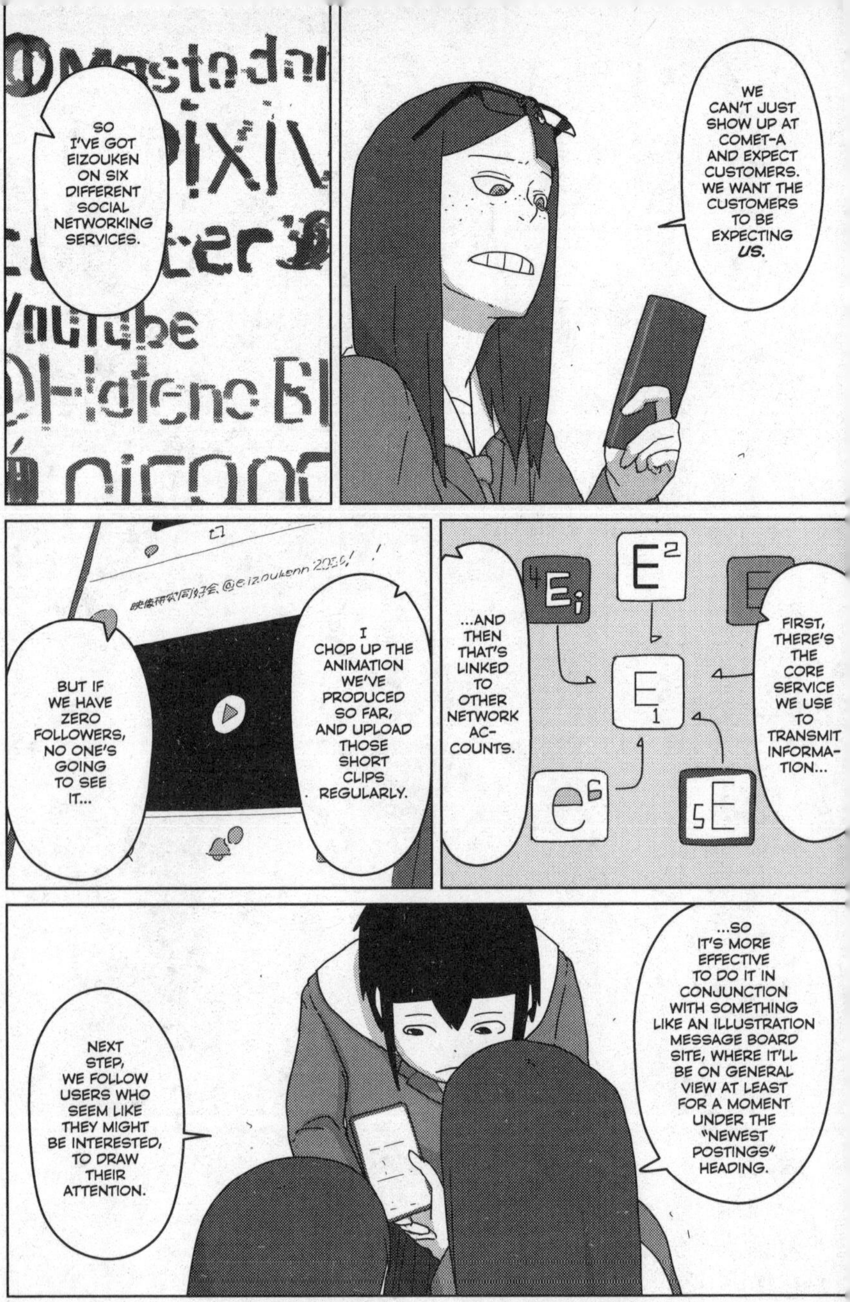
WE CAN'T JUST SHOW UP AT COMET-A AND EXPECT CUSTOMERS. WE WANT THE CUSTOMERS TO BE EXPECTING *US*.
SO I'VE GOT EIZOUKEN ON SIX DIFFERENT SOCIAL NETWORKING SERVICES.
FIRST, THERE'S THE CORE SERVICE WE USE TO TRANSMIT INFORMATION...
...AND THEN THAT'S LINKED TO OTHER NETWORK AC-COUNTS.
I CHOP UP THE ANIMATION WE'VE PRODUCED SO FAR, AND UPLOAD THOSE SHORT CLIPS REGULARLY.
BUT IF WE HAVE ZERO FOLLOWERS, NO ONE'S GOING TO SEE IT...
...SO IT'S MORE EFFECTIVE TO DO IT IN CONJUNCTION WITH SOMETHING LIKE AN ILLUSTRATION MESSAGE BOARD SITE, WHERE IT'LL BE ON GENERAL VIEW AT LEAST FOR A MOMENT UNDER THE "NEWEST POSTINGS" HEADING.
NEXT STEP, WE FOLLOW USERS WHO SEEM LIKE THEY MIGHT BE INTERESTED, TO DRAW THEIR ATTENTION.

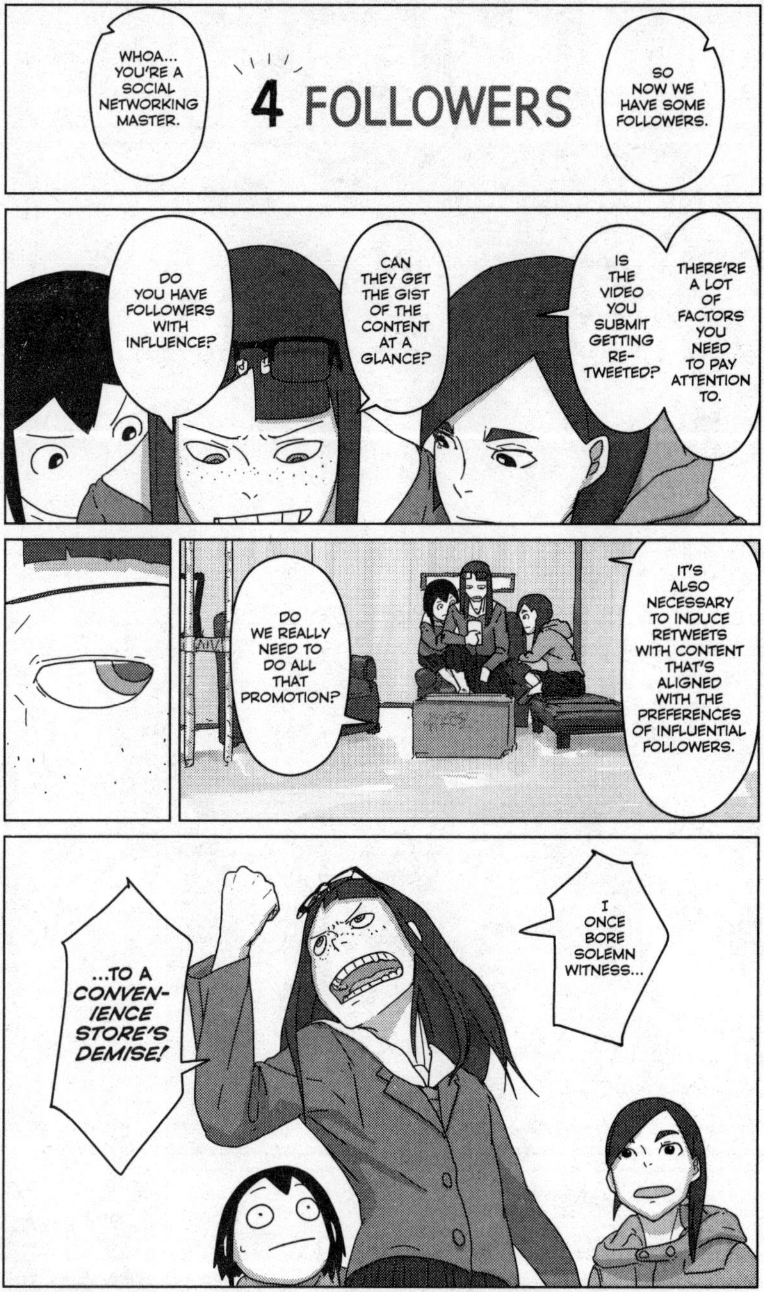
4 FOLLOWERS
SO NOW WE HAVE SOME FOLLOWERS.
WHOA... YOU'RE A SOCIAL NETWORKING MASTER.
THERE'RE A LOT OF FACTORS YOU NEED TO PAY ATTENTION TO.
IS THE VIDEO YOU SUBMIT GETTING RE-TWEETED?
CAN THEY GET THE GIST OF THE CONTENT AT A GLANCE?
DO YOU HAVE FOLLOWERS WITH INFLUENCE?
IT'S ALSO NECESSARY TO INDUCE RETWEETS WITH CONTENT THAT'S ALIGNED WITH THE PREFERENCES OF INFLUENTIAL FOLLOWERS.
DO WE REALLY NEED TO DO ALL THAT PROMOTION?
I ONCE BORE SOLEMN WITNESS...
...TO A CONVEN-IENCE STORE'S DEMISE!

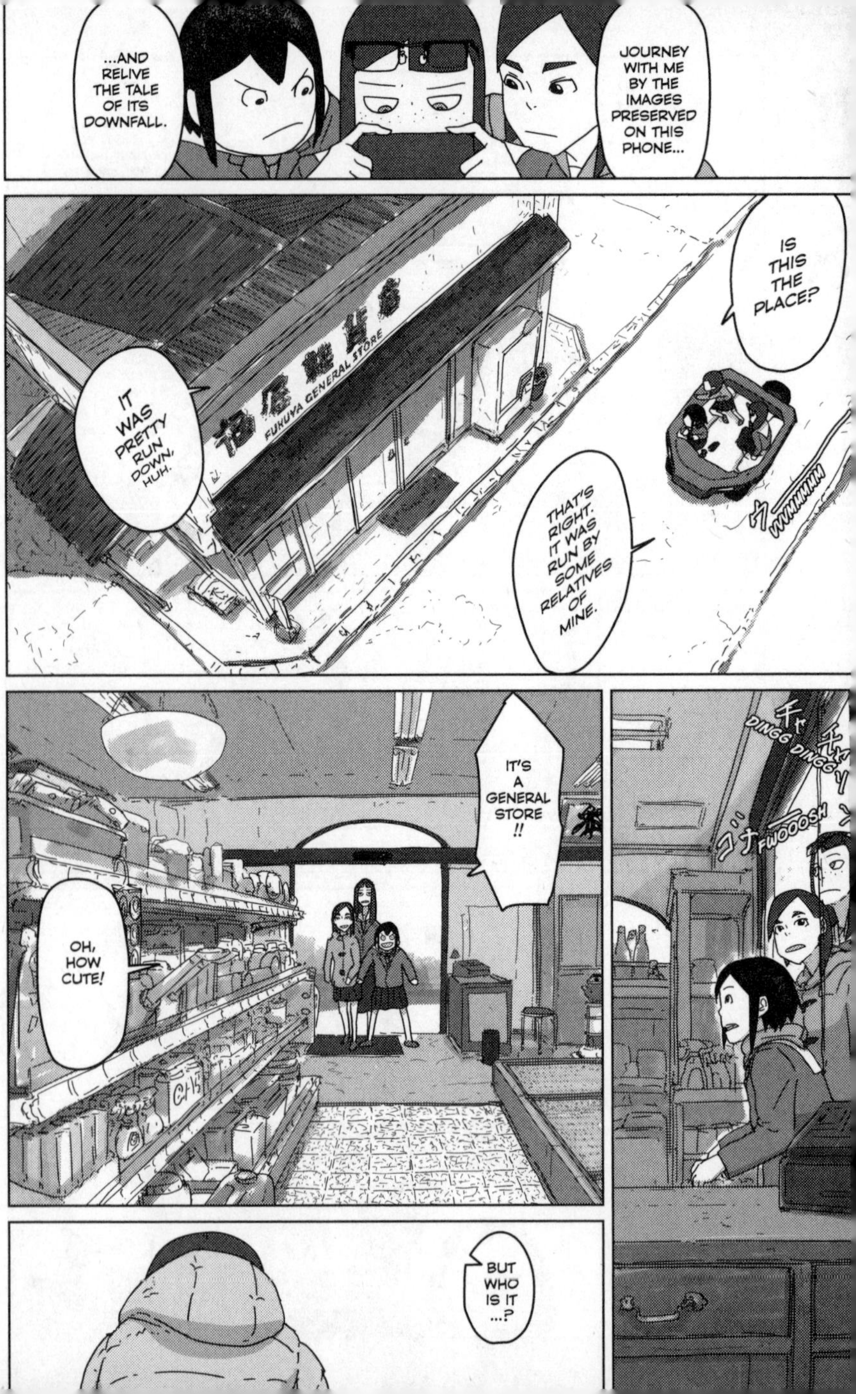
JOURNEY WITH ME BY THE IMAGES PRESERVED ON THIS PHONE...
...AND RELIVE THE TALE OF ITS DOWNFALL.
IS THIS THE PLACE?
VWMMMMM
THAT'S RIGHT. IT WAS RUN BY SOME RELATIVES OF MINE.
FUKUYA GENERAL STORE
IT WAS PRETTY RUN DOWN, HUH.
DINGG DINGG
FWOOOSH
IT'S A GENERAL STORE!!
OH, HOW CUTE!
BUT WHO IS IT ...?

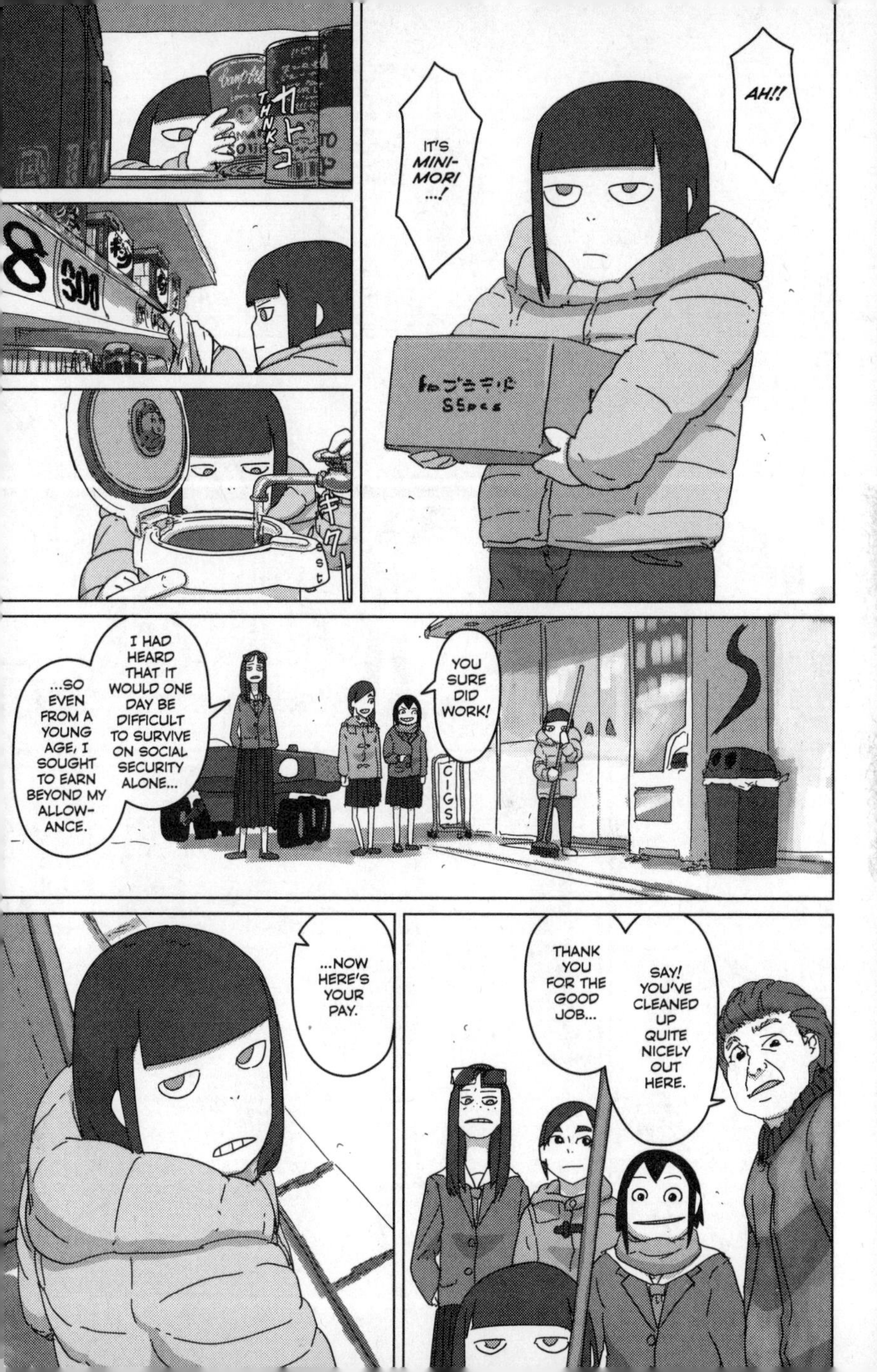
AH!!
IT'S MINI-MORI...!
THNK
YOU SURE DID WORK!
CIGS
I HAD HEARD THAT IT WOULD ONE DAY BE DIFFICULT TO SURVIVE ON SOCIAL SECURITY ALONE...
...SO EVEN FROM A YOUNG AGE, I SOUGHT TO EARN BEYOND MY ALLOW-ANCE.
SAY! YOU'VE CLEANED UP QUITE NICELY OUT HERE.
THANK YOU FOR THE GOOD JOB...
...NOW HERE'S YOUR PAY.

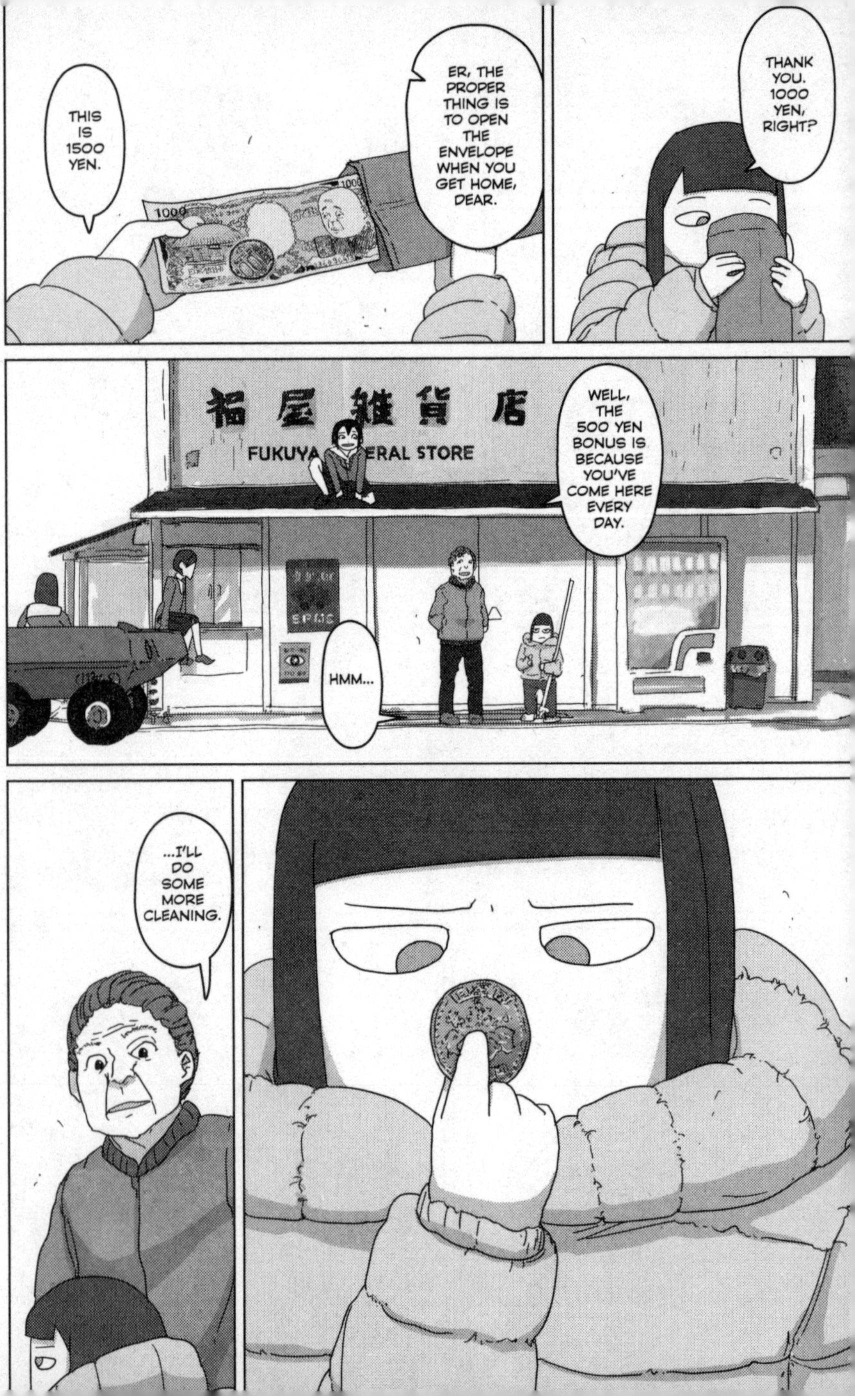
THANK YOU. 1000 YEN, RIGHT?
ER, THE PROPER THING IS TO OPEN THE ENVELOPE WHEN YOU GET HOME, DEAR.
THIS IS 1500 YEN.
福屋雑貨店
FUKUYA
ERAL STORE
WELL, THE 500 YEN BONUS IS BECAUSE YOU'VE COME HERE EVERY DAY.
HMM...
...I'LL DO SOME MORE CLEANING.

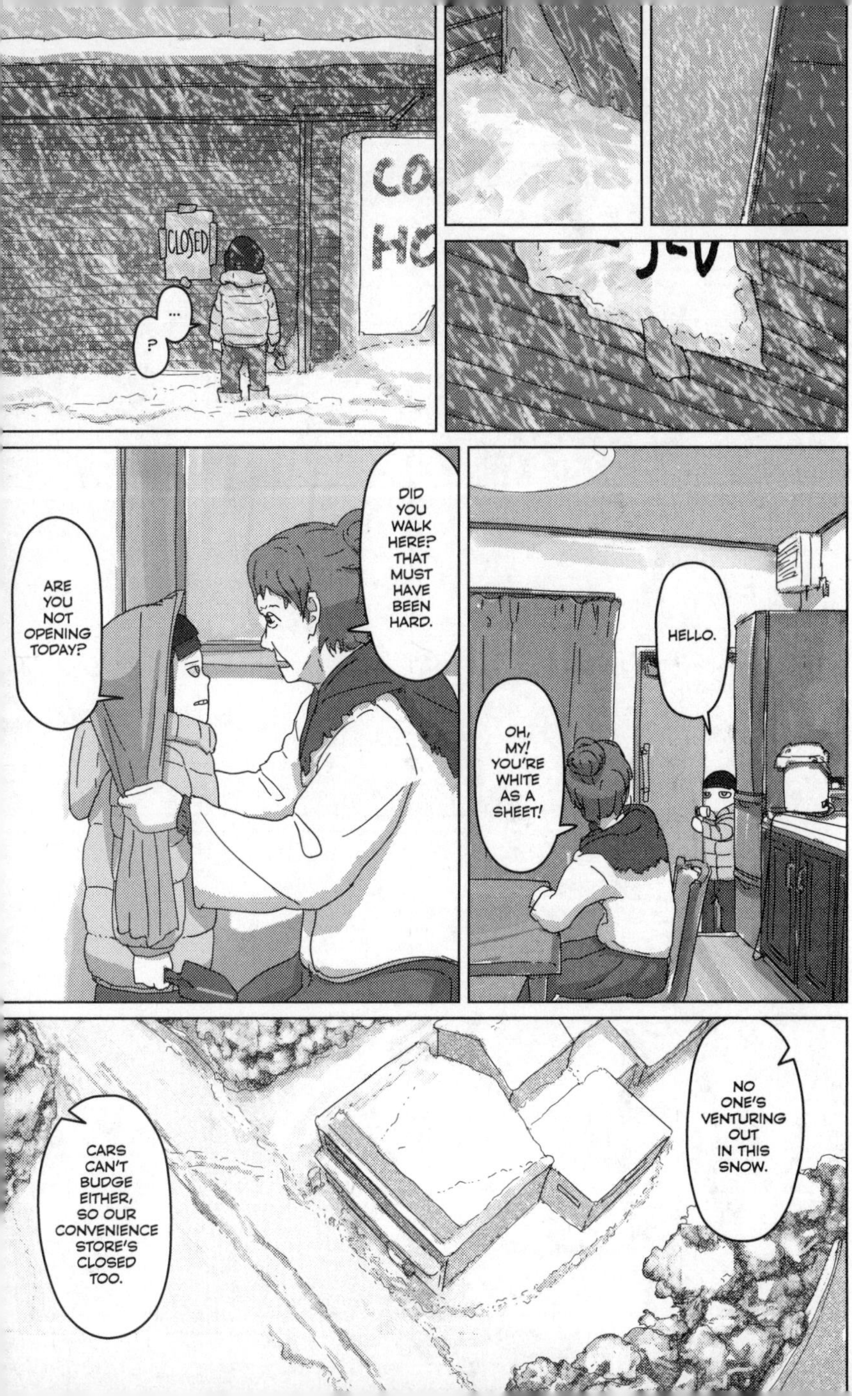
CLOSED
...
?
HELLO.
OH, MY! YOU'RE WHITE AS A SHEET!
DID YOU WALK HERE? THAT MUST HAVE BEEN HARD.
ARE YOU NOT OPENING TODAY?
NO ONE'S VENTURING OUT IN THIS SNOW.
CARS CAN'T BUDGE EITHER, SO OUR CONVENIENCE STORE'S CLOSED TOO.

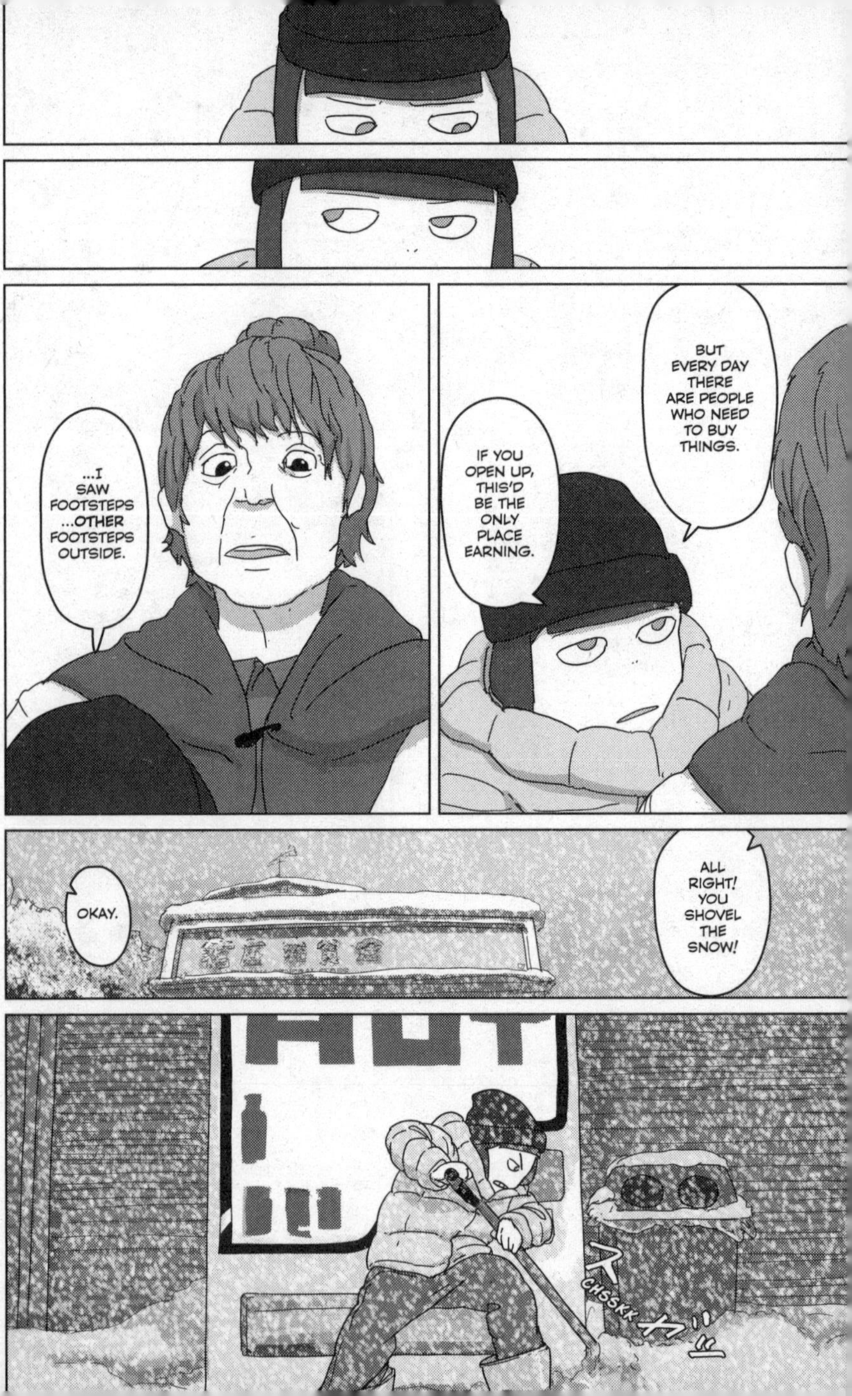
BUT EVERY DAY THERE ARE PEOPLE WHO NEED TO BUY THINGS.
IF YOU OPEN UP, THIS'D BE THE ONLY PLACE EARNING.
...I SAW FOOTSTEPS ...OTHER FOOTSTEPS OUTSIDE.
ALL RIGHT! YOU SHOVEL THE SNOW!
OKAY.
CHSSKK

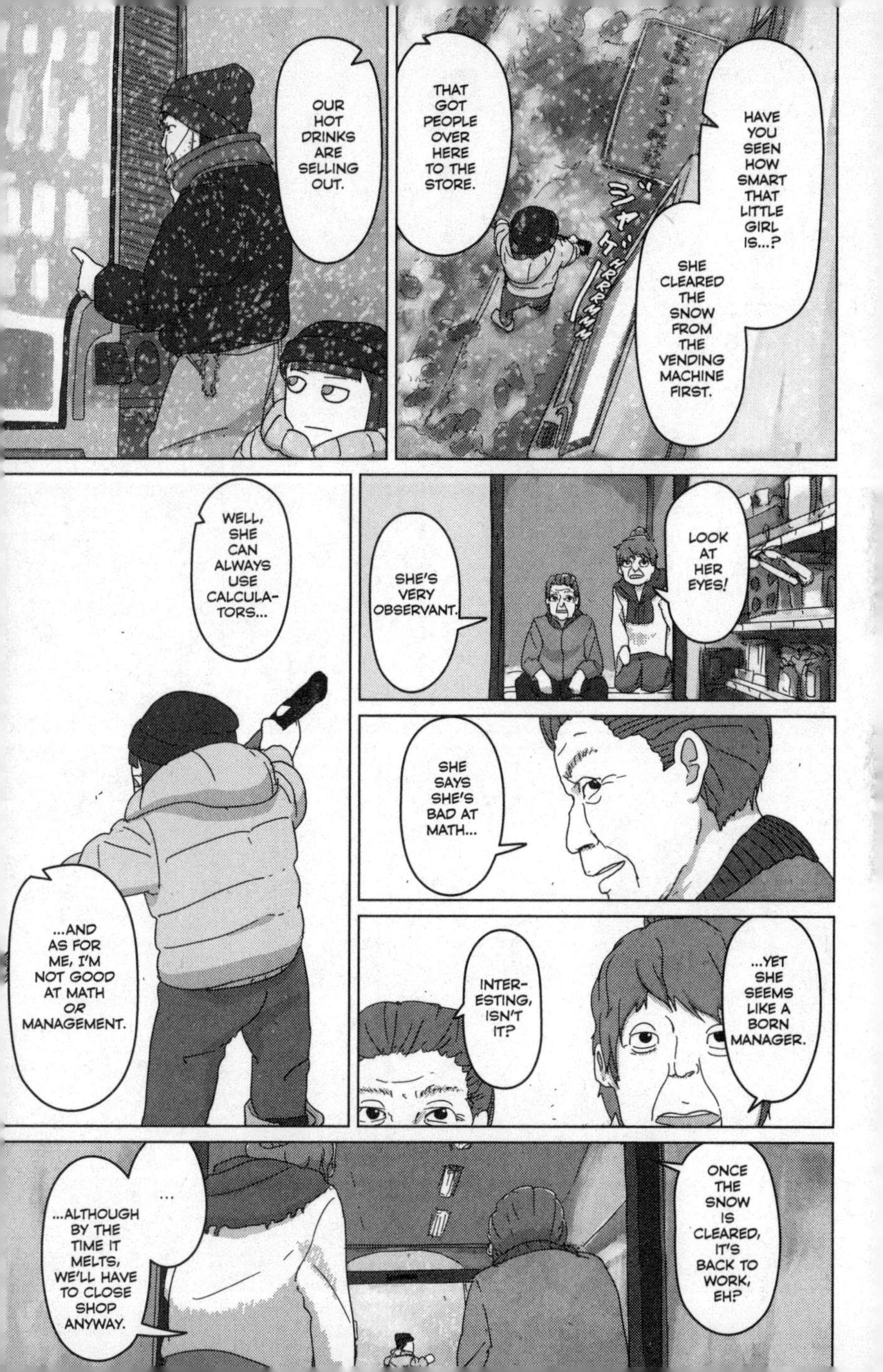
HAVE YOU SEEN HOW SMART THAT LITTLE GIRL IS...?
SHE CLEARED THE SNOW FROM THE VENDING MACHINE FIRST.
HRRRMMM
THAT GOT PEOPLE OVER HERE TO THE STORE.
OUR HOT DRINKS ARE SELLING OUT.
LOOK AT HER EYES!
SHE'S VERY OBSERVANT.
SHE SAYS SHE'S BAD AT MATH...
...YET SHE SEEMS LIKE A BORN MANAGER.
INTER-ESTING, ISN'T IT?
WELL, SHE CAN ALWAYS USE CALCULA-TORS...
...AND AS FOR ME, I'M NOT GOOD AT MATH *OR* MANAGEMENT.
ONCE THE SNOW IS CLEARED, IT'S BACK TO WORK, EH?
...
...ALTHOUGH BY THE TIME IT MELTS, WE'LL HAVE TO CLOSE SHOP ANYWAY.

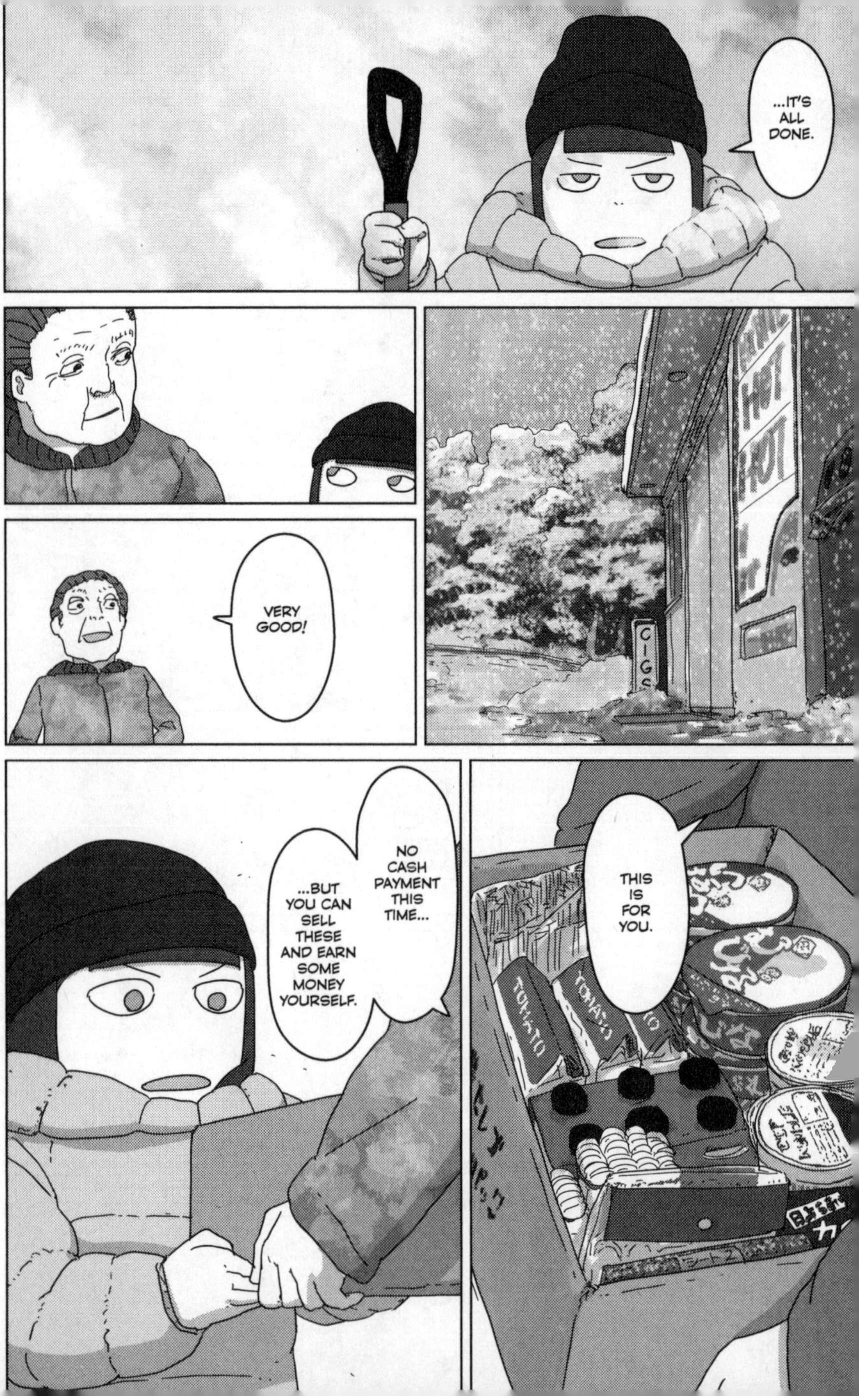
...IT'S ALL DONE.
HOT
HOT
CIGS
VERY GOOD!
THIS IS FOR YOU.
NO CASH PAYMENT THIS TIME...
...BUT YOU CAN SELL THESE AND EARN SOME MONEY YOURSELF.

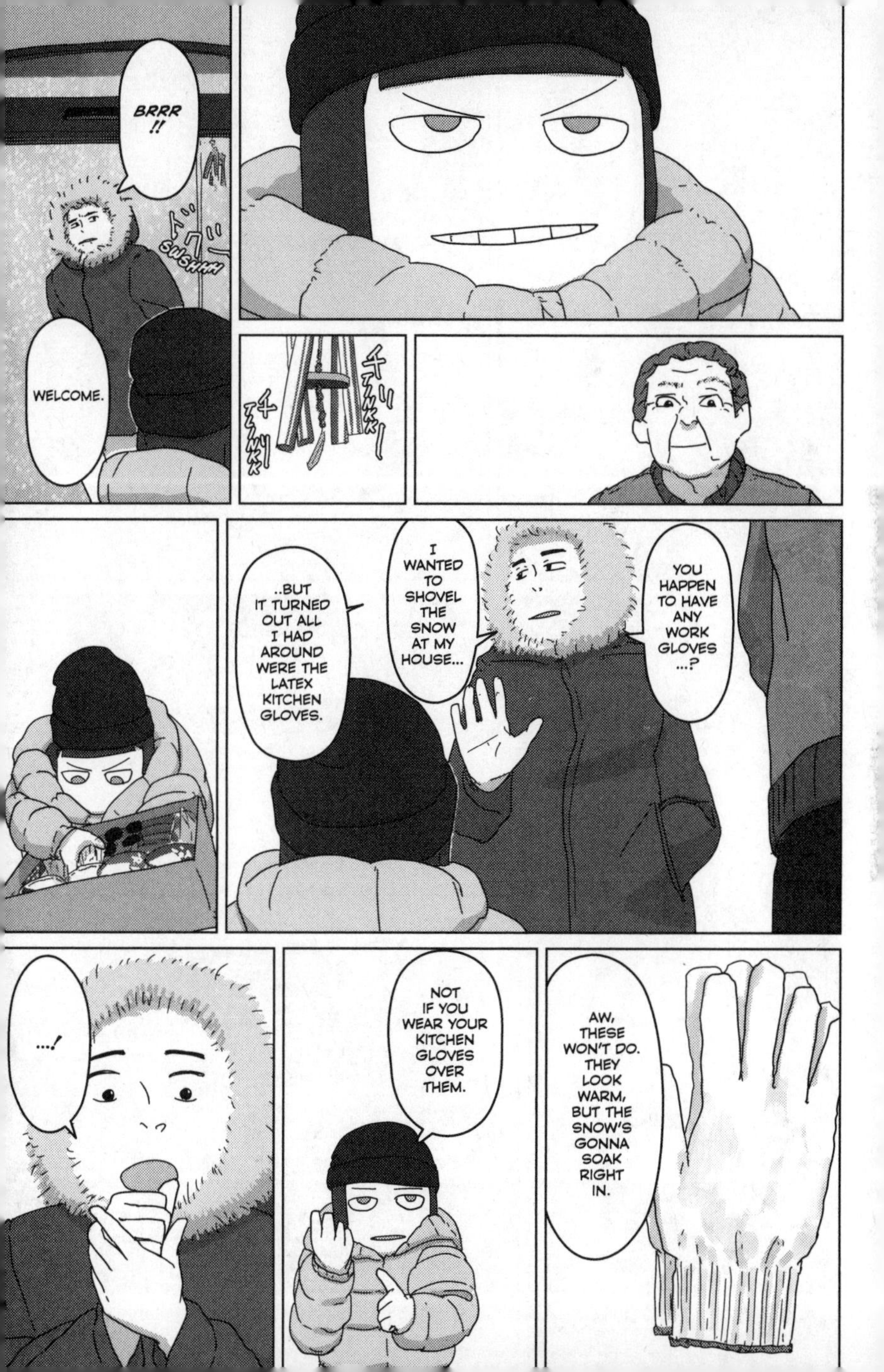

TINKLE
TINKLE
BRRR!!
SWSHHH
WELCOME.
YOU HAPPEN TO HAVE ANY WORK GLOVES ...?
I WANTED TO SHOVEL THE SNOW AT MY HOUSE...
..BUT IT TURNED OUT ALL I HAD AROUND WERE THE LATEX KITCHEN GLOVES.
AW, THESE WON'T DO. THEY LOOK WARM, BUT THE SNOW'S GONNA SOAK RIGHT IN.
NOT IF YOU WEAR YOUR KITCHEN GLOVES OVER THEM.
...!

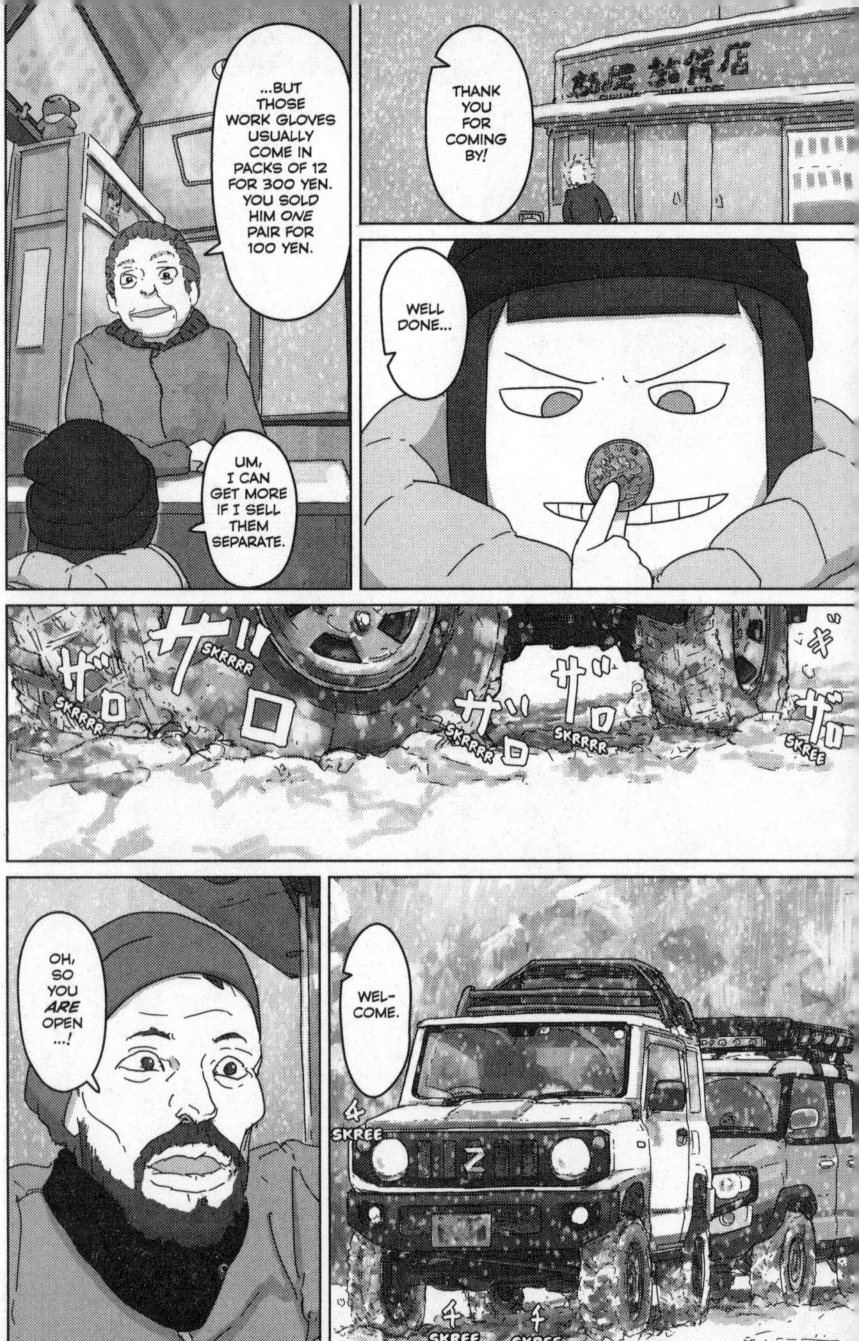
THANK YOU FOR COMING BY!
WELL DONE...
...BUT THOSE WORK GLOVES USUALLY COME IN PACKS OF 12 FOR 300 YEN. YOU SOLD HIM *ONE* PAIR FOR 100 YEN.
UM, I CAN GET MORE IF I SELL THEM SEPARATE.
SKREE
SKRRRR
SKRRRR
SKRRRR
SKRRRR
WEL-COME.
SKREE
SKREE
SKREE
OH, SO YOU ***ARE*** OPEN...!

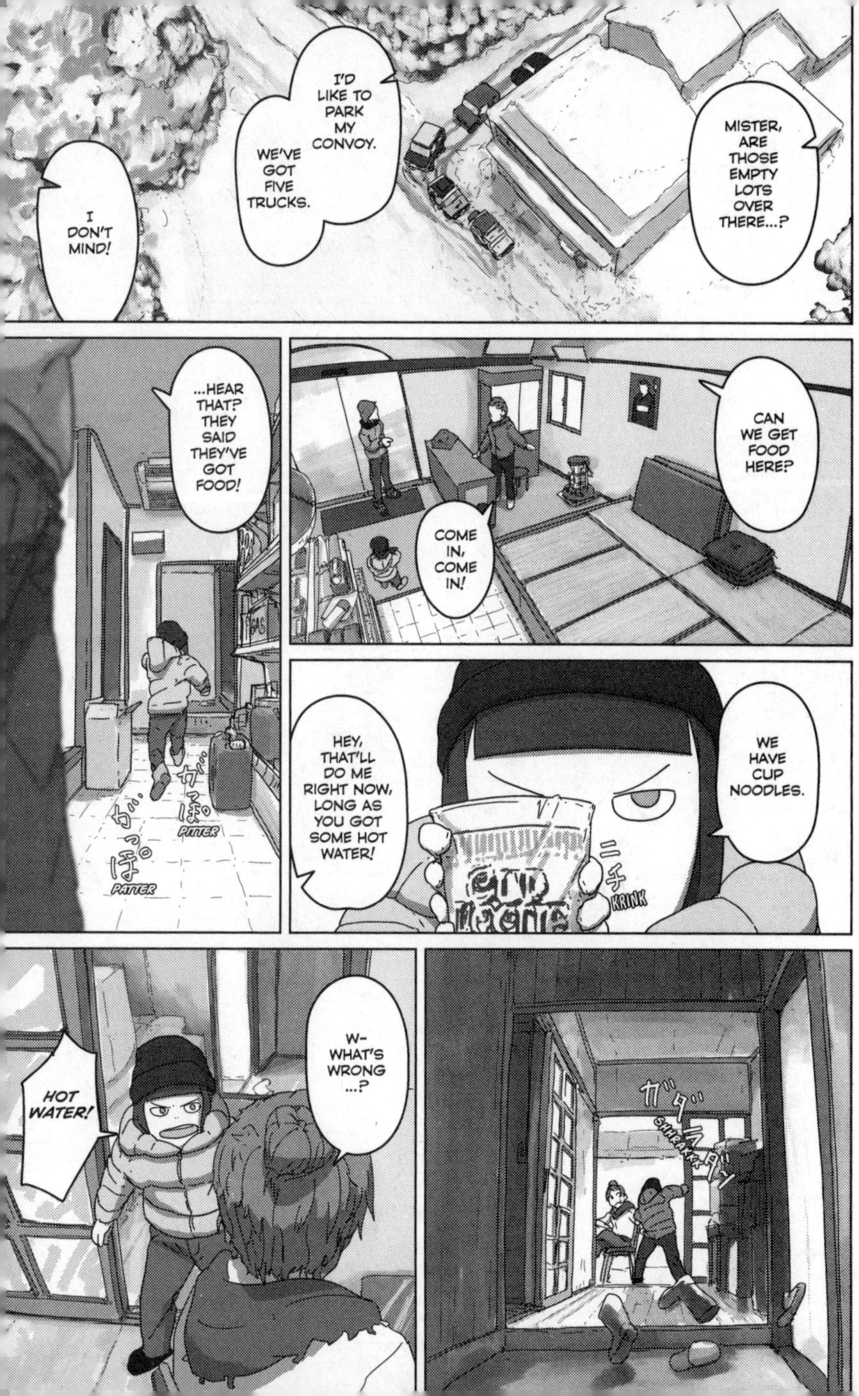
MISTER, ARE THOSE EMPTY LOTS OVER THERE...?
I'D LIKE TO PARK MY CONVOY.
WE'VE GOT FIVE TRUCKS.
I DON'T MIND!
CAN WE GET FOOD HERE?
COME IN, COME IN!
WE HAVE CUP NOODLES.
KRINK
HEY, THAT'LL DO ME RIGHT NOW, LONG AS YOU GOT SOME HOT WATER!
...HEAR THAT? THEY SAID THEY'VE GOT FOOD!
PITTER
PATTER
SHRAKKK
W- WHAT'S WRONG ...?
HOT WATER!

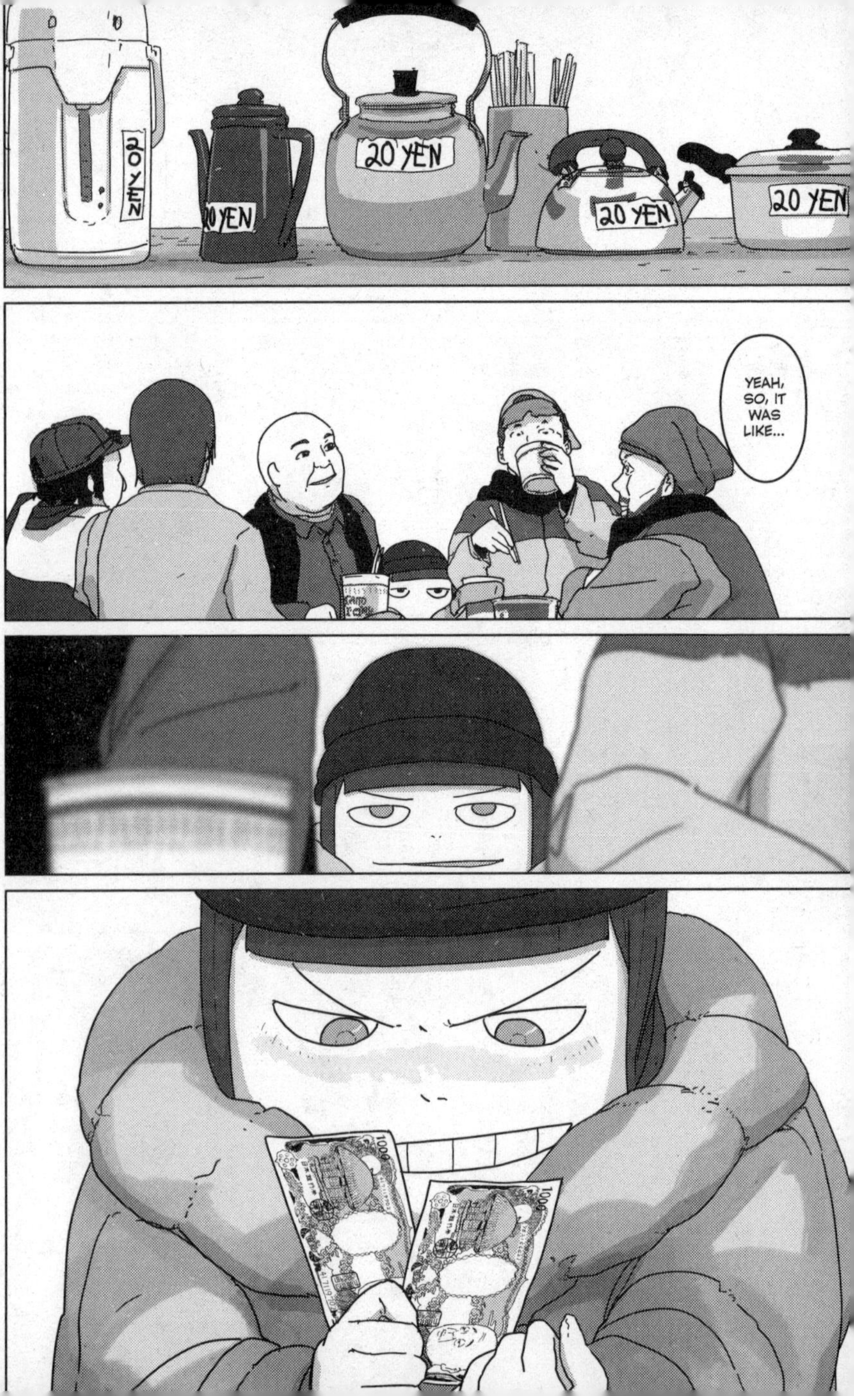

20 YEN
20 YEN
20 YEN
20 YEN
20 YEN
YEAH, SO, IT WAS LIKE...

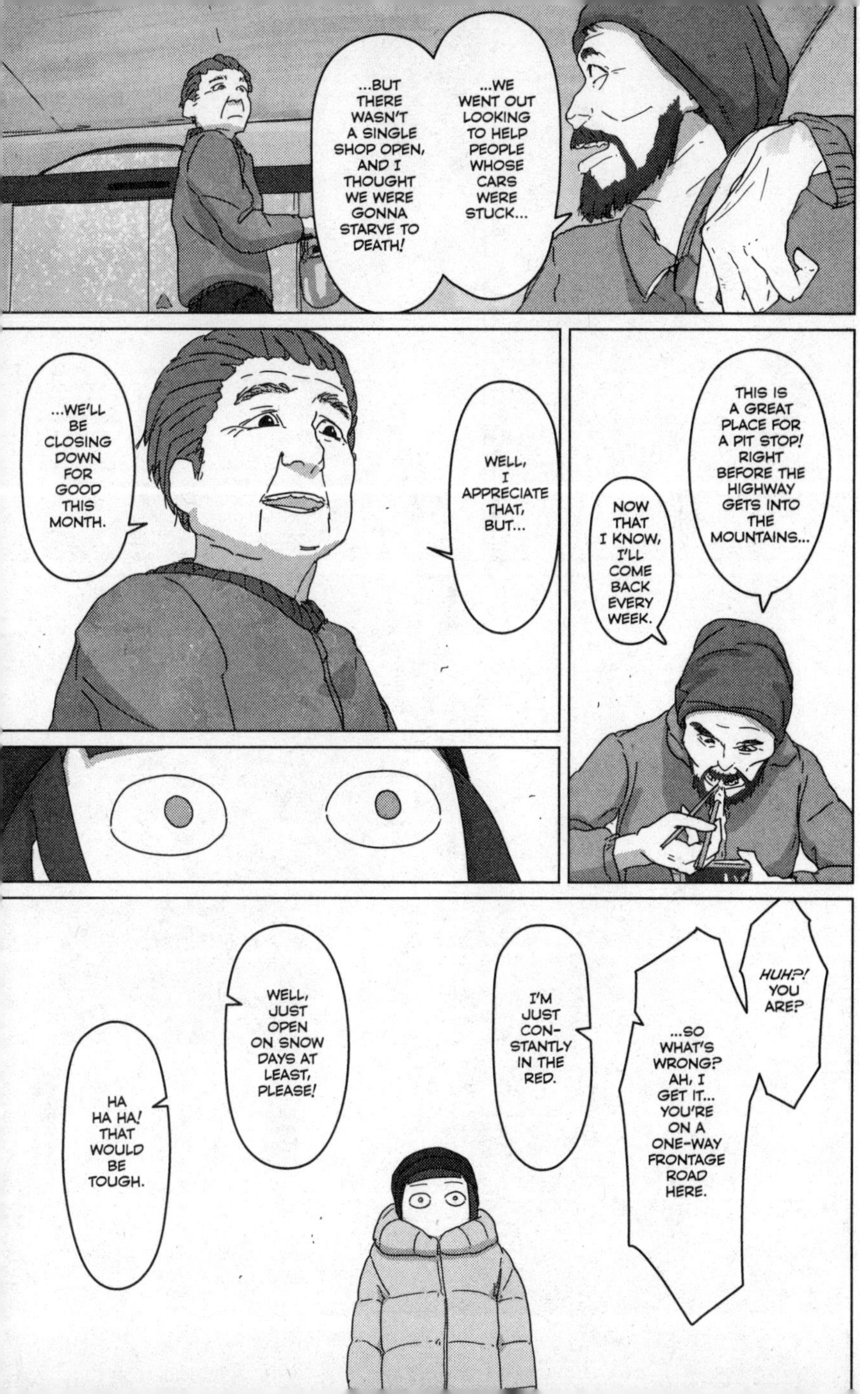
...WE WENT OUT LOOKING TO HELP PEOPLE WHOSE CARS WERE STUCK...
...BUT THERE WASN'T A SINGLE SHOP OPEN, AND I THOUGHT WE WERE GONNA STARVE TO DEATH!
THIS IS A GREAT PLACE FOR A PIT STOP! RIGHT BEFORE THE HIGHWAY GETS INTO THE MOUNTAINS...
NOW THAT I KNOW, I'LL COME BACK EVERY WEEK.
WELL, I APPRECIATE THAT, BUT...
...WE'LL BE CLOSING DOWN FOR GOOD THIS MONTH.
HUH?! YOU ARE?
...SO WHAT'S WRONG? AH, I GET IT... YOU'RE ON A ONE-WAY FRONTAGE ROAD HERE.
I'M JUST CON-STANTLY IN THE RED.
WELL, JUST OPEN ON SNOW DAYS AT LEAST, PLEASE!
HA HA HA! THAT WOULD BE TOUGH.

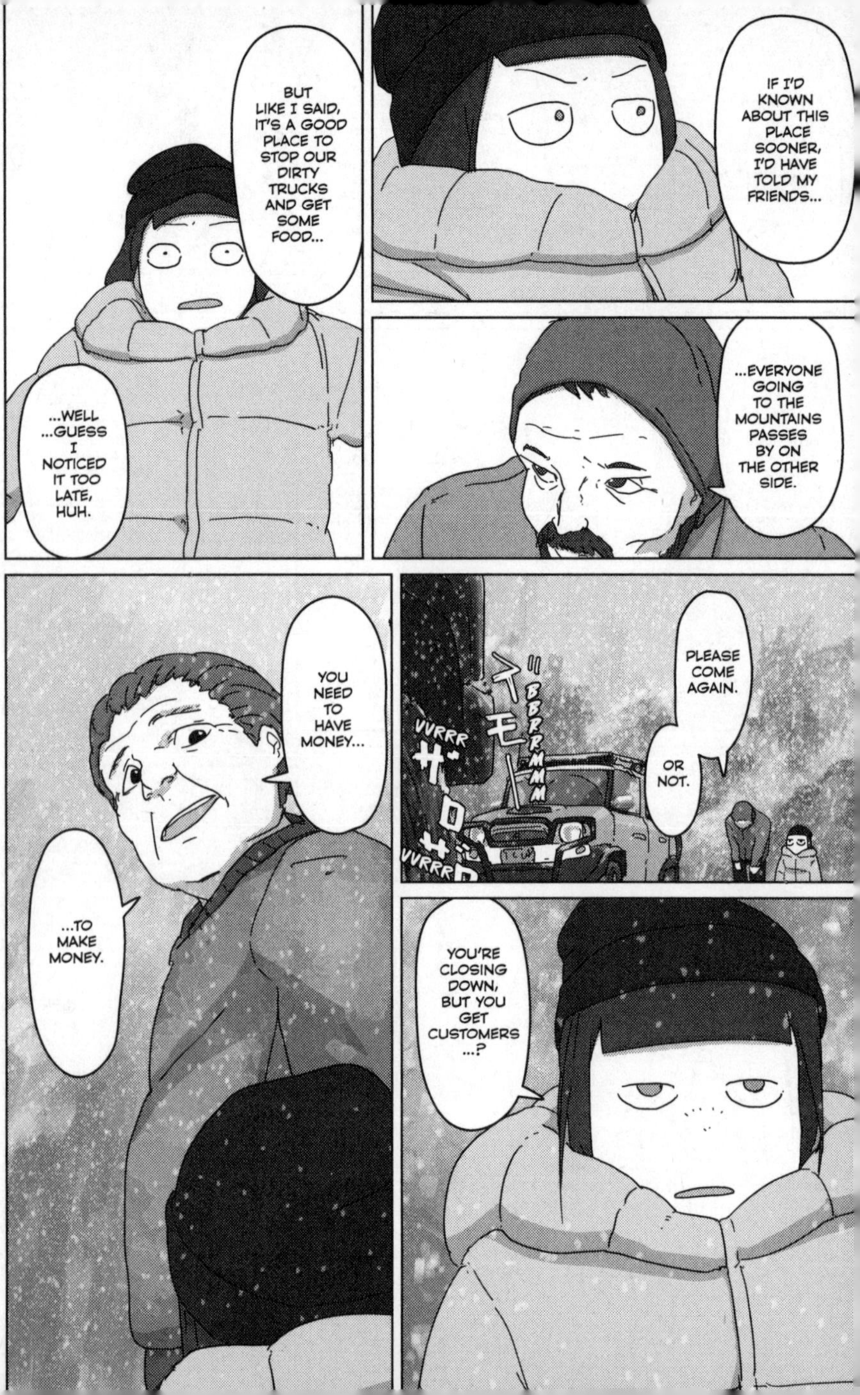
IF I'D KNOWN ABOUT THIS PLACE SOONER, I'D HAVE TOLD MY FRIENDS...
...EVERYONE GOING TO THE MOUNTAINS PASSES BY ON THE OTHER SIDE.
BUT LIKE I SAID, IT'S A GOOD PLACE TO STOP OUR DIRTY TRUCKS AND GET SOME FOOD...
...WELL ...GUESS I NOTICED IT TOO LATE, HUH.
PLEASE COME AGAIN.
OR NOT.
BBRRMMM
VVRRR
VVRRR
YOU'RE CLOSING DOWN, BUT YOU GET CUSTOMERS ...?
YOU NEED TO HAVE MONEY...
...TO MAKE MONEY.

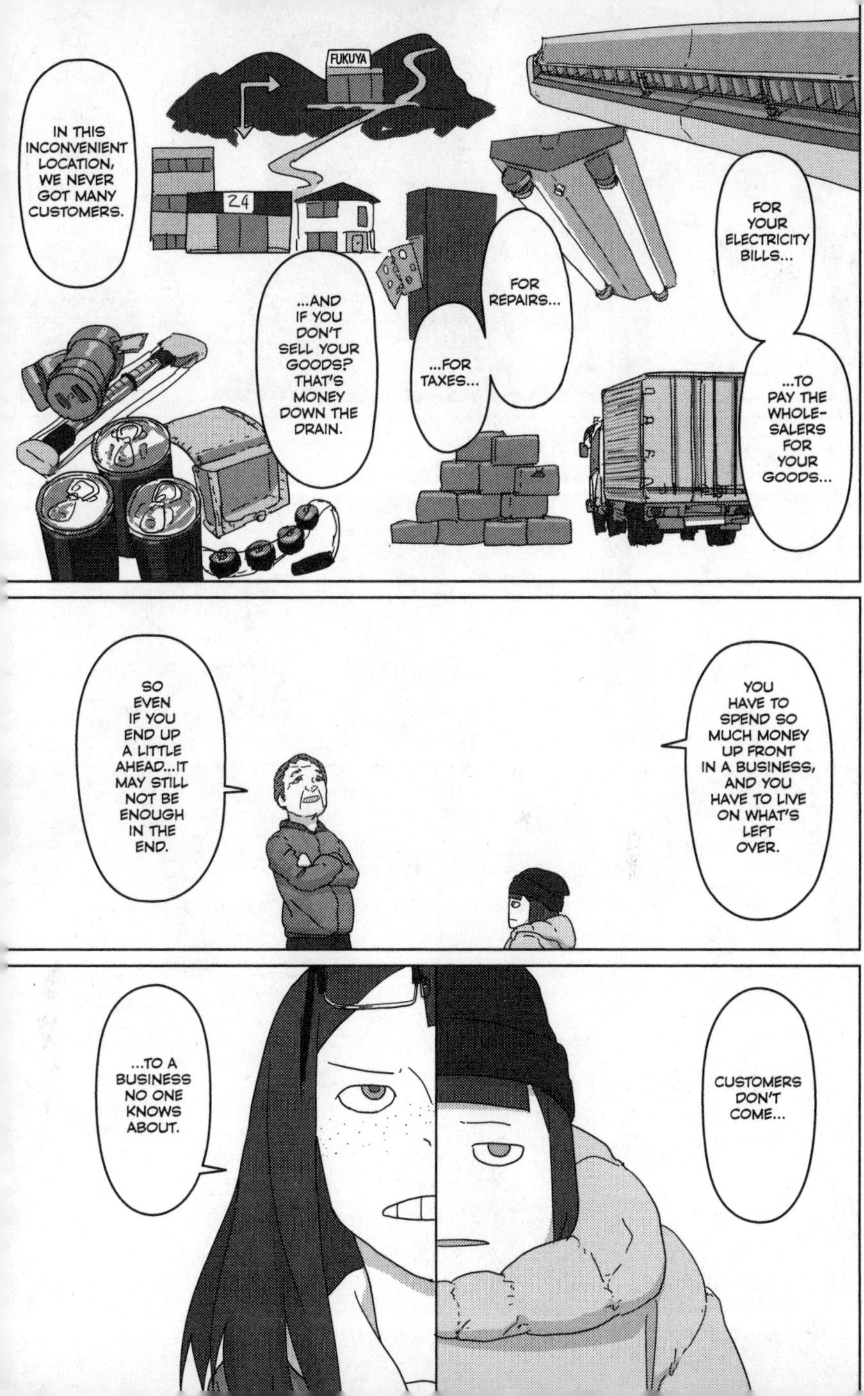
FOR YOUR ELECTRICITY BILLS...
...TO PAY THE WHOLE-SALERS FOR YOUR GOODS...
FOR REPAIRS...
...FOR TAXES...
...AND IF YOU DON'T SELL YOUR GOODS? THAT'S MONEY DOWN THE DRAIN.
FUKUYA
IN THIS INCONVENIENT LOCATION, WE NEVER GOT MANY CUSTOMERS.
24
YOU HAVE TO SPEND SO MUCH MONEY UP FRONT IN A BUSINESS, AND YOU HAVE TO LIVE ON WHAT'S LEFT OVER.
SO EVEN IF YOU END UP A LITTLE AHEAD...IT MAY STILL NOT BE ENOUGH IN THE END.
CUSTOMERS DON'T COME...
...TO A BUSINESS NO ONE KNOWS ABOUT.

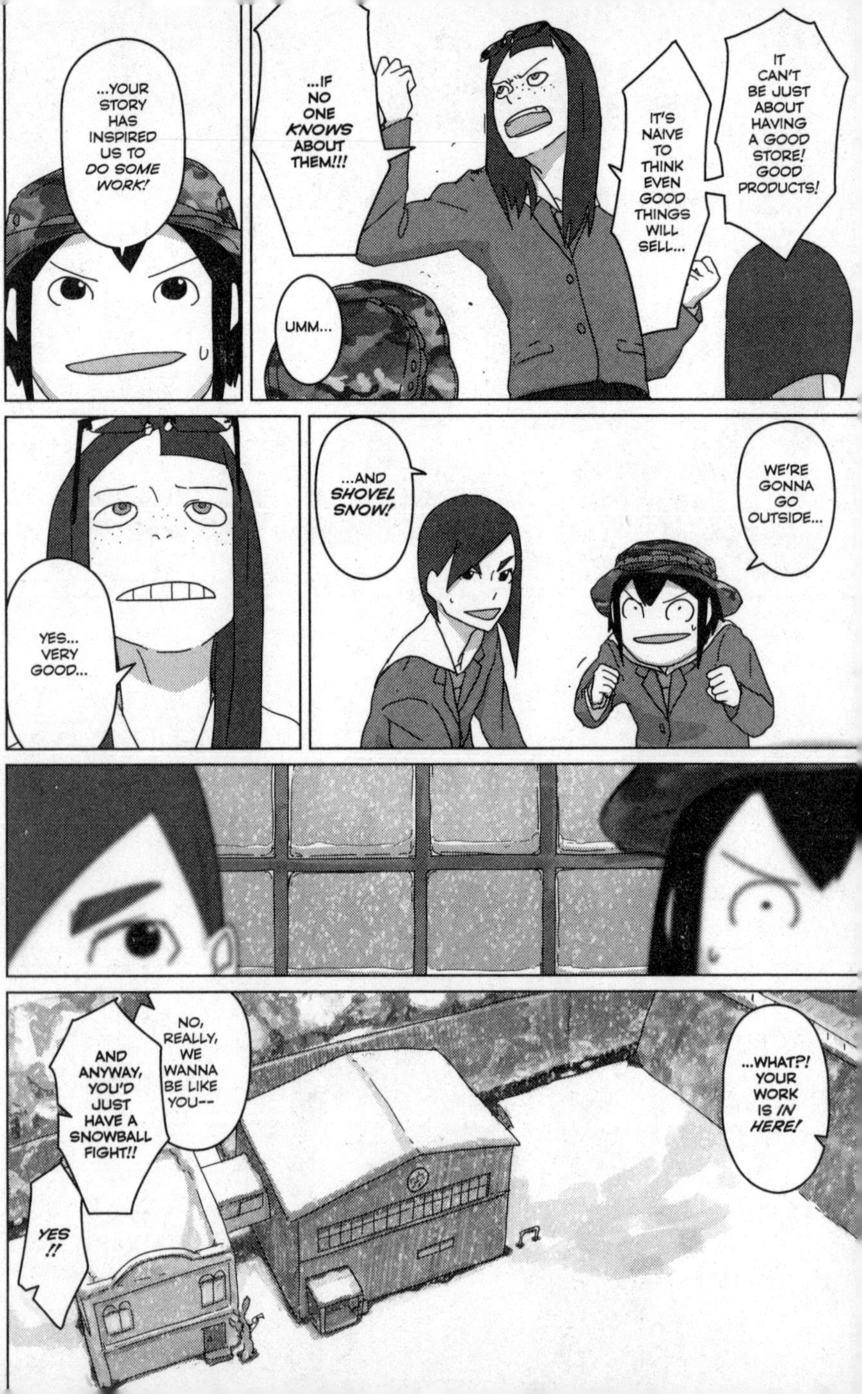
IT CAN'T BE JUST ABOUT HAVING A GOOD STORE! GOOD PRODUCTS!
IT'S NAIVE TO THINK EVEN GOOD THINGS WILL SELL...
...IF NO ONE *KNOWS* ABOUT THEM!!!
UMM...
...YOUR STORY HAS INSPIRED US TO *DO SOME WORK!*
WE'RE GONNA GO OUTSIDE...
...AND *SHOVEL SNOW!*
YES... VERY GOOD...
...WHAT?! YOUR WORK IS *IN HERE!*
NO, REALLY, WE WANNA BE LIKE YOU--
AND ANYWAY, YOU'D JUST HAVE A SNOWBALL FIGHT!!
YES !!

CHAPTER 22: THE BATTLE BEGINS

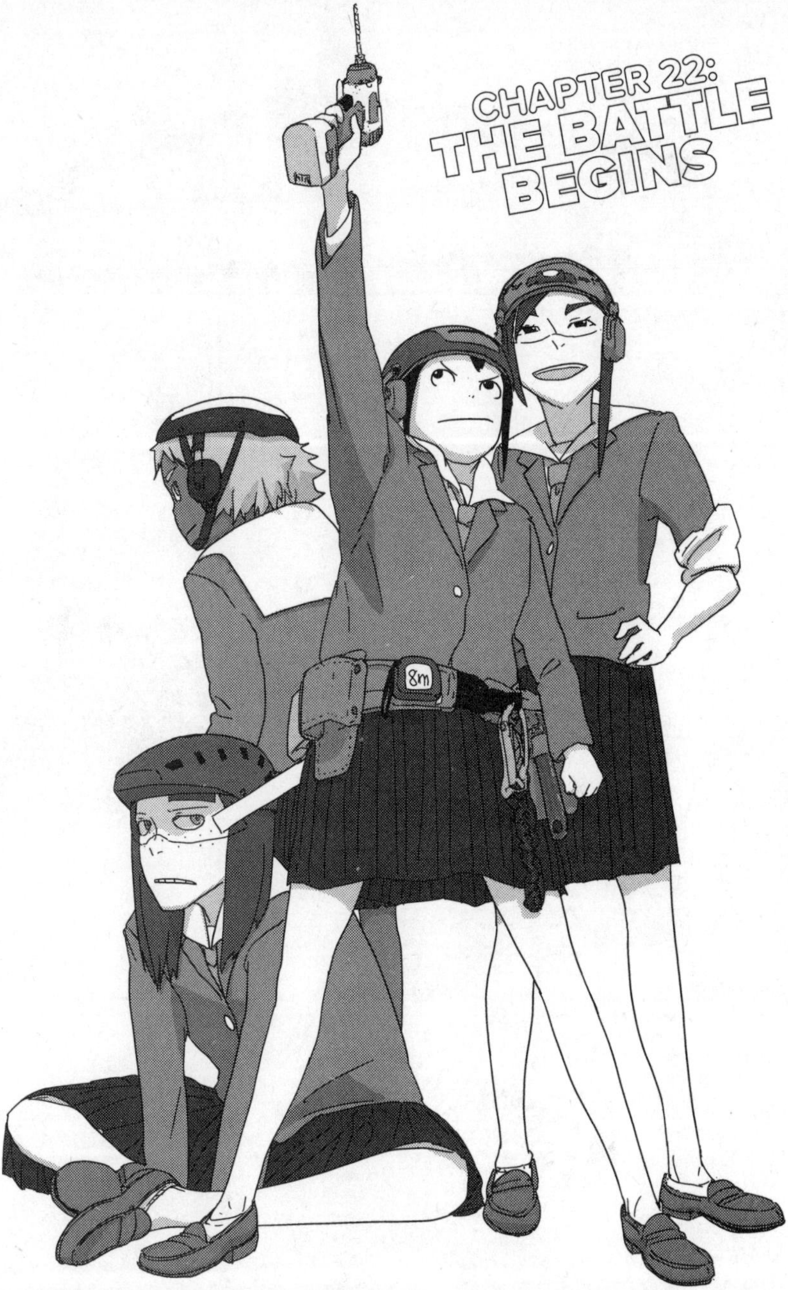
8m

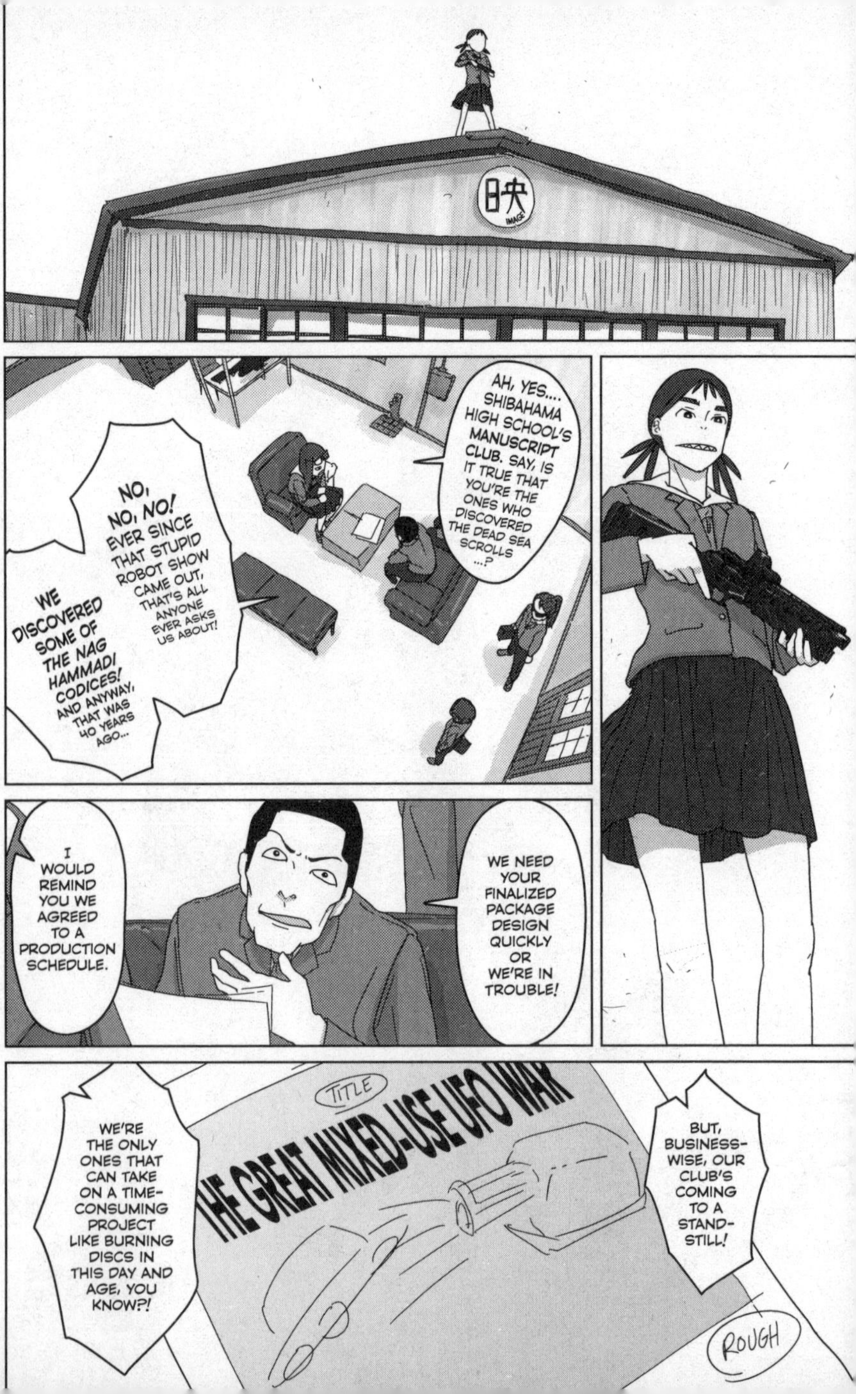

映
IMAGE
AH, YES.... SHIBAHAMA HIGH SCHOOL'S MANUSCRIPT CLUB. SAY, IS IT TRUE THAT YOU'RE THE ONES WHO DISCOVERED THE DEAD SEA SCROLLS ...?
NO, NO, NO! EVER SINCE THAT STUPID ROBOT SHOW CAME OUT, THAT'S ALL ANYONE EVER ASKS US ABOUT!
WE DISCOVERED SOME OF THE NAG HAMMADI CODICES! AND ANYWAY, THAT WAS 40 YEARS AGO...
WE NEED YOUR FINALIZED PACKAGE DESIGN QUICKLY OR WE'RE IN TROUBLE!
I WOULD REMIND YOU WE AGREED TO A PRODUCTION SCHEDULE.
BUT, BUSINESS-WISE, OUR CLUB'S COMING TO A STAND-STILL!
TITLE
THE GREAT MIXED-USE UFO WAR
WE'RE THE ONLY ONES THAT CAN TAKE ON A TIME-CONSUMING PROJECT LIKE BURNING DISCS IN THIS DAY AND AGE, YOU KNOW?!
ROUGH

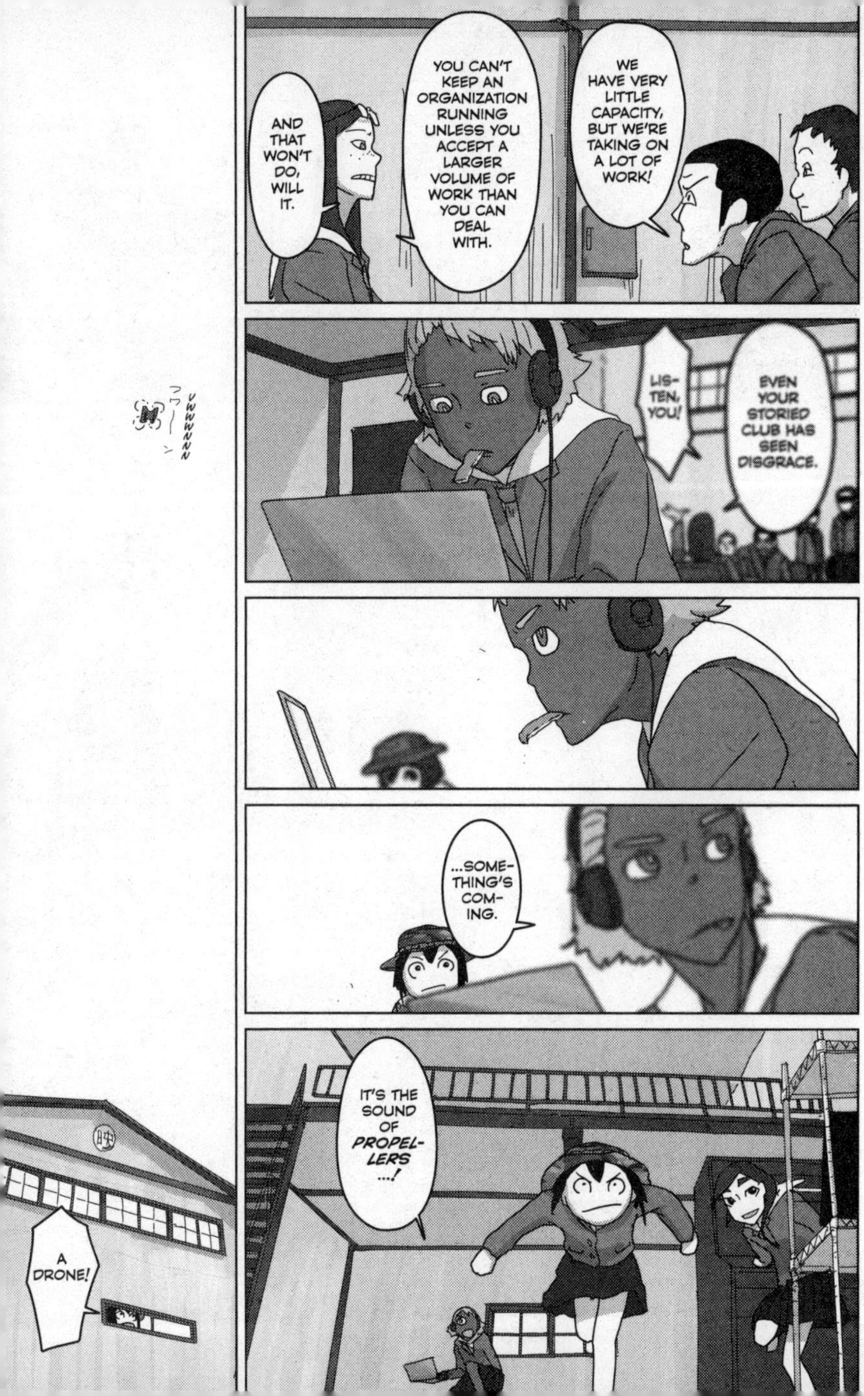
WE HAVE VERY LITTLE CAPACITY, BUT WE'RE TAKING ON A LOT OF WORK!
YOU CAN'T KEEP AN ORGANIZATION RUNNING UNLESS YOU ACCEPT A LARGER VOLUME OF WORK THAN YOU CAN DEAL WITH.
AND THAT WON'T DO, WILL IT.
EVEN YOUR STORIED CLUB HAS SEEN DISGRACE.
LIS-TEN, YOU!
...SOME-THING'S COM-ING.
IT'S THE SOUND OF *PROPEL-LERS*...!
VWWWNNN
A DRONE!

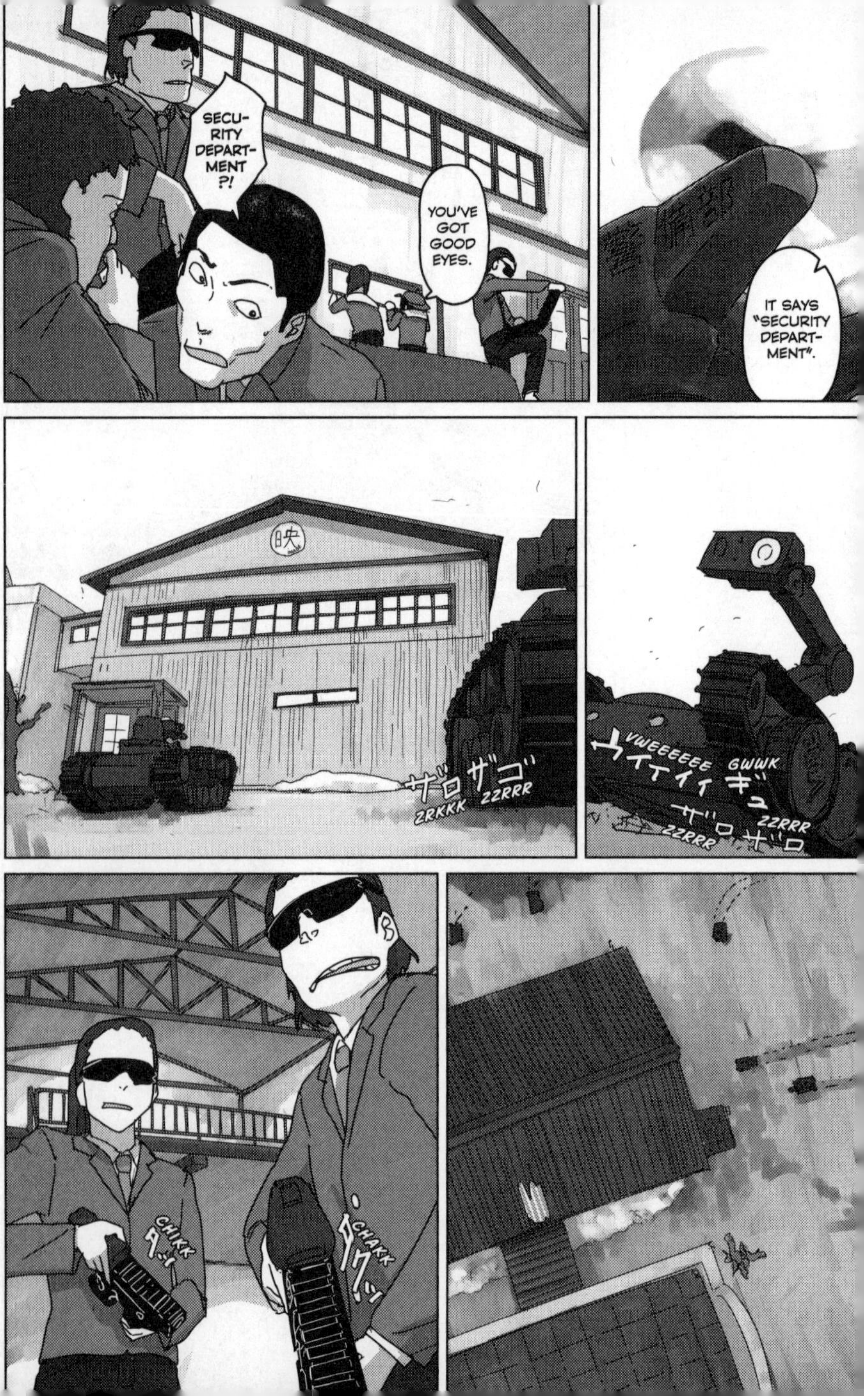
IT SAYS "SECURITY DEPARTMENT".
SECURITY DEPARTMENT?!
YOU'VE GOT GOOD EYES.
VWEEEEEEE ウィィィ
GWWK ギュ
ZZRRR ZZRRR ザロザロ
ザロザゴ ZRKKK ZZRRR
CHAKK タクッ
CHIKK タッ

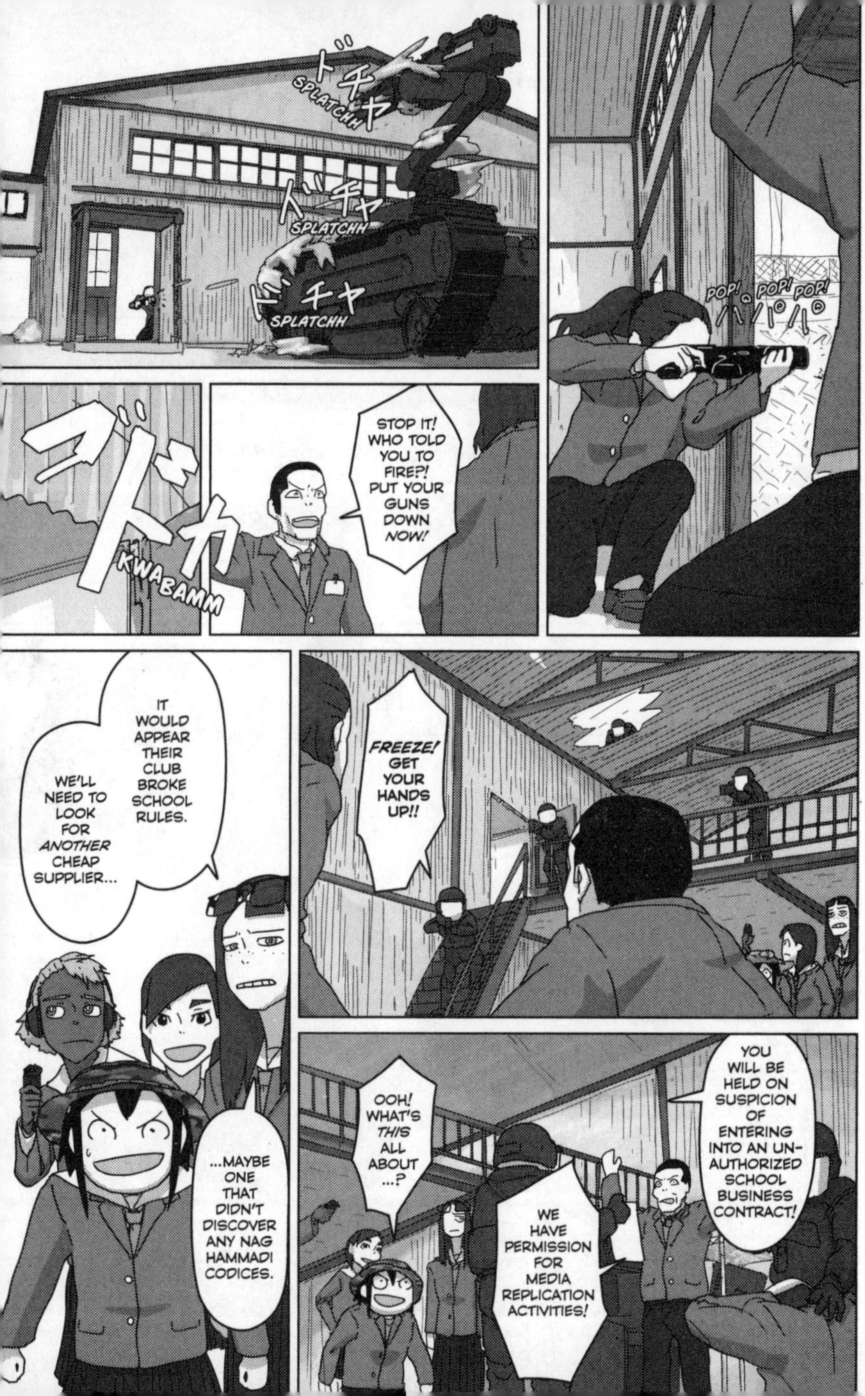
POP! POP! POP!
SPLATCHH
SPLATCHH
SPLATCHH
STOP IT! WHO TOLD YOU TO FIRE?! PUT YOUR GUNS DOWN *NOW!*
KWABAMM
FREEZE! GET YOUR HANDS UP!!
YOU WILL BE HELD ON SUSPICION OF ENTERING INTO AN UN-AUTHORIZED SCHOOL BUSINESS CONTRACT!
OOH! WHAT'S *THIS* ALL ABOUT ...?
WE HAVE PERMISSION FOR MEDIA REPLICATION ACTIVITIES!
IT WOULD APPEAR THEIR CLUB BROKE SCHOOL RULES.
WE'LL NEED TO LOOK FOR *ANOTHER* CHEAP SUPPLIER...
...MAYBE ONE THAT DIDN'T DISCOVER ANY NAG HAMMADI CODICES.

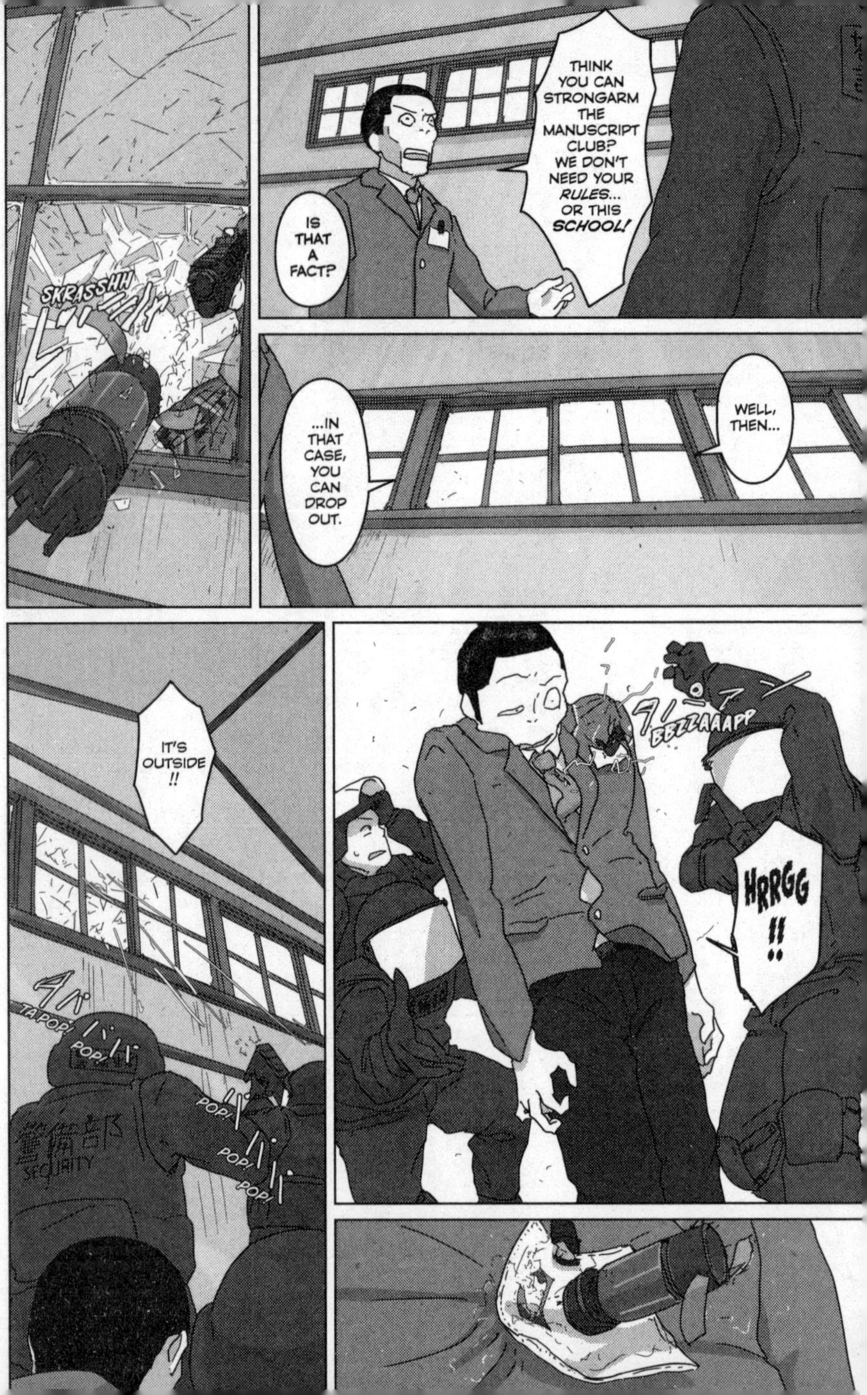
THINK YOU CAN STRONGARM THE MANUSCRIPT CLUB? WE DON'T NEED YOUR *RULES*... OR THIS ***SCHOOL!***
IS THAT A FACT?
WELL, THEN...
...IN THAT CASE, YOU CAN DROP OUT.
SKRASSHH
BBZZAAAPP
HRRGG!!
IT'S OUTSIDE!!
TA POP!
POP!
POP!
POP!
POP!
警備部
SECURITY

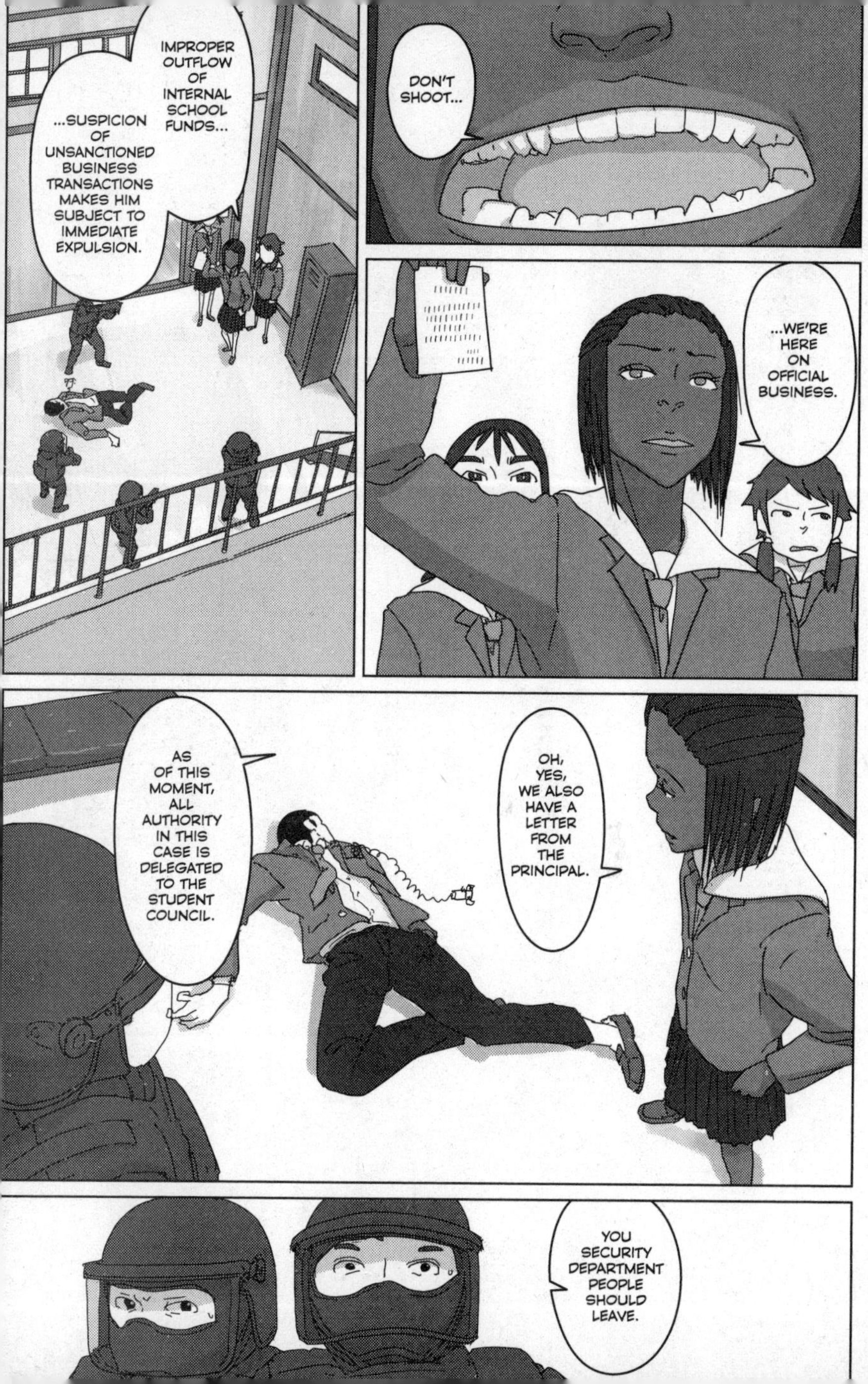
DON'T SHOOT...
...WE'RE HERE ON OFFICIAL BUSINESS.
IMPROPER OUTFLOW OF INTERNAL SCHOOL FUNDS...
...SUSPICION OF UNSANCTIONED BUSINESS TRANSACTIONS MAKES HIM SUBJECT TO IMMEDIATE EXPULSION.
OH, YES, WE ALSO HAVE A LETTER FROM THE PRINCIPAL.
AS OF THIS MOMENT, ALL AUTHORITY IN THIS CASE IS DELEGATED TO THE STUDENT COUNCIL.
YOU SECURITY DEPARTMENT PEOPLE SHOULD LEAVE.

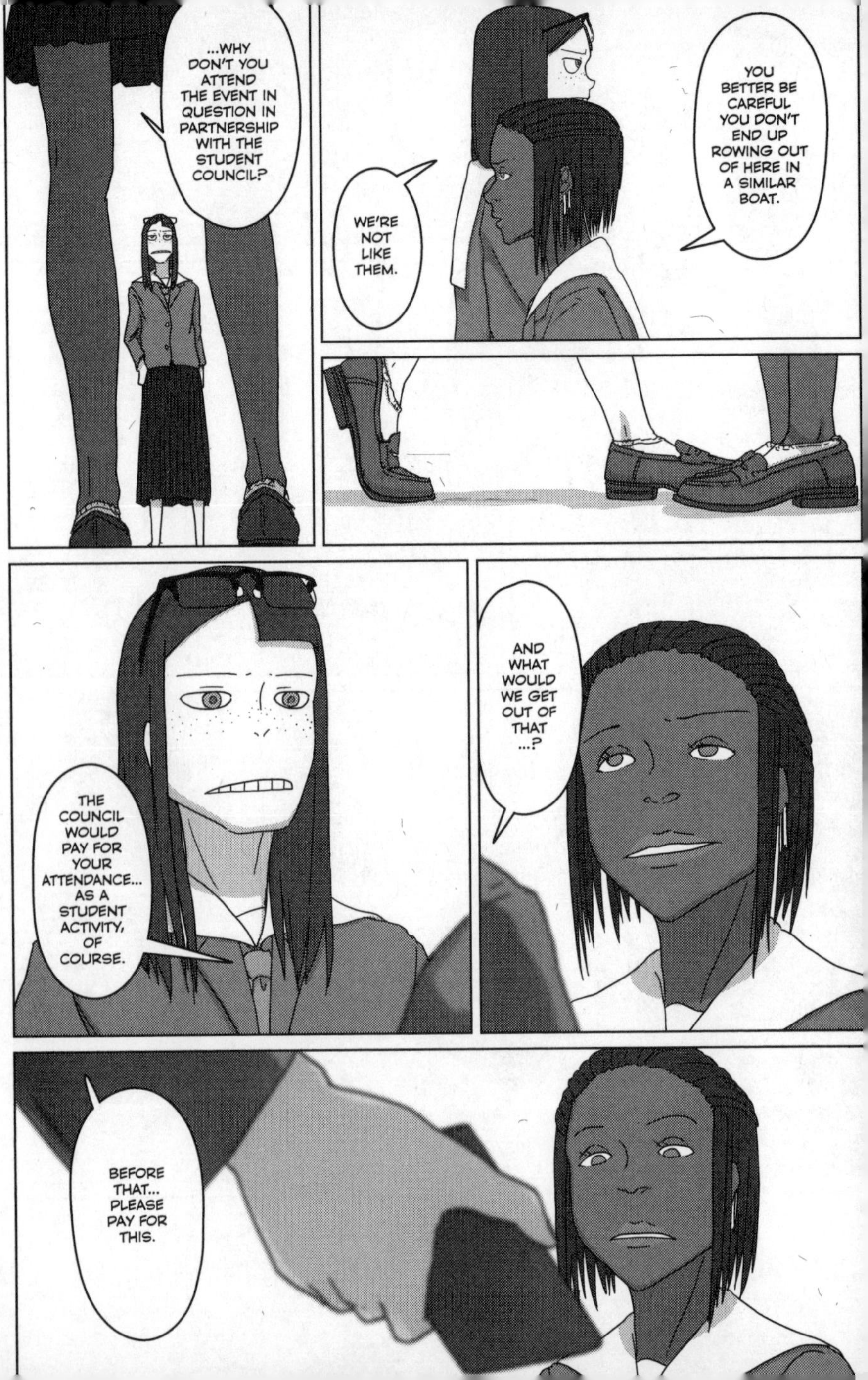
YOU BETTER BE CAREFUL YOU DON'T END UP ROWING OUT OF HERE IN A SIMILAR BOAT.
WE'RE NOT LIKE THEM.
...WHY DON'T YOU ATTEND THE EVENT IN QUESTION IN PARTNERSHIP WITH THE STUDENT COUNCIL?
AND WHAT WOULD WE GET OUT OF THAT ...?
THE COUNCIL WOULD PAY FOR YOUR ATTENDANCE... AS A STUDENT ACTIVITY, OF COURSE.
BEFORE THAT... PLEASE PAY FOR THIS.

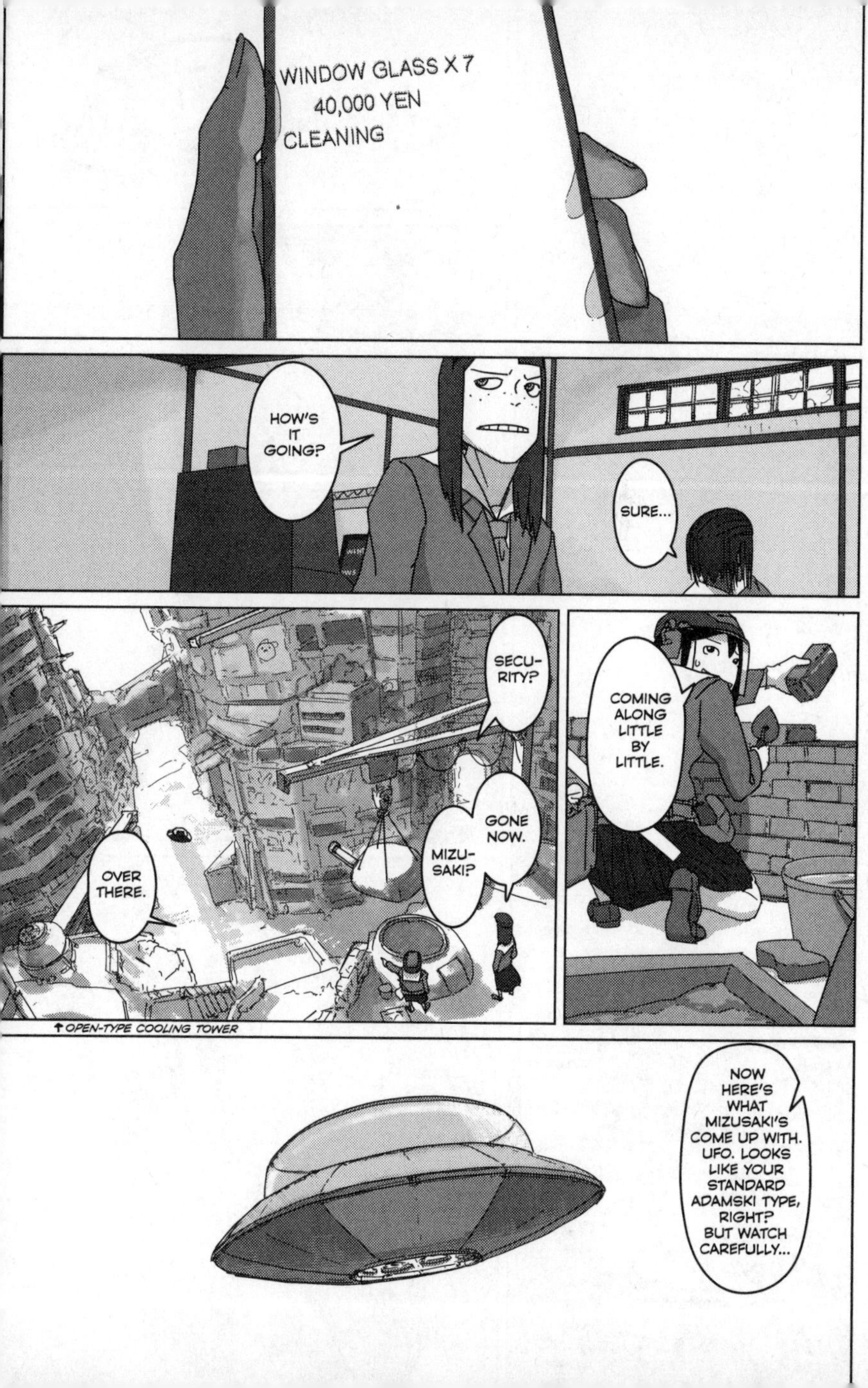
WINDOW GLASS X 7
40,000 YEN
CLEANING
HOW'S IT GOING?
SURE...
COMING ALONG LITTLE BY LITTLE.
SECU-RITY?
GONE NOW.
MIZU-SAKI?
OVER THERE.
↑OPEN-TYPE COOLING TOWER
NOW HERE'S WHAT MIZUSAKI'S COME UP WITH. UFO. LOOKS LIKE YOUR STANDARD ADAMSKI TYPE, RIGHT? BUT WATCH CAREFULLY...

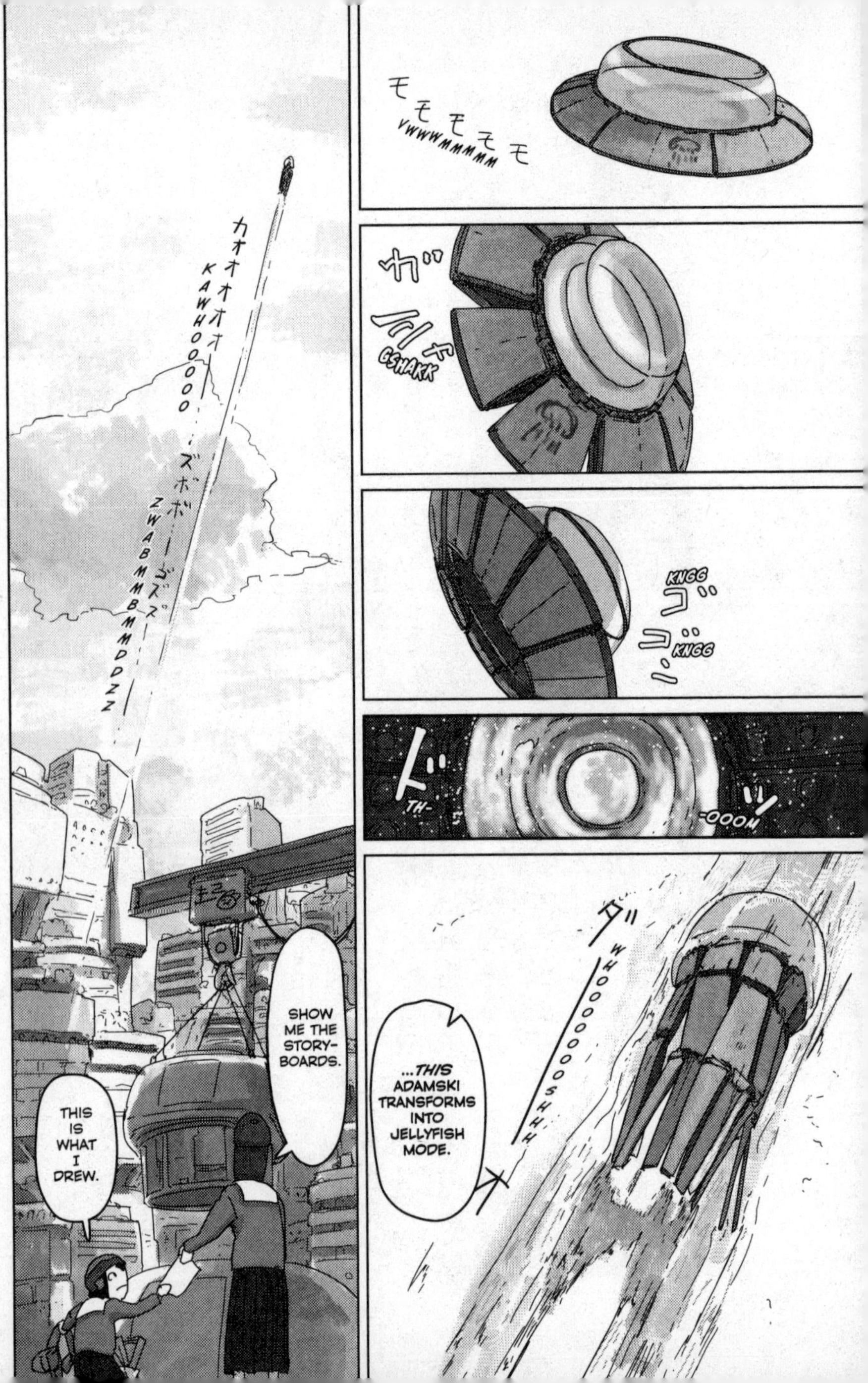

モモモモモ
VWWWMMMMMM
ガシャ
GSHAKK
ゴゴ
KNGG
KNGG
ドン
TH-
-OOOM
...THIS ADAMSKI TRANSFORMS INTO JELLYFISH MODE.
ダッ
WHOOOOOOOOSHHH
カオオオオオ
KAWHOOOOOO
ズボボーゴズズ
ZWABMMBMMDDZZ
SHOW ME THE STORY-BOARDS.
THIS IS WHAT I DREW.

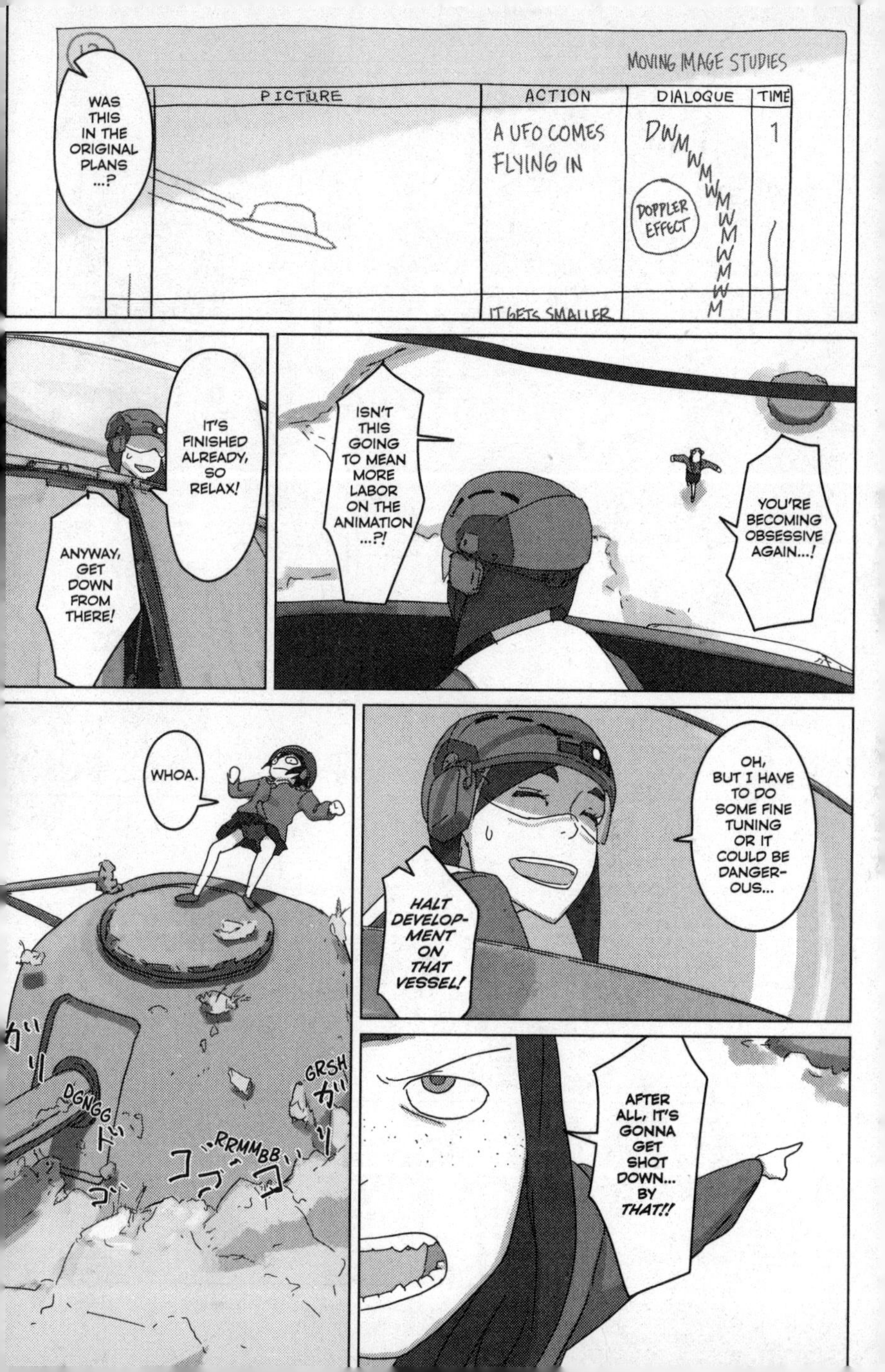
MOVING IMAGE STUDIES
PICTURE
ACTION
DIALOGUE
TIME
A UFO COMES FLYING IN
DWMMMMMMMMMMM
DOPPLER EFFECT
1
IT GETS SMALLER
WAS THIS IN THE ORIGINAL PLANS ...?
YOU'RE BECOMING OBSESSIVE AGAIN...!
ISN'T THIS GOING TO MEAN MORE LABOR ON THE ANIMATION ...?!
IT'S FINISHED ALREADY, SO RELAX!
ANYWAY, GET DOWN FROM THERE!
OH, BUT I HAVE TO DO SOME FINE TUNING OR IT COULD BE DANGER-OUS...
HALT DEVELOP-MENT ON THAT VESSEL!
AFTER ALL, IT'S GONNA GET SHOT DOWN... BY THAT!!
WHOA.
GRSH
DGNGG
RRMMBB

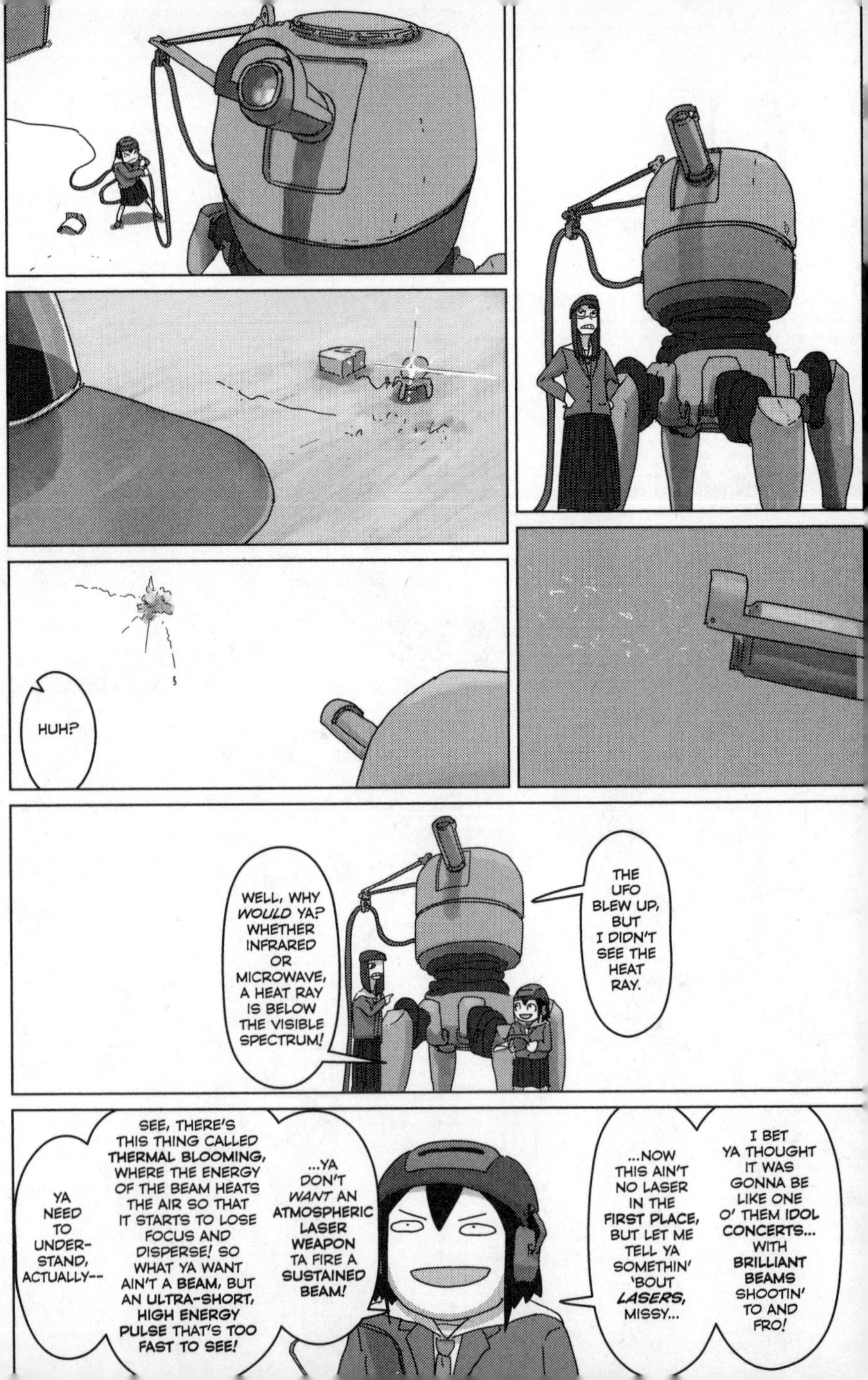
HUH?
THE UFO BLEW UP, BUT I DIDN'T SEE THE HEAT RAY.
WELL, WHY *WOULD* YA? WHETHER INFRARED OR MICROWAVE, A HEAT RAY IS BELOW THE VISIBLE SPECTRUM!
I BET YA THOUGHT IT WAS GONNA BE LIKE ONE O' THEM IDOL CONCERTS... WITH **BRILLIANT BEAMS** SHOOTIN' TO AND FRO!
...NOW THIS AIN'T NO LASER IN THE **FIRST PLACE**, BUT LET ME TELL YA SOMETHIN' 'BOUT ***LASERS***, MISSY...
...YA DON'T *WANT* AN **ATMOSPHERIC LASER WEAPON** TA FIRE A **SUSTAINED BEAM!**
SEE, THERE'S THIS THING CALLED **THERMAL BLOOMING**, WHERE THE ENERGY OF THE BEAM HEATS THE AIR SO THAT IT STARTS TO LOSE FOCUS AND DISPERSE! SO WHAT YA WANT AIN'T A BEAM, BUT AN **ULTRA-SHORT, HIGH ENERGY PULSE** THAT'S TOO FAST TO SEE!
YA NEED TO UNDER-STAND, ACTUALLY--

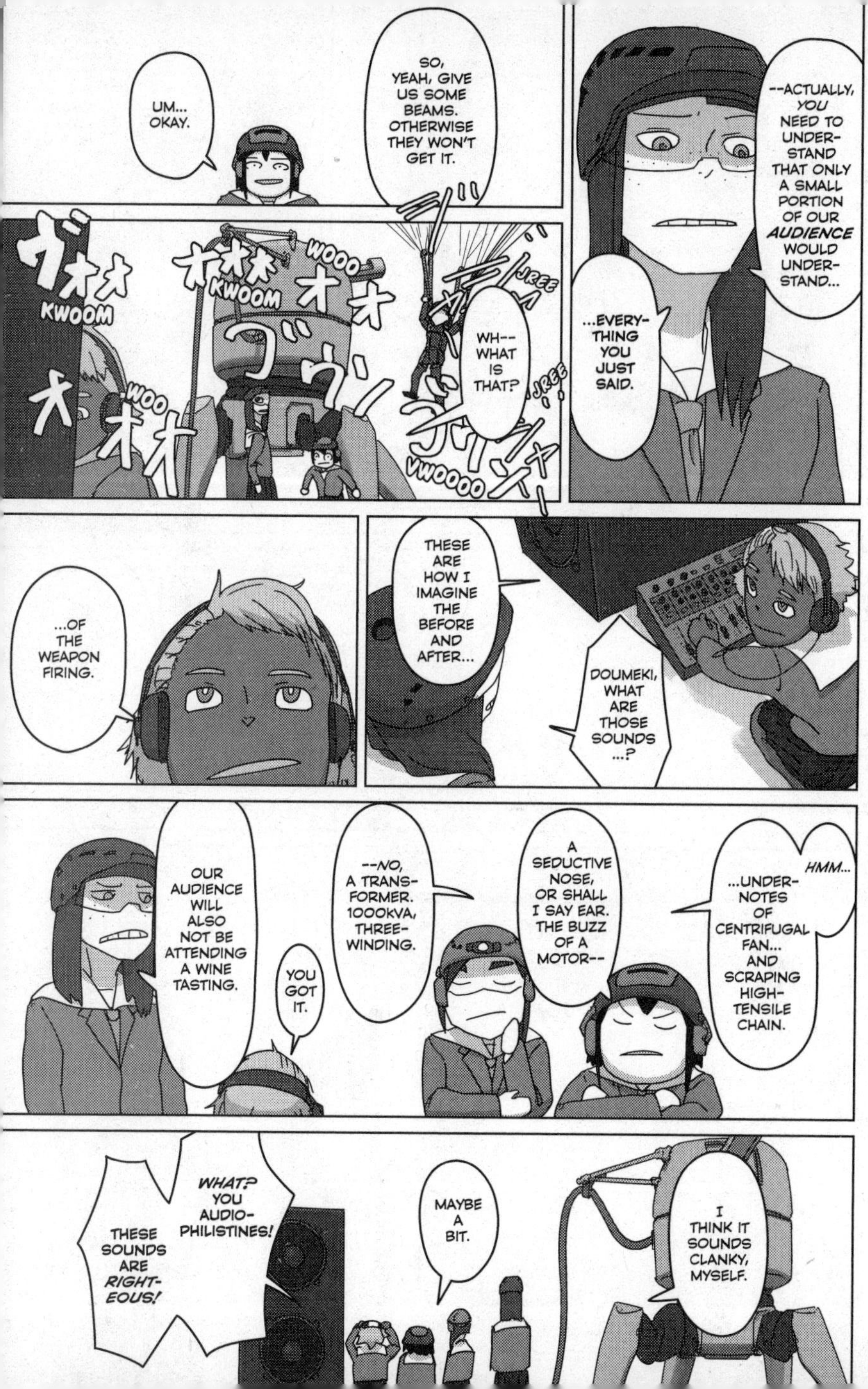
--ACTUALLY, *YOU* NEED TO UNDER-STAND THAT ONLY A SMALL PORTION OF OUR ***AUDIENCE*** WOULD UNDER-STAND...
...EVERY-THING YOU JUST SAID.
SO, YEAH, GIVE US SOME BEAMS. OTHERWISE THEY WON'T GET IT.
UM... OKAY.
JREE
WOOO
KWOOM
KWOOM
WH-- WHAT IS THAT?
JREE
WOO
VWOOOO
DOUMEKI, WHAT ARE THOSE SOUNDS ...?
THESE ARE HOW I IMAGINE THE BEFORE AND AFTER...
...OF THE WEAPON FIRING.
HMM...
...UNDER-NOTES OF CENTRIFUGAL FAN... AND SCRAPING HIGH-TENSILE CHAIN.
A SEDUCTIVE NOSE, OR SHALL I SAY EAR. THE BUZZ OF A MOTOR--
--*NO,* A TRANS-FORMER. 1000KVA, THREE-WINDING.
OUR AUDIENCE WILL ALSO NOT BE ATTENDING A WINE TASTING.
YOU GOT IT.
I THINK IT SOUNDS CLANKY, MYSELF.
MAYBE A BIT.
WHAT? YOU AUDIO-PHILISTINES!
THESE SOUNDS ARE ***RIGHT-EOUS!***

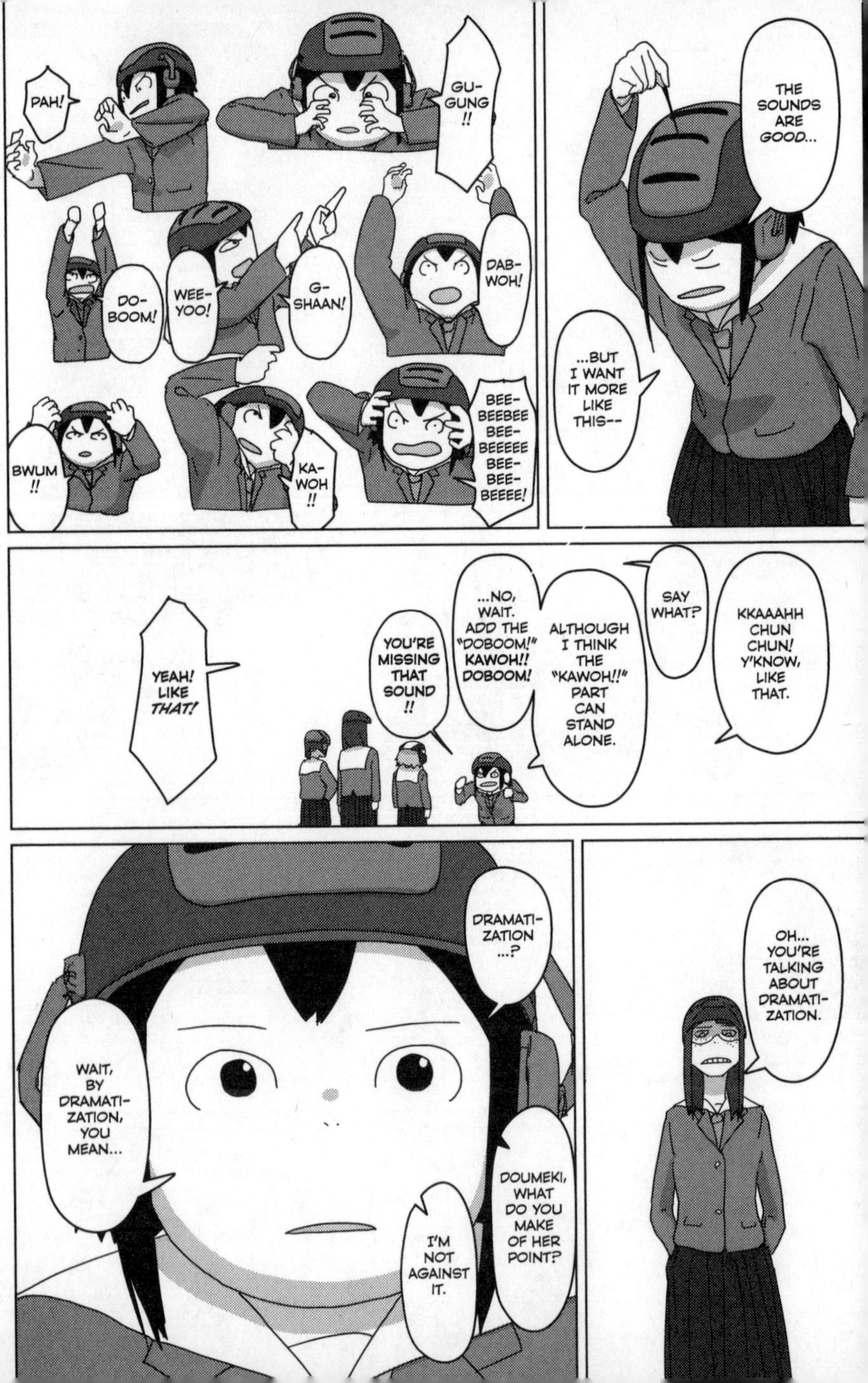
THE SOUNDS ARE GOOD...
...BUT I WANT IT MORE LIKE THIS--
GU-GUNG!!
PAH!
DAB-WOH!
G-SHAAN!
WEE-YOO!
DO-BOOM!
BEE-BEEBEE BEE-BEEEEE BEE-BEE-BEEEE!
KA-WOH!!
BWUM!!
KKAAAHH CHUN CHUN! Y'KNOW, LIKE THAT.
SAY WHAT?
ALTHOUGH I THINK THE "KAWOH!!" PART CAN STAND ALONE.
...NO, WAIT. ADD THE "DOBOOM!" KAWOH!! DOBOOM!
YOU'RE MISSING THAT SOUND!!
YEAH! LIKE *THAT!*
OH... YOU'RE TALKING ABOUT DRAMATI-ZATION.
DRAMATI-ZATION...?
WAIT, BY DRAMATI-ZATION, YOU MEAN...
DOUMEKI, WHAT DO YOU MAKE OF HER POINT?
I'M NOT AGAINST IT.

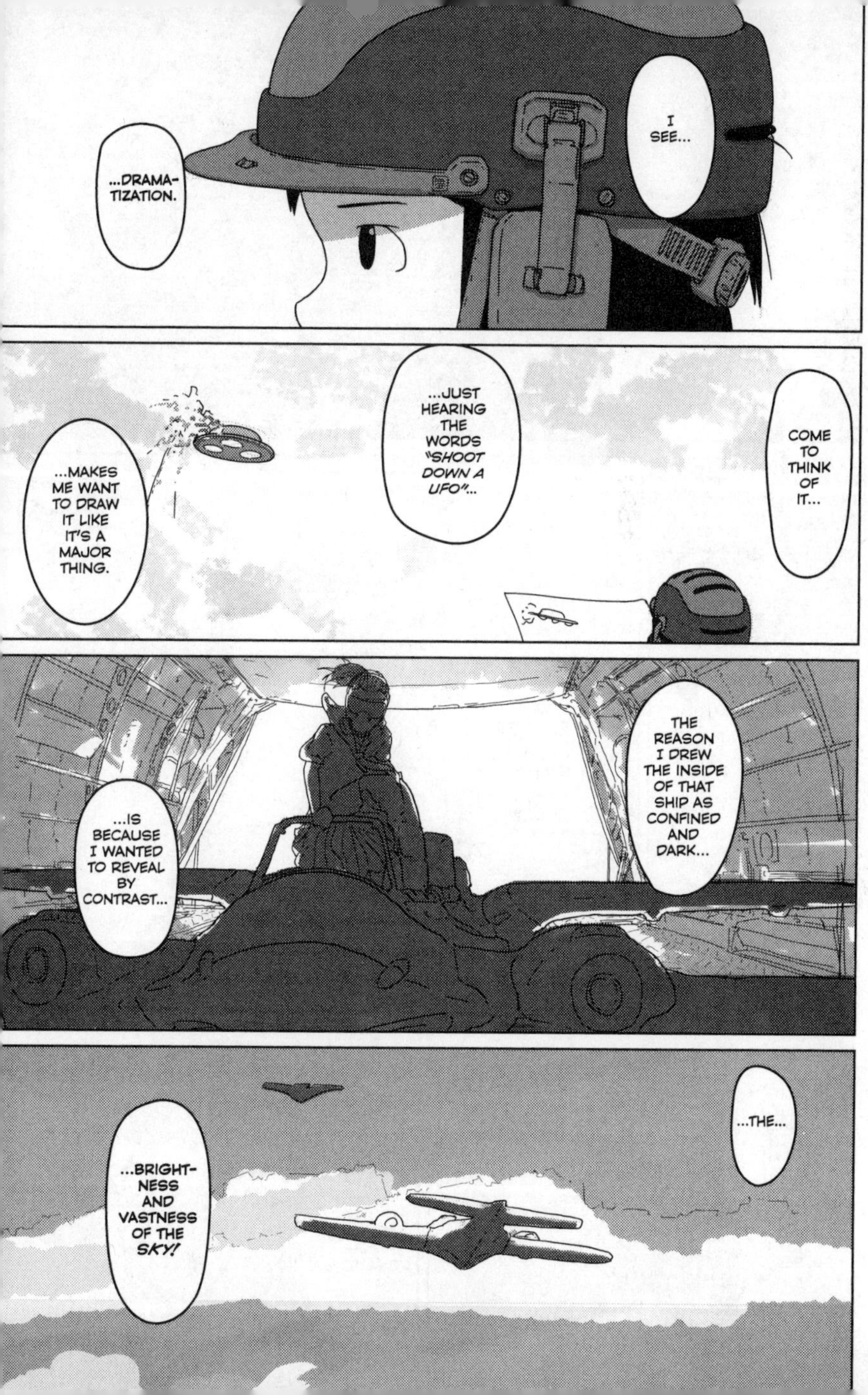
I SEE...
...DRAMATIZATION.
COME TO THINK OF IT...
...JUST HEARING THE WORDS *"SHOOT DOWN A UFO"*...
...MAKES ME WANT TO DRAW IT LIKE IT'S A MAJOR THING.
THE REASON I DREW THE INSIDE OF THAT SHIP AS CONFINED AND DARK...
...IS BECAUSE I WANTED TO REVEAL BY CONTRAST...
...THE...
...BRIGHTNESS AND VASTNESS OF THE *SKY!*

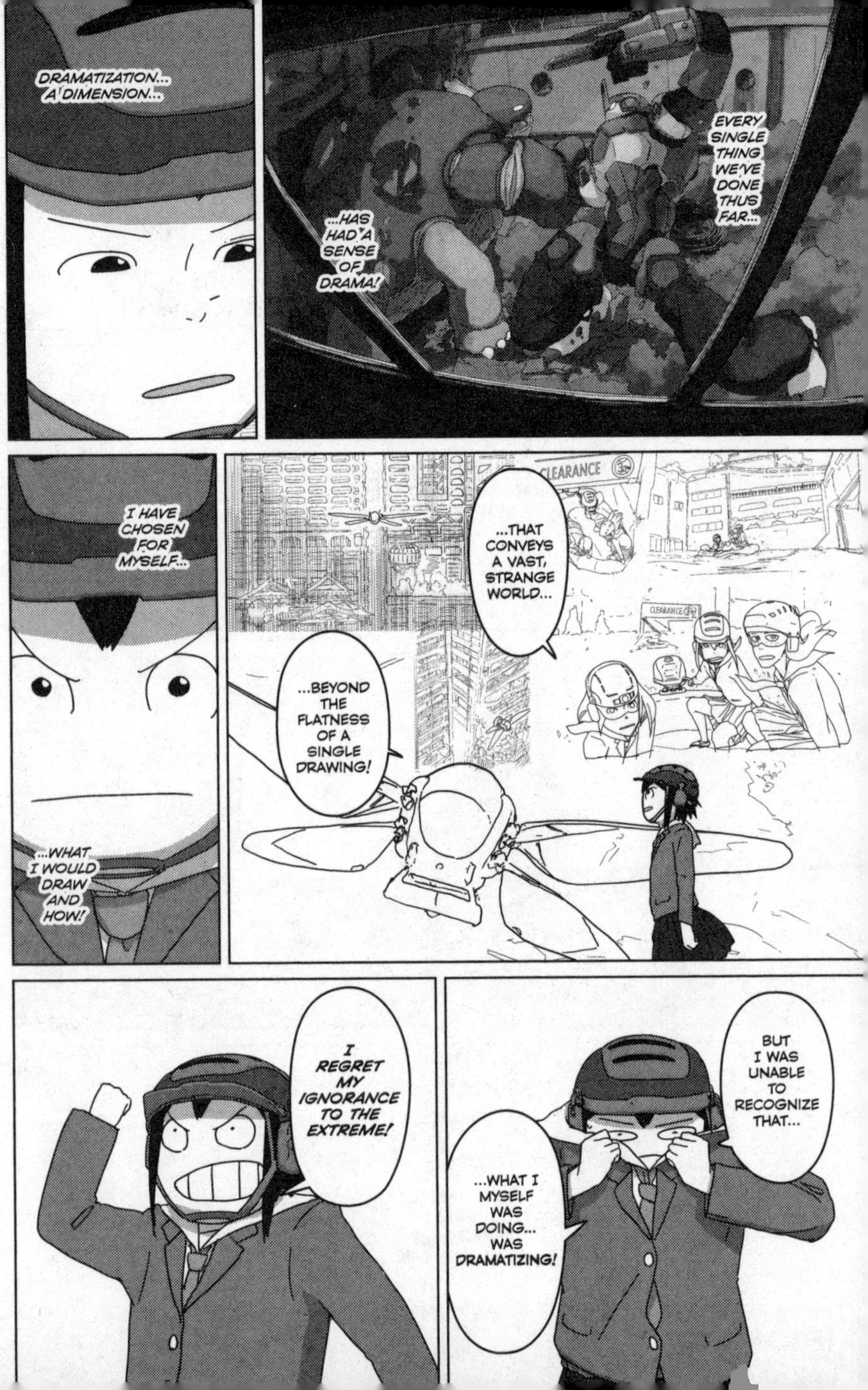
EVERY SINGLE THING WE'VE DONE THUS FAR...
...HAS HAD A SENSE OF DRAMA!
DRAMATIZATION... A DIMENSION...
CLEARANCE
...THAT CONVEYS A VAST, STRANGE WORLD...
CLEARANCE
...BEYOND THE FLATNESS OF A SINGLE DRAWING!
I HAVE CHOSEN FOR MYSELF...
...WHAT I WOULD DRAW AND HOW!
BUT I WAS UNABLE TO RECOGNIZE THAT...
...WHAT I MYSELF WAS DOING... WAS DRAMATIZING!
I REGRET MY IGNORANCE TO THE EXTREME!

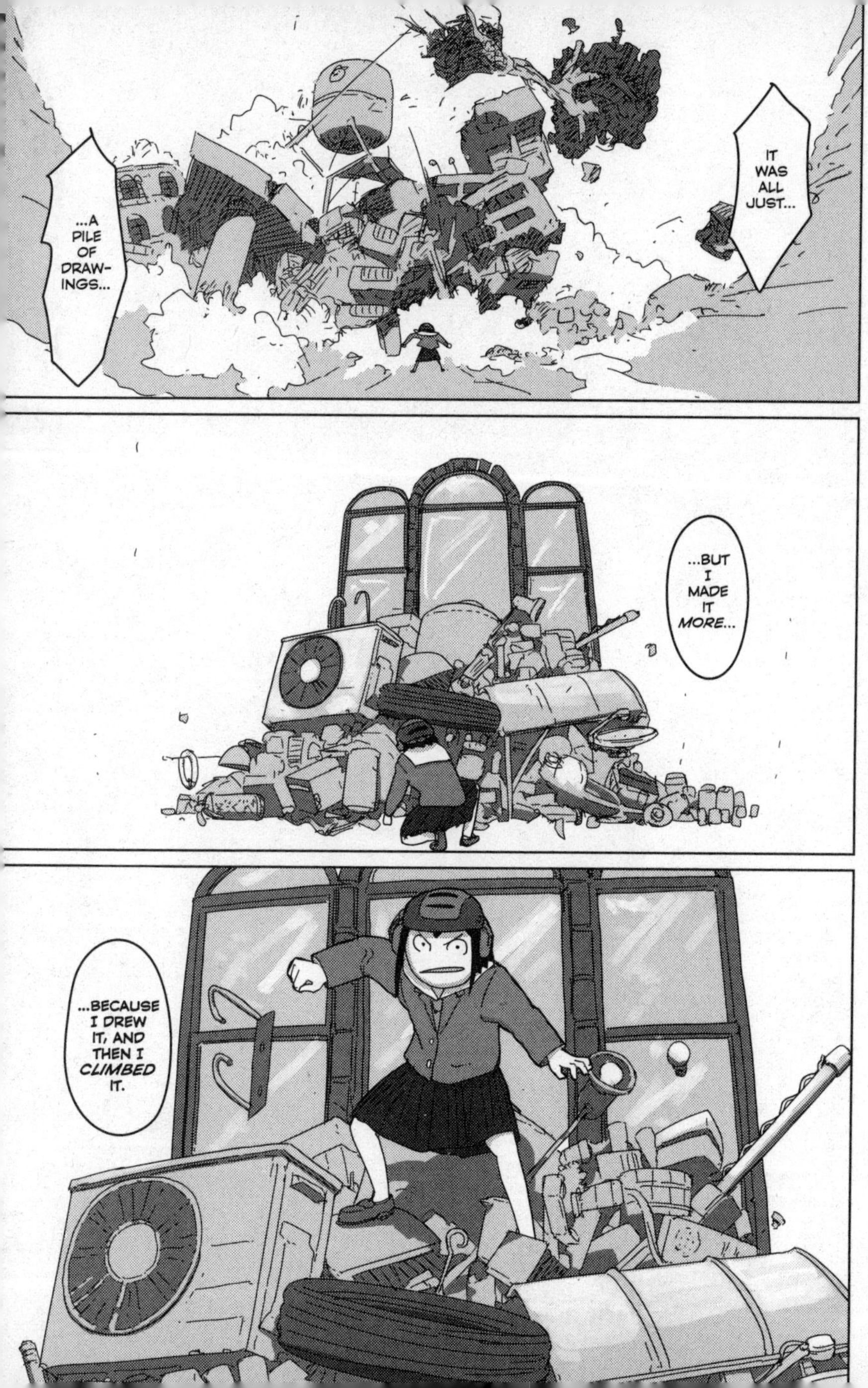
IT WAS ALL JUST...
...A PILE OF DRAWINGS...
...BUT I MADE IT *MORE*...
...BECAUSE I DREW IT, AND THEN I *CLIMBED* IT.

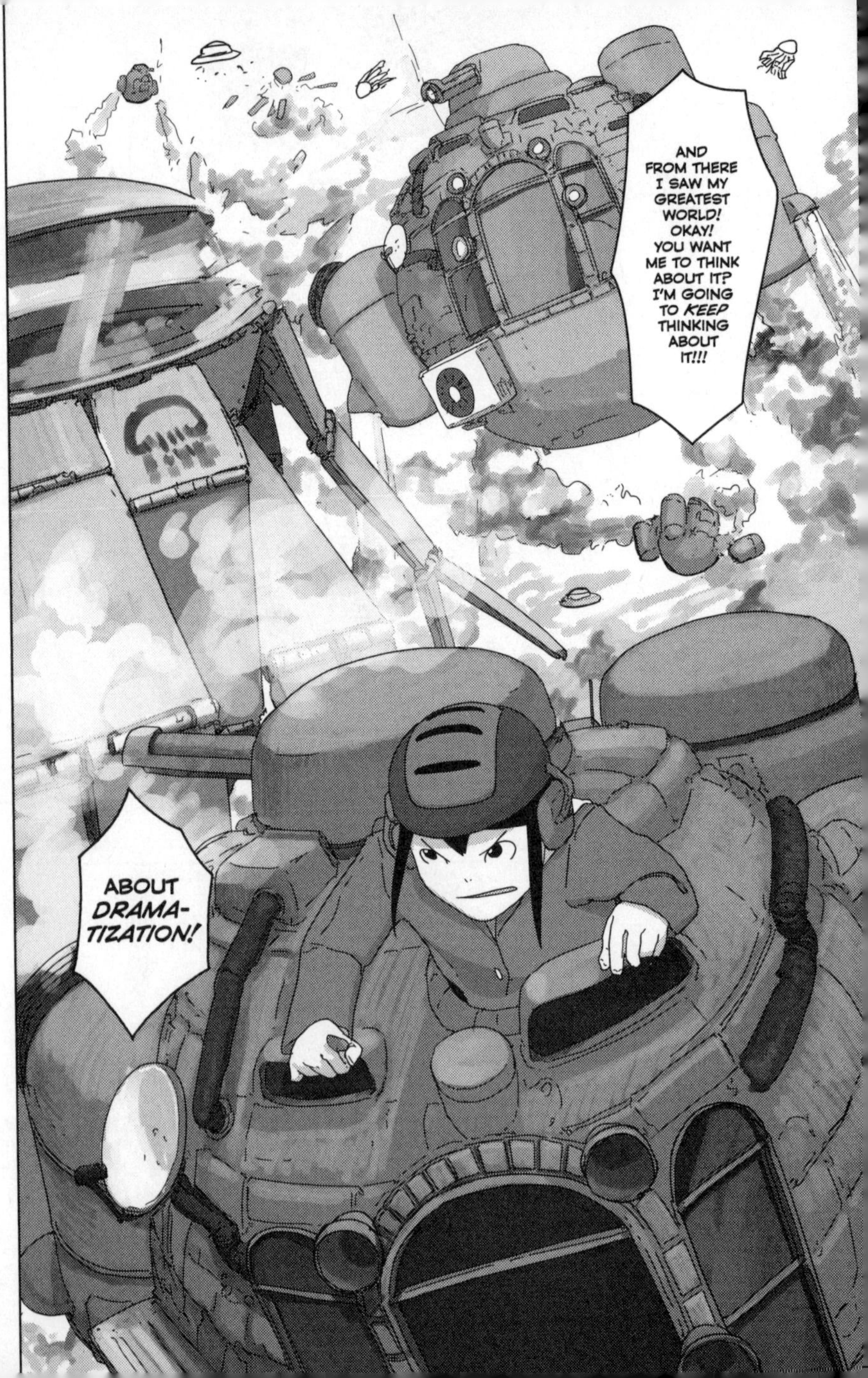
AND FROM THERE I SAW MY GREATEST WORLD! OKAY! YOU WANT ME TO THINK ABOUT IT? I'M GOING TO *KEEP* THINKING ABOUT IT!!!
ABOUT *DRAMA-TIZATION!*

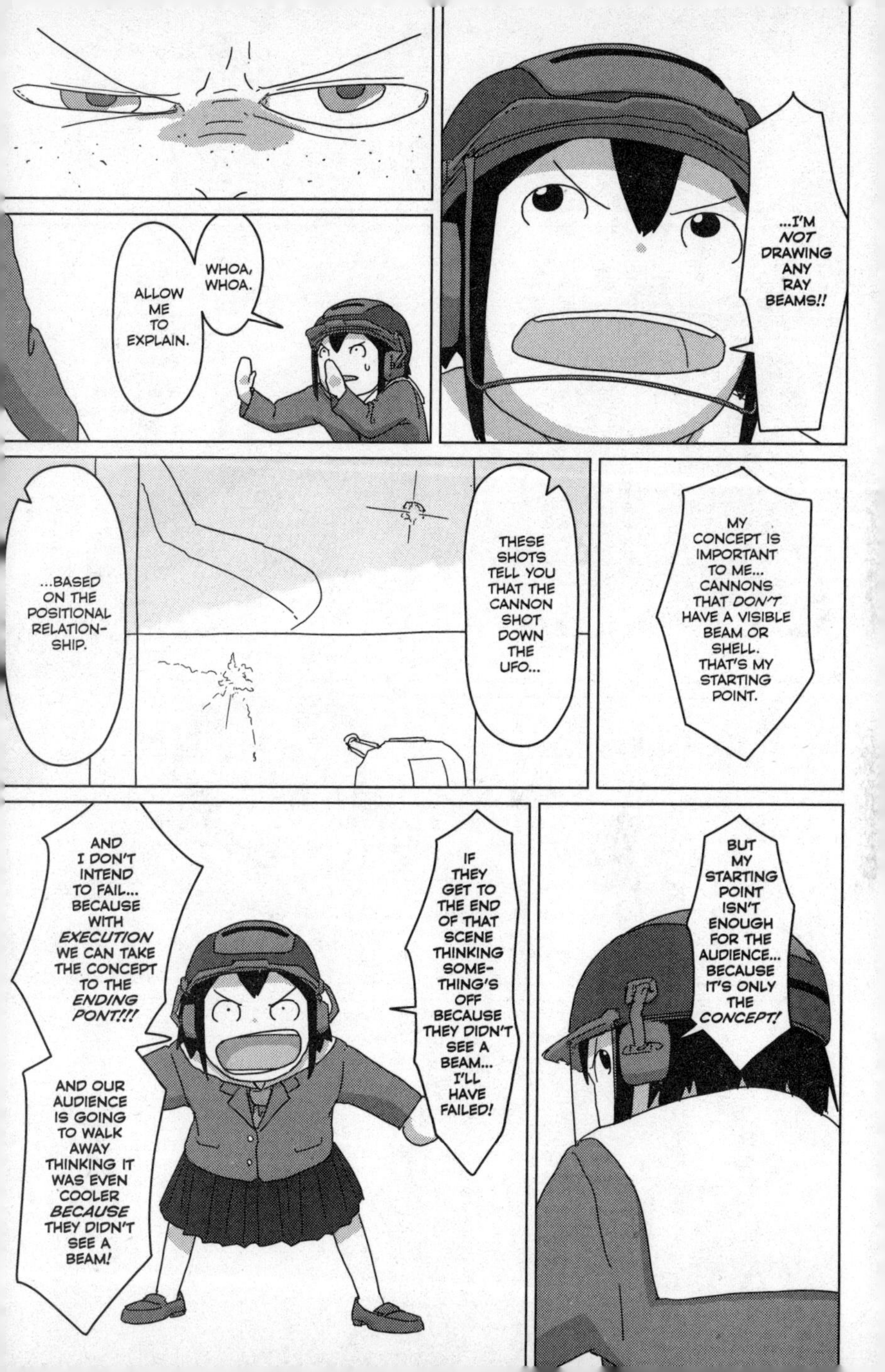
...I'M *NOT* DRAWING ANY RAY BEAMS!!
WHOA, WHOA.
ALLOW ME TO EXPLAIN.
MY CONCEPT IS IMPORTANT TO ME... CANNONS THAT *DON'T* HAVE A VISIBLE BEAM OR SHELL. THAT'S MY STARTING POINT.
THESE SHOTS TELL YOU THAT THE CANNON SHOT DOWN THE UFO...
...BASED ON THE POSITIONAL RELATION-SHIP.
BUT MY STARTING POINT ISN'T ENOUGH FOR THE AUDIENCE... BECAUSE IT'S ONLY THE *CONCEPT!*
IF THEY GET TO THE END OF THAT SCENE THINKING SOME-THING'S OFF BECAUSE THEY DIDN'T SEE A BEAM... I'LL HAVE FAILED!
AND I DON'T INTEND TO FAIL... BECAUSE WITH *EXECUTION* WE CAN TAKE THE CONCEPT TO THE *ENDING PONT!!!*
AND OUR AUDIENCE IS GOING TO WALK AWAY THINKING IT WAS EVEN COOLER *BECAUSE* THEY DIDN'T SEE A BEAM!

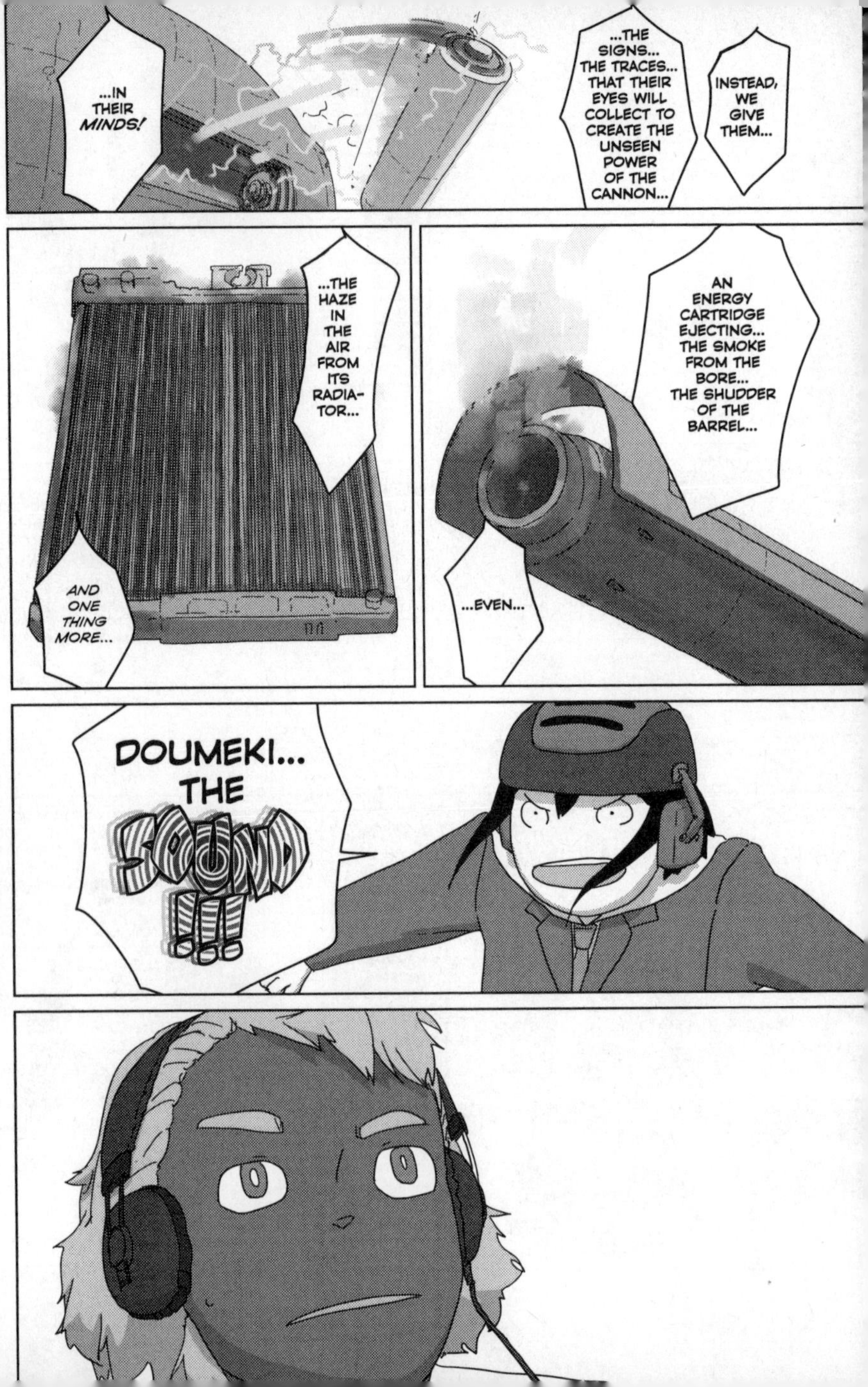
INSTEAD, WE GIVE THEM...
...THE SIGNS... THE TRACES... THAT THEIR EYES WILL COLLECT TO CREATE THE UNSEEN POWER OF THE CANNON...
...IN THEIR *MINDS!*
AN ENERGY CARTRIDGE EJECTING... THE SMOKE FROM THE BORE... THE SHUDDER OF THE BARREL...
...EVEN...
...THE HAZE IN THE AIR FROM ITS RADIATOR...
AND ONE THING MORE...
DOUMEKI... THE SOUND!!!

CHAPTER 23:
SLEEPING ASAKUSA

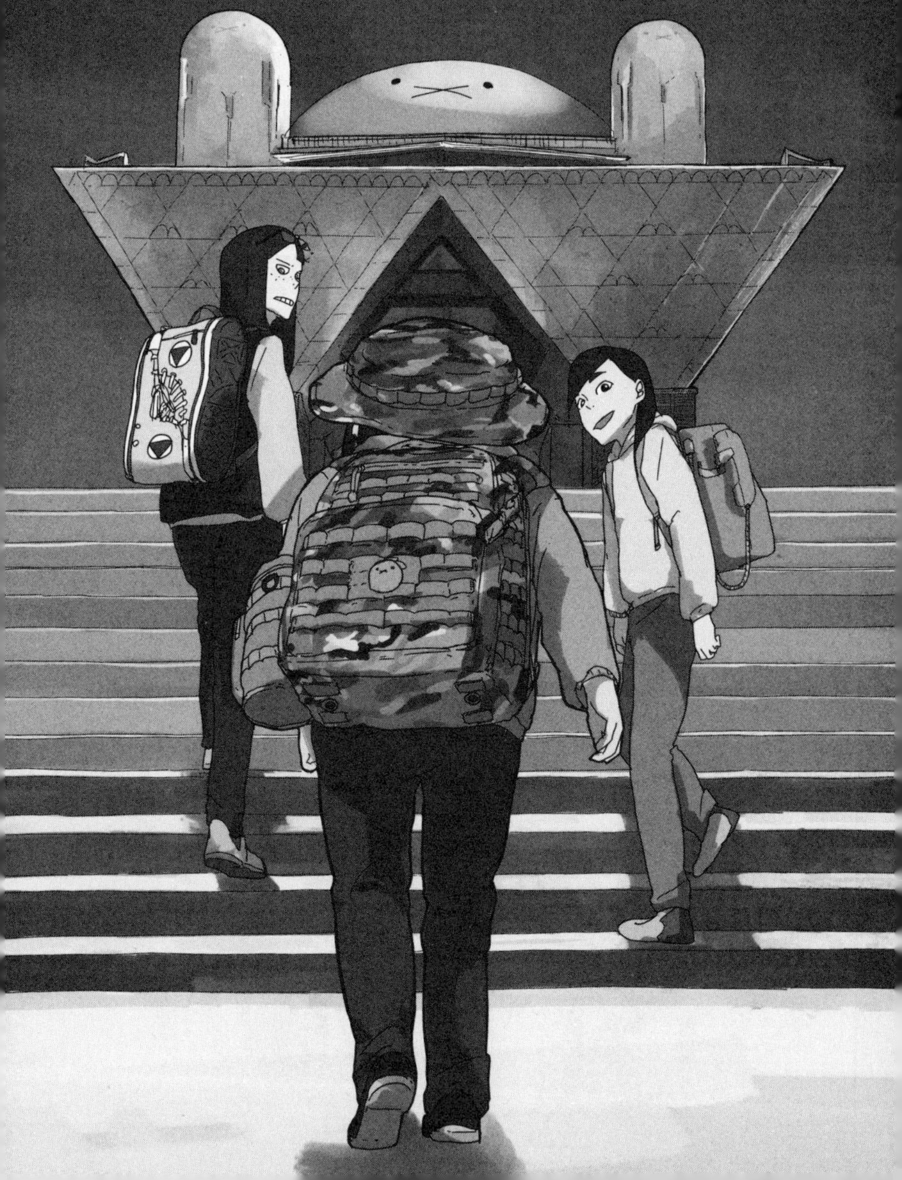

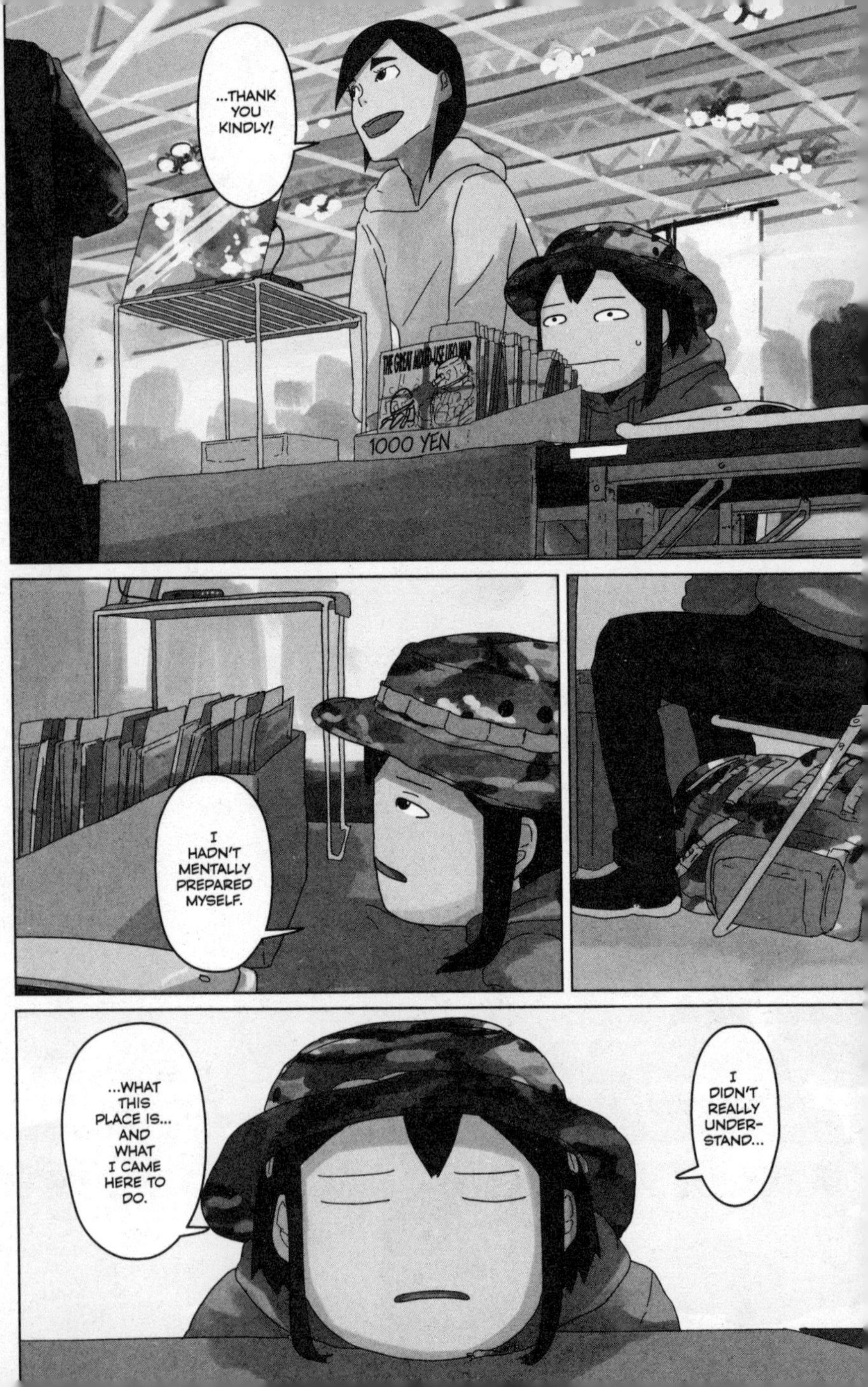
...THANK YOU KINDLY!
THE GREAT MIXED-USE UFO WAR
1000 YEN
I HADN'T MENTALLY PREPARED MYSELF.
I DIDN'T REALLY UNDER-STAND...
...WHAT THIS PLACE IS... AND WHAT I CAME HERE TO DO.

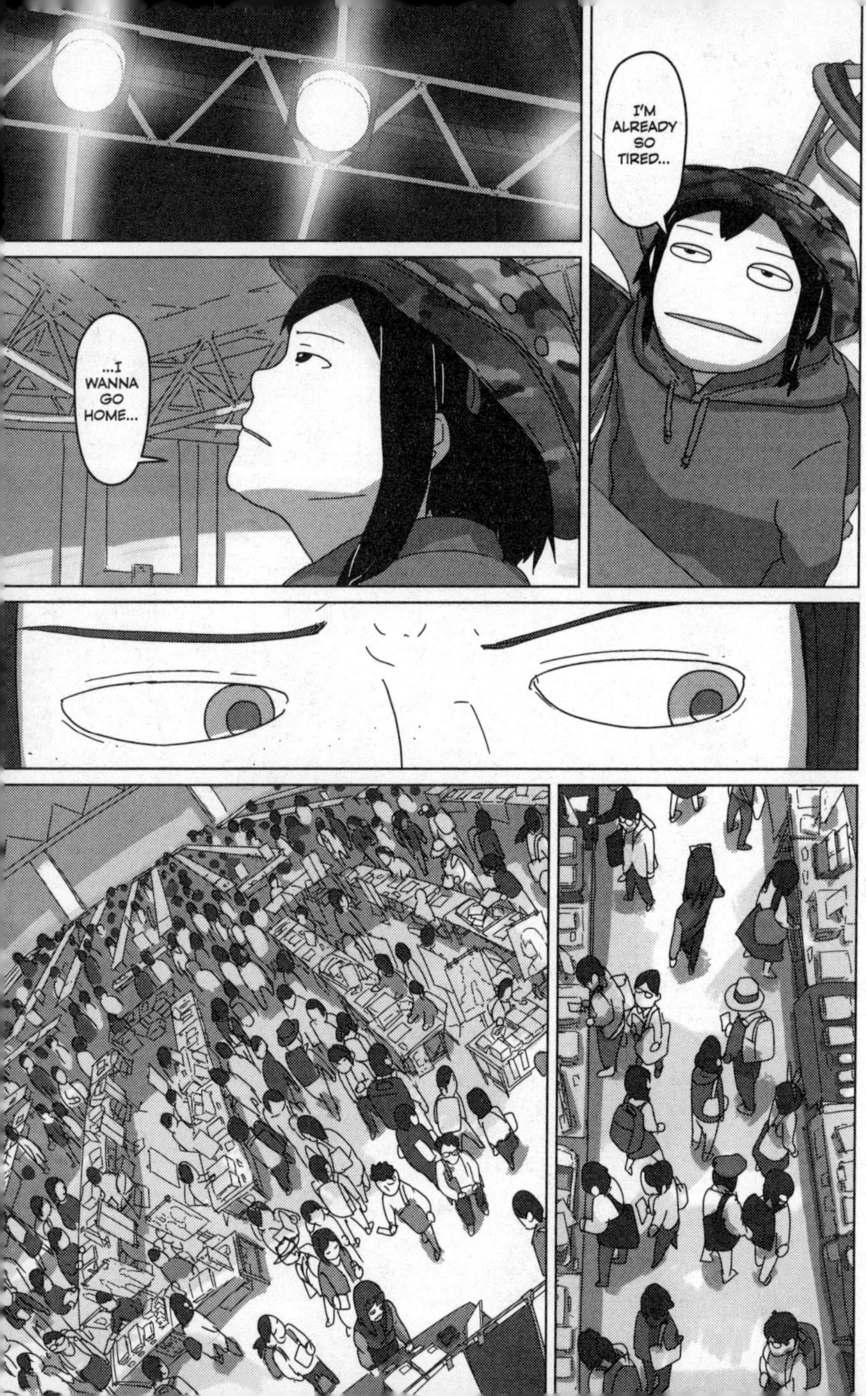
I'M ALREADY SO TIRED...
...I WANNA GO HOME...

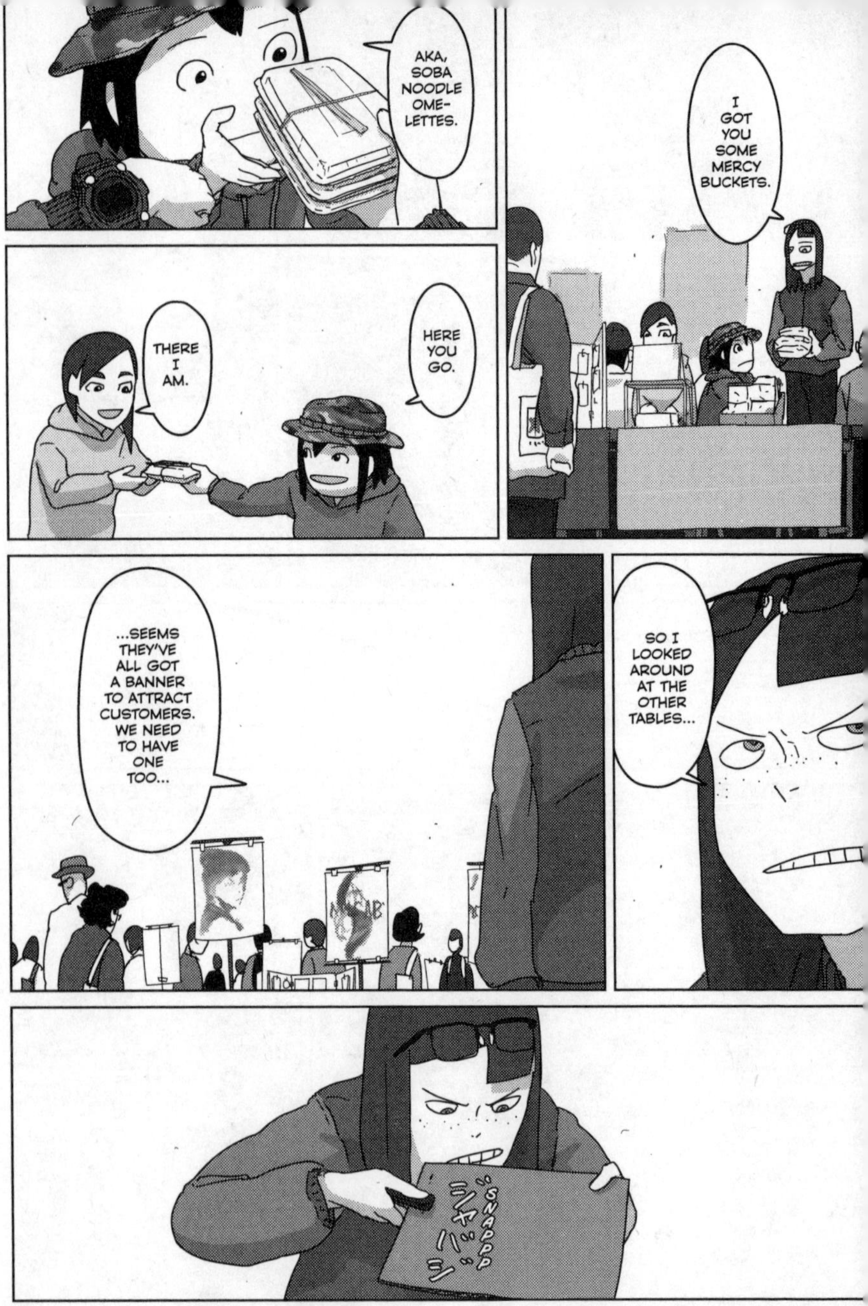
I GOT YOU SOME MERCY BUCKETS.
AKA, SOBA NOODLE OME-LETTES.
HERE YOU GO.
THERE I AM.
SO I LOOKED AROUND AT THE OTHER TABLES...
...SEEMS THEY'VE ALL GOT A BANNER TO ATTRACT CUSTOMERS. WE NEED TO HAVE ONE TOO...
SNAPPP

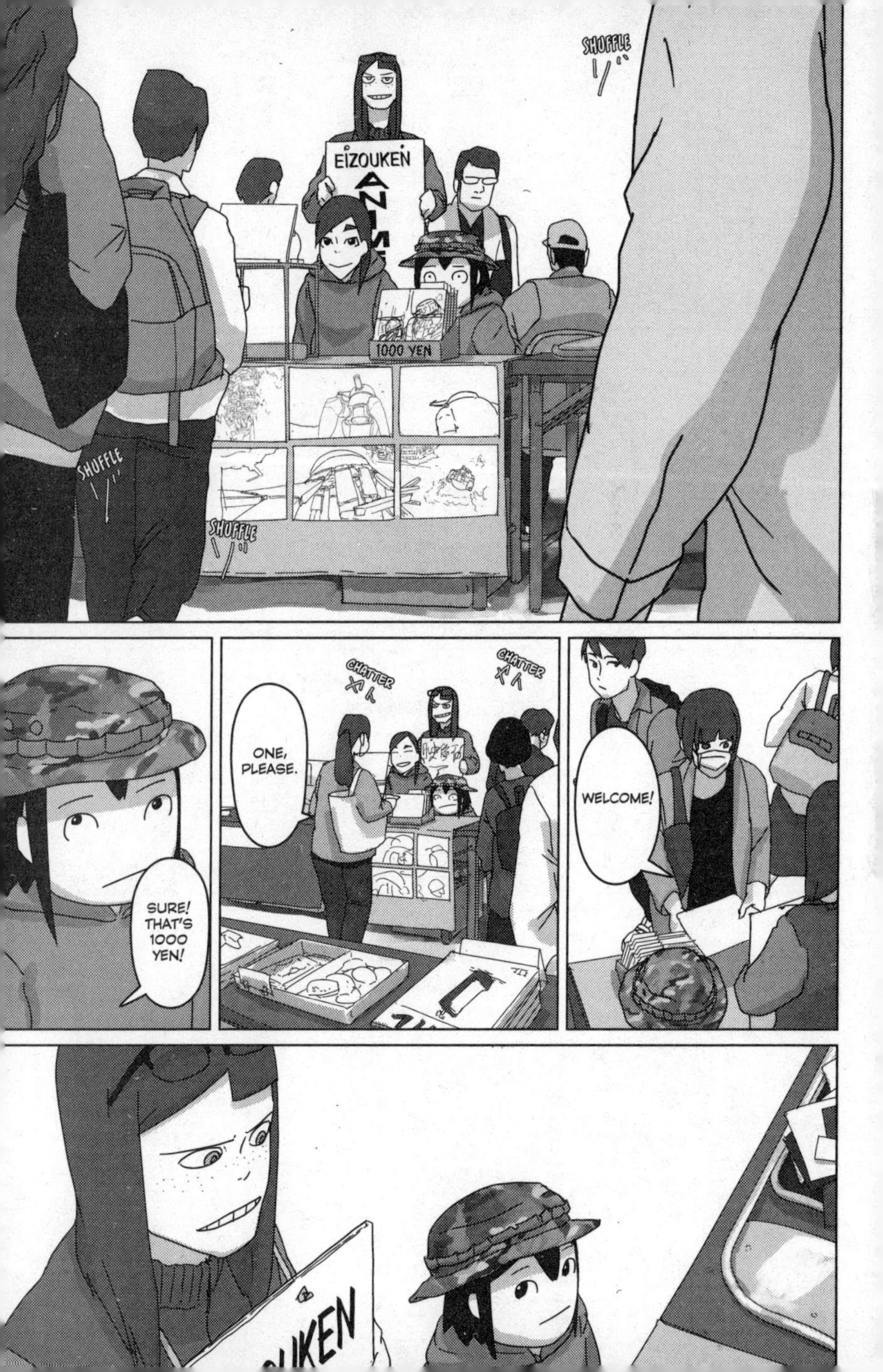
SHUFFLE
EIZOUKEN
1000 YEN
SHUFFLE
SHUFFLE
WELCOME!
CHATTER
CHATTER
ONE, PLEASE.
SURE! THAT'S 1000 YEN!

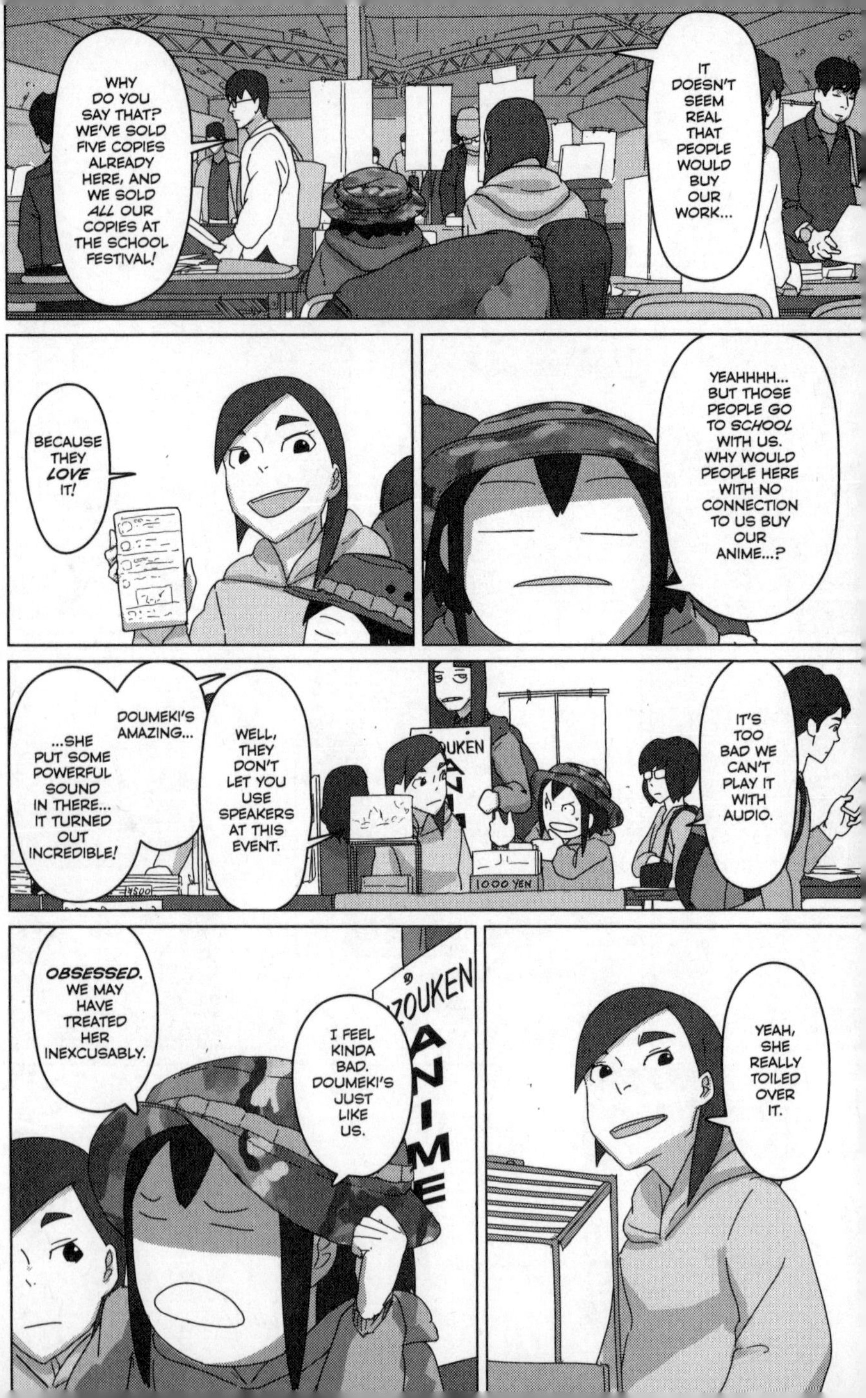
IT DOESN'T SEEM REAL THAT PEOPLE WOULD BUY OUR WORK...
WHY DO YOU SAY THAT? WE'VE SOLD FIVE COPIES ALREADY HERE, AND WE SOLD *ALL* OUR COPIES AT THE SCHOOL FESTIVAL!
YEAHHHH... BUT THOSE PEOPLE GO TO *SCHOOL* WITH US. WHY WOULD PEOPLE HERE WITH NO CONNECTION TO US BUY OUR ANIME...?
BECAUSE THEY ***LOVE*** IT!
IT'S TOO BAD WE CAN'T PLAY IT WITH AUDIO.
WELL, THEY DON'T LET YOU USE SPEAKERS AT THIS EVENT.
DOUMEKI'S AMAZING...
...SHE PUT SOME POWERFUL SOUND IN THERE... IT TURNED OUT INCREDIBLE!
1000 YEN
YEAH, SHE REALLY TOILED OVER IT.
ZOUKEN
ANIME
I FEEL KINDA BAD. DOUMEKI'S JUST LIKE US.
OBSESSED. WE MAY HAVE TREATED HER INEXCUSABLY.

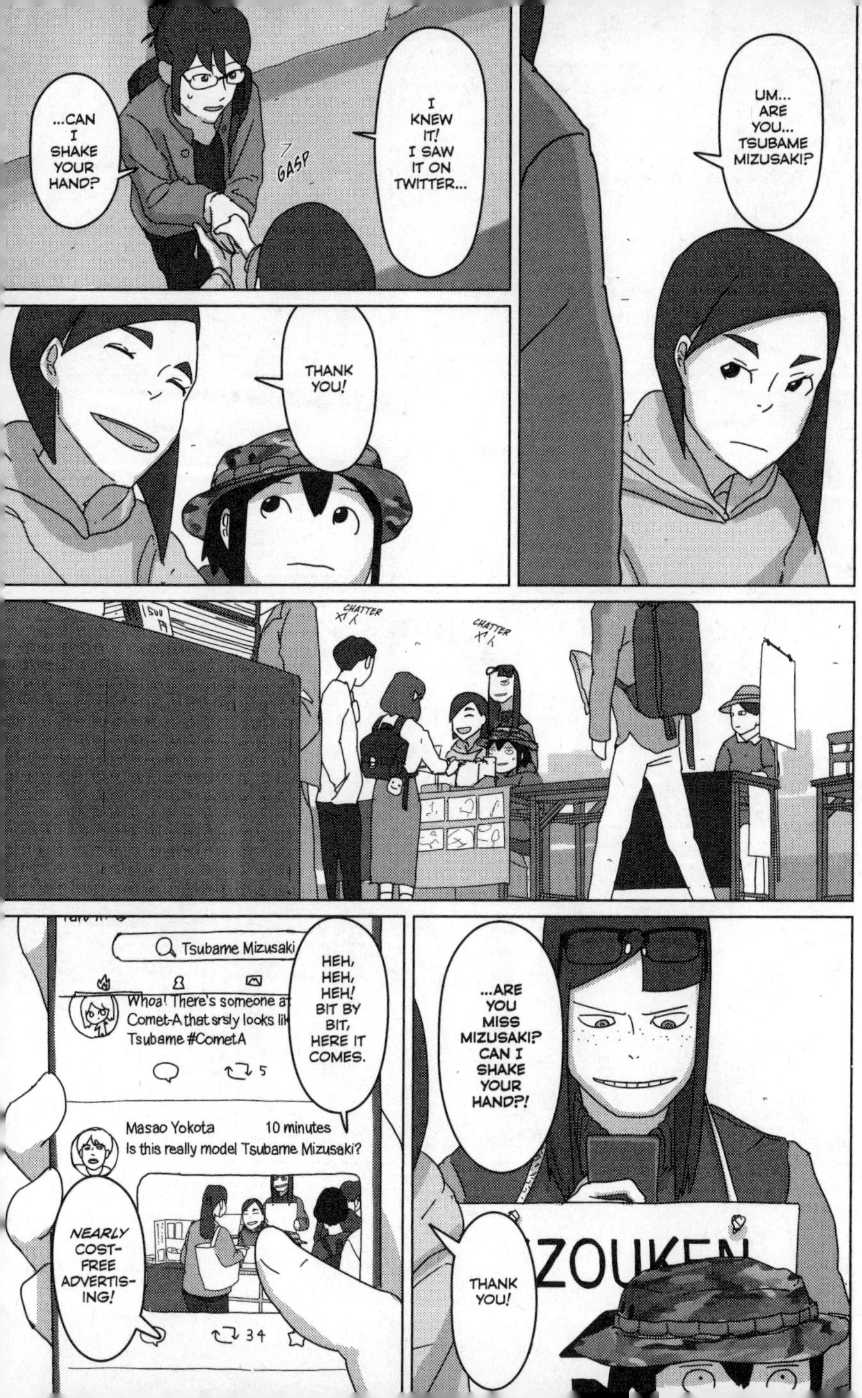

UM... ARE YOU... TSUBAME MIZUSAKI?
I KNEW IT! I SAW IT ON TWITTER...
GASP
...CAN I SHAKE YOUR HAND?
THANK YOU!
CHATTER
CHATTER
...ARE YOU MISS MIZUSAKI? CAN I SHAKE YOUR HAND?!
ZOUKEN
THANK YOU!
Tsubame Mizusaki
Whoa! There's someone at
Comet-A that srsly looks lik
Tsubame #CometA
5
Masao Yokota 10 minutes
Is this really model Tsubame Mizusaki?
34
HEH, HEH, HEH! BIT BY BIT, HERE IT COMES.
NEARLY COST-FREE ADVERTISING!

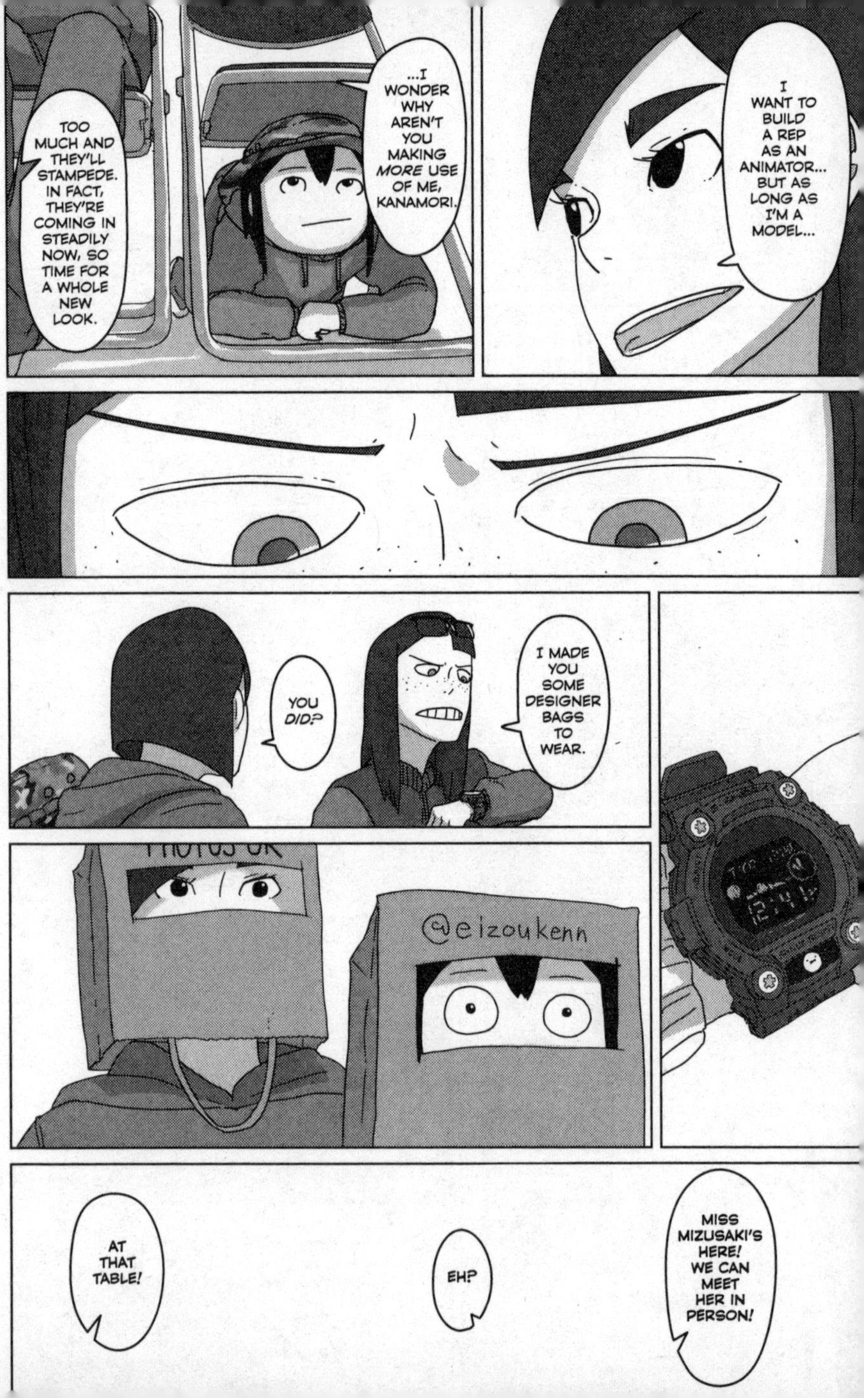
I WANT TO BUILD A REP AS AN ANIMATOR... BUT AS LONG AS I'M A MODEL...
...I WONDER WHY AREN'T YOU MAKING *MORE* USE OF ME, KANAMORI.
TOO MUCH AND THEY'LL STAMPEDE. IN FACT, THEY'RE COMING IN STEADILY NOW, SO TIME FOR A WHOLE NEW LOOK.
I MADE YOU SOME DESIGNER BAGS TO WEAR.
YOU *DID?*
@eizoukenn
MISS MIZUSAKI'S HERE! WE CAN MEET HER IN PERSON!
EH?
AT THAT TABLE!

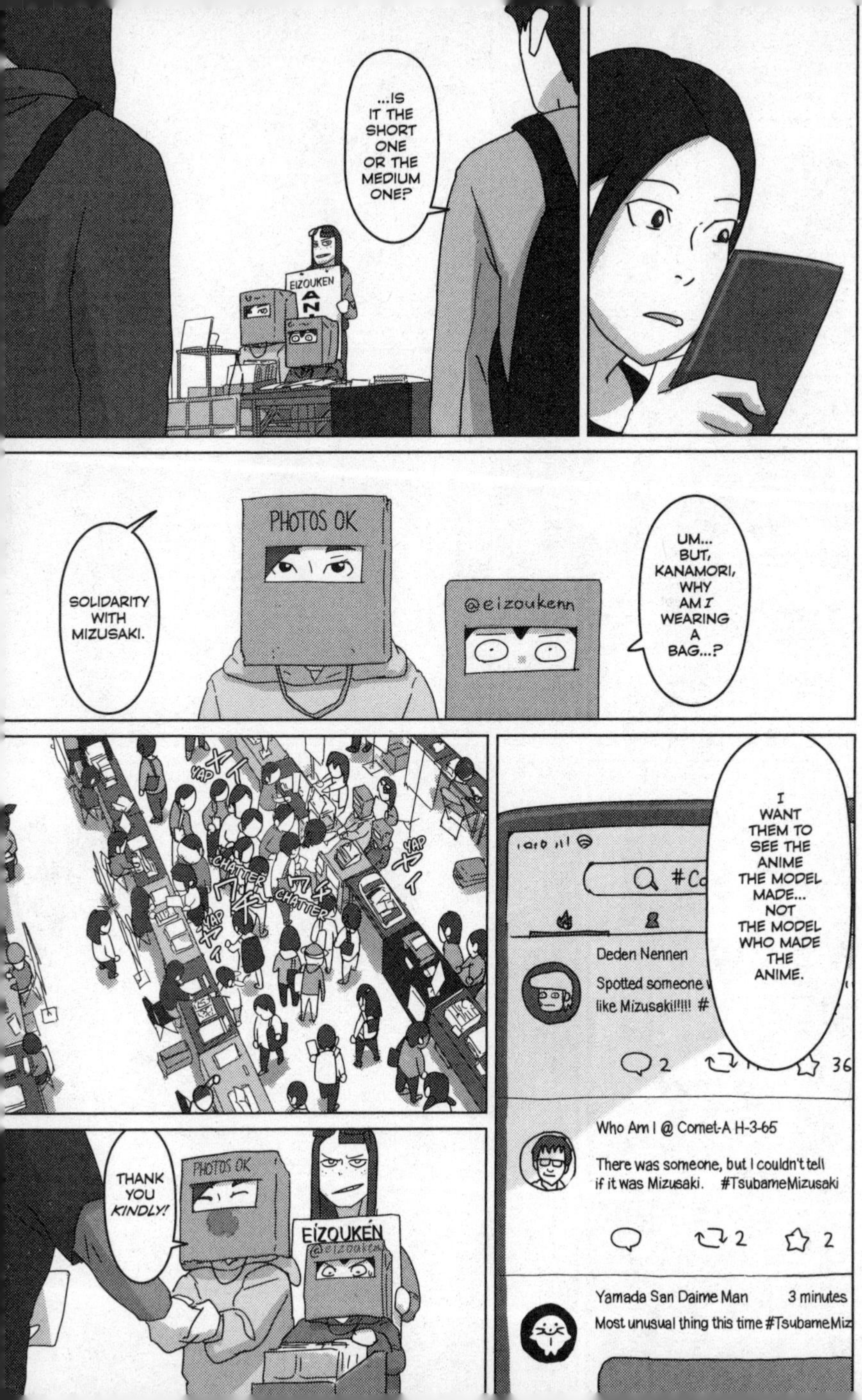
...IS IT THE SHORT ONE OR THE MEDIUM ONE?
EIZOUKEN
UM... BUT, KANAMORI, WHY AM I WEARING A BAG...?
@eizoukenn
PHOTOS OK
SOLIDARITY WITH MIZUSAKI.
I WANT THEM TO SEE THE ANIME THE MODEL MADE... NOT THE MODEL WHO MADE THE ANIME.
Deden Nennen
Spotted someone
like Mizusaki!!!!! #
2
36
Who Am I @ Comet-A H-3-65
There was someone, but I couldn't tell if it was Mizusaki. #TsubameMizusaki
2
2
Yamada San Daime Man
3 minutes
Most unusual thing this time #TsubameMiz
YAP
CHATTER
CHATTER
YAP
YAP
THANK YOU *KINDLY!*
PHOTOS OK
EIZOUKEN

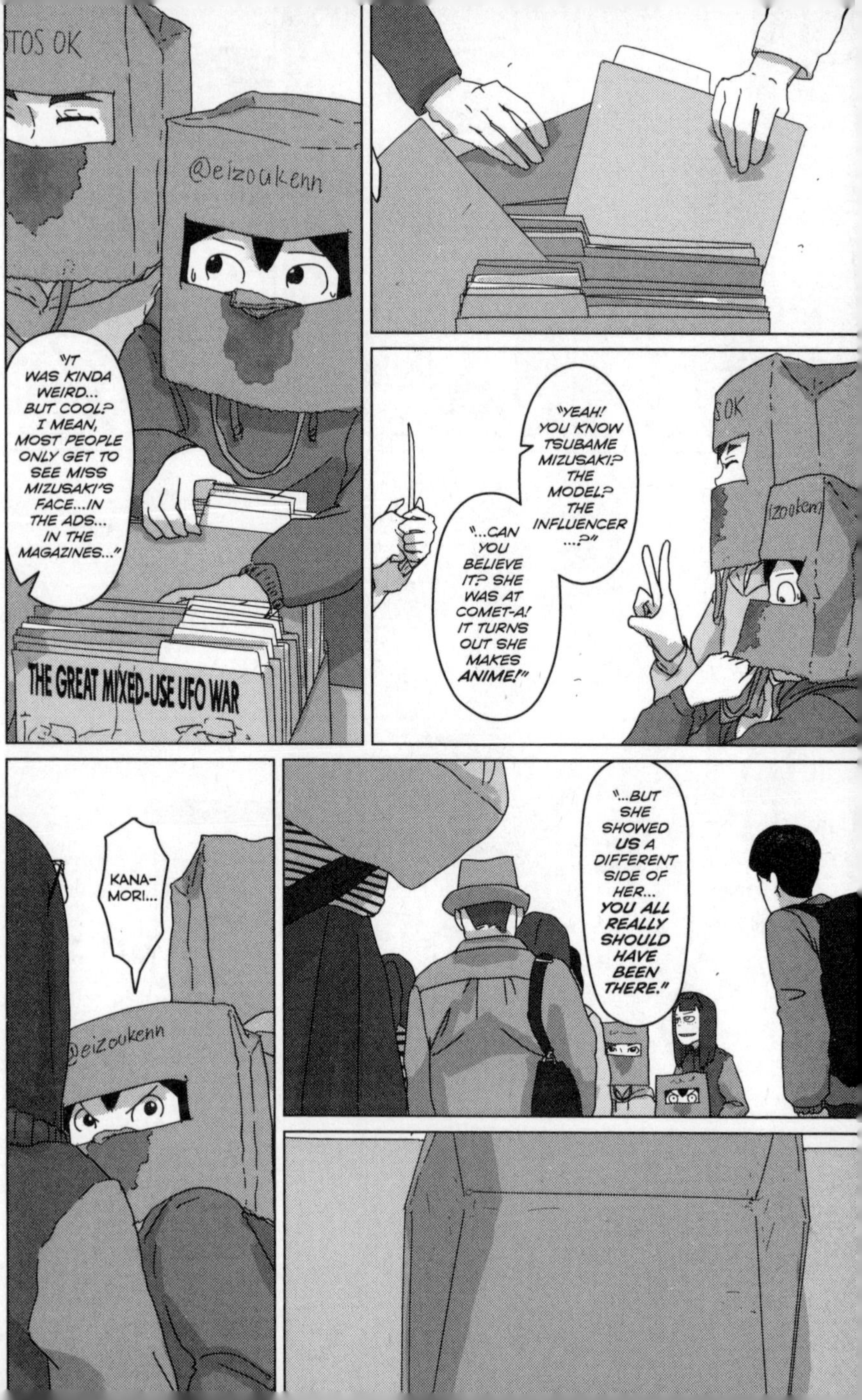
"YEAH! YOU KNOW TSUBAME MIZUSAKI? THE MODEL? THE INFLUENCER ...?"
"...CAN YOU BELIEVE IT? SHE WAS AT COMET-A! IT TURNS OUT SHE MAKES ANIME!"
@eizoukenn
"IT WAS KINDA WEIRD... BUT COOL? I MEAN, MOST PEOPLE ONLY GET TO SEE MISS MIZUSAKI'S FACE...IN THE ADS... IN THE MAGAZINES..."
THE GREAT MIXED-USE UFO WAR
"...BUT SHE SHOWED US A DIFFERENT SIDE OF HER... YOU ALL REALLY SHOULD HAVE BEEN THERE."
KANA-MORI...
@eizoukenn

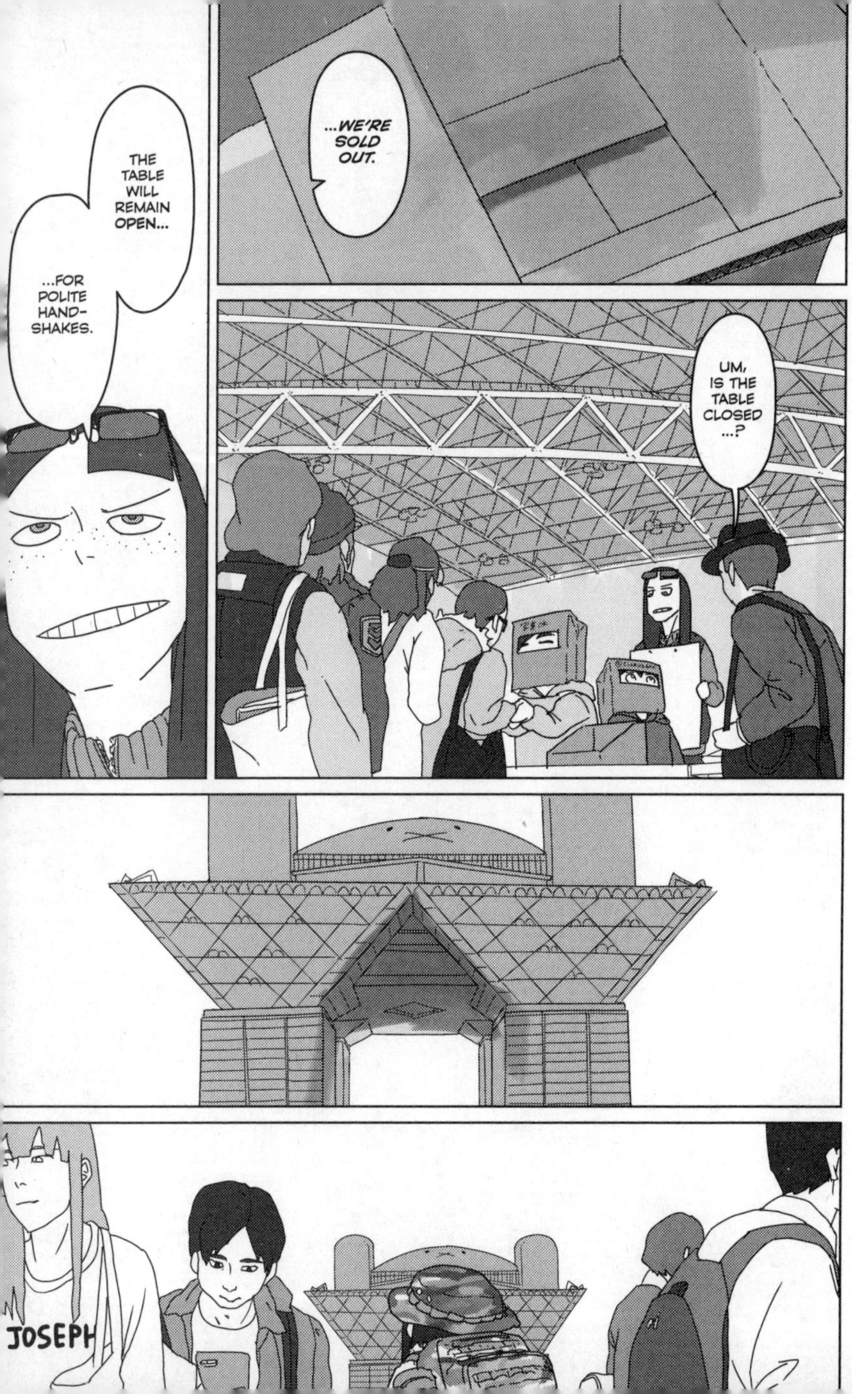
...WE'RE SOLD OUT.
UM, IS THE TABLE CLOSED ...?
THE TABLE WILL REMAIN OPEN...
...FOR POLITE HAND-SHAKES.
JOSEPH

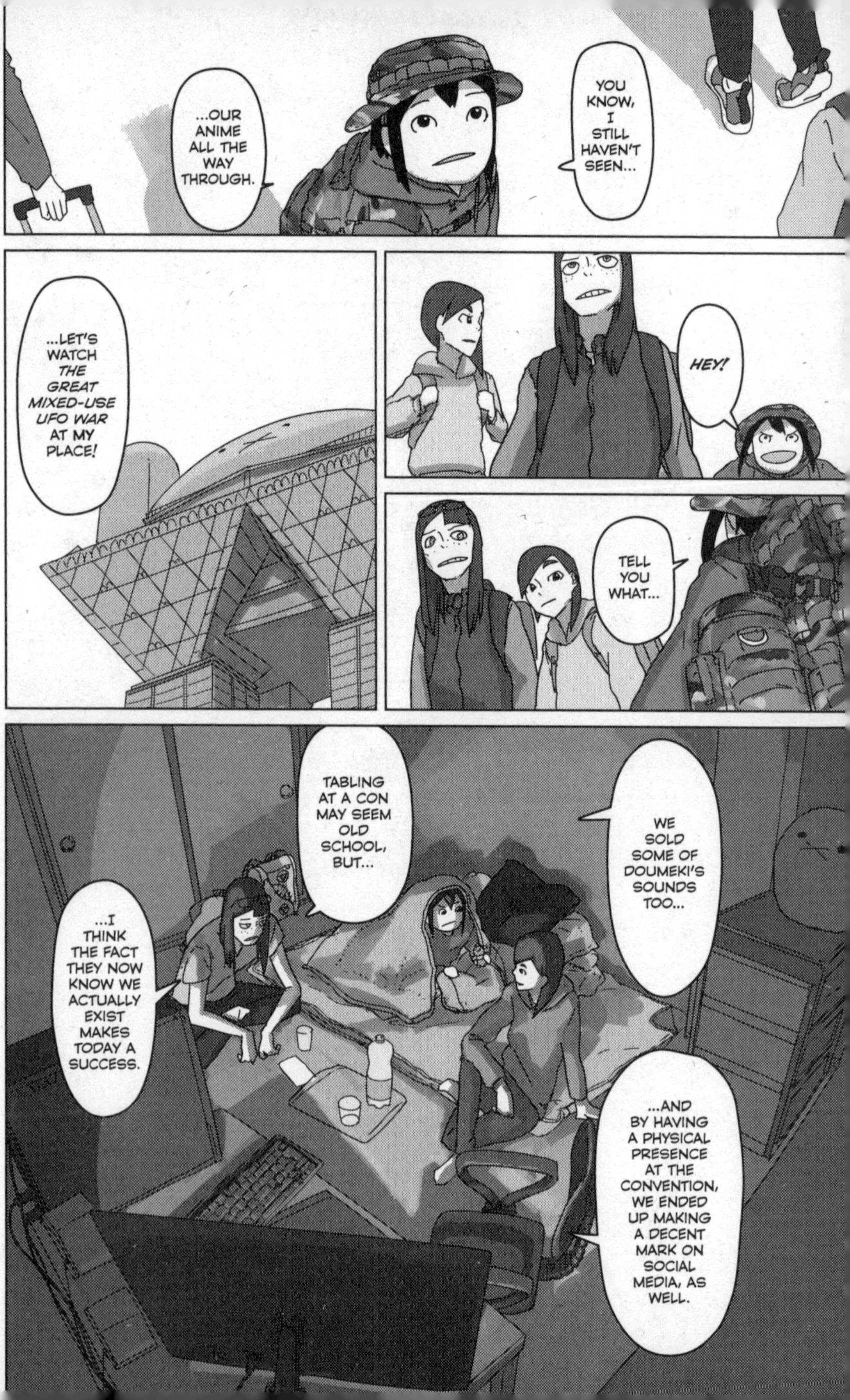

YOU KNOW, I STILL HAVEN'T SEEN...
...OUR ANIME ALL THE WAY THROUGH.
HEY!
TELL YOU WHAT...
...LET'S WATCH *THE GREAT MIXED-USE UFO WAR* AT MY PLACE!
WE SOLD SOME OF DOUMEKI'S SOUNDS TOO...
TABLING AT A CON MAY SEEM OLD SCHOOL, BUT...
...I THINK THE FACT THEY NOW KNOW WE ACTUALLY EXIST MAKES TODAY A SUCCESS.
...AND BY HAVING A PHYSICAL PRESENCE AT THE CONVENTION, WE ENDED UP MAKING A DECENT MARK ON SOCIAL MEDIA, AS WELL.

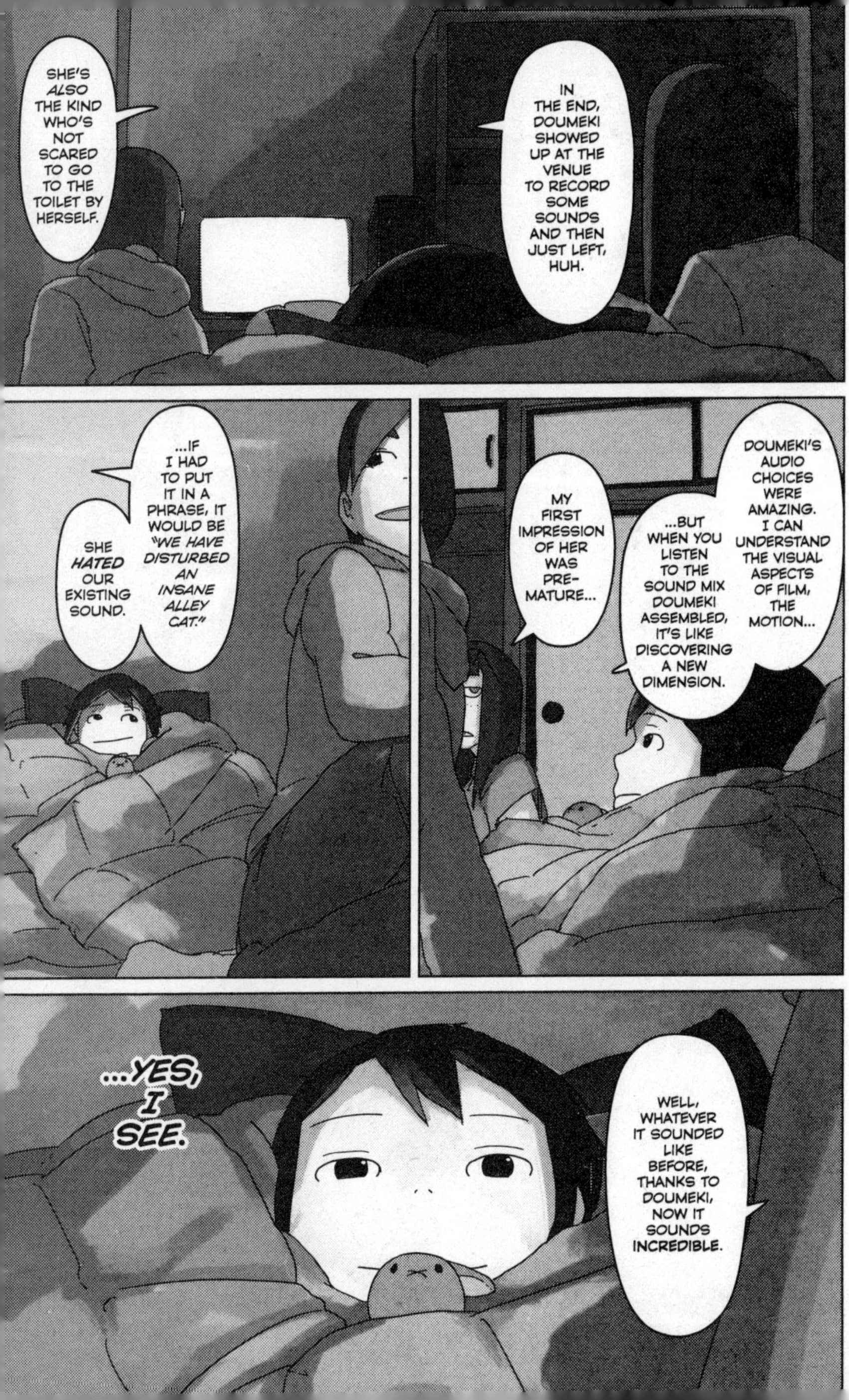
IN THE END, DOUMEKI SHOWED UP AT THE VENUE TO RECORD SOME SOUNDS AND THEN JUST LEFT, HUH.
SHE'S *ALSO* THE KIND WHO'S NOT SCARED TO GO TO THE TOILET BY HERSELF.
DOUMEKI'S AUDIO CHOICES WERE AMAZING. I CAN UNDERSTAND THE VISUAL ASPECTS OF FILM, THE MOTION...
...BUT WHEN YOU LISTEN TO THE SOUND MIX DOUMEKI ASSEMBLED, IT'S LIKE DISCOVERING A NEW DIMENSION.
MY FIRST IMPRESSION OF HER WAS PRE-MATURE...
...IF I HAD TO PUT IT IN A PHRASE, IT WOULD BE "*WE HAVE DISTURBED AN INSANE ALLEY CAT.*"
SHE ***HATED*** OUR EXISTING SOUND.
WELL, WHATEVER IT SOUNDED LIKE BEFORE, THANKS TO DOUMEKI, NOW IT SOUNDS INCREDIBLE.
...YES, I SEE.

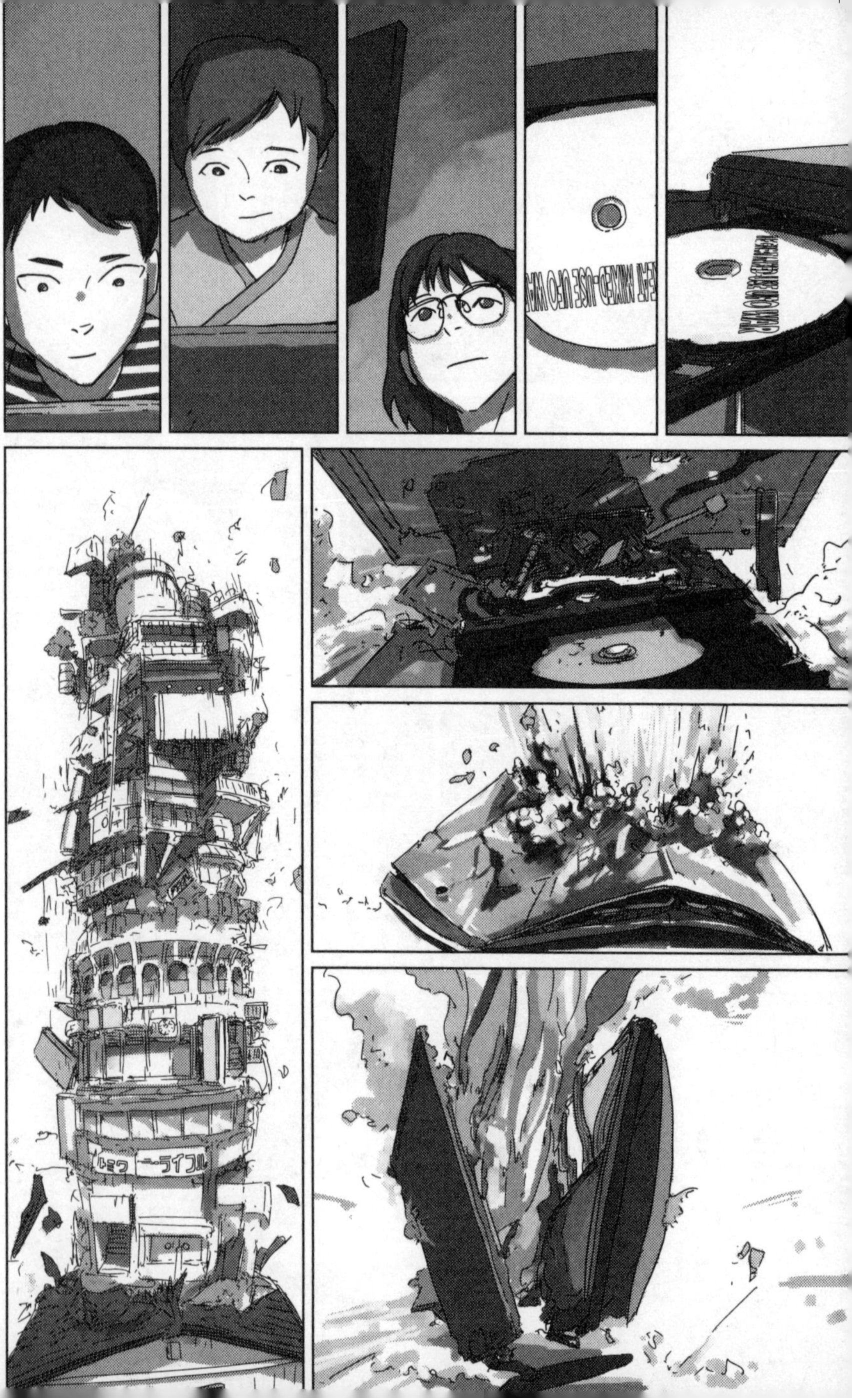
EAT MIXED-USE UFO WA
トミワ
ライフル

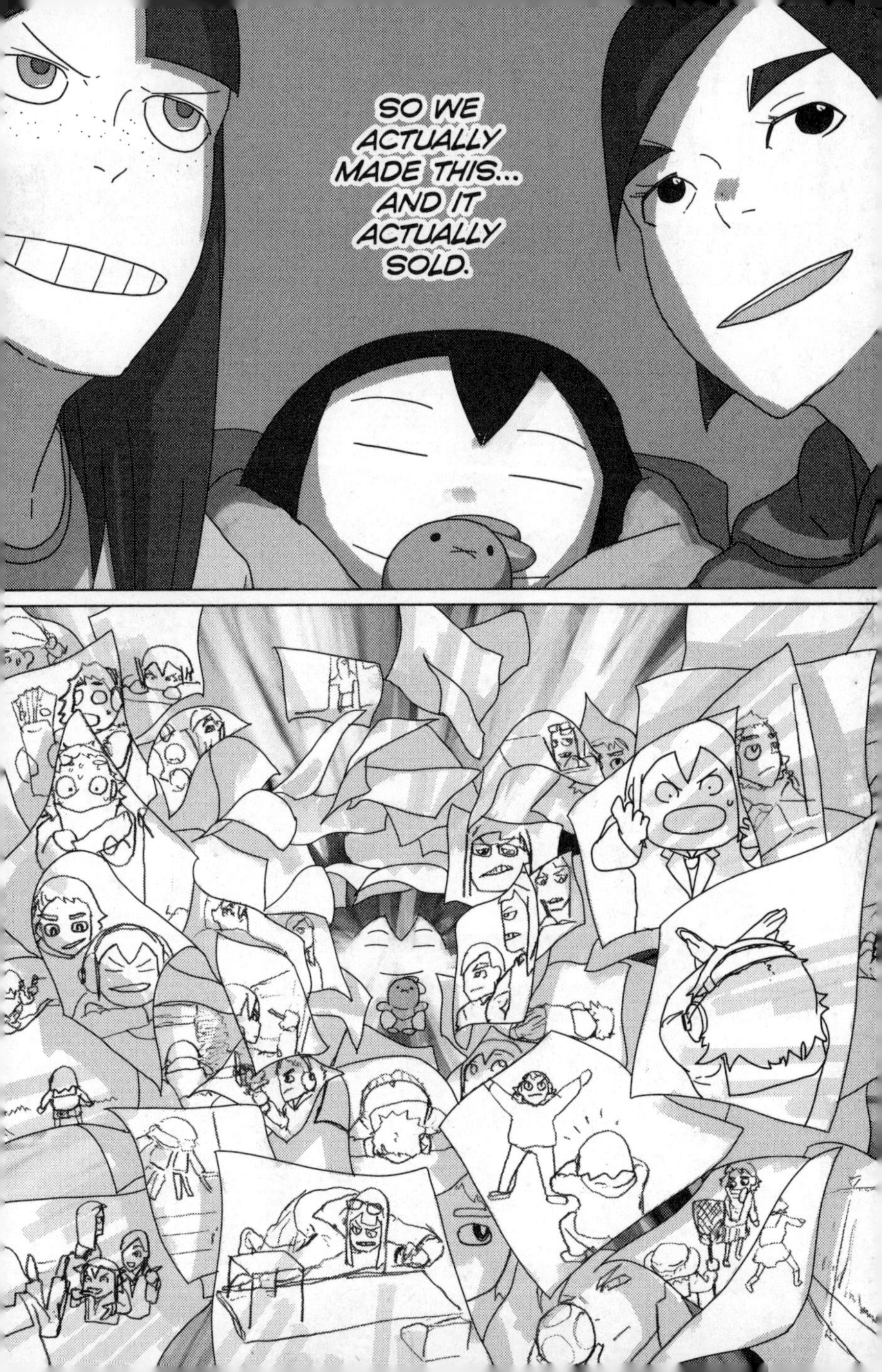
SO WE ACTUALLY MADE THIS... AND IT ACTUALLY SOLD.

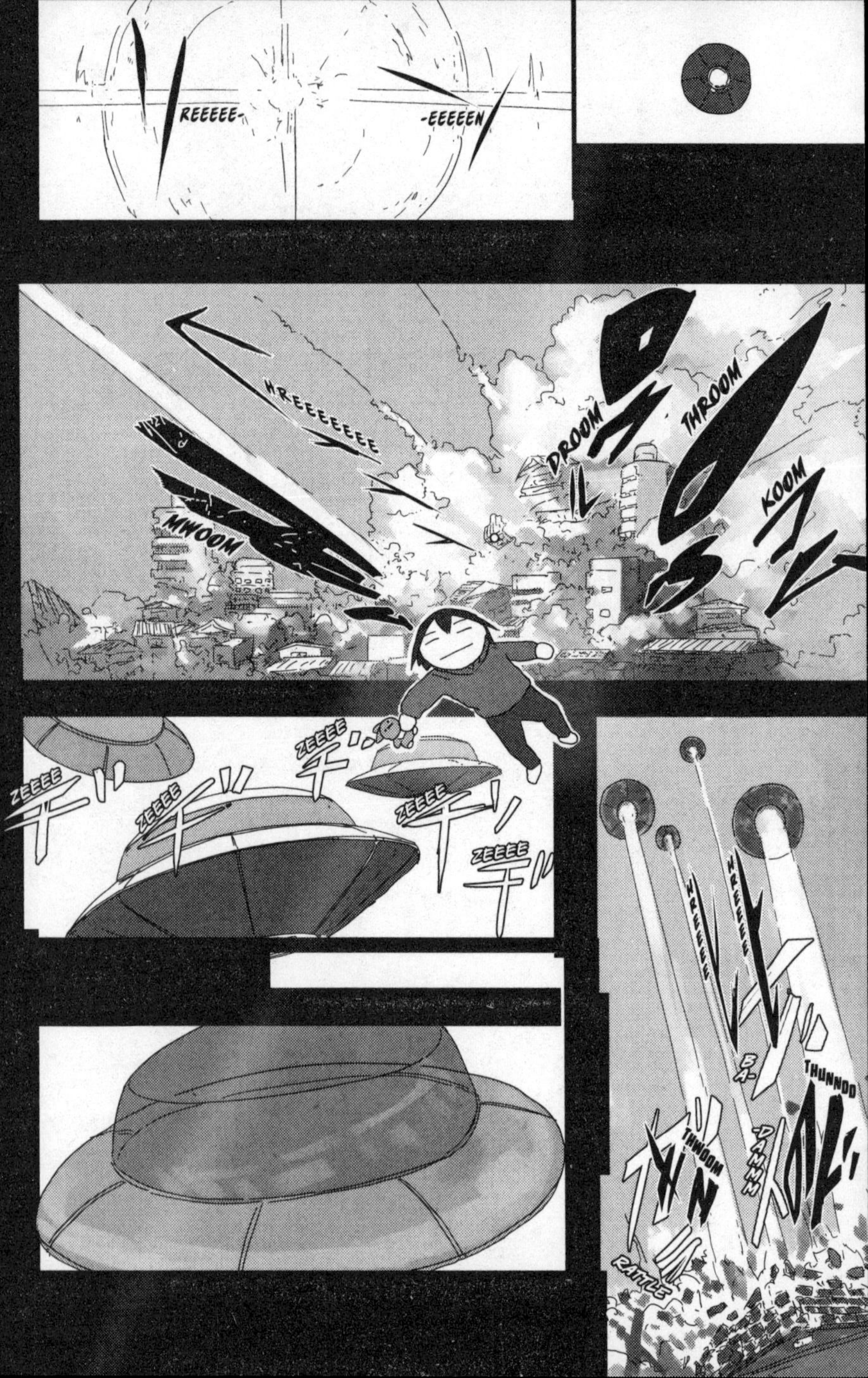
REEEEEE-
-EEEEEN
THROOM
KOOM
DROOM
HREEEEEEEEE
MWOOM
HREEEEEE
HREEEEEE
THUNNDD
BA-
-DAMMM
THWOOM
RATTLE
ZEEEE
ZEEEE
ZEEEE
ZEEEE
ZEEEE

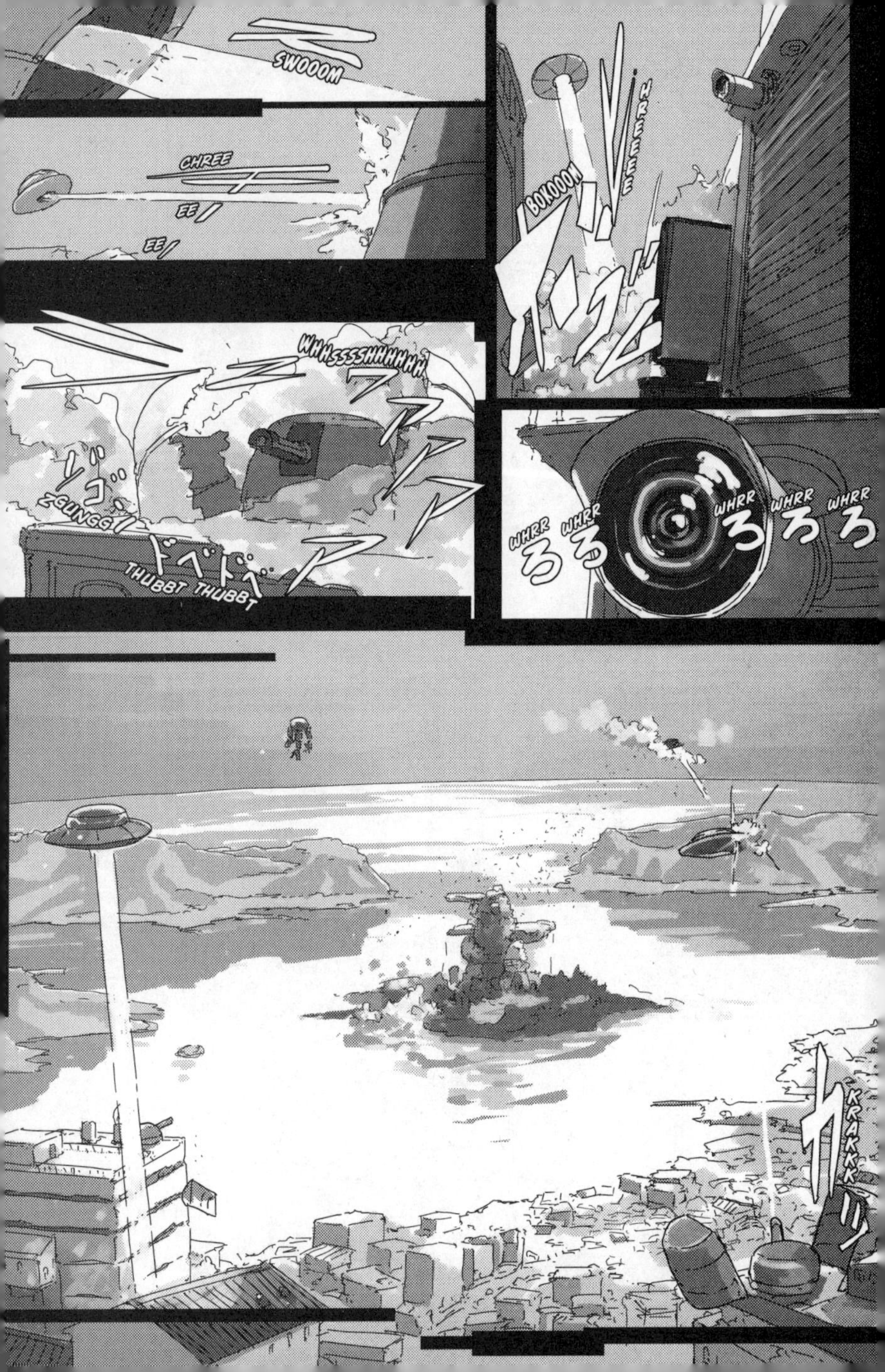
BOKOOOM
HREEEEE
SWOOOM
CHREE
EE!
EE!
WHRR WHRR WHRR WHRR WHRR
WHHSSSSHHHHHH
ZGUNGG
THUBBT THUBBT
KRAKKK

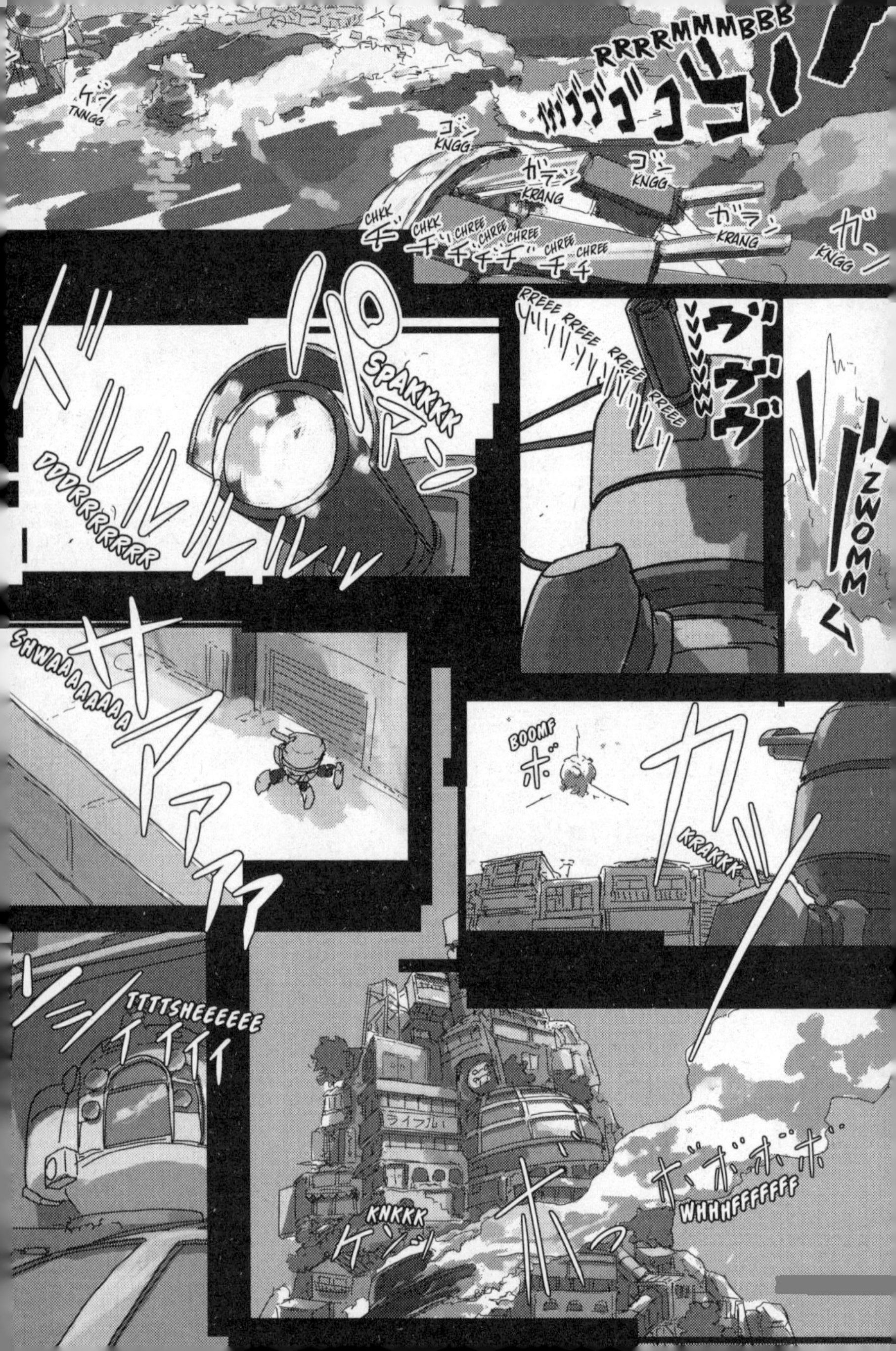

RRRRMMMBBB
KNGG
KRANG
KNGG
KRANG
KNGG
CHKK
CHKK
CHREE
CHREE
CHREE
CHREE
CHREE
TNNGG
ZWOMM
RREEE RREEE RREEE RREEE
SPAKKKKK
DDDRRRRRRRR
BOOMF
KRAKKK
SHWAAAAAAAAA
WHHHFFFFFFF
KNKKK
TTTTSHEEEEEEE

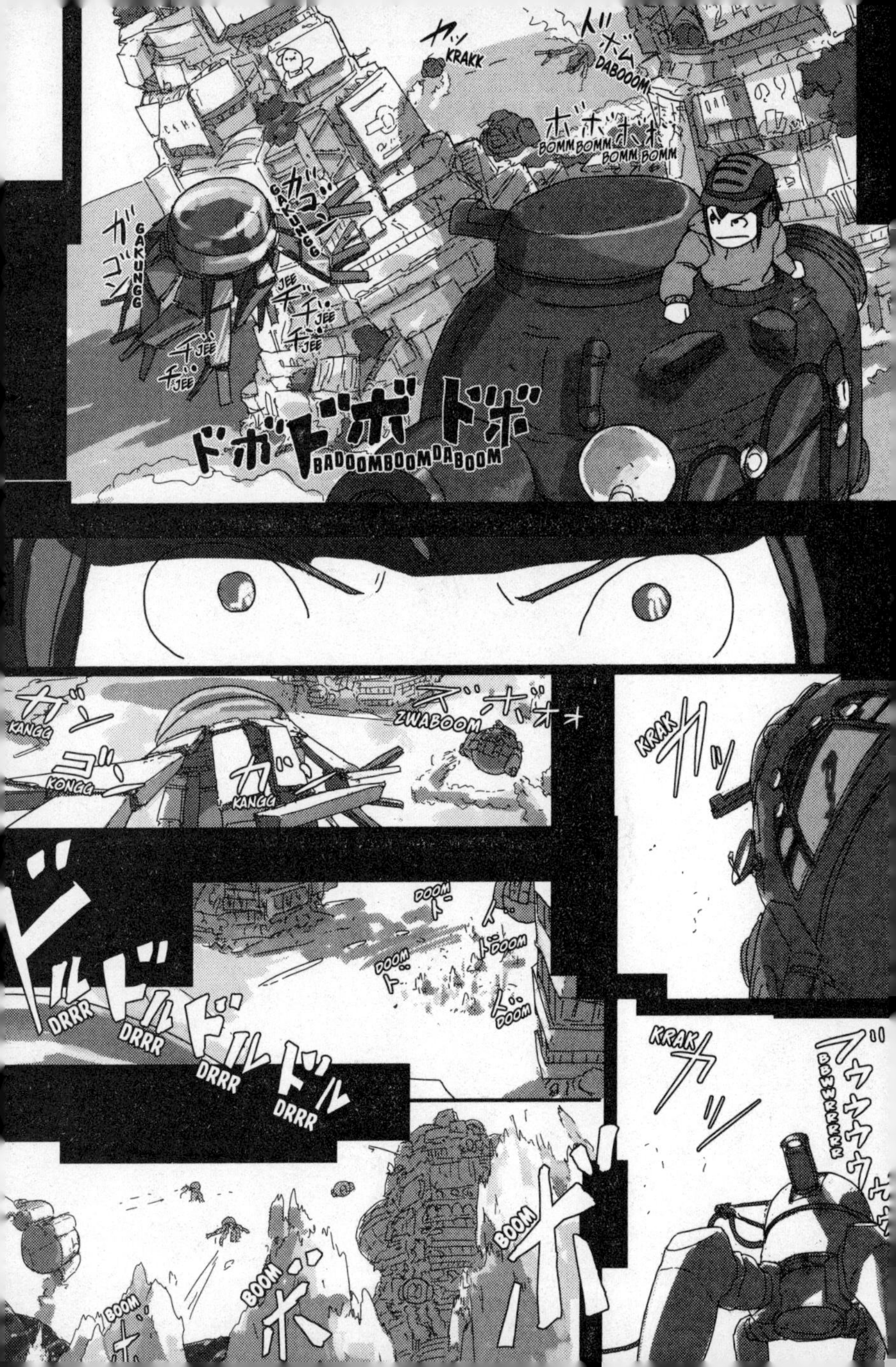

DABOOOM
KRAKK
BOMM BOMM BOMM BOMM
GAKUNGG
GAKUNGG
JEE
JEE
JEE
JEE
JEE
BADOOMBOOMDABOOM
KRAK
ZWABOOM
KANGG
KONGG
KANGG
DOOM
DOOM
DOOM
DOOM
DRRR
DRRR
DRRR
DRRR
BBWRRRRR
KRAK
BOOM
BOOM
BOOM

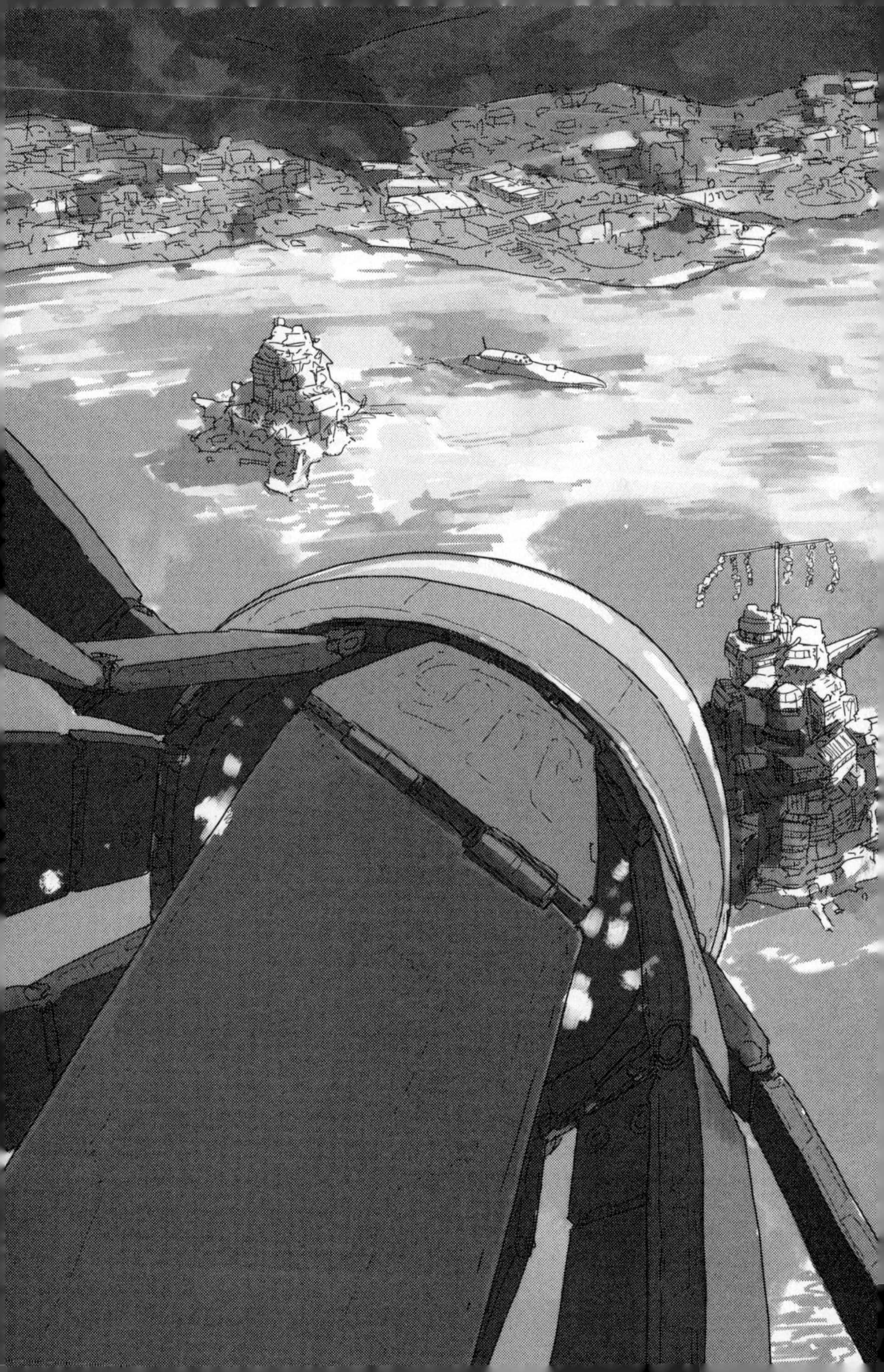

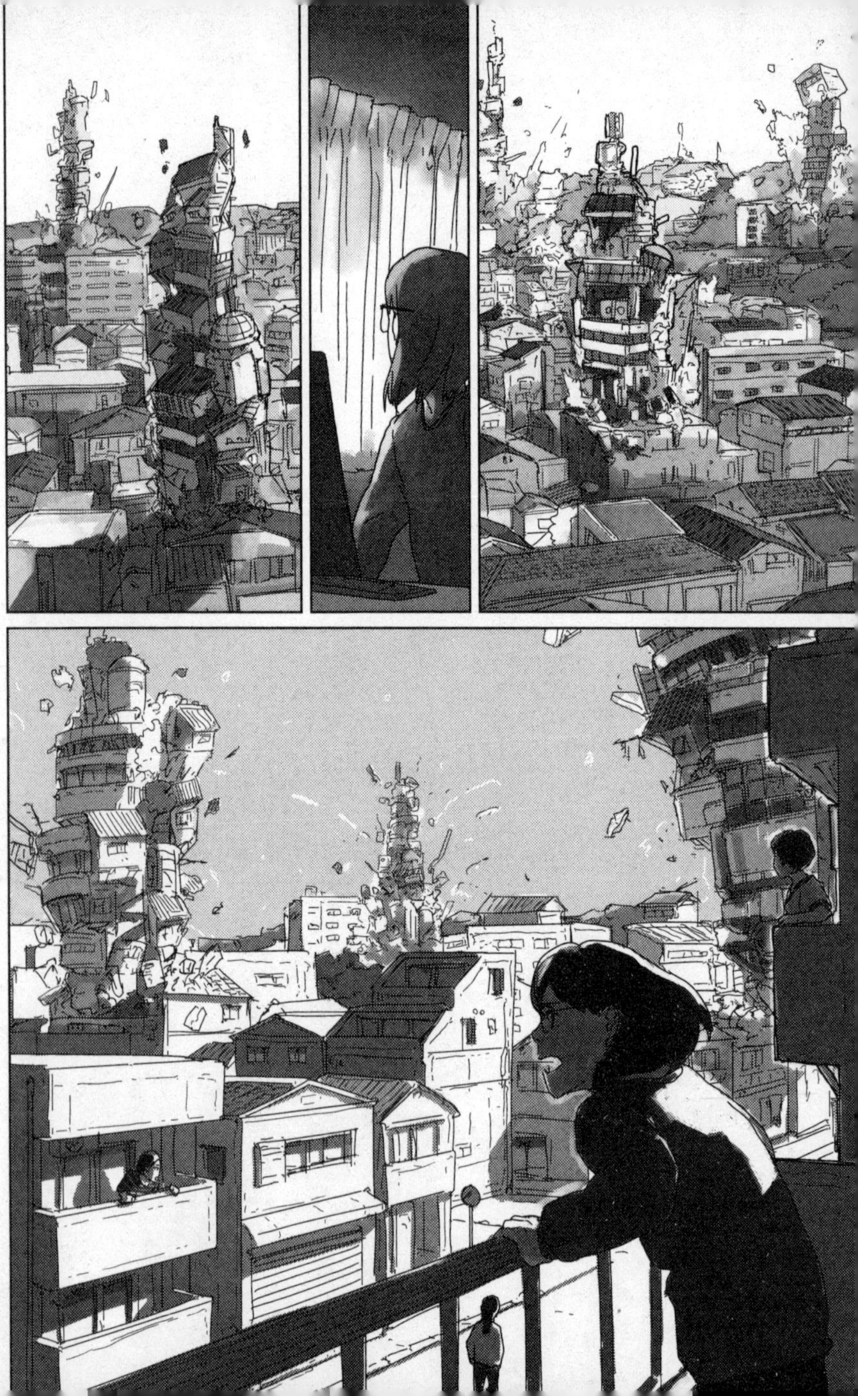

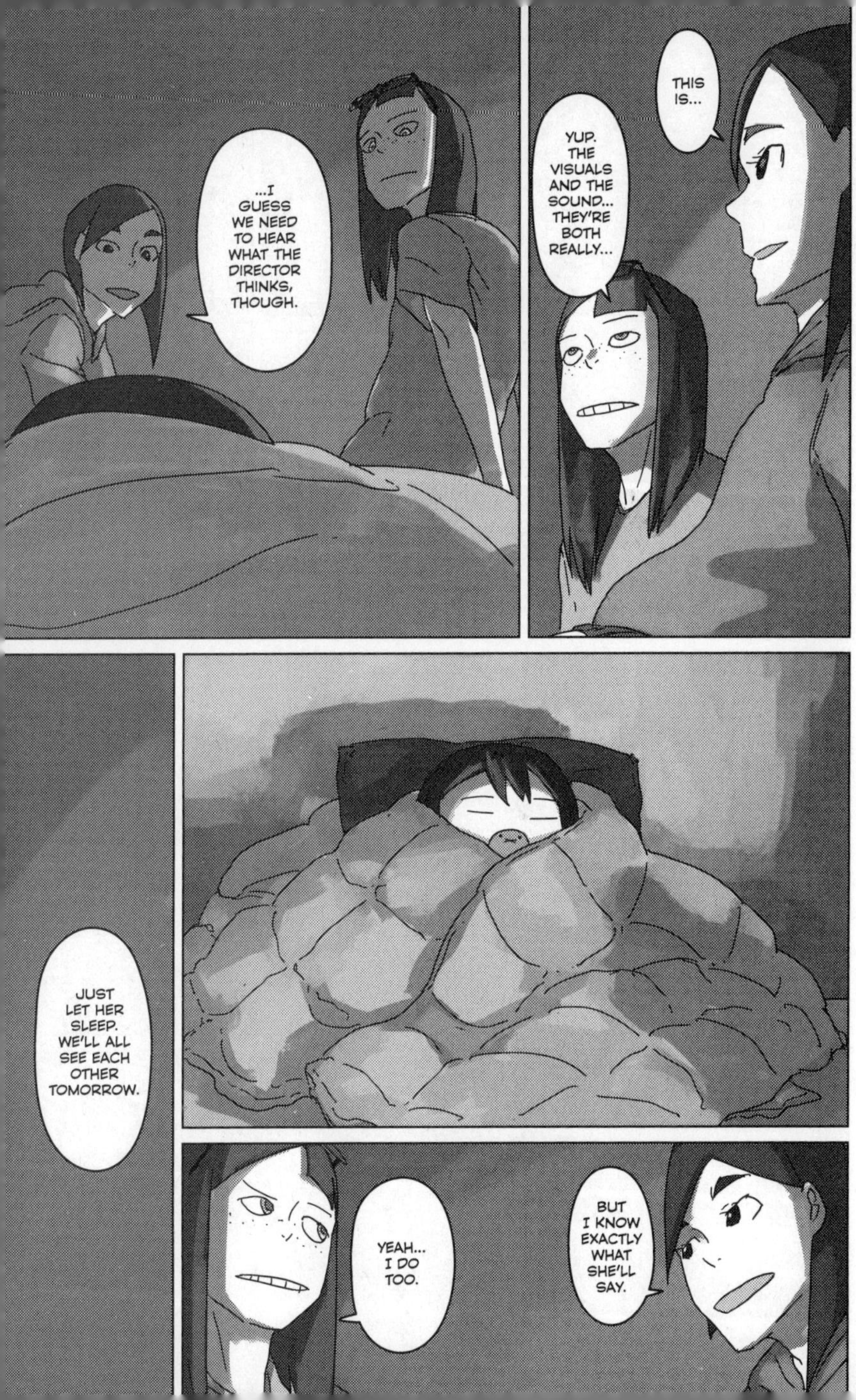
THIS IS...
YUP. THE VISUALS AND THE SOUND... THEY'RE BOTH REALLY...
...I GUESS WE NEED TO HEAR WHAT THE DIRECTOR THINKS, THOUGH.
BUT I KNOW EXACTLY WHAT SHE'LL SAY.
YEAH... I DO TOO.
JUST LET HER SLEEP. WE'LL ALL SEE EACH OTHER TOMORROW.

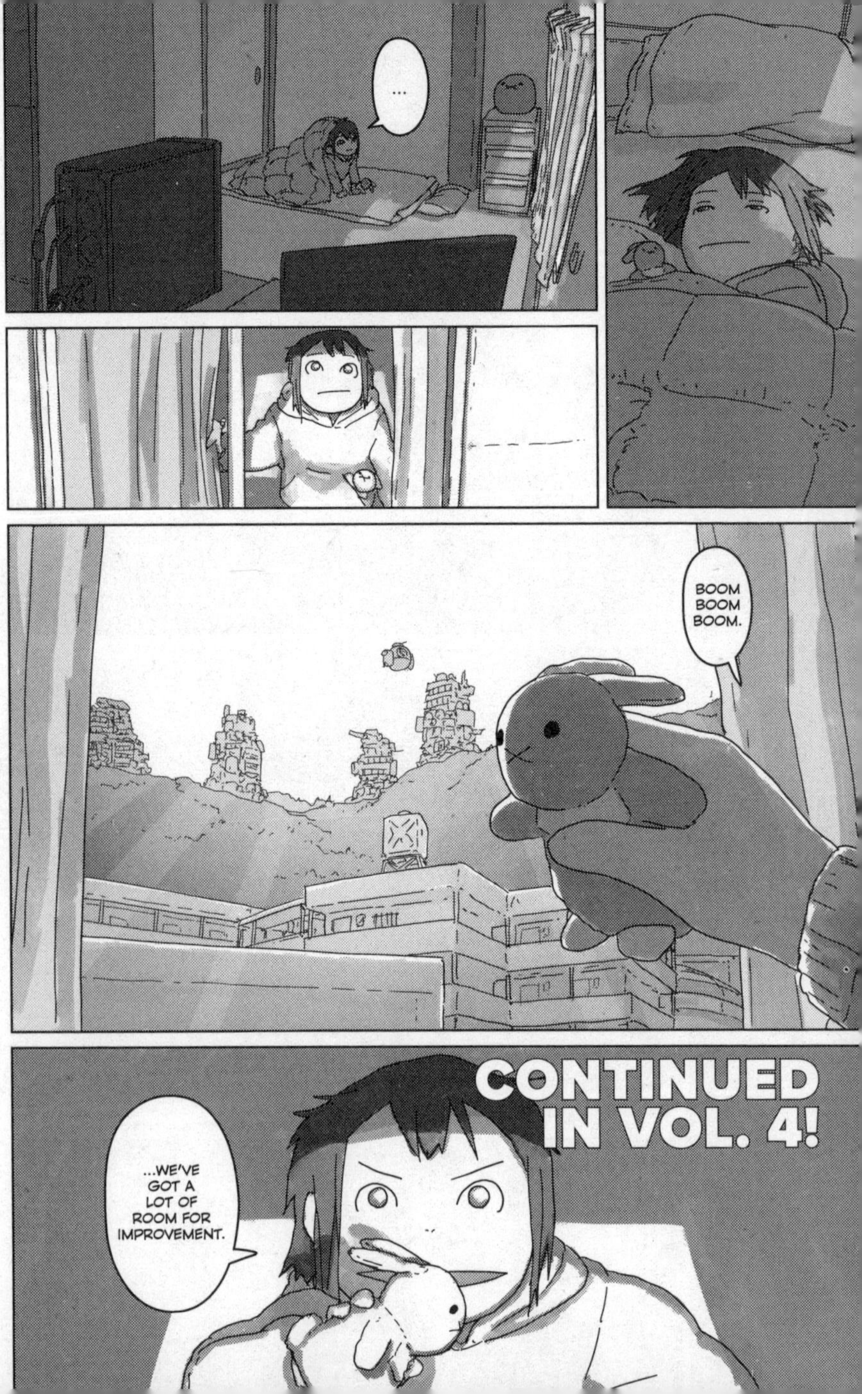
...
BOOM BOOM BOOM.
CONTINUED IN VOL. 4!
...WE'VE GOT A LOT OF ROOM FOR IMPROVEMENT.

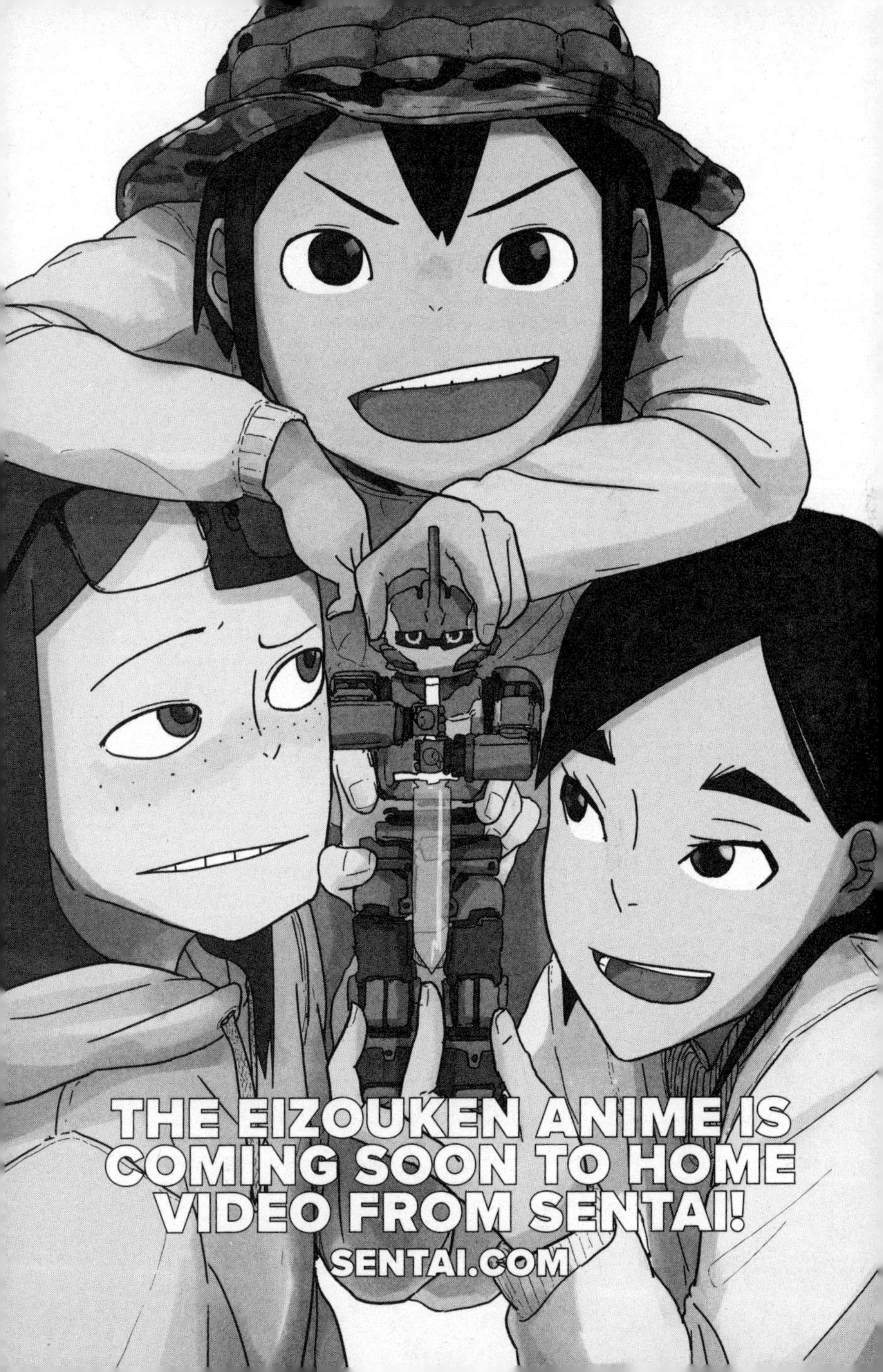
THE EIZOUKEN ANIME IS COMING SOON TO HOME VIDEO FROM SENTAI!
SENTAI.COM

President and Publisher
MIKE RICHARDSON

Editor
CARL GUSTAV HORN

Designer
SKYLER WEISSENFLUH

Digital Art Technician
CHRIS HORN

English-language version produced by Dark Horse Comics

KEEP YOUR HANDS OFF EIZOUKEN!

Published by
Dark Horse Manga
A division of Dark Horse Comics LLC
10956 SE Main Street
Milwaukie, OR 97222

DarkHorse.com

To find a comics shop in your area, visit comicshoplocator.com.

First edition: September 2021
ISBN 978-1-50671-899-6

1 3 5 7 9 10 8 6 4 2

Printed in the United States of America

Neil Hankerson Executive Vice President • Tom Weddle Chief Financial Officer • Dale LaFountain Chief Information Officer • Tim Wiesch Vice President of Licensing • Matt Parkinson Vice President of Marketing Vanessa Todd-Holmes Vice President of Production and Scheduling • Mark Bernardi Vice President of Book Trade and Digital Sales • Ken Lizzi General Counsel • Dave Marshall Editor in Chief • Davey Estrada Editorial Director • Chris Warner Senior Books Editor • Cary Grazzini Director of Specialty Projects • Lia Ribacchi Art Director • Matt Dryer Director of Digital Art and Prepress • Michael Gombos Senior Director of Licensed Publications • Kari Yadro Director of Custom Programs • Kari Torson Director of International Licensing • Sean Brice Director of Trade Sales • Randy Lahrman Director of Product Sales

NOTES ON VOL. 3 BY THE TRANSLATOR AND EDITOR

Welcome back, and good to see you again! Fittingly for the third volume, there's three bits of good news we have to state since last time. First, thanks to your support, we're planning to continue *Eizouken* into volumes 4 and 5, which will take us through all the volumes in Japan thus far—and into new story territory beyond the anime! Second, after a hiatus, the creator, Sumito Oowara, has started up the *Eizouken* manga again in the pages of its home base, Shogakukan's *Monthly Big Comic Spirits*, which means if all goes well there could be a vol. 6, or even beyond! Third, Sentai in Houston (where the editor lived for years—did you know Houston was the first city in the U.S. to have a store specifically dedicated to anime fans?) has announced that they will be releasing the anime version of *Eizouken* on home video! Yes, we indeed have a lot to be thankful for as *Eizouken* fans with this volume. And speaking of this volume . . .

On page 24, panel 1 (and as a setting later in vol. 3), Comet-A is clearly inspired by the doujinshi event, Comitia, and as it becomes an important setting for the end of this story arc, let's talk a little about the original. Although Comitia has been around longer and has hosted more events than any Western anime con—Comitia was founded in 1984, and is held in Tokyo four times a year!—it still seems little known here compared to the famed doujinshi gathering Comiket (Comic Market).

There are reasonable explanations for this. One is sheer size: whereas Comiket may have as many as 35,000 "circles" participating (a circle originally tended to signify a group of creators [like Eizouken], though often now a circle is just one person—it's said that printing prices going down in Japan in the 1980s meant that more people saw the option to publish doujinshi as individuals, rather than needing to pool their expenses with others as was traditional), Comitia may have only 4000—next time you have the chance to go to an artist alley at a con, think about it "only" having 4000 tables ^_^. Comiket is particularly known for its global outreach programs (you may have seen them do presentations at US events such as Sakura-Con and Otakon) and its multilingual staff. Comitia (whose site, comitia.co.jp, is Japanese-only) is basically a Japan-oriented organization—and while often that really means "Tokyo-oriented," there are also autonomous Comitia events in Sapporo, Fukushima, Niigata, Nagoya, Osaka, and Kitakyushu, several of which are themselves held more than once a year.

It certainly isn't the case that Comitia is unconnected to international creators; quite the contrary—however, this has most recently been through their partnership with Japan-based events such as the Tokyo International Comics Festival, an event founded in 2012 by former French diplomat (*le weebisme* is perhaps a tradition dating back to Frederik Schodt, whose dad was in the foreign service) Frédéric Toutlemonde. Toutlemonde's publishing imprint, Euromanga, makes a particular effort to promote European comics translated into Japanese (their best-selling title in Japan, Canales and Guarnido's *Blacksad*, is, I'm proud to say, published in English by Dark Horse). Toutlemonde also makes the argument that young creators outside Japan these days who draw their comics in a "manga style" don't necessarily "copy manga" to any greater extent than young Japanese creators themselves do—because by this point in history the younger generation of global creators have grown up with manga and anime as much as their Japanese counterparts have.

Yet perhaps the largest cultural difference between Comitia and Comiket isn't a matter of size, languages, or localities, but something that calls into question our developed notions of fan conventions and doujinshi events. We might typically picture going to them while cosplaying as characters from shows we like, and buying doujinshi featuring those characters. But neither activity is permitted at Comitia, where the focus is on selling doujinshi that *aren't* based on copyrighted work (unless it's your own copyrighted work). You'll find the full genre diversity in Comitia's doujinshi that you would in a regular bookstore—that is, both fiction doujinshi (fantasy, romance, drama, etc.) and non-fiction doujinshi (travel, food, technology, etc.); adults-only work is permitted, as are doujinshi based on things that are no longer under copyright, such as old literature. And just as at Comiket (or in a typical artist alley, for that matter) "doujinshi" at Comitia is very broadly defined to mean not only printed works but crafts, A/V media, software, etc., so you have a tremendous variety of creative formats as well.

I personally think Japan's culture of fan parody doujinshi based on copyrighted works is amazing, and proves such fan works can coexist alongside (and indeed interact with) a healthy professional industry—the manga industry is about four times the size of the US comics industry in dollar terms, even though Japan has less than 40% of the US population. But even though it's such fan parodies we commonly think of when we hear the term "doujinshi," of course, there's no rule doujinshi have to be based off another's copyrighted work. Many doujinshi are original, and that's always been the case—what makes a doujinshi isn't its content, but the fact it's published through amateur rather than professional routes.

I say "routes" because many professional manga creators, including some released in English by Dark Horse such as Kohta Hirano (*Drifters*, *Hellsing*) and Kenichi Sonoda (*Gunsmith Cats*), still self-publish doujinshi on the side. In other words, although doujinshi are largely associated with amateur creators, it isn't necessarily about whether you're a pro or an amateur, but rather about the way you put your work out. One reason we don't always see a lot of these interesting original Japanese doujinshi of the kind you'd encounter at Comitia showing up at Western anime cons is the same reason Japanese bookstores abroad have only a limited selection of Japanese-language manga in stock compared to what you could find in Japan itself: paper is heavy and costs money to ship overseas, and shelf space is limited, so you have to pick your stock based on what you already expect you can sell (Kanamori nods approvingly ^_^). Therefore, when you see Japanese doujinshi for sale at a Western anime con, they tend to be parodies based on series fans already know and like (and, of course, are looking to find).

Like the rule that the doujinshi you sell at Comitia should reflect your own original creations, Comitia's no-cosplay rule is meant to reflect the notion of one's individual identity (as opposed to temporarily assuming an identity created by or belonging to another, which is generally the method of cosplay). So if you actually *do* happen to wear a certain outfit in your everyday life, it might be permitted, but otherwise not. Since there is no shortage of events in Japan that permit fan parodies and cosplay, I don't begrudge Comitia their different approach, and the fact there have been 137 Comitias to date in Tokyo alone would seem to indicate there's considerable support for that different approach to be found among fans in Japan as well.

There's another quality to Comitia, in that their focus on original doujinshi (by the way, you're certainly allowed to feature your own original work at Comiket too, and many do—it's just that there, it might more easily get drowned out by all the doujinshi based on popular works created by others) is one way of supporting the next generation of creators who'd like to go pro. Yasuhiro Nightow, creator of *Trigun* and *Blood Blockade Battlefront* (both, like *Eizouken*, published in English by Dark Horse!), is one example of such a creator—several of his early stories made their debut at Comitia, as did those of TAGRO (of the *Panty and Stocking with Garterbelt* manga, also available from Dark Horse), as did those of Kaoru Mori, whose works such as *Emma* and *A Bride's Story* you should buy, even if they aren't published by Dark Horse. ^_^

One more thing: I'm drawing a contrast between Comiket and Comitia because they're two successful and influential doujinshi events with distinctly differing philosophies—but it's important to note that they're not the only two doujinshi events in Japan! Just as there are many anime cons in the English-speaking world, there are many, many different doujinshi events in Japan that themselves have a wide variation in policies, ranging in size from huge gatherings to small events, sometimes specializing in works based in a single theme or genre. And that's traditionally the great thing about the Japanese doujinshi scene; you can find a place that fits you, or just fits the mode you're in right now—many people attend *both* Comitia and Comiket!

On page 26, panel 3, Mizusaki is sticking a green foxtail (*Setaria italica*), traditionally used as a *nekojarashi* (cat teaser) into the band of Asakusa's boonie hat. Regarding the scene on page 40, otaku of Japanese mini trucks (also known as kei trucks; related to the better-known kei cars, both named after *keijidōsha*, the category for the smallest street-legal enclosed vehicles in Japan) are invited to identify the exact model of this vehicle, although it looks to the editor like a 1990s Suzuki Carry. As a first-year high school student—high school in Japan is grades 10, 11, and 12—Asakusa is almost certainly too young to legally drive a four-wheel vehicle in Japan, where you must be 18 (you can get a motorcycle license at 16), but it's not like that's going to stop her. I'm *assuming* that's her; the image in panel 2 is small, but it appears to be someone wearing a hat. I'm also not the least bit surprised by the notion Asakusa already knows how to drive; my guess is she could even give piloting an Airbus A380 a shot, provided she had enough books to sit upon.

In response to Doumeki's remark on page 43, panel 4 that "there's no sound in a vacuum," Mizusaki or Asakusa in the original Japanese (we can't see the order in which they're speaking) says 「沙羅双樹」 sarasooju , "sal tree," and the other then replies 「そりゃそうじゃ」 sorya soo ja, "oh, for sure." The scientific name of the sal tree is *Shorea robusta*, which hopefully sounds just as random as the original ^_^ Maybe Eizouken has been paying attention in class, as the opening lines of the classic of Japanese medieval literature, *The Tale of the Heike*, evoke the sal tree (also known as the teak tree), which figures in Buddhist symbology: "The bell of the Gion Temple echoes the impermanence of all things. The pale flowers of the teak tree show the truth that they who prosper must fall." The editor prefers Ippu Nishizawa's 1710 satire *The Gay Tale of the Heike*, which begins, "The bells of the Gion Festival echo the impermanence of all guests. The pale faces under the cherry tree show the truth that they who drink must stagger." You might want to check out Howard Hibbett's *The Floating World in Japanese Fiction*, which you can get for fairly cheap in paperback online, that has a special focus on the illustrated stories (that's right, the light novel is nothing new) of the Genroku period of the late 17th and early 18th century, written for the entertainment of the urban merchant class—who, frankly, seemed to be having a lot more fun with their lives than their samurai masters were.

On page 52, panel 5, Mizusaki, Kanamori, and Doumeki have suddenly donned cliched thieves' garb—Mizusaki in a top hat and cloak reminiscent of Arsene Lupin (the literary creation of Maurice LeBlanc who in turn inspired Monkey Punch to create his supposed descendent, Lupin III), Kanamori with a bandana tied under her nose in the supposed manner of classic Japanese burglars such as Nezumi Kozo, with Doumeki wearing a mask and what looks like a black-and-white striped tank-top pulled over her hoodie—a century ago, such stripes (rather than orange) were the stereotypical prison uniform, passing likewise into pop culture—a famous example being the "Get Out of Jail Free" card in *Monopoly*.

The intelligence service of the same GHQ referenced earlier in *Eizouken* (see the notes on page 162 of vol. 1) investigated several secret Japanese wartime weapons projects, including *Kuwairiki*, referenced on pages 53 and 54. Begun in 1936 under the direction of Lieutenant-General Reikichi Tada, who held a doctorate in engineering and was an advocate for advanced weapons research, "Project Ku" (*Ku-go*) was a high-frequency electromagnetic wave beam, so it could be thought of as a heat beam in the sense of how microwaves cook food. It evidently never left the research stage, and scholar Keiko Nagase-Reimer has documented for the Technical University of Berlin how Project Ku absorbed considerable staff and funds to no avail, even as the war situation grew worse for Japan.

The title page for Chapter 19 on page 57 seems very relevant of late, with Kanamori masked up (evidently in a custom mask, printed with an image of her trademark grill) while Mizusaki and Asakusa take the role of different kinds of viruses trying to infect her. Mizusaki's has a more familiar spherical form, but the mechanical-oriented Asakusa is piloting a bacteriophage—a class of virus that preys on bacteria and archaea. Bacteriophages really do look like that! In the original Japanese on page 63, panel 4, Asakusa thought "*Bancho Sarayashiki!*" *Bancho* is the name of an area near the Imperial Palace in Tokyo, which in the 18th century was the Shogun's palace (the Emperor's palace was in Kyoto during that era) and which was the setting for *Bancho Sarayashiki*, a play whose story eventually became a part of Japanese folklore—Okiku, a servant who breaks a precious plate, is hurled down a well to die (the allusion is expressed here in English as "*This won't end well!!*"), and emerges from it as a vengeful spirit. Written with different kanji than the place name, but pronounced the same, *bancho* also refers to a juvenile delinquent gang leader; readers may have seen it referenced in episode 7 of *Kill La Kill*, when Mako wears a uniform inspired by a classic, stereotypical bancho outfit. In panel 7, Asakusa's remarks refer to the tradition that tanuki will try to pass off leaves or scraps of paper as counterfeit money. "Airy" is used to describe the monorail diagram Asakusa conceived on pages 70-71; the original Japanese term, *kakuu*, likewise in Japanese means both "aerial" and "unreal."

In the original Japanese of page 99, panel 5, Kanamori referred to witnessing the demise of a 「酒屋」, *sakaya*, which is literally a "sake shop" and could also be translated as "liquor store"—but the English used in this edition is generally from a North American perspective, where a "liquor store" implies a place whose primary stock is alcoholic beverages. Rural and small-town *sakaya* in Japan are sometimes closer to a general store or convenience store in terms of what they actually carry—just as you can get alcoholic beverages at a 7-11, but you wouldn't refer to it as a "liquor store." No doubt the store portrayed in this chapter does carry some booze, but you'll notice you don't see any (whereas you do see canned soup, cup noodles, gloves, etc.) and in the original Japanese the name written on the upper story of the shop was in fact 「福屋雑貨店」, "Fukuya General Store." Actually, now that I think about it, this might have been another joke, as "liquor store" is *sakaya*, and "general store" is *zakkaya*. But in any case, please rest assured that we would not attempt to remove references to alcohol. The very first manga I edited was *Evangelion*, so I could never let Misato down like that.

On page 103, panel 4, it is suggested in the original Japanese that Kanamori was too young to properly recognize the kanji for "(business) temporarily closed", 「休業」 and is instead trying to read the first kanji, 「休」 as if it were the kana 「イホ / いほ」, iho. Since *iho* can signify "500" in Japanese, it's very possibly meant to show that bonus is still on her mind. I believe Chapter 21 is also the first time we've seen one of *Eizouken's* flights of fancy to a different place and time initiated by Kanamori, rather than Asakusa or Mizusaki. Of course, although she's usually seen as the sensible one, it was Kanamori who told Asakusa and Mizusaki in vol. 1 that, "We don't have to 'be sensible' yet at our age. We don't have anything to *risk* . . . or lose by **trying!**" In reality, while Kanamori is as much her own person as her partners are, she is like them in that she is also a very passionate individual. Eric Heisserer, who adapted science fiction author Ted Chiang's "Story of Your Life" into the screenplay (for which Heisserer received an Oscar nomination) of the 2016 Denis Villeneuve film *Arrival*, defined a producer in a way I believe applies well to Kanamori: "They fight an invisible war to protect things you never knew were endangered."

Whereas the ancient Dead Sea Scrolls were found in caves in what is now the West Bank and Israel, the Nag Hammadi manuscripts referenced on page 116, panel 3 (Shibahama High School has the most fascinating clubs, you'll agree) were found in what is now Egypt. Their interest is not only for the perspective they provide on early Christian and Gnostic beliefs, but the fact they were indeed, as said, codices rather than scrolls—codices being early forms of books (like the one you're reading right now!) that are made by binding pages to a spine, rather than by attaching pages to each other to be unrolled as with a scroll. You probably picked up on it, but this whole scene is a riff on the opening of the original manga and movie *Ghost in the Shell*, beginning with Shock Troop Commander Kyu Ajima waiting up on the roof like Major Kusanagi, and lines like "Stop it! Who told you to fire?! Put your guns down *now!*" which is a direct quote. The unnamed perp from the Manuscript Club is lucky, however, that the Student Council's techniques are not as gory as those of Section 9.

On page 142, panel 2, Asakusa's method of attempting to stay incognito is extremely endearing, although I think anybody who's worked an artist alley table has felt like doing that at one point, no matter how dirty the floor. Likewise perhaps the bags over the face, although they may be found in violation of the rules at the real Comitia, unless you can demonstrate you also bag your face in daily life. Comitia, by the way, respects that attendees may want the option to protect their privacy, but requests if so they do it through the methods Japanese people might employ in ordinary public situations, such wearing a face mask (not a character mask, but the kind we've all worn recently) and/or sunglasses. I like how the bags are shown by the next page to already be getting moist from exhalations, and by the page after that, Asakusa's is starting to lose structural integrity around the nose and mouth regions (note her adjusting the bag on page 144, panel 2, and then the flap of loosening paper peeking out the visor in panel 3). Also, is "@ eizoukenn" an attempt at plausible deniability with the school? "What, us, Eizouken, sell at Comet-A? You must have mistaken us for *Eizoukenn*, that mysterious group whose identity is known to none, for they wear crude masks fashioned from brown paper bags."

On page 147, panel 1, you may recall that Kanamori said something similar to Asakusa on page 7 of vol. 1. This is referring to 「連れ ション」, *tsure-shon*, "pee company" ("pee pals"?), meaning students who always go to the school bathroom as a posse. There were students at my school who did that, and come to think of it, there are plenty of adults who do it when they go out clubbing or to a bar or restaurant with their friends. There isn't anything necessarily wrong with it, but I get the impression that to Kanamori, it's more socializing than she can grasp—that her perspective is, "do you even have to *pee* as a group?"

SPECIAL BONUS! We'd like to forward some notes covering not only this volume, but the two previous volumes, written by the creator of *Keep Your Hands off Eizouken!* himself, Sumito Oowara!

Oowara-sensei's comments on vol. 1 are as follows: "Shibahama High School is located on a lake, so it's believed it takes no countermeasures against salt (water) damage. It's necessary to keep a close eye on the positions of the furnishings and equipment in Eizouken's clubhouse, as they change regularly. Asakusa's 'nice stick' (introduced on page 41) is from a *Prunus × yedoensis* 'Yoshino cherry'. Eizouken didn't actually use tin sheets for the roof repairs, but transparent polycarbonate corrugated sheets, to allow light in. The reason they don't look transparent when they're looking up at the repairs at the end of Chapter 4 is because they're covered with tarps until the caulking dries!" The editor notes that in vol. 3, page 119, panel 5, you can see one of the security department police (first witnessed in vol. 1 beating back the audience during the student council meeting) peeking through one of transparent sheets on the roof.

On vol. 2, Oowara comments: "About those floating round particles in the very first panel? They're not ghosts. It's just an effect of light in a dusty room. (On page 10), consider the power strip plug coming loose from the wall, and the AC adapter coming loose from the power strip, as happening at the exact same moment. Asakusa's method of collecting fallen leaves (page 88, panel 5) is to use a garden spade with an oar-rowing like motion. And regarding vol. 3: "The grass Kanamori and Asakusa are harvesting (in Chapter 19) is *Sasa veitchii* (Kuma bamboo grass); the state of the leaves of course depends on the season. Despite Asakusa and Doumeki's speculations (on page 33), the true monetary value of the Audio Club's sound library is unknown. The reason Asakusa can tell (on page 50, panel 1) that it was a former power station is because of the conduit seen in the next panel to convey water downhill to a hydroelectric generator. Besides the mic mounted on the tripod, Doumeki also uses a stethoscope-like device (on page 55, panel 3) to gather sound transmitted through the pole by direct contact. Asakusa's bike in the monorail diagram (in the lower right of page 70) doesn't have a saddle, as it's intended for off-road use." And regarding the driving scene on page 40, we are assured by the creator that, "The Shibahama High School Auto Club has been granted a 'License to Drive on School Grounds' from the Student Council for their activities." And here I was, as editor, worried about the Japanese government's driving laws—I should have remembered that in manga and anime, the only law in high school that counts is that of the student council ^_^ We'll look forward to seeing you all again in vol. 4 and beyond!

—CGH

LOOK AT THIS

(the other way)

Sayaka Kanamori would like to thank you for your purchase of *Keep Your Hands off Eizouken!* and reminds all customers that this manga reads in the traditional Japanese style, right-to-left. To get your money's worth, please flip the book around and begin reading.

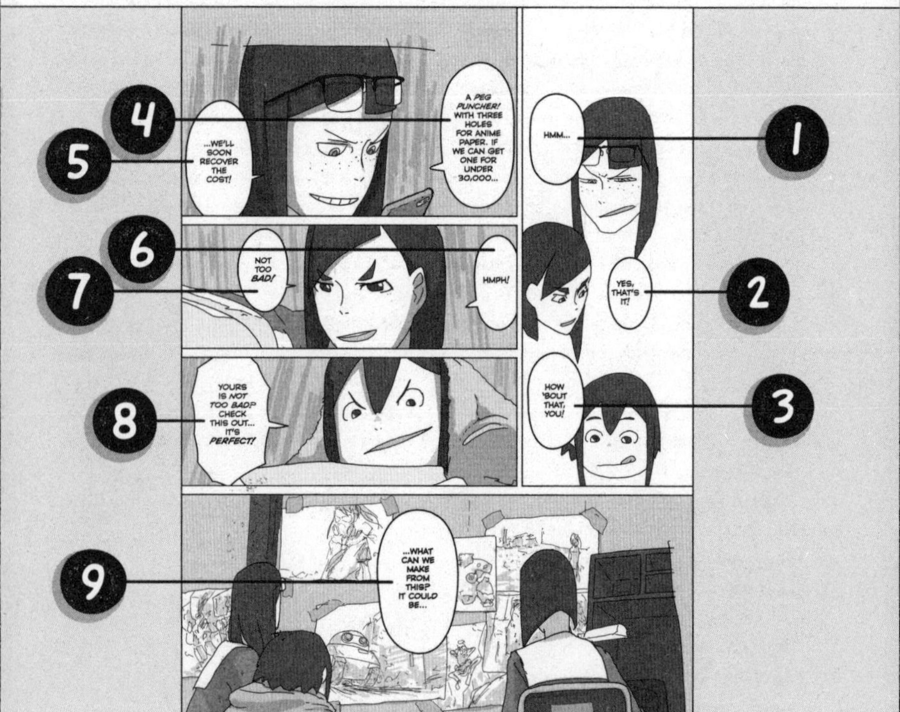

1
HMM...
2
YES, THAT'S IT!
3
HOW 'BOUT THAT, YOU!
4
A PEG PUNCHER! WITH THREE HOLES FOR ANIME PAPER. IF WE CAN GET ONE FOR UNDER 30,000...
5
...WE'LL SOON RECOVER THE COST!
6
HMPH!
7
NOT TOO BAD!
8
YOURS IS NOT TOO BAD? CHECK THIS OUT... IT'S PERFECT!
9
...WHAT CAN WE MAKE FROM THIS? IT COULD BE...

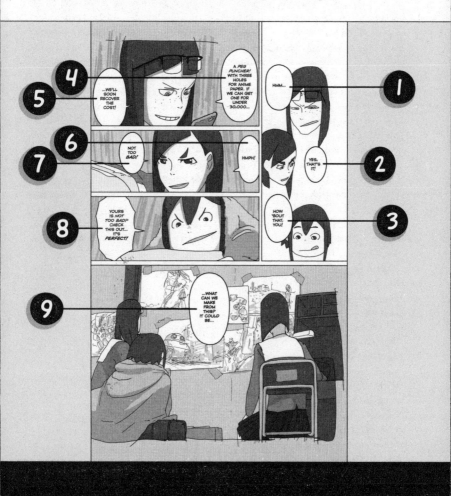